The Qur'an

A Translation for the 21st Century

ADIL SALAHI

The Qur'an: A Translation for the 21st Century

Published by:

THE ISLAMIC FOUNDATION

Markfield Conference Centre, Ratby Lane,
Markfield, Leicestershire LE67 9SY, United Kingdom
E-mail: publications@islamic-foundation.com
Website: www.islamic-foundation.com

Quran House, PO Box 30611, Nairobi, Kenya
PMB 3193, Kano, Nigeria

Distributed by:
Kube Publishing Ltd.
Tel: +44(01530) 249230, Fax: +44(01530) 249656
E-mail: info@kubepublishing.com

British Library Cataloguing-in-Publication Data

A catalogue record for this book is available from the British Library

ISBN: 978-0-86037-725-2 Paperback

ISBN: 978-0-86037-750-4 Hardback

ISBN: 978-0-86037-755-9 e-book

Typeset by: S4Carlise
Front Cover Calligraphy: Shutterstock
Cover design by: Inspiral Design
Printed by: IMAK offset, Turkey

Table of Contents

Introduction

The Qur'an is God's word which He revealed to Prophet Muhammad through the Angel Gabriel. God had earlier revealed Scriptures to different prophets, including the Torah, the Psalms and the Gospel. The Qur'an is clearly intended to be God's final message to mankind, setting out the way of life God wants people to lead. It sets their lives on the right course and ensures their happiness in this world and the next. In this present life, they have through God's message what satisfies their physical and spiritual needs and gives them a sense of complete fulfilment. Implementation of the Qur'an in this present life ensures for them admittance into Heaven in the life to come. This means a second life of perfect bliss and happiness, as well as enjoyment of what is even better, namely that God is pleased with them.

The Qur'an was revealed in parts during the period from the beginning of Muhammad's prophethood in 610 to shortly before he passed away in 632. Although the revelations given to Prophet Muhammad (peace be upon him) included much more than the Qur'an. The Qur'an is given in God's own word, while the rest of His revelation was expressed by Prophet Muhammad in his words and style. The two complement each other and together form the Islamic message.

The Qur'an is God's own word, and it has been preserved in its original form over the fourteen centuries of Islamic history. This is due, first and foremost, to the fact that God has guaranteed its preservation: '*It is We Ourselves who have bestowed this reminder from on high, and it is We who shall preserve it intact*'. (15: 9) When the Prophet received a surah or a passage of the Qur'an, he immediately dictated it to one or more of his scribes. Many of his Companions memorised it. When he passed away, his successor as head of the Muslim state, Abu Bakr, ordered the collation of a complete copy of the Qur'an to serve as reference. This was a meticulous exercise completed during Abu Bakr's reign which lasted less than two years. The task was entrusted to Zayd ibn Thabit who had learnt the complete Qur'an by heart under the Prophet's own instruction and guidance. Zayd gathered the written parts together, requiring two independent witnesses to testify that they were present when the Prophet dictated it to the scribe who kept it. Thus, authenticity was perfectly assured through the four people involved up to that point: the scribe, the two witnesses and Zayd, plus the written copy. However, Abu Bakr, 'Umar, 'Uthman and 'Ali, all of whom knew the full Qur'an by heart, further checked the complete copy. The whole exercise was repeated again less than fifteen years later, when reference copies were produced by a committee headed by Zayd himself and who was helped by three more of the Prophet's Companions who also knew the Qur'an by heart. These copies were checked against the original copy collated during Abu Bakr's reign. A copy was then sent to each of the main cities of the Muslim state, with a reciter who memorised the Qur'an in full to teach people its proper recitation.

The Qur'an is recited every day by every Muslim who keeps up his or her prayer. It is recited in prayer and at other times, because its recitation is an act of worship. Millions of people have learned its entirety by heart throughout every generation since it was first revealed 1,400 years ago. Nearly every Muslim memorises parts of it, and most recite a portion of it every day. Those who know it by heart read it in full once a week in order to retain it in their immediate memory. None feels this to be a demanding task, even though it takes at least an hour and a half every day. On the contrary, they approach it with the eagerness of one who feels it adds to their happiness.

No religious book is read and recited or listened to as frequently as the Qur'an. Yet those who recite it are always eager to do more. The question is whether this is due only to the religious aspect or if there is something more about the Qur'an? The religious factor is undoubtedly very important, but what is there about the Qur'an that attracts non-Muslim Arabs to memorise some passages of it? Indeed, some of them read it in its entirety time after time.

We need to remember that the Qur'an was revealed during a time when the Arabs were very proud of their language and used it so skilfully as to include fine forms of expressive speech. Moreover, they attached great importance to poetry. As they were largely unlettered people, poetry was the way they recorded their history, highlighted their bright moments, expressed their sorrows, extolled the merits of their departed elders, described their happiest events, reviled their enemies and recorded the lessons they learnt through hard experience. They chanted it in their social gatherings, and through poetry their news travelled from one part of Arabia to another. It also served as their formal and social media. What is special about Arabic poetry is that a poem may run into hundreds of lines, maintaining the same metre and rhyme, without giving even a hint of affectation or the rhyming word sounding laboured. In this they benefited by the fact that Arabic is a derivative language, which means that a three-consonant root can generate words in double figures in the forms of verbs, nouns, adjectives and adverbs bearing the same meaning as the root and adding varying connotations.

For example, if we take the Arabic root *h-d-th*, meaning to do and to speak, we may derive the following fifteen words: happened, narrated, speaker, interlocutor, spokesman, spoken statement, converse, conversation, accident, recent, made something new, invented a new thing, event, innovated, recently, and the causer of an event.[1] Furthermore, the root will also provide several more words delivering yet greater subtleties in each instance.

In the tribal society of Arabia, with tribes often raiding each other for plunder or revenge, the rise of a poet was an occasion for great celebration, because he could always highlight the merits of his tribe and revile its opponents. The fact that poetry is easily memorised and survives for a considerable length of time added to its importance.

When Prophet Muhammad (peace be upon him) recited passages of the Qur'an to the Arabs, in his efforts to advocate his message, they could not place it in any form of speech they knew. For certain, they realised that, despite its use of rhyme at times and having rhythm, it was not poetry. The Prophet appreciated poetry and could distinguish what was fine and what was of low standard, and he listened to some recitals of fine poetry, but he never expressed himself in any form that could be described as akin to poetry. He did not even quote any line of poetry in his speech. Discerning Arabs were quick to recognise that the Qur'an was of a much superior quality than even the finest of their poetry. Hence, when anyone suggested that his opponents should describe Muhammad as a poet, the suggestion was rejected out of hand. Having listened to two passages of the Qur'an, al-Mafruq ibn 'Amr, the head of the major Arabian tribe, the Shayban, said to the Prophet: 'What you say is not the word of a human being. Had it been human speech we would have recognised it'.[2]

One of the finest aspects of the Qur'an's style is the combination of word economy and expansive expression. Many literary critics have expressed wonder at how the Qur'an presents its ideas with the number of words it uses: it is a case of full meaning with minimum words, and this is consistent throughout, even when it provides detailed legislation. One clear example is the system of inheritance which assigns shares to different heirs, covering all situations and relations that may arise in any family and leaving no room for dispute.

---

1   These Arabic words are: *hadatha, haddatha, muhaddith, muhadith, mutahaddith, hadith, hadatha, muhadathah, hadeth, hadeeth, ahdatha, istahdath, hadath, mustahdath, hadeethan,* and *muhdith.*

2   The two passages the Prophet recited to the Shayban group of pilgrims were verses 151–153 of Surah 6, and verse 90 of Surah 16.

The whole system is outlined in verses 11, 12 and 176 of the fourth surah, Women. Together these verses use no more than 209 words in 22 lines.

The Qur'an tells stories of earlier prophets and their communities. Brevity is again a main feature of its style. In the story of the birth of Jesus in Surah 19, only seven words separate the angel's announcement to Mary that he was to give her a son and her being in labour. Yet the difficulties around her virgin pregnancy and the need to hide from curious eyes is perfectly accounted for. Surah 12 devotes 98 of its 111 verses to the story of Prophet Joseph, from his childhood to the reunion with his parents after he was appointed to a high position in the government of Egypt. The story runs in 28 scenes and there are gaps between some of them and at times the gap could stretch over several years. Yet at no point does the reciter or the listener feel that any part of the story is left out. On the contrary, they feel that they are given all necessary details. For example, one scene closes with Joseph's brothers in Egypt finding themselves at a loss because of the arrest of their youngest brother when they had most solemnly pledged to their father that they would return him safely. Their eldest is telling them to go back and explain what happened to their father and give him all the necessary evidence confirming the truth of their report. The next scene opens immediately, with their father giving his reaction to their report. Thus, their journey from Egypt to Palestine, their feelings as they arrived, their reluctance to speak to their father as they were conscious of their guilt over Joseph's disappearance are all left out, but the story is felt to be complete. Furthermore, the story identifies lessons to be learned and clearly illustrates concepts for believers to uphold.

A unique feature of the Qur'an's style is that outlined by Sayyid Qutb in his pioneering work *Artistic Imagery in the Qur'an*, published in 1945. Qutb says:

> Painting images is the Qur'an's preferred method of expression. It presents abstract concepts, psychological feelings, real events, visible scenes, people's types and human nature in clear images that we can mentally see before us. It then gives the painted image real life and successive movement. It thus gives the abstract idea shape or movement; presents a psychological feeling in a scene or a painting; shows human nature and types of people alive before our very eyes. Events, scenes and stories are all

shown full of life and movement. When dialogue is added to these, all elements are completed for us to imagine what is on show. Once the Qur'an starts its presentation of these, the reciter and listeners become the audience watching the story unfold. They are transported to the stage where the story took place or where the event will happen. As one scene or movement follows another, listeners forget that they are merely listening to words being recited. Instead, they feel that they are actually watching those very scenes and events.[3]

An excellent translator will be able to express the ideas and meanings of the author and put these in a way that enables the reader in the target language to fully understand the original text. However, each language has its own characteristics and what is easily manipulated in one language may not be achievable in another. This feature of the Qur'anic style is one of the difficulties that a translator of the Qur'an faces.

Another aspect of the Qur'anic style is its rhythm. Rhythm runs throughout the Qur'an, and it varies to suit the nature of the surah and its subject matter. Indeed it varies within the same surah, even in shorter ones. Sometimes the beat is strong and fast, while at others it is soft and slow. At other times these two combinations are reversed. Yet there is no metre to adhere to anywhere. Arabic poetry has no less than 17 different metres, but none of them is employed in the Qur'an. Nevertheless, one only needs to listen to the Qur'an being recited by an expert reciter to realise that music runs throughout it. At least two translators of the Qur'an were largely motivated to undertake the task by their love of its music. These were the late Arthur Arberry and N.J. Dawood; neither of whom was a Muslim, and both tried to give rhythm to their texts, despite the fact that their approaches were fundamentally different. In several conversations with Mr Dawood, he spoke to me about his feelings when he listened to a good recitation of the Qur'an. Professor Arberry wrote in the Introduction to his translation:

There is a repertory of familiar themes running through the whole Koran; each Sura elaborates or adumbrates one or more – often many – of these. Using the language of music,

---

3   Sayyid Qutb, *Artistic Imagery in the Qur'an*, p. 34. (Publisher, place and date are not mentioned.)

each Sura is a rhapsody composed of whole or fragmentary leitmotivs; the analogy is reinforced by the subtly varied rhythmical flow of the discourse...

During the long months, the dark and light months, of labouring at this interpretation... I have been reliving those Ramadan nights of long ago, when I would sit on the veranda of my Gezira[4] house and listen entranced to the old, white-bearded Sheykh who chanted the Koran for the pious delectation of my neighbour.

We may say that the superior literary excellence of the Qur'anic style, its brevity, music and other unique aspects make the Qur'an very hard to translate, or even 'untranslatable'. Yet there has been no shortage of attempts to translate the Qur'an. The first English translation by George Sale was published in 1734, followed in 1861 by Rodwell's and in 1880 by Palmer's. English translations by Muslims started to appear early in the 20th century, followed by two widely circulated versions; one by Abdullah Yusuf Ali and the other by Muhammad Marmaduke Pickthall. Both appeared in the 1930s. Then Arberry's and Dawood's appeared in the 1950s. The later part of the 20th century saw the publication of several other translations, perhaps reaching double figures, and the trend continues in the present century. At least two have already appeared and I know of two more currently being prepared. Most of these are by Muslim scholars. Each of these translations, as well as the ones I have not mentioned, has its merits, particularly when we take their dates into consideration.

However, this multiplicity of rendering the same original text begs the question: why should anyone redo what has already been done? The answer is the feeling everyone who is familiar with both Arabic and English experiences: the product falls far short of what the original is like. How can it be otherwise when the text of the translation is the word of a human being while the original is the word of God?

Should a person who undertakes the task of producing a new translation of the Qur'an consult the work of those who preceded him in this endeavour? Undoubtedly he should, just as he looks through the commentaries produced by Muslim scholars over the centuries. There is no harm in using similar words. Indeed this is inevitable,

---

4   At the time, Gezira was one of the most prestigious areas of Cairo.

because the original text is the same. Yet the method and style may be remarkably different.

* * *

Many years ago, a student who was preparing a Ph.D. thesis on Qur'anic translations asked me if I wished to produce a new translation of the Qur'an. My answer was definitely in the negative. Yet at the time I was heavily committed to the translation of *In the Shade of the Qur'an*, an 18-volume translation of Sayyid Qutb's priceless commentary on the Qur'an. Needless to say, the work involved rendering the meaning of the Qur'an into English. Even when I finished that work, at the end of 2007, I had no intention of producing the translation of the Qur'an separately. However, many friends have encouraged me to do so, and this despite the reluctance I expressed given the great gulf between the Arabic text and the work I did.

I have now, however, yielded to these requests, accepting the counter argument that the Qur'an does its work and addresses people's hearts even when it speaks to them only through the poor language of feeble humans. Its message comes across despite the many shortcomings of human expression. Even in the original, its address touches the hearts of Arabs who never went to school or learnt to read and write, despite the fact that their language is far removed from that of the people of Arabia at the time the Qur'an was revealed. Therefore, it is right to express the meaning of the Qur'an in today's language, so that its message is more readily available to English readers. Therefore, I have now reappraised my earlier work and introduced some changes which, I hope, improve upon it.

I have endeavoured to put the meanings of the Qur'anic verses and surahs in simple and straightforward form, so that the 21st century reader may find it easy to access. I hope that in this way, my contribution is worthwhile. I am indebted to many of my predecessors and I hope that their work has helped me to avoid the pitfalls this task presents.

No one can or may translate the Qur'an without consulting the commentaries and interpretations written by renowned scholars over the fourteen centuries of Islamic history. As many sentences in the Qur'an are understood in more than one way, these commentaries may highlight meanings that are seen to be secondary in others. Translators may take one or the other, and as a result there will be differences in the way they render their meanings. On the other hand, translators themselves may read verses differently, or highlight

certain shades of meaning more than others. All these are factors that
have led to great variations in the way the meanings of the Qur'an are
rendered in different translations. However, the overriding difficulty
is that the power and richness of expression provided in the original
Arabic text, as revealed by God Himself, cannot then be matched in
human language.

* * *

I have kept footnotes to the minimum, so as to allow the text to
deliver its own core message. I realise that some verses and surahs
must be understood against the background of the events they relate
to, but as the Qur'an is a book for all time, I have not sought to give
such explanations following our scholars' agreed view that Qur'anic
texts should be taken in their general meanings, rather than with the
peculiarity of relevant events. The event only helps to understand
the reason for revelation, but the message is everlasting. In my short
introductions to the surahs I point out the events to which they relate,
so that readers who wish to delve further into these can easily find
their references.

* * *

I strongly recommend readers listen to recitations of the Qur'an in
Arabic. There are a number of reciters whose works are available
on YouTube. The one I admire most is Muhammad Siddiq al-
Minshawi who passed away in 1969. He recorded the entire Qur'an
in different forms, and there are recordings made in radio studios for
various Arab broadcasts, as well as recordings of recitations given
in mosques and private homes. When searching, readers should key
in his full name, because three others of his family, with the same
middle name and surname, have recordings available on YouTube:
Muhammad, however, is the best. His recordings of the entire Qur'an
are available in *mujawwad* and *murattal* forms. The first is better,
slower and more musical, while the second is faster, maintaining the
same rhythm throughout. I suggest that readers may begin with the
following surahs:

- Surah 12 which relates the story of Joseph.
- Surah 19 which relates the story of Mary and the virgin birth
  of Jesus, as also mentions several other prophets.
- Surah 20 which devotes a large part of its verses to the history
  of Prophet Moses.

- Surah 26 which devotes a long section to Prophet Moses and his argument with Pharaoh before it gives short accounts of several other prophets.
- Surah 40 which gives a presentation of the argument given by a good believer who belonged to Pharaoh's household.

Other fine reciters include: Kamil Yusuf al-Bahteemi, Mahmood Khaleel al-Husari, Abd al-Basit Abd al-Samad. One of the best reciters is Muhammad Rifaat, but sadly his recordings are not of fine quality as he suffered from an illness affecting his throat which forced him to stop recording in 1943; he died in 1950. Mahmood al-Shareef is also a fine Palestinian reciter and his method is close to that of Muhammad Rifaat.

Surah 1   The Opening

This surah sums up the Islamic concept of God's Oneness and man's relationship with God. It is a relationship based on God's never-failing mercy and man's accountability, coupled with a prayer for guidance that ensures happiness in the life to come. A Muslim is required to recite this surah in every obligatory or voluntary prayer, which means that a Muslim recites this surah at least 17 times every day mentioning God's mercy no less than 68 times.

The Opening

1 In the Name of God, the Lord of Grace, the Ever-Merciful[1] **2** Praise be to God, the Lord of all the worlds, **3** The Lord of Grace, the Ever-Merciful, **4** Master of the Day of Judgement. **5** You alone do we

---

1   Every surah of the Qur'an starts with the phrase *Bismillah al-Rahman al-Rahim*. The only exception is Surah 9, Repentance, which exposes the nature of hypocrisy and makes clear that hypocrites are devoid of God's mercy. The phrase itself comprises four Arabic words, the first two of which mean 'In the name of God'. The other two words add two attributes of God derived from the same root, *rahama*, signifying grace and mercy. While the second of these attributes, *al-Rahim*, is commonly used as a superlative form of granting mercy, the first, *al-Rahman*, is used only to refer to God. In fact, it was never used in Arabic before Islam. It is commonly accepted as a proper noun referring to God, just like His most common Arabic name, Allah.

When we look carefully at the usage of *al-Rahman* in the Qur'an we note that it consistently bears connotations of power, creation, might and dominion alongside those of grace and mercy. Therefore, an accurate translation of the term should bring out these additional connotations. This is perhaps most clearly apparent where it is employed in Surahs 50 *Qaf*, 67 *Dominion*, 20 *TaHa*, and 19 *Mary*. The word occurs once in the first of these surahs, four times each in the second and the third and no less than fourteen times in the fourth. A discerning look at these instances will not fail to reveal that the connotations of creation, revelation, power, ability to punish, smite and destroy are equally, if not more, prominent than those of grace, mercy and compassion. Therefore, we can say that *al-Rahman* connotes 'the exercise of mercy on the basis of free choice by one who is able to inflict severe punishment without fear of any consequence'. Therefore, it is translated wherever it occurs in this work as 'The Lord of Grace'.

By contrast *al-Rahim* stresses the availability of God's mercy in all situations and to all creatures. People only need to appeal for it and it is certain to be granted. Indeed, it is given at all times without such appeals. There are numerous aspects of God's mercy that people enjoy, and often without appreciation or gratitude. Therefore, I render it as the 'The Ever-Merciful'.

worship[2] and to You alone do we turn for help. **6** Guide us on the straight path, **7** The path of those on whom You have bestowed Your favours, not those who have incurred Your wrath, nor those who have gone astray.

---

2   'Worship' in Islam has a much wider sense than the offering of certain duties and voluntary actions, such as prayer, fasting and extolling God's praises. As the essence of Islam is man's submission to God in all life affairs, every action a human being does may be considered as an act of worship when it is done with the right intention, with proper observation of Islamic principles and regulations, and aimed to earn God's pleasure.

Surah 2   The Cow

This is the longest surah in the Qur'an, composed of 286 verses of varying length. It was revealed in Madinah, over a period of seven years, yet it reflects a clear unity of theme. It consists of an introduction, four main topics and a conclusion.

The introduction takes up the first 20 verses, starting with a statement defining the Qur'an as God's book detailing His final message to mankind, and dividing people into three groups with regard to their attitude to the Qur'an: believers, unbelievers and hypocrites. The first topic is an address to all mankind calling on them to believe in Islam and follow its guidance. This is followed by the story of the creation of man and his placement on earth. All this takes up to the end of verse 39.

The second topic is presented in 123 verses (40–162) making a special appeal to the people of earlier divine revelations to discard all the distortion they introduced into their faiths and to accept the new and final version of the divine faith, i.e. Islam. Here the discourse covers four areas: an account of the history of the Jews after Moses (verses 40–74); the Jews in Madinah at the time of the revelation of the Islamic message (75–121); an account of the believers in the divine faith since Abraham (122–134), and the Muslims at the time of Prophet Muhammad (135–162).

Once the second topic is concluded, a passage of 15 verses (163–177) provides an introduction for what is to follow. These verses focus on three points: the Oneness of the Creator; that He is the One who commands and must be obeyed; and an outline of the legislation to be detailed in the third subject which takes up 106 verses (178–283). Under this topic various areas of legislation are included, relating to worship such as fasting and pilgrimage, as well as financial transactions, looking after the poor, family relations, divorce, child care, fighting and the observance of sanctities. As this makes up a wealth of legislation, the surah provides a relaxing passage (verses 204–214) giving a general admonition to mankind and a clear advice to believers to maintain the pure faith.

The fourth subject is summed up in one verse (284) defining the highest form of belief which is attained only by the elite of the elite of believers.

The conclusion is given in the final two verses which are in perfect harmony with its five opening verses. The opening outlines

essential qualities of believers and the conclusion shows them as
good and devout.

The Cow

In the Name of God, the Lord of Grace, the Ever-Merciful

1 *Alif. Lam. Mim.*[3] **2** This is the Book, there is no doubt about it:
a guidance for the God-fearing.[4] **3** Those who believe in what lies
beyond the reach of human perception,[5] attend regularly to prayer and
give generously of what We bestow upon them. **4** Those who believe
in what has been revealed to you and what was revealed before you,
and are certain of the Hereafter. **5** Those follow their Lord's guidance,
and they shall surely prosper. **6** For the unbelievers, it is alike whether
you forewarn them or not, they will not accept the faith. **7** God has
sealed their hearts and ears; their eyes are covered; and a grievous
punishment awaits them. **8** There are some who say: 'We believe in
God and the Last Day', yet, in truth, they do not believe. **9** They
seek to deceive God and the believers, but they are only deceiving
themselves, though they may not realise it. **10** There is sickness in
their hearts, and God has aggravated their sickness. Painful suffering
awaits them for the lies they keep telling. **11** When it is said to them:
'Do not spread corruption in the land', they say: 'We are but doers
of good'. **12** But, they indeed are the ones who do spread corruption,
though they do not realise it. **13** When it is said to them, 'Believe

---

3   Several surahs begin with separate letters of the Arabic alphabet.
Commentators have different views on these, but the view that receives most
approval is that they represent an aspect of the challenge the Qur'an makes to
the Arabs to produce anything like it. These letters tell them that the Qur'an is
composed of words and letters of their language, but it is inimitable and despite
their excellent poetic standard, they remain incapable of producing something
even remotely comparable to it.

4   The Arabic term *taqwa*, which is a quality of good believers, is derived
from a root that connotes feelings of awe, caution, and seeking protection.
A believer fears to incur God's displeasure through committing what He has
forbidden. In Islamic terminology, *taqwa* has added connotations of loving God
and being ready and willing to do His bidding.

5   'Beyond the reach of human perception' is my preferred translation
of the Qur'anic Arabic term '*ghayb*', which is derived from a root that means
absence. Many translators of the Qur'an render it as 'the unseen', but this is a
much narrower sense than what the term conveys. *Ghayb* refers to what cannot be
reached by any human sense or faculty.

as other people have believed', they say, 'Are we to believe as the fools believe?' It is indeed they who are fools, though they do not know it. **14** When they meet the believers, they say, 'We believe', but when they are alone with their devilish allies, they say, 'We are with you; we are only mocking'. **15** God will put them to derision and let them continue their transgression, blundering blindly along. **16** These are the ones who barter away guidance for error. Their transaction is profitless and they will receive no guidance. **17** They are like one who sought to kindle a fire, and as it lit up all around him God took away their light and left them in darkness, unable to see anything.[6] **18** Deaf, dumb and blind, they can never return to the right path. **19** Or, when there is a storm-cloud, dark, charged with thunder and lightning, they thrust their fingers in their ears at every thunder-clap, for fear of death; but God encompasses the unbelievers. **20** The lightning all but snatches away their sight; whenever it flashes over them they walk on, but when darkness overtakes them they stand still. Should God will it, He would take away their hearing and their sight, for God has power over all things. **21** Mankind, worship your Lord who has created you and those who lived before you, so that you may become God-fearing. **22** He made the earth a couch for you, and the heavens a ceiling. He sent down water from the sky to bring forth fruits for your sustenance. Do not, then, knowingly set up equals to God. **23** If you are in doubt as to what We have revealed to Our servant, then produce one surah comparable to it and call upon all your witnesses, other than God, if what you say is true. **24** But if you fail, as you will certainly do, then guard yourselves against the Fire, fuelled by humans and stones, prepared for the unbelievers. **25** To those who believe and do good deeds give the good tidings that they shall reside in gardens through which running waters flow. Whenever they are offered fruits therefrom, they say, 'We have been given the same before', for they shall be provided with what looks similar. They shall also have pure spouses and they shall reside there for ever. **26** God does not disdain to give a parable of a gnat, or a higher creature.

---

6   This verse provides an early example of the principle of 'word economy' which is characteristic of the Qur'anic style. Hypocrites are compared to a person lighting up a fire to see what is around him. Once the comparison has been set, the verse immediately focuses on the hypocrites themselves. It does not mention anything further about the man and his fire. This explains the usage of the plural pronoun while the example uses the singular form. Such changes in use of pronouns, verbs and nouns are very frequent in the Qur'an, keeping the reciter and listener always on the alert.

Those who believe know that it is the truth from their Lord, while the unbelievers ask, 'What could God mean by such a parable?' In this way, God lets many go astray and gives guidance to many others, but none does He leave to go astray except the evildoers, **27** who violate God's covenant[7] after having accepted it, and cut asunder what He has ordered to be joined, and spread corruption in the land. They are the losers. **28** How can you reject God who has given you life after you were dead? He will cause you to die again then He will bring you back to life. To Him you shall return. **29** It is He who created for you all that is on earth. He then turned to heaven and fashioned it into seven heavens. He has knowledge of all things.

30 Your Lord said to the angels, 'I am appointing a vicegerent on earth'. They said, 'Will You appoint on it someone who would spread corruption and shed blood, whereas we celebrate Your praises and extol Your holiness?' He said, 'I surely know that of which you have no knowledge'. **31** And He taught Adam the names of all things and then turned to the angels and said, 'Tell Me the names of these things, if what you say is true'. **32** They said, 'Limitless are You in Your glory! We only know what You have taught us. Indeed, You alone are all-knowing, wise'. **33** He said, 'Adam! Tell them their names'. When he had told them all their names, He said, 'Have I not said to you that I know all that is in the heavens and the earth, and I know all that you reveal and conceal?' **34** When We said to the angels, 'Prostrate yourselves before Adam', they did so except for Iblis[8] who refused, swelled in insolence, and was thus an unbeliever. **35** And We said to Adam, 'Dwell you with your spouse in Paradise and eat freely whatever you wish of its fruit, but do not come near this one tree, lest you would be wrongdoers'. **36** But Satan lured them away from it [Paradise] and thus caused them to be ousted from where they had been. We said, 'Get you down. You shall be enemies to one another. On earth you shall have an abode and sustenance, for a while'. **37** Thereupon Adam received from his Lord certain words, and He accepted his repentance; for He alone is the One who accepts repentance, the Ever-Merciful. **38** We said, 'You shall all descend from it [Paradise]. Guidance shall reach you from Me. Those who follow My guidance shall have nothing to fear nor shall they grieve.

---

7   The basic covenant between man and God is man's obligation to acknowledge God as his Creator and the only God in the universe and to turn to Him in worship and submission.

8   Iblis is Satan's name.

39 But those who deny and gainsay Our revelations shall have the Fire, wherein they shall abide.

40 Children of Israel! Remember My favour which I have bestowed on you. Fulfil your covenant with Me and I will fulfil Mine with you; and of Me alone stand in awe. **41** Believe in what I have revealed, confirming that which you already have, and be not the first to reject it. Do not barter away My revelations for a paltry price, and fear Me alone. **42** Do not overlay the truth with falsehood, nor knowingly suppress the truth. **43** Attend regularly to your prayers, pay your zakat,[9] and bow down in prayers with those who bow down. **44** How can you bid others to be righteous and forget yourselves, even when you read the Scriptures? Do you not understand? **45** Seek strength in patient perseverance and in prayer, which is indeed a demanding task except for the devout, **46** who know that they shall meet their Lord and to Him they shall ultimately return. **47** Children of Israel! Remember My favour which I bestowed on you, and that I have preferred you over all people. **48** Fear the day when no soul shall avail another in any way, nor shall intercession be accepted from any of them, nor ransom taken from them, and none shall receive help. **49** And remember how We delivered you from Pharaoh's people, who afflicted you with cruel suffering, killing your sons and sparing only your women. That was a grievous trial from your Lord. **50** We parted the sea for you, led you to safety and drowned Pharaoh's people before your very eyes. **51** And [remember, too], when We appointed for Moses forty nights, and in his absence you took to worshipping the calf, and thus became wrongdoers. **52** Yet even after that We pardoned you, so that you might be thankful. **53** We gave Moses the Scriptures and the Standard [by which to distinguish right from wrong], so that you might be rightly guided. **54** Moses said to his people, 'You, my people, have wronged yourselves by worshipping the calf. Turn, then, in repentance to your Maker and slay one another. That will be better for you in your Maker's sight'. Thus, He accepted your repentance; for He is the One to accept repentance, the Ever-Merciful. **55** And

---

9   Zakat is an Islamic worship, and it is one of the five pillars on which the structure of Islam is built. The word is derived from a root in Arabic that signifies growth. We may explain it as 'obligatory charity', because it is incumbent on all Muslims who own more than a specified threshold, and it is paid out annually. Eight categories of people may benefit by it. No one else has any claim to it. These categories are specified in Verse 9: 60. All divine religions have in common the belief in God's Oneness, attending to prayers and payment of zakat. Other details, however, differ.

[remember] when you said, 'Moses, we will not believe in you until we see God in person'. You were then struck by a thunderbolt while you were looking on. **56** But We raised you again after you had been as dead, so that you might be thankful. **57** We caused the clouds to provide shade for you, and sent down for you manna and quails. 'Eat of the good things We have provided for you.' Indeed, to Us they did no harm, but themselves did they wrong. **58** And [remember] when We said, 'Enter this city, eat of its abundant food as you may desire, prostrate yourselves as you enter the gates and say: "Lord, relieve us of our burden". We will then forgive you your sins and We will richly reward those who do good'. **59** But the wrongdoers among them substituted other words for those which they had been given. Therefore, We let loose against them a scourge from heaven in requital for their transgression. **60** And [remember] when Moses prayed for water for his people We said to him, 'Strike the rock with your staff'. Twelve springs gushed forth from it. Each tribe knew their drinking place. 'Eat and drink of what God has provided and do not persistently spread corruption in the land.' **61** And [remember] when you said, 'Moses! We can no longer put up with one kind of food. Pray to your Lord, then, to bring forth for us some of what the earth produces of green herbs, cucumber, garlic, lentils and onions'. He said, 'Would you take a lesser thing in exchange for what is much better? Go down to any land and you shall have what you asked for'. Ignominy and humiliation were stamped upon them and they incurred the wrath of God, because they denied His revelations and slew prophets against all right, and because they persisted in their disobedience and transgression. **62** Those who believe, and those who are Jews, and Christians and Sabians[10] – anyone who believes in God and the Last Day, and does what is right, shall have their reward with their Lord. They have nothing to fear nor shall they grieve. **63** We accepted your solemn pledge and raised Mount Sinai above you, saying, 'Take with firmness and strength what We have given you, and bear in mind all its contents, so that you may remain God-fearing'. **64** Yet after that you turned away, and but for God's grace and mercy you would have surely been among the losers. **65** You are well aware of those of you who broke the Sabbath. To them We said, 'Be as despicable apes'. **66** Through that [punishment] We set an example to their own

---

10   The Sabians are considered to be a religious group who believed in God's Oneness and followed a prophet sent before Jesus Christ. Some scholars mention that they followed Prophets Zachariah and John.

time and for all times to come, and an admonition to the God-fearing. **67** When Moses said to his people, 'God commands you to sacrifice a cow', they said, 'Are you mocking at us?' He said, 'God forbid that I should be so ignorant'. **68** They said, 'Pray on our behalf to your Lord to make plain to us what kind of cow she should be.' He said, 'He says let her be neither an old cow nor a young heifer, but of an age in between. Do, then, as you are commanded'. **69** They said, 'Pray on our behalf to your Lord to make clear to us of what colour she should be'. [Moses] replied, 'He says let her be a yellow cow, bright of hue, pleasing to the beholder'. **70** They said, 'Pray on our behalf to your Lord to make plain to us of what exact type she should be, for to us cows are much alike. We shall, God willing, be guided aright'. **71** [Moses] answered, 'He says let her be a cow, not broken-in to plough the earth or water the tillage, free of all fault, without markings of any other colour'. Said they, 'Now you have given the right description'. They sacrificed her, although they had almost left it undone. **72** Having slain a human being, you cast the blame on one another for this [murder]. God would definitely reveal what you have concealed. **73** We said, 'Strike him with a piece of it. Thus God brings the dead back to life and shows you His signs, so that you may use your reason'. **74** Yet after all this, your hearts hardened until they were as hard as rocks or even harder; for there are rocks from which rivers gush forth; others split so that water flows through them, and some other rocks fall down for fear of God. Indeed, God is not unaware of what you do.

75 Do you hope that they will accept your message when some of them would listen to the word of God then, having understood it, knowingly distort it? **76** When they meet the believers, they say, 'We believe', but when they find themselves alone, they say to one another, 'Need you tell them that which God has disclosed to you? They will only use it in argument against you before your Lord? Will you not use your reason?' **77** Do they not know that God is well aware of all that they conceal and all that they reveal? **78** There are among them illiterate people who have no real knowledge of the Scriptures, entertaining only wishful beliefs and conjecture. **79** Woe, then, to those who write down, with their own hands, [something which they claim to be of] the Scriptures, and then say, 'This is from God', in order to get for it a trifling price. Woe to them for what their hands have written and woe to them for what they earn. **80** They declare, 'The Fire will not touch us except for a few days'. Say, 'Have you received such a promise from God – for God never breaks His promise – or do

you attribute to God something of which you have no knowledge?'
81 Indeed, those who earn evil and become engulfed by their sin
are destined for the Fire where they shall abide, **82** but those who
believe and do righteous deeds are destined for Paradise where they
shall abide. **83** We made this covenant with the Children of Israel:
'Worship none but God; show kindness to parents and kinsfolk and to
the orphans and the poor; speak kindly to all people; attend regularly
to your prayers and pay the obligatory charity'. But, except for a few,
you turned away and paid no heed. **84** We made a covenant with you
that you shall not shed your own blood or drive yourselves out of
your own homeland. You acknowledged all that and bore witness to
it. **85** Yet there you are, slaying yourselves, and driving some of your
own people out of their homes, collaborating against them in sin and
injustice. Had they come to you as captives you would have ransomed
them. Their expulsion is indeed forbidden to you. Do you, then,
believe in some parts of the Scriptures and deny others? Those of you
who do this will have nothing for their reward other than ignominy
in this life and, on the Day of Resurrection, they shall be committed
to a most grievous suffering. For God is not unaware of what you do.
86 Such are the ones who buy the life of this world at the price of
the life to come. Their suffering shall not be alleviated, nor shall
they receive any succour. **87** We gave Moses the Book and caused a
succession of messengers to follow him. To Jesus, son of Mary, We
gave clear proofs and supported him with the Holy Spirit. Why is it
that every time a messenger comes to you with a message that does
not suit your fancies, you glory in your arrogance, charging some
(messengers) with lying and slaying others? **88** They say, 'Our hearts
are sealed'. No! God has cursed them for their disbelief. They have
but little faith. **89** And now that a Book confirming their own has come
to them from God, and they had repeatedly forecast its coming to the
unbelievers, they have denied what they know to be the truth. God's
curse be upon the unbelievers! **90** Vile is that for which they have
bartered their souls, because they have denied what God has revealed,
grudging that He should, by His grace, send down His revelations to
whom He chooses from among His servants. Thus they have incurred
God's wrath over and over again. Ignominious suffering is in store
for the unbelievers. **91** When it is said to them, 'Believe in what God
has revealed', they say, 'We believe in what has been revealed to us'.
They deny everything else, although it is the truth, corroborating the
revelations they have. Say, 'Why, then, did you in the past kill God's
prophets, if you were true believers?' **92** Moses came to you with

clear proofs, but in his absence you transgressed, worshipping the calf. **93** We accepted your solemn pledge, and We raised Mount Sinai above you, saying, 'Take with firmness and strength what We have given you and hearken to it'. They said, 'We hear but we disobey'. For their unbelief they were made to drink the calf into their hearts. Say, 'Vile is that which your faith enjoins upon you, if indeed you are believers'. **94** Say, 'If the ultimate abode with God is yours alone, to the exclusion of all others, then wish for death, if your claim is true'. **95** But they will never wish for it because of what their hands have wrought in this life. God is well aware of the wrongdoers. **96** Indeed, you shall find that they cling to life more eagerly than any other people, even more than the idolaters. Each one of them would love to live a thousand years, although the grant of a long life could not save him from punishment. God sees all that they do. **97** Say, 'Whoever is an enemy of Gabriel should know that he revealed it [the Qur'an] to your heart by God's leave'. It confirms the Scriptures revealed before it, and is a guidance and joyful tiding for believers. **98** Whoever is an enemy of God, His angels, His messengers, and to Gabriel and Michael will surely find that God is indeed the enemy of the unbelievers. **99** We have sent down to you clear revelations: none will deny them except the evildoers. **100** Is it always to be the case that every time they make a solemn pledge some of them will violate it? The truth is that most of them do not believe. **101** And now that a Messenger from God has come to them, confirming what is already in their possession, some of those who had been given the Scriptures cast God's Book behind their backs as though they know nothing. **102** They follow what the devils relate of Solomon's kingdom. Solomon never disbelieved, but the devils did. They instruct people in witchcraft which was certainly not revealed to the two angels, Harut and Marut, at Babylon. Yet these two [angels] never taught anyone without first declaring, 'We are but a temptation to evil, so do not renounce your faith'. From these two, some people learned what they would use to cause discord between a man and his wife. However, with that knowledge they can harm no one except by God's leave. Indeed, they learn what harms them and brings them no profit. They knew full well that whoever contracted such a deal would have no share in the life to come. Vile indeed is what they had sold their souls for, if they but knew it! **103** Had they embraced the faith and been God-fearing, God's reward would have been far better for them, if they but knew it.

104 Believers, do not say [to the Prophet]: 'Listen to us', but say: 'Have patience with us', and hearken. Grievous suffering awaits the unbelievers. **105** Neither the unbelievers among the people of earlier revelations nor the idolaters would like to see any blessing ever bestowed upon you by your Lord. But God favours with His mercy whom He wills; His grace is infinite. **106** Any revelation We annul or consign to oblivion We replace with a better or similar one. Do you not know that God has power over all things? **107** Do you not know that God has sovereignty over the heavens and the earth, and that apart from God you have no one to protect you or give you help? **108** Do you wish to ask of the Messenger who has been sent to you the same as was formerly asked of Moses? He who barters faith for unbelief has surely strayed away from the right path. **109** Many among the people of earlier revelations would love to lead you back to unbelief, now that you have embraced the faith. This they do out of deep-seated envy, after the truth has become manifest to them; so forgive and forbear until God makes known His decree. Indeed, God has power over all things. **110** Attend regularly to your prayer and pay zakat; for, whatever good you do for your own sake you shall find it with God. God sees all that you do. **111** They declare, 'None shall enter Paradise unless he is a Jew or a Christian'. Such are their wishful fancies. Say, 'Produce your proof, if what you say is true'. **112** Indeed, whoever surrender themselves to God, while doing good works, shall have their reward with their Lord; they shall have nothing to fear nor shall they grieve. **113** The Jews say the Christians have no basis for their faith and the Christians say the Jews have no basis for their faith. Yet they both recite the Scriptures. Those devoid of knowledge say likewise, and on the Day of Judgement God shall judge between them on all their disputes. **114** Who is more unjust than he who forbids God's name to be mentioned in His places of worship, and seeks to destroy them? Such people have no right to enter them except with fear in their hearts. They shall suffer ignominy in this world and grievous suffering awaits them in the life to come. **115** To God belong the East and the West: wherever you turn there will be the face of God. Truly, God is limitless in His bounty and He knows all. **116** They say, 'God has taken to Him a son'. Limitless is He in His glory! His is all that is in the heavens and on earth; all things are devoutly obedient to Him. **117** He is the Originator of the heavens and the earth. When He wills something to be, He need only say, 'Be', and it is. **118** Those devoid of knowledge say, 'Why does not God speak to us, nor is a sign shown to us?' The same demands were made by people before them: their hearts are all alike. We have made the signs very clear for those with firm conviction. **119** We have sent you with the truth; a bearer of glad tidings and a warner. You shall not be questioned about those who are destined for the blazing Fire. **120** Never will the Jews nor yet the Christians be pleased with you unless you follow their faith. Say, 'God's guidance is the only true guidance'. Should you follow their desires after all the knowledge that has come to you, you would have none to protect you from God, nor to give you help. **121** Those to whom We have given the Book, and who recite it as it ought to be recited, truly believe in it; those who deny it are utter losers. **122** Children of Israel! Remember My favour which I bestowed on you, and that I have preferred you over all people. **123** Fear the Day when no soul shall avail another in any way, nor shall ransom be accepted from any of them, nor shall intercession be of any benefit, and none shall receive help.

124 When his Lord tested Abraham with certain commandments and he fulfilled them, He said, 'I have appointed you a leader of mankind'. Abraham asked, 'And what of my descendants?' God said, 'My covenant does not apply to the wrongdoers'. **125** We made the House [i.e. the Kaʿbah] a resort for mankind and a sanctuary: 'Make the place where Abraham stood as a place of prayer'. We assigned to Abraham and Ishmael the task of purifying My House for those who walk around it, those who sojourn there for meditation and those who bow down and prostrate themselves in prayer. **126** Abraham said, 'Lord, make this a land of security and make provisions of fruits for those of its people who believe in God and the Last Day'. God said, 'And as for he who disbelieves, I shall let him enjoy life for a while and then I shall drive him to suffering through the Fire; and what a terrible end!' **127** As Abraham and Ishmael raised the foundations of the House, [they prayed]: 'Our Lord, accept this from us; You are the One that hears all and knows all'. **128** 'Our Lord, make us surrender ourselves to You, and make out of our offspring a community that will surrender itself to You. Show us our ways of worship and accept our repentance; You are the One who accepts repentance, the Ever-Merciful. **129** Our Lord, send them a Messenger from among themselves who shall declare to them Your revelations, and instruct them in the Book and in wisdom, and purify them. You are the Mighty One, the Wise'. **130** Who but a foolish person would turn away from the faith of Abraham? We raised him high in this life, and in the life to come he shall be among the righteous. **131** When his Lord said to him, 'Submit yourself', he said, 'I have submitted myself to the Lord of all the worlds'. **132** Abraham enjoined the same on his children, and so did Jacob, saying, 'My children, God has given you the purest faith. Do not let death overtake you before you have submitted yourselves to God'. **133** Were you present when death approached Jacob? He asked his children, 'Whom will you worship when I am gone?' They replied, 'We will worship your God, the God of your forefathers Abraham, Ishmael and Isaac, the One God. To Him do we submit ourselves'. **134** That community have passed away. Theirs is what they had earned and yours is what you have earned. You shall not be questioned about what they did. **135** They say, 'Follow the Jewish faith – or, follow the Christian faith – and you shall be rightly guided'. Say, 'No. We follow the faith of Abraham, who was truly devoted to God, and was not of those who associated partners with God'. **136** Say [all of you], 'We believe in God and in what has been revealed to us, and in what was revealed to Abraham, Ishmael, Isaac, Jacob and their descendants, and in what was given to Moses and Jesus, and in what all prophets have been given by their Lord. We make no distinction between any of them, and to God we have surrendered ourselves'. **137** If they come to believe in the way you believe, they will be rightly guided; but if they turn away, they will be in schism, but God will protect you from them; He hears all and knows all. **138** [This message takes its] hue from God; who can give a better hue than God? Him alone do we worship. **139** Say, 'Would you dispute with us about God? He is our Lord and your Lord. To us our deeds shall be credited and to you, your deeds. To Him alone are we devoted'. **140** Do you claim that Abraham, Ishmael, Isaac, Jacob and the tribes were Jews or Christians? Say, 'Do you know better than God?' Who is more wicked than one who suppresses a testimony he has received from God? God is not unmindful of what you do. **141** That community have passed away. Theirs is what they earned and yours is what you have earned. You shall not be questioned about what they did.

142 The weak-minded among people will say, 'What has turned them away from the direction of prayer which they have so far observed?' Say, 'To God belong the East and the West. He guides whomever He wills to a straight path'. **143** Thus, We have made you the community [ummah] of the middle way, so that you may stand witness against the rest of mankind, and the Messenger shall be a witness against you. We appointed the direction of prayer which you formerly followed in order that We might distinguish those who follow the Messenger from those who turn on their heels. It was indeed a hard test except for those whom God has guided. God would never have let your faith be in vain. God is ever compassionate and merciful to mankind. **144** We have seen you often turn your face towards heaven. We shall, therefore, make you turn in prayer towards a direction you will be happy with. Turn your face, then, towards the Sacred Mosque; and wherever you all may be, turn your faces [in prayer] towards it. Those who have been granted revelations in the past know well that it is the truth from their Lord. God is not unaware of what they do. **145** Were you to bring every possible sign before those who had been granted revelations, they would not follow your direction of prayer. And neither may you follow their direction of prayer, nor would they even follow one another's direction. If you were to follow their whims and desires after all the knowledge that has been given to you, you would certainly be among the wrongdoers. **146** Those to whom We granted revelation know it as well as they know their own children, but some of them knowingly conceal the truth. **147** This is the truth from your Lord; never, then, be among the doubters. **148** Each one has a goal towards which he turns; so vie with one another in good works. Wherever you may be, God will bring you all together. God has power over all things. **149** From wherever you may come forth, turn your face [in prayer] towards the Sacred Mosque. It is indeed the truth from your Lord. God is not unaware of what you do. **150** From wherever you may come forth, turn your face [in prayer] towards the Sacred Mosque; and wherever you all may be, turn your faces towards it, so that people may have no argument against you, except those who are bent on wrongdoing. Have no fear of them, but fear Me, so that I may perfect My grace on you, and that you may be rightly guided. **151** Thus, We have sent forth to you a Messenger from among yourselves to recite to you Our revelations, purify you, and instruct you in the Book and in wisdom and teach you what you did not know. **152** Remember Me, then, and I will remember you; give thanks to Me and never deny Me.

153 Believers, seek strength in patience and prayer. God is with those who are patient. **154** Do not say of those who are killed in God's cause, 'They are dead'. They are alive, although you do not perceive that. **155** We shall certainly try you with a certain measure of fear and hunger, and with diminution of wealth, lives and crops. But give glad tidings to those who remain patient in adversity; **156** who, when a calamity befalls them, say, 'To God we belong, and to Him we shall return'. **157** On such people, blessings and mercy are bestowed by their Lord; Such people will be rightly guided.

158 Safa and Marwah are among the symbols set up by God. Whoever visits the Sacred House for pilgrimage or 'umrah, would do no wrong to walk to and fro between them. He who does good of his own accord shall find that God is most thankful, all-knowing. **159** Those who conceal the clear proofs and guidance We bestowed from on high, after We have expounded it clearly for mankind in the Book, shall be cursed by God and by others who curse. **160** Excepted, however, shall be those who repent, mend their ways and make known the truth: from these I shall accept their repentance; for I alone accept repentance and I am the Ever-Merciful. **161** Those who reject the faith and die unbelievers shall incur the curse of God, the angels and all mankind. **162** They shall remain under that curse forever, their torment shall not be alleviated, nor shall they have respite. **163** Your God is the One God: there is no deity but He, the Lord of Grace, the Ever-Merciful. **164** In the creation of the heavens and the earth; in the alternation of night and day; in the vessels that sail through the sea with what is useful for mankind; in the water God sends down from the sky giving life to the earth after it had been lifeless, causing all manner of living creatures to multiply on it; in the movement of the winds, and the clouds that run their courses between sky and earth: in all this there are signs for people who use their reason. **165** Yet, there are people who worship beings other than God, giving them a status equal to His, loving them as God alone should be loved; whereas the believers love God more than all else. If the wrongdoers could but see, as see they will when they are made to suffer, that all might belongs to God alone, and that He is stern in retribution. **166** [On that Day] those who were followed will disown their followers and they all shall see their punishment, while all their ties are severed. **167** The followers will say, 'Would that we had another chance so that we can disown them as they have disowned us!' Thus, will God show them their works [in a way which causes them] bitter regrets. They shall never come out of the Fire. **168** Mankind, eat of what is lawful and wholesome on earth and do not follow Satan's footsteps: he is indeed an open enemy for you. **169** He enjoins you only to commit evil and indecency and to attribute to God something of which you have no knowledge. **170** When it is said to them, 'Follow what God has revealed', they say, 'No; but we will follow only what we found our forefathers believing in'. Why, even if their forefathers did not use reason at all, and followed no guidance? **171** The unbelievers are like the one who shouts to that which hears nothing but a call and a cry. Deaf, dumb and blind, they understand nothing. **172** Believers, eat of the wholesome things We have provided for you, and give thanks to God, if it is truly Him that you worship. **173** He has only forbidden you carrion, blood, the flesh of swine, and that on which a name other than God's has been invoked. But he who is driven by necessity, not intending to transgress nor exceeding his need, incurs no sin. God is much-forgiving, merciful. **174** Those who suppress any part of the Scriptures God has revealed, and barter it away for a paltry price, eat nothing but fire in their bellies. God will not speak to them on the Day of Resurrection, nor will He purify them. Painful suffering awaits them. **175** It is they who barter guidance for error and forgiveness for suffering. How great is their endurance of the Fire! **176** That is because God has revealed the Book with the truth. Those who are at variance with the Book are most deeply in the wrong. **177** Righteousness is not that you turn your faces towards the East or the West, but truly righteous is he who believes in God, the Last Day, the angels, the Book, and the prophets; and gives his money, much as he may cherish it, to his kinsfolk, orphans, the needy, a stranded wayfarer, beggars, and for the freeing of slaves; who attends to his prayers and pays zakat; and [truly pious are] they who keep their promises once made, and are patient in misfortune and adversity and in time of peril. Such are those who have proved themselves true, and such are the God-fearing.

178 Believers, just retribution is prescribed for you in cases of killing: a free man for a free man, a slave for a slave, and a female for a female. If something [of his guilt] is remitted to a person by his brother, this shall be pursued with fairness, and restitution to his fellow-man shall be made in a goodly manner. This is an alleviation from your Lord, and an act of His grace. He who transgresses thereafter shall face grievous suffering. **179** There is life for you, men of understanding, in this law of just retribution, so that you may remain God-fearing. **180** It is prescribed for you, when death approaches any of you and he is leaving behind some property, to make bequests in favour of his parents and other near of kin in fairness. This is a duty incumbent on the God-fearing. **181** If anyone alters a will after having come to know it, the sin of acting thus shall fall only on those who have altered it. God hears all and knows all. **182** If, however, one fears that the testator has committed a mistake or a wrong, and brings about a settlement between the parties concerned, he will incur no sin thereby. God is indeed much-forgiving, ever-merciful. **183** Believers, fasting is decreed for you as it was decreed for those before you, so that you may be God-fearing. **184** [Fast] on a certain number of days.

But whoever of you is ill, or on a journey, shall fast instead the same number of days later on. Those who find fasting a strain too hard to bear may compensate for it by feeding a needy person. He who does good of his own account does himself good thereby. For to fast is to do good to yourselves, if you only knew it. **185** It was in the month of Ramadan that the Qur'an was revealed: a guidance for mankind and a self-evident proof of that guidance and a standard to distinguish right from wrong. Therefore, whoever of you is present in that month shall fast throughout the month; but he who is ill or on a journey shall fast instead the same number of days later on. God desires that you have ease. He does not desire that you be afflicted with hardship. You are, however, required to complete the necessary number of days and to extol and glorify God for having guided you aright and to tender your thanks. **186** If My servants ask you about Me, well, I am near; I answer the prayer of the supplicant when he calls to Me. Let them then respond to Me, and believe in Me, so that they may follow the right way. **187** It is lawful for you to be intimate with your wives during the night preceding the fast. They are as a garment for you, as you are for them. God is aware that you have been deceiving yourselves in this respect, and He has turned to you in His mercy and pardoned you. So, you may now lie with them and seek what God has ordained for you. Eat and drink until you can see the white streak of dawn against the blackness of the night. Then resume the fast till nightfall. Do not lie with your wives when you are in retreat in the mosques. These are the bounds set by God, so do not come near them. Thus God makes clear His revelations to people, that they may remain God-fearing. **188** Do not devour one another's property wrongfully, nor bribe with it the judges in order that you may sinfully, and knowingly, deprive others of any part of what is rightfully theirs.

189 They ask you about the new moons. Say, 'They are signs for people to mark fixed periods of time, and for the pilgrimage'. Righteousness does not mean that you enter houses from the rear, but truly righteous is he who fears God. Enter houses by their doors and fear God, so that you may be successful. **190** Fight for the cause of God those who wage war against you, but do not commit aggression. Indeed, God does not love aggressors. **191** Slay them wherever you may come upon them, and drive them away from wherever they drove you away; for oppression is even worse than killing. Do not fight them near the Sacred Mosque unless they fight you there first. Should they fight you, then kill them. Such is the reward of the unbelievers. **192** But if they desist, know that God is much-forgiving, ever-merciful.

193 Fight them until there is no more oppression, and submission is made to God alone. If they desist, let there be no hostility except against the wrongdoers. **194** A sacred month for a sacred month: for just retribution also applies to the violation of sanctity. If anyone commits aggression against you, attack him just as he has attacked you. Have fear of God, and be sure that God is with those who are God-fearing. **195** Give generously for the cause of God and do not with your own hands throw yourselves to ruin. Persevere in doing good, for God loves those who do good. **196** Perform to their completion both the pilgrimage and the 'umrah purely for God's sake. If you are prevented from doing so, then make whatever offering you can easily afford. Do not shave your heads until the offerings have reached their appointed destination. If any of you is ill or suffers from an ailment of the head, he shall redeem himself by fasting, or alms, or sacrifice. When you are in safety, then he who takes advantage of performing the 'umrah before the pilgrimage shall make whatever offering he can easily afford; but he who lacks the means shall fast three days during the pilgrimage and seven more days on returning home; that is, ten days in all. All this applies to those whose families are not resident in the vicinity of the Sacred Mosque. Fear God, and know well that He is severe in retribution. **197** The pilgrimage takes place in the months appointed for it. Whoever undertakes the pilgrimage in those months shall, while on pilgrimage, abstain from lewdness, all wicked conduct and wrangling. Whatever good you do God is well aware of it. Provide well for yourselves: the best provision of all is to be God-fearing. Fear Me, then, you who are endowed with insight. **198** It is no sin for you to seek the bounty of your Lord. When you surge downward from 'Arafat, remember God at al-Mash'ar al-Haram. Remember Him who has given you guidance. Before this you were certainly in error. **199** Surge onward from the place where all other pilgrims surge and pray to God to forgive you. He is much-forgiving, ever-merciful. **200** When you have fulfilled your sacred duties, remember God as you remember your fathers – nay with a yet keener remembrance. Some people say, 'Our Lord, give us abundance in this world'. They shall have no share in the rewards of the life to come. **201** There are others who say, 'Our Lord, grant us what is good in this world and what is good in the life to come and protect us from the torment of the Fire'. **202** These shall have their portion in return for what they have earned; for God is swift in reckoning. **203** Give glory to God during certain appointed days. Those who hasten their departure after two days incur no sin, and those who stay longer incur no sin, provided that they are truly God-fearing. Have fear of God and know well that you shall all be gathered before Him.

204 There is a kind of man who pleases you greatly in the present life by what he says, and he cites God as witness to what is in his heart, whereas he is the most hostile of adversaries. **205** Yet, no sooner does he turn his back than he strives to spread corruption in the world, destroying crops and progeny. God does not love corruption. **206** When it is said to him, 'Have fear of God', his false pride drives him into sin. Therefore, Hell will be his allotted portion, and how vile a resting place. **207** But there is also a kind of man who would willingly sell himself, seeking God's pleasure. God is most compassionate to His servants. **208** Believers, submit all of you to God and do not follow Satan's footsteps. He is indeed your open foe. **209** If you should stumble after all evidence of the truth has come to you, then know that God is almighty, wise. **210** Are they waiting for God to reveal Himself to them in the shadows of clouds, together with the angels? The case will have been settled then. To God shall all things return. **211** Ask the Children of Israel how many a veritable sign We have given them. He who alters the grace of God after it has been bestowed on him [should know that] God is severe in punishment. **212** The life of this world has been made alluring to the unbelievers; hence, they scoff at those who believe; but those that fear God shall be above them in rank on the Day of Resurrection. God grants sustenance to whom He wills beyond all reckoning. **213** All mankind were once one single community. Then God sent forth prophets to give them good tidings and to warn them, and with them He sent down the Book, setting forth the truth, to judge between people over all on which they differed. Yet none other than those who had been given the Book started, out of injustice to one another, to dispute it after clear evidence of the truth had come to them. God, by His will, guided the believers to the truth concerning that which they had differed. God guides whom He will to the straight path. **214** Do you reckon that you will enter Paradise while you have not suffered like those [believers] who passed away before you? Affliction and adversity befell them, and so terribly shaken were they that the messenger and the believers with him would exclaim, 'When will God's help come?' Surely, God's help is close at hand.

215 They ask you what they should spend [in charity]. Say 'Anything good you spend of your wealth should go to parents and the near of kin, to orphans and the needy, and to travellers in need. God is well aware of whatever good you do'. **216** Fighting is ordained for you, even though it is hateful to you. But it may well be that you hate a thing while it is good for you, and it may well be that you love a thing while it is bad for you. God knows, whereas you do not know. **217** They ask you about fighting in the sacred month. Say, 'Fighting in it is a grave offence, but to turn people away from God's path, to disbelieve in Him and in the Sacred Mosque, and to expel its people from it – [all this] is far more grave in God's sight'. Religious persecution is worse than killing. They shall not cease to fight you until they force you to renounce your faith, if they can. But whoever of you renounces his faith and dies an unbeliever, his works shall come to nothing in this world and in the world to come. Such people are destined for Hell, wherein they shall abide. **218** Those who have believed and those who have forsaken their homeland and striven hard for God's cause are indeed the ones who may look forward to God's mercy. God is much-forgiving, ever-merciful. **219** They ask you about intoxicants and games of chance. Say, 'In both there is great evil although they have some benefits for people, but their evil is far greater than their benefit'. They ask you what they should spend in charity; say, 'Whatever you can spare'. Thus God makes plain His revelations so that you may reflect **220** upon this life and the life to come. They ask you about orphans; say, 'To improve their conditions is best. If you mix their affairs with yours, remember that they are your brothers. God knows him who spoils things and him who improves. Had God so willed, He would indeed have overburdened you. God is indeed almighty, wise'.

221 Do not marry women who associate partners with God unless they embrace the true faith. Any believing bondwoman is certainly better than an idolatress, even though the latter may well please you. And do not give your women in marriage to men who associate partners with God unless they embrace the true faith. Any believing bondman is certainly better than an idolater, even though the latter may well please you. These invite to the Fire; whereas God invites to Paradise and to the achievement of forgiveness by His leave. He makes plain His revelations to mankind so that they may bear them in mind. **222** They ask you about menstruation. Say: 'It is an unclean condition; so keep aloof from women during menstruation, and do not draw near to them until they are cleansed. When they have cleansed themselves, you may go in unto them in the proper way, as God has bidden you. God loves those who turn to Him in repentance, and He loves those who keep themselves pure'. **223** Your wives are your tilth; go, then, to your tilth as you may desire, but first provide something for your souls. Fear God and know that you shall meet Him. Give the happy news to the believers. **224** Do not allow your oaths in the name of God to become an obstacle to your being kind and God-fearing, or to promoting peace among people. God hears all and knows all. **225** God shall not take you to task for oaths which you may have uttered without thought, but He will take you to task for what your hearts have conceived in earnest. God is much-forgiving, clement. **226** Those who take an oath that they will not approach their wives shall have four months of grace. If they go back on their oaths, God is much-forgiving, ever-merciful; **227** And if they are resolved on divorce, [let them remember that] God hears all and knows all. **228** Divorced women shall wait, by themselves, for three monthly courses. It is unlawful for them to conceal what God might have created in their wombs, if they believe in God and the Last Day. During this period, their husbands are entitled to take them back, if they desire reconciliation. Women shall, in all fairness, enjoy rights similar to those exercised against them, although men have an advantage over them. God is almighty, wise. **229** Divorce may be [revoked] twice, whereupon a woman may either be retained in fairness or released with kindness. It is unlawful for you to take back from women anything of what you have given them [as dowry], unless they both [husband and wife] fear that they may not be able to keep within the bounds set by God. If you have cause to fear that they would not be able to keep within the bounds set by God, it shall be no offence for either of them if she gives up whatever she may in order to free herself. These are the bounds set by God; do not, then, transgress them. Those who transgress the bounds set by God are wrongdoers indeed. **230** Should he divorce her [a third time], she shall not thereafter be lawful for him to remarry until she has wedded another husband. If the latter then divorces her it shall be no offence for either of the two if they return to one another, if they feel that they will be able to keep within the bounds set by God. Such are the bounds set by God. He makes them plain for people who have knowledge. **231** When you have divorced women and they have reached the end of their waiting-term, either retain them with fairness or let them go with fairness. Do not retain them out of malice in order to hurt them. He who does so wrongs his own soul. Do not take God's revelations in a frivolous manner. Remember the blessings God has bestowed upon you, and all the revelation and wisdom He has bestowed upon you from on high in order to admonish you. Fear God and know well that He has full knowledge of everything. **232** And when you have divorced women and they have reached the end of their waiting-term, do not prevent them from marrying their husbands if they have agreed with each other in a fair manner. This is an admonition for everyone of you who believes in God and the Last Day. That is more virtuous for you, and purer. God knows, whereas you do not know. **233** Mothers may breast-feed their children for two whole years; [that is] for those who wish to complete the suckling. The father of the child is responsible to provide in a fair manner for their sustenance and clothing. No human being shall be burdened with more than he is well able to bear. Neither shall a mother be allowed to cause her child to suffer, nor shall a father cause suffering to his child. The same shall apply to the father's heir. If, by mutual consent and after due consultation, the parents choose to wean the child, they will incur no sin thereby. Nor shall it be any offence on your part if you engage wet nurses for your children, provided that you hand over what you agreed to pay, in a fair manner. Fear God, and know that God sees all that you do. **234** Those of you who die leaving wives behind, their wives shall wait, by themselves, for four months and ten days. When they have reached the end of their waiting-term, you shall incur no sin in whatever they may do with themselves in a lawful manner. God is aware of all that you do. **235** You will incur no sin if you give a hint of a marriage offer to [widowed] women or keep such an intention to yourselves. God knows that you will entertain such intentions concerning them. Do not, however, pledge your troth in secret; but speak only in a decent manner. Furthermore, do not resolve on actually making the marriage tie before the prescribed term [of waiting] has run its course. Know well that God knows what is in your minds, so have fear of Him; and know that God is much-forgiving, clement. **236** You will incur no sin if you divorce women before having touched them or settled a dowry for them. Provide for them, the rich according to his means and the straitened according to his means. Such a provision, in an equitable manner, is an obligation binding on the righteous. **237** If you divorce them before having touched them but after having settled a dowry for them, then give them half of that which you have settled, unless they forgo it or he in whose hand is the marriage tie forgoes it. To forgo what is due to you is closer to being righteous. Do not forget to act benevolently to one another. God sees all that you do. **238** Attend regularly to your prayers, particularly the middle prayer, and stand up before God in devout obedience. **239** If you are in fear, pray walking or riding. When you are again secure, remember God, since it is He who has taught you what you did not know. **240** Those of you who die leaving their wives behind, shall bequeath to their wives provisions for one year without their being obliged to leave [their deceased husbands' homes]. Should they leave home [of their own accord], you shall incur no sin for what they may do with themselves in a lawful manner. God is almighty, wise. **241** Divorced women shall have a provision according to what is fair. This is an obligation on the God-fearing. **242** Thus God makes clear to you His revelations that you may understand.

243 Are you not aware of those who left their homes in their thousands for fear of death? God said to them: 'Die', and later He brought them back to life. Surely, God grants limitless bounty to mankind, but most people are ungrateful. **244** Fight for the cause of God and know that God hears all and knows all. **245** Who will offer God a generous loan, which He will repay multiplied many times over? It is God who straitens people's circumstances and it is He who gives abundantly; and to Him you shall all return. **246** Are you not aware of those elders of the Children of Israel, after the time of Moses, when they said to one of their prophets, 'Appoint for us a king, and we shall fight for the cause of God'. He said, 'Would you, perchance, refuse to fight if fighting is ordained for you?' They said, 'Why should we not fight for the cause of God when we have been driven out of our homes and our families[11]?' Yet, when fighting was ordained for them, they turned back, save for a few of them. God is fully aware of the wrongdoers. **247** Their prophet said to them, 'God has appointed Saul [Talut] to be your king'. They said, 'How can he have the kingship over us when we are better entitled to it than he is? Besides, he has not been given abundance of wealth'. He said, 'God has chosen him in preference to you, and endowed him abundantly with knowledge and physical stature. God grants His dominion to whom He will. He is munificent, all-knowing'. **248** Their prophet also said to them, 'The sign of his kingship is that a casket shall be brought to you, wherein you shall have peace of reassurance from your Lord, and a legacy left behind by the House of Moses and the House of Aaron. It will be borne by angels. That will be a sign for you, if you are true believers'. **249** And when Saul set out with his troops, he said, 'God will now put you to the test by a river. He who drinks from it will not belong to me, but he who does not taste its water will indeed belong to me, except him who takes a scoop with his hand'. They all drank [their fill] of it, except for a few of them. When he and those who

---

11　　Literally: 'when we have been driven out of our homes and our sons', but it is not unusual in Arabic to refer to one's family as one's children.

kept faith with him crossed the river, they said, 'No strength have we today to stand up to Goliath and his forces'. But those of them who were certain that they would meet their Lord said, 'How often has a small host triumphed over a large host by God's grace. God is with those who remain patient in adversity'. **250** And when they came face to face with Goliath and his troops, they prayed, 'Our Lord, grant us patience in adversity, make firm our steps, and grant us victory over the unbelievers'. **251** They routed them, by God's will. David slew Goliath, and God bestowed on him the kingdom and wisdom, and taught him whatever He willed. Had it not been for the fact that God repels one group of people by another, the earth would have been utterly corrupted. God is limitless in His bounty to all the worlds. **252** These are the revelations of God. We recite them to you in all truth, for you are indeed one of Our messengers.

253 Those are the messengers! We have exalted some of them above others. To some God spoke directly, and some He raised in rank. We gave Jesus, the son of Mary, clear signs and strengthened him with the Holy Spirit. Had God so willed, those who succeeded them would not have fought against one another after the clear proofs had come to them. But they differed with one another: some of them accepted the faith and some rejected it. Yet had God so willed, they would not have fought one another. But God does whatever He wills. **254** Believers, spend [for God's cause] out of that with which We have provided you before there comes a Day when there will be no trading, or friendship or intercession. Truly, the unbelievers are the wrongdoers. **255** God: there is no deity but Him, the Ever-Living, the Eternal Master of all. Neither slumber nor sleep overtakes Him. His is all that is in the heavens and all that is on earth. Who is there that can intercede with Him, except by His permission? He knows all that lies open before them and all that lies hidden from them; whereas they cannot attain to anything of His knowledge save as He wills. His throne extends over the heavens and the earth, and the preservation of both does not weary Him. He is the Most High, the Most Great. **256** There shall be no compulsion in religion. The right way is henceforth distinct from error. He who rejects false deities[12]

---

12   The Arabic term for 'false deities' is *taghut*, meaning tyranny, a word denoting anything or anyone that takes hold of the mind or suppresses the truth, or transgresses the laws and limits set by God. It refers to forces and systems that disregard the divine religious, moral, social and legal order and operate in this life on values and principles not sanctioned by God or derived from His guidance and teachings.

and believes in God has indeed taken hold of a most firm support that never breaks. God hears all and knows all. **257** God is the patron of the believers. He leads them out of darkness into the light. As for the unbelievers, their patrons are false deities who lead them out of light into darkness. Those are the people destined for the Fire, therein to abide. **258** Are you not aware of him who argued with Abraham about his Lord simply because God had given him kingship? Abraham said, 'My Lord gives life and causes death'. 'I, too', said he, 'give life and cause death'. Abraham said, 'Well, God causes the sun to rise in the east; cause it, then, to rise in the west'. Thus the unbeliever was dumbfounded. God does not guide the wrongdoers. **259** Or, [are you not aware] of him who, passing by a township which had fallen into utter ruin, exclaimed: 'How can God bring this town back to life now that it is dead?' Thereupon God caused him to be dead for a hundred years, then brought him back to life, and said, 'How long have you remained thus?' He said, 'I have remained thus a day or part of a day'. God said, 'No. You have remained thus for a hundred years. Just look at your food and drink: none of it has rotted. And look at your ass. We will make you a sign for mankind. Look you at the bones, how We put them up and then clothe them with flesh'. When it had all become clear to him, he said, 'I know now that God has power over all things'. **260** When Abraham said, 'My Lord, show me how You give life to the dead', He replied, 'Have you, then, no faith?' 'Indeed, I have', said Abraham, 'but I only wish my heart to be fully reassured'. God said, 'Take four birds and draw them close to you, then [having cut them into pieces] place a part of them on each mountain. Then call them back and they will come to you in haste. Know that God is almighty, wise'.

261 The case of those who spend their property for the cause of God is like that of a grain that brings forth seven ears, each bearing a hundred grains. God gives manifold increase to whom He wills. God is munificent, all-knowing. **262** Those who spend their property for the cause of God and do not follow their spending by vaunting their own generosity, or by hurting others, shall have their reward with their Lord. They have nothing to fear, nor shall they grieve. **263** A kind word with forgiveness is better than charity followed by injury. God is free of all wants, clement. **264** Believers, do not render your charitable deeds worthless by vaunting your generosity and hurting others, as does he who spends his wealth to impress people, while he believes neither in God nor in the Last Day. Such a person is like a smooth rock covered with earth. Then heavy rain falls on it and leaves it hard and bare. Such as these shall gain nothing from their works. God does not guide the unbelievers. **265** But those who give away their money out of a genuine desire to please God, and out of their own inner certainty, are like a garden on a hillside. When heavy rain falls on it, it yields up twice its normal produce. If no heavy rain falls on it, then a light drizzle [will suffice]. God sees all that you do. **266** Would any of you wish to have a garden of palm-trees and vines, through which running waters flow, bringing forth all kinds of fruits, then to be well advanced in age, with helpless offspring; and then a fiery whirlwind smites it and leaves it all burnt down? Thus God makes plain to you His revelations, so that you may reflect. **267** Believers, spend on others out of the good things you have earned, and out of that which We bring forth for you from the earth. Do not choose for your spending the inferior things which you yourselves would not accept without turning your eyes away in disdain. Know that God is free of all want, ever to be praised. **268** Satan promises you poverty and bids you to commit indecency, whereas God promises you His forgiveness and bounty. God is munificent, all-knowing. **269** He grants wisdom to whom He wills. He who is granted wisdom has indeed been granted abundant good. Yet only those with sound minds would take heed. **270** Whatever charity you give or vows you make are known to God. The evildoers shall have none to help them. **271** If you give your charity openly, that is well; but if you give it to the poor in private, it is even better for you, and will atone for some of your bad deeds. God is aware of all you do. **272** It is not for you to make people follow the right guidance. It is God who guides whom He wills. Whatever good you may spend in charity is for your own good. You should only give out of pure dedication to God. And whatever good you give in charity will be repaid to you in full, and you shall not be wronged. **273** [Give] to the needy who, being wholly preoccupied with God's cause, are unable to go about earning their livelihood. The unthinking take them for men of wealth on account of their restrained behaviour. You can recognise them by their special mark: they do not beseech people for alms. Whatever good you give is certainly known to God. **274** Those who give out of their possessions by night and by day, in private and in public, shall have their reward with their Lord. They have nothing to fear and they shall not grieve.

275 Those who gorge themselves on usury cannot rise up except as he may rise up whom Satan has confounded with his touch. That is because they say, 'Trade is just the same as usury', whereas God has made trade lawful and usury forbidden. He who receives an admonition from his Lord, and thereupon desists [from usury] may retain his past gains, and it will be for God to judge him. Those who revert to the practice [of usury] are indeed the inmates of the Fire, wherein they shall abide. **276** God blots out usury and causes charitable offerings to grow and increase. God does not love confirmed unbelievers who persist in wrongdoing. **277** Those that have faith and do good deeds, attend regularly to their prayers and pay zakat, shall have their reward with their Lord. They shall have nothing to fear, nor shall they grieve. **278** Believers, fear God and give up what remains outstanding of usury gains, if you are true believers. **279** If you do not, then war is declared against you by God and His Messenger. If you repent, however, you shall remain entitled to your principal. Thus, you shall commit no wrong, nor suffer any wrong yourselves. **280** If [the debtor] is in straitened circumstances, grant him a delay until a time of ease. And if you waive [the debt entirely] as a gift of charity, it will be better for you, if you but knew it. **281** Fear the Day when you shall all return to God; when every soul shall be repaid in full for what it had earned, and none shall be wronged.

282 Believers, when you contract a debt for a fixed term, put it in writing, and let a scribe write it down for you with fairness. No scribe shall refuse to write as God has taught him. So he shall write. And let the one who incurs the liability [the debtor] dictate; and [in so doing] let him be conscious of God his Lord and not diminish anything of it. If he who incurs the liability is weak of mind or body, or unable to dictate himself, then let his guardian dictate with fairness. Call in two of your men to act as witnesses, but if two men are not available, then a man and two women, whom you consider acceptable as witnesses, so that if either of them should make a mistake, the other will remind her. Witnesses must not refuse when they are called in. Do not be averse to writing down debts, be they small or great, together with the time when they fall due; that is more equitable in the sight of God and lends greater credence to the testimony and is more likely to spare you any doubt. In the case of a commercial deal transacted on the spot, you shall incur no sin by not writing it down. Have witnesses when you make business deals; but let no harm be suffered by scribe or witness; if you do [harm them], that is sinful on your part. Have fear of God, for it is God who teaches you. God has knowledge of all things. **283** If you are on a journey and cannot find a scribe, pledges taken in hand [are sufficient]. If you trust one another, let him who is trusted fulfil his trust, and let him fear God, his Lord. You shall not withhold testimony, for he that withholds testimony is sinful at heart. God has full knowledge of all you do. **284** To God belongs all that is in the heavens and the earth. Whether you make known what is in your minds or conceal it, God will bring you to account for it. He will then forgive whom He wills and punish whom He wills. God has power over all things.

285 The Messenger believes in what has been revealed to him by his Lord, and so do the believers. Each one of them believes in God, His angels, His books, and His messengers. We make no distinction between any of His messengers. And they say, 'We hear and we obey. Grant us Your forgiveness, our Lord; to You we shall all return'. **286** God does not charge a soul with more than it can bear. In its favour shall be whatever good it does, and against it whatever evil it does. Our Lord, do not take us to task if we forget or unwittingly do wrong. Our Lord, do not lay on us a burden such as that You laid on those before us. Our Lord, do not burden us with what we do not have the strength to bear. Pardon us, and forgive us our sins, and bestow Your mercy on us. You are our Lord Supreme; grant us victory against the unbelievers.

Surah 3   Al 'Imran

This surah was revealed in Madinah when the first Muslim state was taking shape and the Muslim community were facing an array of hostile forces. Its first major section engages in a long discussion with these different groups who were hostile to the new divine message of Islam. It outlines the truth of God and the fact that He is the Creator of the universe and the One who conducts its affairs. The true nature of the Islamic message is also established and its focus on God's Oneness is emphasised. It gives examples of God's will, which is free and unrestricted by any force or law. The stories of Zachariah, Mary and the birth of first John and then Jesus are told in detail.

The Qur'an provides guidance to mankind over all generations. Therefore, when it relates a story, an historical event or a contemporary episode, it shows it against a universal background, so as to make its lessons relevant to all human generations, not only to the time of its occurrence. Therefore, it explains the motives of the enemies of Islam and shows that they are not limited to those who take an open stance of hostility, trying to crush Islam in open warfare. Instead, there are also hostile factions that take a more wicked and subtle stance, scheming against Islam to destroy its very fabric.

The second part of the surah (verses 121–179) deals with the Battle of Uhud and its effects on the Muslim community and the new Muslim state. This was the second major battle in Islam's history. The first encounter, the Battle of Badr, ended in a resounding victory for the Muslims. At Uhud, the Muslims suffered a military defeat because they disobeyed the Prophet. It tells the Muslims that it is not enough that they believe in Islam to guarantee victory every time they face their enemies in battle. Rather, they need to live up to the principles and values Islam lays down. Otherwise, their belief has no practical effect.

The final part of the surah outlines the characteristics of the Muslim community, describing the relationship between man and God as Islam wants its followers to view it.

Al 'Imran

In the Name of God, the Lord of Grace, the Ever-Merciful

1 *Alif. Lam. Mim.* **2** God: there is no deity but Him, the Ever-Living, the Eternal Master of all. **3** He has revealed to you this Book with the truth, confirming what was revealed before it; and He has already revealed the Torah and the Gospel **4** before this as guidance for people. And He has revealed the Criterion [to distinguish the true from the false]. Those who disbelieve in God's revelations shall endure grievous suffering. God is Mighty, able to requite. **5** Nothing on earth or in the heavens is hidden from God. **6** It is He who shapes you in the wombs as He pleases. There is no deity save Him, the Almighty, the Wise. **7** He it is who has sent down to you the Book, containing verses which are clear and precise – and these are the essence of the Book – and others are equivocal. Those whose hearts have swerved from the truth pursue that part of it which is equivocal, seeking to create dissension and trying to give it an arbitrary meaning. None knows its final meaning other than God and those who are firmly grounded in knowledge. They say: 'We believe in it; it is all from our Lord'. But only those who are endowed with insight take heed. **8** Our Lord, let not our hearts swerve from the truth after You have guided us; and bestow on us mercy from Yourself. You are indeed the Great Giver. **9** Our Lord, You will indeed gather mankind together to witness the Day of which there is no doubt. Surely, God never fails to keep His promise. **10** As for those who disbelieve, neither their riches nor their offspring will in the least avail them against God; it is they who shall be the fuel of the Fire. **11** Just like the cases of the people of Pharaoh and those before them: they disbelieved Our revelations; therefore, God took them to task for their sins. God's punishment is severe indeed. **12** Say to those who disbelieve: 'You shall be overcome and gathered unto Hell, an evil resting place. **13** You have had a sign in the two armies which met in battle. One was fighting for God's cause, the other an army of unbelievers. They saw with their very eyes that the others were twice their own number. But God strengthens with His succour whom He wills. In this there is surely a lesson for all who have eyes to see'. **14** Alluring to man is the enjoyment of worldly desires through women and offspring, heaped-up treasures of gold and silver, horses of high mark, cattle and plantations. These are the comforts of this life. With God is the best of all goals. **15** Say: 'Shall I tell you of better things than these? For the God-fearing there are, with their Lord, gardens through which running waters flow where they shall dwell forever, and spouses of perfect chastity, and God's good pleasure. God is mindful of His servants, **16** those who say: "Our Lord, we have indeed accepted the faith. Forgive us our sins and keep us safe from the torments of the Fire". **17** They are the patient in adversity, the true to their word, the devoted who spend in the cause of God, and those who pray for forgiveness at the time of dawn'.

18 God Himself bears witness, and so do the angels and men of knowledge, that there is no deity other than Him, the executor of Justice. There is no deity save Him, the Almighty, the Wise. **19** The only true faith acceptable to God is [man's] self-surrender to Him. Disagreements spread, through mutual aggression, among those who were given revelations only after knowledge had been granted to them. He who denies God's revelations will find that God is indeed swift in reckoning. **20** If they argue with you, say: 'I have surrendered my whole being to God, and so have all who follow me'. Say to those who were given revelations and to unlettered people, 'Will you also surrender yourselves (to God)?'; If they surrender, they are on the right path. But if they turn away, then your only duty is to convey your message. God is watching over His servants. **21** Those who deny God's revelations, and slay the prophets against all right and slay people who enjoin equity among all people: promise them a painful suffering. **22** It is they whose works shall come to nothing in this world and in the life to come; and they shall have none to help them. **23** Have you considered the case of those who have received a share of revelation? When they are called upon to accept the judgement of God's Book in their affairs, some of them turn away and pay no heed. **24** For they claim: 'The Fire will most certainly not touch us save for a limited number of days'. They are deceived in their own faith by the false beliefs they used to invent. **25** How, then, will it be with them when We shall gather them all together to witness the Day about which there is no doubt, when every soul will be paid in full what it has earned, and they shall not be wronged? **26** Say: 'Lord, Sovereign of all dominion, You grant dominion to whom You will and take dominion away from whom You will. You exalt whom You will and abase whom You will. In Your hand is all that is good. You are able to do all things. **27** You cause the night to pass into the day, and You cause the day to pass into the night. You bring forth the living from the dead, and You bring forth the dead from that which is alive. You grant sustenance to whom You will, beyond all reckoning'. **28** Let not the believers take unbelievers for their allies in preference to the believers. He who does this has cut himself off from God, unless it be that you protect yourselves against them in this way. God warns you to beware of Him: for to God you shall all return. **29** Say: 'Whether you conceal what is in your hearts or bring it into the open, it is known to God. He knows all that is in the heavens and all that is on earth; and God has the power to accomplish anything'. **30** On the Day when every soul will find itself confronted with whatever good it has done and whatever evil it has done, they will wish that there were a long span of time between them and that Day. God warns you to beware of Him; and God is most compassionate towards His servants. **31** Say: 'If you love God, follow me; God will love you and forgive you your sins. God is much-forgiving, ever-merciful'. **32** Say: 'Obey God and the Messenger'. If they turn their backs, God does not love the unbelievers.

33 God raised Adam and Noah, and the House of Abraham and the House of 'Imran above all mankind. **34** They were the offspring of one another. God hears all and knows all. **35** 'Imran's wife said: 'My Lord, I vow to you that which is in my womb, to be devoted to Your service. Accept it from me. You alone are the One who hears all and knows all'. **36** When she had given birth she said: 'My Lord, I have given birth to a female' – God well knew to what she would give birth – 'The male is not like the female. I have named her Mary and I seek Your protection for her and her offspring against Satan, the accursed'. **37** Her Lord graciously accepted her. He made her grow up a goodly child, and placed her in the care of Zachariah. Whenever Zachariah visited her in the sanctuary he found her provided with food. He would say: 'Mary, where has this come to you from?' She would answer: 'It is from God. God gives sustenance to whom He wills, beyond all reckoning'. **38** At that point, Zachariah prayed to his Lord, saying: 'Lord, bestow on me, out of Your grace, goodly offspring. Indeed, You hear all prayers'. **39** Thereupon, the angels called out to him as he stood praying in the sanctuary: 'God gives you the happy news of [the birth of] John, who shall confirm the truth of a word from God. He shall be noble, utterly chaste and a prophet from among the righteous'. **40** [Zachariah] said: 'Lord, how can I have a son when old age has already overtaken me and my wife is barren?' He answered: 'Thus it is. God does what He wills'. **41** [Zachariah] said: 'Lord, grant me a sign'. He replied: 'Your sign shall be that for three days you will not speak to people except by gestures. Remember your Lord unceasingly and glorify Him in the early hours of night and day'. **42** The angels said: 'Mary, God has chosen you and made you pure, and raised you above all the women of the world. **43** Mary, Remain truly devout to your Lord, prostrate yourself [to Him] and bow down with those who bow down in worship'. **44** This is an account of something which remained beyond the reach of your perception We now reveal to you. You were not present with them when they cast lots as to which of them should have charge of Mary; nor were you present when they contended about it with one another. **45** The angels said: 'Mary, God sends you the happy news, through a word from Him, [of a son] whose name is the Christ, Jesus, son of Mary, honoured in this world and in the life to come, and shall be among those who are favoured by God. **46** He shall speak to people in his cradle, and as a grown man, and shall be of the righteous'. **47** Said she: 'My Lord, How can I have a son when no man has ever touched me?' [The angel] answered: 'Thus it is. God creates what He wills. When He wills a thing to be, He only says to it "Be", and it is. **48** He will teach him the book and wisdom, and the Torah and the Gospel, **49** and will make him a messenger to the Israelites. "I have brought you a sign from your Lord. I will fashion for you out of clay the likeness of a bird. I shall breathe into it and, by God's leave, it shall become a living bird. I will heal the blind and the leper, and bring the dead back to life by God's leave. I will announce to you what you eat and what you store up in your houses. Surely, in all this there is a sign for you, if you are truly believers. **50** And [I have come] to confirm that which has already been sent down of the Torah and to make lawful to you some of the things which were forbidden you. I have come to you with a sign from your Lord; so remain conscious of God and obey me. **51** God is indeed my Lord and your Lord, so worship Him alone. That is the straight path".' **52** When Jesus became conscious of their rejection of the faith, he asked: 'Who will be my helpers in the cause of God?' The disciples replied: 'We are [your] helpers in God's cause. We believe in God. Bear you witness that we have surrendered ourselves to Him. **53** Our Lord, we believe in what You have bestowed from on high, and we follow the messenger, so write us down among those who bear witness [to the truth]'. **54** They schemed, and God also schemed. God is the best of schemers. **55** God said: 'Jesus, I shall gather you and cause you to ascend to Me, and I shall cleanse you of those who disbelieve, and I shall place those who follow you above those who disbelieve until the Day of Resurrection. Then to Me you shall all return, and I shall judge between you with regard to everything on which you used to differ. **56** As for those who disbelieve I shall inflict on them severe suffering in this world and in the life to come; and they shall have none to help them'. **57** But to those who believe and do good works, He will grant their reward in full. God does not love the wrongdoers. **58** This which We recite to you is a revelation and a wise reminder. **59** The case of Jesus in the sight of God is the same as the case of Adam. He created him of dust and then said to him: 'Be', and he was. **60** This is the truth from your Lord: be not, then, among the doubters. **61** If anyone should dispute with you about this [truth] after all the knowledge you have received, say: 'Come. Let us summon our sons and your sons, our women and your women, and ourselves and yourselves; then let us pray humbly and solemnly and invoke God's curse upon the ones who are telling a lie. **62** This is indeed the truth of the matter. There is no deity save God. Indeed, it is God Who is the Mighty, the Wise'. **63** And if they turn away, God has full knowledge of those who spread corruption. **64** Say: 'People of earlier revelations. Let us come to an agreement which is equitable between you and us: that we shall worship none but God, that we shall associate no partners with Him, and that we shall not take one another for lords beside God'. And if they turn away, then say: 'Bear witness that we have surrendered ourselves to God'.

65 People of earlier revelations! Why do you argue about Abraham when both the Torah and the Gospel were only revealed after his time? Have you no sense? **66** You have indeed argued about that of which you have some knowledge; why then do you argue about that of which you have no knowledge at all? God knows, whereas you do not know. **67** Abraham was neither a Jew nor a Christian; but he was wholly devoted to God, having surrendered himself to Him. He was not of those who associate partners with God. **68** The people who have the best claim to Abraham are those who followed him, and this Prophet and those who are true believers. God is the Guardian of the believers. **69** A party of the people of earlier revelations would love to lead you astray; but they lead astray none but themselves, although they may not perceive it. **70** People of earlier revelations! Why do you disbelieve in God's revelations when you yourselves bear witness [to their truth]? **71** People of earlier revelations! Why do you cloak the truth with falsehood, and knowingly conceal the truth? **72** A party of the people of earlier revelations say [to one another]: 'Declare at the beginning of the day, that you believe in what has been revealed to the believers, and then deny it at the end of the day, so that they may go back on their faith. **73** But do not really trust anyone except those who follow your own faith.' – Say: 'All true guidance is God's guidance' – 'That anyone may be given the like of what you have been given. Or that they should contend against you before your Lord.' Say: 'Grace is in God's hand: He bestows it on whom He wills. God is munificent and all-knowing'. **74** He singles out for His mercy whom He wills. And God's grace is great indeed.

75 Among the people of earlier revelations there is many a one who, if you trust him with a treasure, will return it to you intact; and there is among them many a one who, if you trust him with a small gold coin, will not return it to you, unless you keep standing over him. For they say: 'We have no obligation to keep faith with Gentiles'. Thus they deliberately say of God what they know to be a lie. **76** Indeed those who fulfil their pledges and guard themselves against evil [enjoy God's love]; for God loves the righteous. **77** Those who barter away their covenant with God and their oaths for a trifling gain will have no share in the life to come. God will neither speak to them, nor cast a look on them on the Day of Resurrection, nor will He cleanse them of their sins. Theirs will be a painful suffering. **78** There are some among them who twist their tongues when quoting the Scriptures, so that you may think that [what they say] is from the Scriptures, when it is not from the Scriptures. They say: 'It is from God', when it is not from God. Thus, they deliberately say of God what they know to be a lie. **79** It is not conceivable that any human being to whom God had given revelation and wisdom and prophethood would subsequently say to people: 'Worship me instead of God'. But rather 'Be devoted servants of God, by virtue of spreading the knowledge of the Scriptures and your constant study of them'. **80** Nor would he bid you to take the angels and the prophets as your gods. Would he bid you to be unbelievers after you have surrendered yourselves to God? **81** God made a covenant with the prophets: 'If, after what I have bestowed on you of the Scriptures and wisdom, there comes to you a messenger confirming the truth of what you have in your possession, you shall believe in him and you shall help him. Do you', said He, 'affirm this and accept the obligation I lay upon you in these terms?' They answered: 'We do affirm it'. Said He: 'Then bear witness, and I am also a witness with you'. **82** Then those who turn away afterwards are indeed transgressors. **83** Do they seek a religion other than God's, when every soul in the heavens and the earth has submitted to Him, willingly or by compulsion, and to Him they shall all return? **84** Say: 'We believe in God and in that which has been bestowed from on high upon us, and that which has been bestowed on Abraham, Ishmael, Isaac, Jacob and their descendants, and that which has been vouchsafed by their Lord to Moses and Jesus and all the prophets. We make no distinction between them. To Him do we surrender ourselves'. **85** He who seeks a religion other than self-surrender to God, it will not be accepted from him, and in the life to come he will be among the lost. **86** How shall God guide people who have lapsed into disbelief after having accepted the faith and having borne witness that this messenger is true, and after having received clear evidence of the truth? God does not guide the wrongdoers. **87** Of such people the punishment shall be the curse of God, the angels and all men. **88** Under it they shall abide. Neither their suffering shall be lightened, nor shall they be granted respite. **89** Excepted shall be those who afterwards repent and mend their ways; for God is much-forgiving, ever-merciful. **90** But those who return to disbelief after having accepted the faith and then grow more stubborn in their rejection of the faith, their repentance will not be accepted. For they are those who have truly gone astray. **91** As for those who disbelieve and die unbelievers, not even the earth full of gold shall be accepted from any one of them, were he to offer it in ransom. They shall have grievous suffering and they shall have none to help them. **92** You will never attain to true piety unless you spend on others out of what you dearly cherish. God has full knowledge of what you spend.

93 All food was lawful to the Children of Israel except what Israel forbade himself, in the days before the Torah was bestowed from on high. Say: 'Bring the Torah and recite it, if what you say is true. **94** Those who fabricate lies about God after this are indeed wrongdoers'. **95** Say: 'God speaks truth. Follow, then, the creed of Abraham, who turned away from all that is false and was not one of those who associate partners with God'. **96** The first House [of worship] ever set up for mankind was indeed the one at Bakkah: rich in blessing; and a source of guidance to all the worlds, **97** full of clear messages. It is the place whereon Abraham once stood; and whoever enters it finds inner peace. Pilgrimage to this House is a duty owed to God by all people who are able to undertake it. As for those who disbelieve, God does not stand in need of anything in all the worlds. **98** Say: 'People of earlier revelations, why do you disbelieve in God's revelations, when God Himself is witness to all that you do?' **99** Say: 'People of earlier revelations, why do you try to turn those who have come to believe away from the path of God, seeking to make it appear crooked, when you yourselves bear witness [to its being straight]? God is not unaware of what you do'. **100** Believers, if you pay heed to some of those who have been given revelations, they will cause you to renounce the truth after you have accepted the faith. **101** But how can you sink into disbelief when God's revelations are being recited to you and His Messenger is in your midst? He who holds fast to God has already been guided along a straight path. **102** Believers! Fear God as you rightly should, and do not allow death to overtake you before you have surrendered yourselves truly to Him. **103** Hold fast, all of you together, to the bond with God and do not be disunited. And remember the blessings God has bestowed on you: how, when you were enemies [to one another] He united your hearts and, by His grace, you have become brothers; and how, when you were on the brink of an abyss of fire, He saved you from it. Thus God makes clear His revelations to you, so that you may be rightly guided. **104** Let there become of you a nation who invite to all that is good, enjoin the doing of what is right and forbid what is wrong. Such are they who shall prosper. **105** Do not follow the example of those who became divided and fell into conflict with one another after clear proofs had come to them. For these there will be grievous suffering, **106** on the Day when some faces will shine with happiness and some faces will be blackened. Those whose faces are blackened [shall be told]: 'Did you disbelieve after having embraced the faith? Taste, then, this suffering for having sunk into disbelief'. **107** Those with shining faces shall be in God's grace; they abide there forever. **108** These are revelations from God. We recite them to you in truth. God wills no injustice to His creatures. **109** To God belongs all that is in the heavens and all that is on earth; to Him shall all things return. **110** You are the best community that has ever been raised for mankind; you enjoin the doing of what is right and forbid what is wrong, and you believe in God. Had the people of earlier revelations believed, it would have been for their own good. Few of them are believers, while most of them are evil-doers. **111** They cannot harm you beyond causing you some trifling hurt; and if they fight against you they will turn their backs upon you in flight. Then they will receive no help. **112** Ignominy shall be pitched over them wherever they may be, save when they have a bond with God and a bond with men. They have incurred the wrath of God and humiliation shall overshadow them. That is because they persisted in denying God's revelations and killing the prophets against all right. That is because they persisted in their disobedience and transgression. **113** They are not all alike. Of the people of earlier revelations there are some upright people who recite the revelations of God in the depth of the night, and prostrate themselves in worship. **114** They believe in God and the Last Day and enjoin the doing of what is right and forbid what is wrong and vie with one another in doing good works. These belong to the righteous. **115** Whatever good they do, they shall never be denied its reward. God knows those who fear Him. **116** As for the unbelievers, neither their riches nor their children will avail them in any way against God. It is they who are destined for the Fire, where they will abide. **117** Whatever they spend in this present life is like a biting, icy wind which smites the harvest of people who have wronged themselves, laying it to waste. It is not God who does them wrong; they wrong themselves. **118** Believers, do not take for your intimate friends men other than your own folk. They will spare no effort to corrupt you. They love to see you in distress. Their hatred has already become apparent by [what they say with] their mouths, but what their hearts conceal is much worse. We have made revelations plain to you, if you will only use your reason. **119** See for yourselves how it is you who love them and they do not love you. You believe in all revelations. When they meet you they say: 'We, too, are believers'. But when they find themselves alone, they bite their fingertips with rage against you. Say: 'Perish in your rage'. God is fully aware of what is in the hearts [of people]. **120** When good fortune comes your way, it grieves them; and if evil befalls you, they rejoice. If you persevere and fear God, their machinations cannot harm you in any way. God encompasses all that they do.

121 Remember when you set out from your home at an early hour to assign the believers to their battle posts. God hears all and knows all. **122** Two of your groups were about to lose heart, but God was their protector. In God shall the believers trust. **123** God gave you victory at Badr when you were utterly weak. Therefore, fear God, that you may have cause to be grateful. **124** You said to the believers: 'Is it not enough for you [to know] that your Lord should send down three thousand angels to support you?' **125** Indeed, He will, if you are patient in adversity and fear God, and if they [the unbelievers] suddenly attack you, your Lord will supply you with five thousand angels swooping down. **126** God made this only as a happy news for you, so that your hearts might take comfort from it. Victory comes only from God, the Mighty, the Wise. **127** It is in order to destroy some of the unbelievers, and so abase others that they lose and withdraw. **128** You, [Prophet], have no say in the matter. [It is for Him] to accept their repentance or punish them. They are wrongdoers. **129** To Him belongs all that is in the heavens and the earth; He forgives whom He wills and punishes whom He wills. God is much-forgiving, ever-merciful. **130** Believers, do not gorge yourselves on usury, doubling [your money] again and again. Have fear of God, so that you may prosper. **131** Guard yourselves against the Fire which has been prepared for the unbelievers; **132** and obey God and the Messenger, that you may be graced with mercy.

133 Hasten, all of you, to the achievement of your Lord's forgiveness, and a Paradise as vast as the heavens and the earth, prepared for the God-fearing, **134** who spend [in His way] in time of plenty and in time of hardship, and restrain their anger, and forgive their fellow men. God loves the benevolent. **135** Those who, when they commit a gross indecency or wrong themselves, remember God and pray for the forgiveness of their sins – for who but God can forgive sins? – and do not knowingly persist in doing the wrong they may have done. **136** These shall have the reward of forgiveness from their Lord, and gardens underneath which rivers flow, where they shall abide. Excellent is the reward for those who labour [well].

137 Many patterns have passed away before you. Go about the earth and see what was the fate of those who described the truth as lies. **138** This is a plain exposition for mankind, as well as a guidance and an admonition for the God-fearing. **139** Do not be faint of heart, and do not grieve; for you shall gain the upper hand if you are truly believers. **140** If misfortune befalls you, a similar misfortune has befallen other people as well. Such days [of fortune and misfortune] We deal out in turn among men. God wants to mark out those who truly believe and choose from among you such as [with their lives] bear witness to the truth. God does not love the wrongdoers. **141** And God wants to test and prove the believers, and to blot out the unbelievers. **142** Do you reckon that you can enter Paradise unless God has identified those among you who strive hard [in His cause], and who are patient in adversity? **143** Surely, you used to wish for death before you came face to face with it. Now you have seen it with your own eyes. **144** Muhammad is only a messenger: all messengers have passed away before him. If, then, he dies or is slain, will you turn about on your heels? He that turns about on his heels will not harm God in any way. God will reward those who are grateful [to Him]. **145** No one can die except by God's leave, at a term appointed. He who desires the reward of this world, We shall give him thereof; and to him who desires the reward of the life to come, We shall give thereof. We shall reward those who are grateful to Us. **146** Many a prophet has fought with many devout men alongside him. They never lost heart on account of what they had to suffer in God's cause, and neither did they weaken nor succumb. God loves those who are patient in adversity. **147** All that they said was this: 'Our Lord! Forgive us our sins and our excesses in our affairs. Make firm our steps, and give us victory over the unbelievers'. **148** God has granted them the reward of this life and the best reward of the life to come. God loves those who do their duty well.

149 Believers, if you obey those who have rejected the faith, they will cause you to turn back on your heels, and you will be the losers. **150** Indeed, God alone is your Lord Supreme and He is the best of all who bring succour. **151** We shall strike terror in the hearts of unbelievers because they associate partners with God – something for which He has never granted any warrant. Their abode is the Fire, and evil indeed is the dwelling place of the wrongdoers. **152** God fulfilled to you His promise when, by His leave, you were about to destroy them. But then you lost heart and disagreed with one another concerning [the Prophet's command] and disobeyed after God had brought you within view of that for which you were longing. Some of you cared only for this world and some cared for the life to come. Then He turned you away from them so that He may put you to a test. But now He has forgiven you, for God is gracious to the believers. **153** [Remember] when you ran away, up into the mountain, paying no heed to anyone, while the Messenger was at your rear calling out to you. Therefore, He rewarded you with sorrow after sorrow so that you may not grieve over what had escaped you, nor over what had befallen you. God is aware of all that you do. **154** Then, after sorrow, He let peace fall upon you, in the shape of a slumber which overtook some of you, while others, who cared mainly for themselves, entertained wrong thoughts about God – thoughts of pagan ignorance. They ask: 'Have we any say in the matter?' Say: 'All power of decision rests with God'. They conceal in their minds what they do not disclose to you. They say: 'Had we had any say in the matter, we should not have been slaughtered here'. Say: 'Had you stayed in your homes, those of you who were destined to be killed would have gone to their deathbeds'. For it was God's will to put to a test all that you entertain in your minds and to render pure what you may have in your hearts, God is fully aware of what is in people's bosoms. **155** As for those of you who turned away on the day when the two hosts met in battle, Satan caused them to slip only in consequence of something that they themselves had done. But now God has pardoned them. Indeed, God is much-forgiving, clement. **156** Believers, be not like those who disbelieve and say of their brethren, when they travel on earth or go forth to war, 'Had they stayed with us they would not have died, nor would they have been killed', so that God places a source of despair in their hearts. It is God alone who grants life and causes death. God sees all that you do. **157** If you should be slain or die in God's cause, surely forgiveness by God and His grace are better than all the riches they amass. **158** If you should die or be slain, it is to God that you shall be gathered.

159 It is by God's grace that you deal gently with them. Had you been harsh and hard-hearted, they would surely have broken away from you. Therefore, pardon them and pray for them to be forgiven and consult with them in the conduct of public affairs. When you have resolved about a course of action, put your trust in God. God loves those who put their trust in Him. **160** If God helps you, none can overcome you; but if He should forsake you, then who is it that can help you besides Him? It is in God that the believers should put their trust. **161** It does not behove a prophet to act dishonestly, for he who acts dishonestly shall be faced with his dishonesty on the Day of Resurrection. Everyone will then be paid in full what he has earned, and none shall be wronged. **162** Can he who strives after God's pleasure be compared to one who has incurred God's wrath and whose abode is Hell? How evil such a goal is. **163** They have different standings in God's sight. God sees all that they do. **164** Indeed, God bestowed a favour on the believers when He sent them a messenger from among themselves, to recite to them His revelations, and to purify them, and teach them the Book and wisdom, whereas before that they were surely in plain error.

165 Why, when a calamity befell you, after you had inflicted twice as much [on your enemy], did you exclaim, 'How has this come about?' Say: 'It has come from your own selves'. Surely, God has the power over all things. **166** That which befell you, on the day when the two hosts met in battle, happened by God's leave, so that He might mark out the true believers. **167** And [He might] mark out the hypocrites. When these were told, 'Come, fight in God's cause', or 'Defend yourselves', they answered, 'Had we known there would be a fight, we would certainly have followed you'. On that day they were nearer unbelief than faith, uttering with their mouths something different to what was in their hearts, but God knew fully well all that they tried to conceal. **168** Such were they who, having themselves stayed behind, said of their brothers: 'If only they had listened to us, they would not have been slain'. Say to them: 'Ward off death from yourselves, then, if what you say be true'. **169** Do not think of those who are slain in God's cause as dead. They are alive, and well provided for by their Lord. **170** Happy they are with what God has granted them. They rejoice that those [of their brethren] who have been left behind and have not yet joined them have nothing to fear, nor have they [cause] to grieve. **171** They rejoice in the happy news of God's blessing and bounty, and in the fact that God will not suffer the reward of the believers to be lost. **172** Those who responded to the call of God and the Messenger after misfortune had befallen them: a great reward awaits those of them who continued to do good and feared God. **173** When other people warned them: 'A big force has gathered against you, so fear them', that only strengthened their faith and they answered: 'God is enough for us; He is the best Guardian'. **174** So they earned God's grace and bounty, suffering no harm. For they had striven to please God, whose bounty is limitless. **175** It is but Satan who prompts people to fear his allies: so, have no fear of them, but fear Me if you are truly believers. **176** Be not grieved by those who hasten on to disbelief. They cannot harm God in any way. It is God's will not to assign to them any share in the [blessings of the] life to come. Grievous suffering awaits them. **177** Indeed, those who have bought disbelief at the price of faith cannot harm God in any way. Painful suffering awaits them. **178** Let not those who disbelieve imagine that our giving them rein bodes well for their own souls. We only give them rein so that they may grow in sinfulness. A humiliating suffering awaits them. **179** It is not God's purpose to leave the believers in your present state except to set apart the bad from the good. And it is not God's purpose to reveal to you what is kept beyond the reach of human perception. But God favours from among His messengers whomever He wills. Believe, therefore, in God and His messengers. If you believe and are God-fearing, you shall have a great reward.

180 Let not those who miserly cling to all that God has bestowed on them of His bounty think that this is good for them. Indeed, it is bad for them. That to which they miserly cling will hang around their necks on the Day of Resurrection. To God belongs the heritage of the heavens and the earth, and God is well aware of all that you do. **181** God has certainly heard the words of those who said: 'God is poor, and we are rich'. We shall record what they have said, and also their slaying of prophets against all right and We shall say: 'Taste now the torment of burning. **182** This is on account of what your own hands have wrought. Never does God do the slightest injustice to His servants'. **183** They declare: 'God has charged us not to believe in any messenger unless he brings us an offering which the fire consumes'. Say: 'Messengers came to you before me with clear evidence of the truth, and with that which you describe. Why, then, did you slay them, if what you say is true?' **184** Then, if they charge you with falsehood, before your time other messengers were also charged with falsehood when they came with clear evidence of the truth, and books of divine wisdom and with the light-giving revelation. **185** Every soul shall taste death, and you shall be paid on the Day of Resurrection only that which you have earned. He who shall be drawn away from the Fire and brought into Paradise shall indeed have gained a triumph. The life of this world is nothing but an illusory enjoyment. **186** You shall most certainly be tried in your possessions and in your persons; and you shall hear much hurting abuse from those who were given revelations before you and from those who set up partners with God. But if you persevere and continue to fear God – that is indeed a matter requiring strong resolve. **187** God has made a covenant with those who were granted revelations (when He bade them): 'Make it known to mankind and do not conceal it'. But they cast it behind their backs and bartered it away for a trifling price. Evil is that which they have taken in exchange for it. **188** Do not think that those who exult in their deeds and love to be praised for what they have not done will escape punishment. Painful suffering awaits them. **189** To God belongs the dominion of the heavens and the earth; and He has power over all things.

190 In the creation of the heavens and the earth, and in the succession of night and day, there are indeed signs for men endowed with insight, **191** who remember God when they stand, sit and lie down, and reflect on the creation of the heavens and the earth: 'Our Lord, You have not created all this in vain. Limitless are You in Your glory. Guard us, then, against the torment of the Fire. **192** Our Lord, him whom You shall commit to the Fire, You will have condemned to disgrace. The wrongdoers shall have none to help them. **193** Our Lord, we have heard the voice of one who calls to faith, [saying], "Believe in your Lord", and we have believed. Our Lord, forgive us, then, our sins and efface our bad deeds and let us die with the truly virtuous. **194** Our Lord, grant us what You have promised us through Your messengers, and do not disgrace us on the Day of Resurrection. Surely, You never fail to fulfil Your promise'. **195** Their Lord answers them: 'I will not suffer the work of any worker among you, male or female, to be lost. Each of you is an issue of the other. Therefore, those who migrate and are driven out of their homes and suffer persecution in My cause, and fight and are slain [for it] – I shall indeed efface their bad deeds and admit them to gardens through which running waters flow, as a reward from God. With God is the best of rewards'. **196** Let not the unbelievers' prosperity in the land deceive you. **197** It is but a brief enjoyment. Then, Hell shall be their abode. What an evil abode. **198** As for those who fear their Lord, theirs shall be gardens through which running waters flow, in which they shall abide, a gift of welcome from God. That which is with God is best for the truly virtuous. **199** There are indeed among the people of earlier revelations some who believe in God and in what has been bestowed from on high upon you and in what has been bestowed upon them, humbling themselves before God. They do not barter away God's revelations for a trifling price. They shall have their reward with their Lord. God is swift in reckoning. **200** Believers, be patient in adversity, and let your patience never be exhausted, be ever ready and fear God so that you may prosper.

Surah 4   Women

This is the second longest surah in the Qur'an and it was revealed in Madinah, contributing to the moulding of the first Muslim community. From reading the surah and relating its verses to the different events that took place in the Madinan period we may conclude that its revelation stretched over a period from the end of the third year to the beginning of the ninth year of the Prophet's migration to Madinah.

The surah deals with different aspects of the life of the new Muslim society, removing the lingering values of the old system. Most importantly, the surah seeks to establish the rights of the vulnerable in society, administering justice to all. Thus, we note that its legislation ensures the rights of orphans, establishing their inheritance rights and putting in place the detailed Islamic system of inheritance that gives every heir, man, woman or child their fair shares (verses 6–14 and 176). The surah gives women their full rights of ownership and financial independence, doing away with the traditions of the preceding ignorant society that rendered the status of women so low that, in certain cases, a widow could be considered part of the estate left by her deceased husband. Legislation concerning women is given in various parts of the surah.

In all its legislation, the surah relates the new laws to the central principle of the Islamic faith that gives the authority to legislate to God alone. Thus, the concept of God in Islam is further clarified as is the relationship between God and man. Where particular incidents that took place during the Prophet's lifetime are addressed, the Qur'an gives its laws a general application so that the incident serves as a background, while the implementation of the law is required to be for all time.

Essentially, the surah stresses the need to ensure justice to all. Indeed, it gives a ruling that established the innocence of a Jew in Madinah who was falsely accused of theft by his neighbours who pretended to be Muslims (verses 105–113). The surah includes some provisions relating to fighting and war ethics.

Women

In the Name of God, the Lord of Grace, the Ever-Merciful

1 Mankind, fear your Lord, who has created you from a single soul, and from it created its mate, and from the two of them spread abroad

so many men and women. Fear God, in whose name you appeal to one another, and be mindful of your ties of kinship. Indeed, God is ever watching over you. **2** Give the orphans their property. Do not substitute bad things of your own for their good things, and do not absorb their wealth into your own wealth. That is surely a grave sin of injustice. **3** If you fear that you may not deal fairly by the orphans, you may marry of other women as may be agreeable to you, two or three or four. But if you fear that you will not be able to maintain fairness between them, then marry only one, or those whom your right hands possess. That makes it more likely that you will not do injustice. **4** Give women their dowry as a free gift; but if they, of their own accord, choose to give up to you a part of it, then you may take it with pleasure. **5** Do not give to the feeble-minded your wealth which God has assigned to you in trust. Make provisions for them and clothe them out of it and speak to them in a kindly way. **6** Test the orphans [in your charge] until they reach a marriageable age; then, if you find them of sound judgement, hand over to them their property, and do not consume it by wasteful and hasty spending before they come of age. Let him who is rich abstain generously [from his ward's property], but he who is poor may partake of it in a fair manner. When you hand over to them their property, let there be witnesses on their behalf. God is sufficient as a reckoner. **7** Men shall have a share in what parents and kinsfolk leave behind, and women shall have a share in what parents and kinsfolk leave behind; whether it be little or much. It is an apportioned share. **8** When other kinsfolk, orphans and needy people are present at the distribution of inheritance, give them something out of it, and speak to them in a kindly way. **9** Let those who, if they themselves had to leave behind weak offspring, would feel fear on their account, be afraid [to wrong the orphans in their charge], let them fear God and speak in a just manner. **10** Those who devour the property of orphans unjustly, only swallow fire into their bellies. They will be made to endure a blazing Fire. God has this to enjoin on you with regard to your children: The male shall have a share equal to that of two females. If there are more than two women, they shall have two-thirds of what [their parents] leave behind; and if there is only one, she shall have one-half of it. **11** As for the parents [of the deceased], each of them shall have one-sixth of what he leaves behind, in the event of his having a child; but if he leaves no children, and his parents be his heirs, then his mother shall have one-third; and if he has brothers and sisters, his mother shall have one-sixth after any bequest he may have made, or any outstanding debt [has been deducted from the total estate]. With regard to your parents and your children, you do not know which of them is of more benefit to you. This is, therefore, an ordinance from God. God is all-knowing, wise. **12** You shall inherit one-half of what your wives leave behind, provided that they have left no child; but if they have left a child, then you shall have one-quarter of what they leave behind, after [deducting] any bequest they may have made or any outstanding debt. And they [your widows] shall inherit one-quarter of what you leave behind, provided that you have left no child; but if you have left a child, then they shall have one-eighth of what you leave behind, after [deducting] any bequest you may have made or any outstanding debt. If a man or a woman has no heir in the direct line, but has a brother or a sister, then each of them shall inherit one-sixth; but if there be more, then they shall share in one-third, after [deducting] any bequest which may have been made or any outstanding debt, neither of which having been intended to harm [the heirs]. This is a commandment from God; and God is all-knowing, clement. **13** These are the bounds set by God. Whoever obeys God and His Messenger, him will He admit into gardens through which running waters flow, there to dwell forever. That is the supreme triumph. **14** But whoever disobeys God and His Messenger, and transgresses His bounds, him will He commit to the Fire, there to abide forever; and shameful torment awaits him.

15 As for those of your women who are guilty of gross immoral conduct, call upon four from among you to bear witness against them. If they so testify, then confine the guilty women to their houses until death takes them or God opens another way for them. **16** And the two from among you who are guilty of the same, punish them both. If they repent and mend their ways, then leave them alone. God is the acceptor of repentance, the Ever-Merciful. **17** God will indeed accept the repentance of only those who do evil out of ignorance, and then repent shortly afterwards. It is they to whom God turns in His mercy. God is all-knowing, wise. **18** Repentance shall not be accepted from those who indulge in their evil deeds and, when death comes to any of them, he says: 'I now repent'; nor from those who die as unbelievers. For those We have prepared painful suffering. **19** Believers, it is unlawful for you to inherit women against their will, or to bar them from remarrying so that you may make off with part of what you have given them, except when they are guilty of a flagrant indecency. Consort with them in a goodly manner. Even if you are averse to them, it may well be that you are averse to something in which God has placed much good. **20** If you wish to take one wife in place of another and you have given the first one a large dowry, do not take away anything of it. Would you take it away though that constitutes a gross injustice and a manifest sin? **21** How can you take it away when each of you has been privy with the other, and they have received from you a most solemn pledge? **22** Do not marry women whom your fathers have previously married, unless it be a thing of the past. Surely, that is an indecent, abominable and evil practice. **23** Forbidden to you [in marriage] are your mothers, your daughters, your sisters, your aunts paternal and maternal, your brother's daughters and your sister's daughters, your mothers who have given suck to you, your suckling sisters, the mothers of your wives, your stepdaughters – who are your foster children – born to your wives with whom you have consummated your marriage; but if you have not consummated your marriage with them, you will incur no sin [by marrying their daughters],[13] and the wives of your own begotten sons; and [you are forbidden] to have two sisters as your wives at one and the same time, unless it be a thing of the past. God is much-forgiving, ever-merciful. **24** And [forbidden to you are] all married women, other than those whom your right hands possess. This is God's ordinance, binding upon you. Lawful to you are all women other than these, provided that, offering them of your own possessions, you seek to take them in wedlock, not in fornication. To those with whom you seek to enjoy marriage, you shall give the dowries due to them; but you will incur no sin if you agree among yourselves on any voluntary arrangement even after what has been stipulated by way of duty. God is indeed all-knowing, wise. **25** Any of you who, owing to circumstances, is not in a position to marry a free believing woman may marry a believing maiden from among those whom your right hands possess. God knows all about your faith: you belong to one another. Marry them, then, with their people's consent and give them their dowries in an equitable manner, as chaste women who give themselves in honest wedlock, not in fornication, nor as women who have secret love companions. If after their marriage, they are guilty of gross immoral conduct, they shall be liable to half the penalty to which free women are liable. This provision applies to those of you who fear to stumble into sin. Yet it is better for you to be patient. God is much-forgiving, ever-merciful. **26** God wants to make all this clear to you and to guide you in the [righteous] ways of life of

---

13   This is permissible only in the case when the marriage to the mother is terminated by divorce or death before it has been consummated.

those who have preceded you, and to turn to you in His mercy. God is all-knowing, wise. **27** And God wants to turn to you in His mercy, while those who follow their lusts want you to go very far astray. **28** God wants to lighten your burdens; for man has been created weak.

29 Believers, do not devour each other's wealth illegally, unless it be through trade which you conduct by mutual consent. Do not kill yourselves, for God is merciful to you. **30** Whoever does this with malicious intent and by way of wilful wrongdoing, We shall make to suffer the Fire. That is very easy for God. **31** If you avoid the most serious of what you are forbidden, We will erase your bad deeds, and shall cause you to enter an abode of glory. **32** Do not covet the bounties God has bestowed more abundantly on some of you than on others. Men shall have a benefit of what they earn and women shall have a benefit of what they earn. Therefore, ask God to give you out of His bounty. God is a witness of everything. **33** To everyone have We appointed heirs to property left by parents and relatives. As for those with whom you have made covenants give them their share. God is indeed witness to all things. **34** Men shall take full care of women with the bounties with which God has favoured some of them more abundantly than others, and with what they may spend of their own wealth. The righteous women are devout, guarding the intimacy which God has ordained to be guarded. As for those women from whom you have reason to fear rebellion, admonish them [first]; then leave them alone in bed; then beat them.[14] Then, if they pay you heed, do not seek any pretext to harm them. God is indeed most high,

---

14   In most, if not all, translations of the Qur'an, this phrase is rendered, 'and beat them'. I, however, do not feel that this reflects the intended meaning. According to the *Cambridge English Dictionary*, beat is defined as 'to hit someone repeatedly'. In other dictionaries an intention to cause pain or injury is added. This is definitely different from what the measure recommended in this verse means. Nor do we find in English a synonym or analogous word that fits the context. Therefore, we need to explain the recommended measure. To do so, we must, of necessity, resort to the Prophet's own guidance and the linguistic usage of the word.

    1. As regards the Prophet's own action, 'A'ishah reports: 'God's Messenger never beat anyone with his hand, not a woman, not a servant, except when he fought for God's cause'. When a maid angered him, he said to her: 'Had it not been for my fear of God, I would have punished you with this toothbrush'. When his wives jointly pressurised him for a more comfortable living, he admonished them, and when the admonition did not work, he stayed away from them for a month. He then gave them a free choice: either to remain with him or to be divorced in an amicable and honourable way. They all chose to stay with him. Moreover, he continually stressed that a man who beats his wife is not a

great. **35** If you have reason to fear that a breach may occur between a [married] couple, appoint an arbiter from among his people and an arbiter from among her people. If they both want to set things aright, God will bring about their reconciliation. God is indeed all knowing, aware of all things.

36 Worship God alone and do not associate with Him any partners. Be kind to your parents and near of kin, to orphans, the needy, the neighbour who is related to you and the neighbour who is a stranger, the friend by your side, the wayfarer, and those whom your right hands possess. God does not love those who are arrogant and boastful; **37** [nor] those who are miserly and bid others to be miserly, and conceal whatever God has bestowed on them of His bounty. We have prepared humiliating suffering for the unbelievers. **38** And [God does not love] those who spend their wealth for the sake of ostentation, and do not believe in God and the Last Day. He who chooses Satan for a companion, an evil companion has he. **39** What would they have to fear if they would only believe in God and the Last Day, and spend [in charity] out of that with which He has provided

---

good person and counselled his Companions and his followers never to resort to such measures.

2. The Arabic root *darb* is used in the Qur'an in various forms 17 times. Few of these are intended in the sense of hitting, and one or two carry different senses, but the sense that is clear in most instances is that of 'separation, isolation, abandoning, staying away from, etc.'. The question that arises here is in which sense is the word used in this verse?

Essentially, this verse and the following one mention four different measures to be resorted to in cases of rebellion that threatens the continuity of marriage. These measures are meant to provide a gradual course which means that they have to be followed in sequence, not as alternatives available all the time. In other words, admonition is the first step. Only when it is not heeded may the next measure of using separate beds be resorted to. The third measure is the one we are trying to understand. The fourth, which is stated in the next verse, is to refer the matter for arbitration by a relative of each of the couple. The two arbiters should try to work out reconciliation between man and wife. Thus, we have three measures resorted to within the family home, with no interference by even close relatives, while the fourth seeks reconciliation with the help of relatives. Could this come about after the man had beaten his wife? Would the beating not have forestalled the efforts of arbiters? In other words, any such beating would have polarised the situation and made both parties stick to their original stances.

Looking at all these factors, I agree with Dr Abd al-Hameed Abu Sulaiman that the phrase *wa-dribuhunn* is used here in the sense of separation, rather than any physical punishment. This separation means that the husband stays away from the family home for a few days, so as to give a chance for tempers to cool down and both husband and wife to think about their situation in a cooler and wiser way.

them. Indeed God has full knowledge of them. **40** Indeed God does not wrong anyone by as much as an atom's weight. And if there be a good deed, He will multiply it, and will bestow a great reward out of His grace. **41** How will it be [on Judgement Day] when We shall bring a witness from every community, and call you as a witness against these people? **42** Those who disbelieved and disobeyed God's Messenger will on that Day wish that the earth may swallow them. They shall be able to conceal nothing from God. **43** Believers, do not attempt to pray when you are drunk, [but wait] until you know what you are saying; nor when you are in a state of ceremonial impurity,[15] except if you are on your way, until you have bathed. But if you are ill, or travelling, or if one of you has come from the toilet, or if you have cohabited with a woman and can find no water, then have recourse to pure dust, passing therewith lightly over your faces and your hands. God is indeed most lenient, much-forgiving.

44 Are you not aware of those who, having been granted a share of divine revelations, now barter it away for error, and want you too to lose your way? **45** But God knows best who your enemies are. God is sufficient for you as a patron, and God is sufficient to give succour. **46** Among those of the Jewish faith there are some who take (revealed) words out of their context and say: 'We have heard, but we disobey' and, 'Hear; may you be bereft of hearing', and, 'Hearken to us'. Thus they distort the phrases with their tongues and imply that the true faith is false. Had they but said: 'We have heard and we pay heed', and 'Hear us and have patience with us', it would have been for their own good and more proper. God has rejected them for their disbelief. It is only a few of them that believe. **47** O you who have been given revelations! Believe in what We have bestowed from on high confirming that which you already have, lest We obliterate faces and turn them backward, or We reject them as We rejected the Sabbath-breakers: for God's will is always done. **48** For a certainty, God does not forgive that partners are associated with Him. He forgives any lesser sin to whomever He wills. He who associates partners with God contrives an awesome sin indeed. **49** Are you aware of those who consider themselves pure? It is indeed God who causes whom He wills to grow in purity. None shall be wronged by as much as a

---

15   Men are considered to be in a state of ceremonial impurity as a result of semen ejaculation with desire, whether this takes place through sexual intercourse, masturbation, or a wet dream. Women are in this state as a result of sexual intercourse or during menstruation.

hair's breadth. **50** Behold how they fabricate lies against God. This is enough as an obvious sin [for anyone]. **51** Are you not aware of those who, having been granted a share of divine revelations, now believe in falsehood and arrogant deviation [from divine faith]? And they say to the unbelievers that they are better guided than the believers. **52** These are the ones whom God has rejected; anyone whom God rejects shall find none to succour him. **53** Have they, perchance, a share in [God's] dominion? If so, they would not give other people so much as [would fill] the groove of a date-stone. **54** Do they, perchance, envy other people for what God has given them out of His bounty? We have indeed given revelation and wisdom to the House of Abraham, and We did bestow on them a mighty dominion. **55** Some of them believe in him and some turn away from him. Sufficient scourge is the fire of Hell. **56** Those who disbelieve in Our revelations We shall, in time, cause them to endure fire: every time their skins are burnt off, We shall replace them with new skins, so that they may taste suffering [in full]. God is indeed almighty, wise. **57** But those who believe and do righteous deeds We shall admit into gardens through which running waters flow, where they shall abide beyond the count of time. There they shall have pure spouses, and We shall admit them into a cool, dense shade.

58 God commands you to deliver whatever you have been entrusted with to their rightful owners, and whenever you judge between people, to judge with justice. Most excellent is what God exhorts you to do. God hears all and sees all. **59** Believers, obey God and obey the Messenger and those from among you who have been entrusted with authority. If you are in dispute over anything, refer it to God and the Messenger, if you truly believe in God and the Last Day. This is the best [for you], and most suitable for final determination. **60** Are you not aware of those who claim that they believe in what has been bestowed from on high upon you, as well as in what was bestowed from on high before you? They seek the judgement of false gods, although they are bidden to deny them. But Satan wants to lead them far astray. **61** When it is said to them, 'Come to that which God has bestowed from on high, and to the Messenger', you see the hypocrites turn away from you with aversion. **62** But how will it be when calamity befalls them [on the Day of Judgement] because of what their hands have done in this world? They would then come to you, swearing by God, 'Our aim was but to do good, and to bring about harmony'. **63** As for them – God knows all that is in their hearts. So leave them alone, and admonish them, and speak to them a word to reach their very souls. **64** We have sent every messenger so that he should be obeyed by God's leave. If, when they have wronged themselves, they would but come to you and pray to God to forgive them, and the Messenger prayed for their forgiveness, they would surely find that God is the one to accept repentance, ever-merciful. **65** But no, by your Lord! They do not really believe unless they make you judge in all disputes between them, and then find in their hearts no bar to an acceptance of your decisions and give themselves up in total submission. **66** Yet if We were to order them, 'Lay down your lives', or, 'Forsake your homelands', only a very few of them would do it; but if they would do what they are admonished to do, it would indeed be for their own good and apt to strengthen them greatly [in faith]. **67** And We should indeed grant them, out of Our grace, a mighty reward, **68** and indeed guide them along a straight path. **69** All who obey God and the Messenger shall be among those upon whom God has bestowed His blessings: the prophets, and those who never deviate from the truth, and the martyrs and the righteous ones. How goodly a company are these! **70** Such is God's bounty, and sufficient it is that God knows all.

71 Believers, be fully prepared against danger, and go to war either in small groups or all together. **72** There are indeed among you such as would lag behind, and then, if a calamity befalls you, say, 'God has bestowed His favours upon me in that I was not present with them!' **73** But if good fortune comes to you from God, he is sure to say – just as if there had never been any question of love between you and him – 'Oh, would that I had been with them; I would surely have had a [share in a] mighty triumph'. **74** Let them fight in God's cause – all who are willing to barter the life of this world for the life to come. To him who fights in God's cause, whether he be slain or be victorious, We shall grant a richly reward. **75** And why should you not fight in the cause of God and the utterly helpless men, women and children who are crying, 'Our Lord! Deliver us from this land whose people are oppressors, and send forth to us, out of Your grace, a protector, and send us one that will help us'. **76** Those who believe fight in the cause of God, and those who reject the faith fight in the cause of evil. Fight, then, against the friends of Satan. Feeble indeed is the cunning of Satan. **77** Are you not aware of those who have been told, 'Hold back your hands [from fighting], and attend regularly to prayer, and pay your zakat?' When, at length, the order for fighting was issued to them, some of them stood in awe of men as one should stand in awe of God – or in even greater awe – and said, 'Our Lord! Why have you ordered us to fight? If only You have granted us a delay for a little while!' Say, 'Brief is the enjoyment of this world, whereas the life to come is the best for all who are God-fearing. None of you shall be wronged by as much as a hair's breadth'. **78** Wherever you may be death will overtake you, even though you be in towers built up strong and high. Yet, when a good thing happens to them, some [people] say, 'This is from God', whereas when evil befalls them, they say, 'This is from you!' Say, 'All is from God'. What is amiss with these people that they are in no wise near to grasping the truth of what they are told? **79** Whatever good happens to you is from God; and whatever evil befalls you is from yourself. We have sent you as a Messenger to all mankind. Enough is God for a witness. **80** He who obeys the Messenger obeys God thereby. As for those who turn away – We have not sent you to be their keeper. **81** And they say, 'We do obey you', but when they leave you, some of them devise, in secret, something different from what you advocate. All the while God records what they thus devise in secret. Leave them, then, alone, and place your trust in God. Sufficient is God for a guardian. **82** Will they not, then, try to understand the Quran? Had it issued from any but God, they would surely have found in it many an inner contradiction! **83** If any matter pertaining to peace or war comes to their knowledge, they make it known to all and sundry; whereas, if they would only refer it to the Messenger and to those from among them entrusted with authority, those of them who are engaged in obtaining intelligence would know it. Were it not for God's bounty to you, and His grace, all but a few of you would certainly have followed Satan. **84** Fight, then, in God's cause, since you are responsible only for your own self, and encourage the believers. God may well curb the might of the unbelievers; for God is the strongest in might, and in the ability to deter. **85** Whoever rallies to a good cause shall have a share in its [benefit], and whoever rallies to an evil cause shall have a share in its [burden]. God watches over everything. **86** When a greeting is offered you, answer it with an even better greeting, or [at least] with its like. God keeps count of all things.

87 God, save whom there is no deity, will surely gather you all together on the Day of Resurrection, which is sure to come, no doubt. Whose word could be truer than God's? **88** How could you be divided into two groups concerning the hypocrites, when God Himself has cast them off because of their guilt? Do you seek to guide those whom God has let go astray? For him whom God lets go astray you can never find any way. **89** They would love to see you disbelieve as they themselves disbelieve, so that you may be all alike. Do not, therefore, take them for your allies, until they migrate for God's cause. If they turn against you, then seize them and kill them wherever you may find them. Do not take any of them for your ally or supporter. **90** Except in the case of those of them who have ties with people to whom you yourselves are bound by a covenant, or those who come to you because their hearts shrink from the thought of fighting you or fighting their own people. Had God so willed, He would have given them power over you, and they would have fought you. Therefore, if they leave you alone, and do not make war on you, and offer you peace, God has given you no way against them. **91** You will find others who would like to be safe from you as well as to be safe from their own people. Whenever they are called back to sedition they plunge headlong into it. If they do not leave you alone, and do not offer you peace and do not stay their hands, seize them and kill them wherever you come upon them. Over these We have given you a clear authority. **92** Never should a believer kill another believer, unless it be by mistake. He who kills a believer by mistake must free a believing soul from bondage and pay an indemnity to his family, unless they forgo it by way of charity. If the victim belonged to a people who are at war with you, while he himself was a believer, then let his killer free a believing soul from bondage. If he [the victim] belonged to a people with whom you are bound by a covenant, then the penalty is an indemnity to be paid to his family and the freeing of a believing soul from bondage. He who cannot afford the wherewithal must fast for two consecutive months. This is the atonement ordained by God. God is all-knowing, wise. **93** He who deliberately kills a believer, his punishment is Hell, therein to abide permanently. God will be angry with him, and will reject him, and will prepare for him a dreadful suffering. **94** Believers, when you go on an expedition to serve the cause of God, use your discernment and do not – out of a desire for the fleeting gains of this worldly life – say to one who offers you the greeting of peace: 'You are not a believer': for with God are abundant gains. Thus have you been in days gone by. But God has bestowed on you His grace. Therefore, use your discernment. Indeed God is always aware of what you do.

95 Those of the believers who remain passive, other than the disabled, are not equal to those who strive hard in God's cause with their possessions and their lives. God has exalted those who strive hard with their possessions and their lives far above the ones who remain passive. To each God has promised the ultimate good, yet God has preferred those who strive hard over those who remain passive with a mighty reward: **96** degrees of honour, forgiveness of sins and His grace. God is much-forgiving, ever-merciful. **97** To those whom the angels gather in death while they are still wronging themselves, the angels will say: 'What were you doing?' They will answer: 'We were oppressed on earth'. [The angels] will say: 'Was not God's earth so spacious that you might have migrated and settled elsewhere?' Such will have their abode in Hell, a certainly evil end. **98** Excepted are the men, women, and children who, being truly helpless, can devise nothing and can find no way. **99** These God may well pardon, then, for God is indeed most lenient, much-forgiving. **100** Anyone who migrates for God's cause will find on earth many places for refuge and great abundance. He who leaves his home, fleeing from evil unto God and His Messenger, and is then overtaken by death, his reward is reserved for him with God. God is much-forgiving, ever-merciful. **101** When you go forth on earth, you will incur no sin by shortening your prayers, if you have reason to fear that the unbelievers may cause you affliction. Truly, the unbelievers are your sworn enemies. **102** When you are with the believers and about to lead them in prayer, let one group of them stand up with you, holding on to their weapons. Then, after they have prostrated themselves, let them be behind you, while the other group, who have not yet prayed, shall come forward and pray with you, and let these be on their guard, holding on to their weapons. The unbelievers would love to see you oblivious of your weapons and your equipment, so that they might swoop on you with one assault. But it is no offence for you to lay down your arms [while you pray] if you are bothered by heavy rain, or suffering from illness; but you must always be on your guard. God has prepared humiliating suffering for the unbelievers. **103** And when you have performed your prayers, remember God standing, sitting, and lying down. When you are again secure, observe your prayers [fully]. Indeed, prayer is a time-related duty, binding on all believers. **104** Do not be faint of heart when you seek out the [enemy] host. If you happen to suffer pain, they also suffer pain as you do; while you hope to receive from God what they can never hope for. God is indeed all-knowing, wise.

105 We have bestowed this Book on you from on high, setting forth the truth, so that you may judge between people in accordance with what God has taught you. Hence, do not contend with those who betray their trust. **106** Seek God's forgiveness, for God is indeed much-forgiving, ever-merciful. **107** And do not argue on behalf of those who are false to their own selves. Indeed God does not love those who betray their trust and persist in sinful action. **108** They conceal their doings from men, but they cannot conceal them from God; for He is present with them when, in the darkness of the night, they agree all manner of sayings which displease Him. God certainly encompasses [with His knowledge] whatever they do. **109** You may well argue on their behalf in the life of this world, but who is there to argue on their behalf with God on the Day of Resurrection, or who will be their advocate? **110** He who does evil or wrongs his own soul, and then prays to God to forgive him, shall find God much-forgiving, ever-merciful. **111** For he who commits a sin, does so to his own hurt. God is indeed all-knowing, wise. **112** But he who commits a fault or a sin and then throws the blame therefore on an innocent person, burdens himself with both falsehood and a flagrant sin. **113** But for God's grace to you and His mercy, some of them would indeed endeavour to lead you astray. Yet none but themselves do they lead astray. Nor can they harm you in any way. It is God who has bestowed this Book on you from on high and given you wisdom, and has taught you what you did not know. God's favour on you is great indeed.

114 No good comes out of much of their secret talks; except for one who enjoins charity, or justice, or setting things right between people. To him who does this out of a longing for God's goodly acceptance We shall in time grant a rich reward. **115** But as for him who, after guidance has been plainly conveyed to him, puts himself in contention with God's Messenger and follows a path other than that of the believers – him shall We leave to that which he himself has chosen, and shall cause him to endure Hell. How evil a journey's end. **116** For a certainty, God does not forgive that partners should be associated with Him, but He forgives any lesser sin to whomever He wills. He who associates partners with God has indeed gone far astray. **117** In His stead, they invoke only lifeless symbols – thus invoking none but a rebellious Satan, **118** whom God has rejected, for he had said: 'Of Your servants I shall indeed take my due share, **119** and shall certainly lead them astray, and fill them with vain desires; and I shall command them – and they will slit the ears of cattle [in idolatrous sacrifice]; and I shall command them – and they will corrupt God's creation'. But all who take Satan rather than God for their master do incur a manifest loss. **120** He [Satan] holds out promises to them, and fills them with vain desires, but whatever Satan promises is meant only to deceive them. **121** Such as these have Hell as their dwelling place. They shall find no way to escape from it. **122** Yet those who believe and do righteous deeds We shall bring into gardens through which running waters flow, wherein they will abide beyond the count of time. This is, in truth, God's promise. Whose word could be truer than God's? **123** It may not accord with your wishful thinking, nor with the wishful thinking of the people of earlier revelations. He who does evil shall be requited for it, and shall find none to protect him from God, and none to bring him support. **124** But anyone, be it man or woman, who does good deeds and is a believer, shall enter Paradise and shall not suffer the least injustice. **125** Who could be of better faith than he who surrenders himself completely to God, does what is good, and follows the creed of Abraham, who turned away from all that is false? For God has taken Abraham for a friend. **126** To God belongs all that is in the heavens and all that is on the earth; and indeed God encompasses everything.

127 They ask you for rulings concerning women. Say, 'God [Himself] gives you His rulings concerning them, as well as what is conveyed to you through this Book about orphan women whom you deny what has been assigned to them, and you are disinclined to marry them; and concerning helpless children, and about your duty to treat orphans with fairness. Whatever good you may do, God knows it fully. **128** If a woman has reason to fear ill-treatment or desertion by her husband, it shall not be wrong for the two of them if they should try to set things peacefully to rights between them; for peace is best. Avarice is ever-present in human souls. If you act with kindness and are God-fearing, surely God is aware of all that you do. **129** In no way can you maintain equity between your wives, even though you may be keen to do so. Do not, then, be totally partial towards one to the exclusion of the other, leaving her, as it were, in a state of suspense. If you put things to rights and are God-fearing, God is indeed much-forgiving, ever-merciful. **130** But if the two separate, God shall provide for each of them out of His abundance: God is indeed munificent, wise'. **131** To God belongs all that is in the heavens and all that is on earth. We have indeed enjoined those who were granted revelations before your time, as well as yourselves, to always be God-fearing. If you disbelieve, know that to God belongs all that is in the heavens and all that is on earth. God is free of all want, ever to be praised. **132** And to God belongs all that is in the heavens and all that is on earth. Sufficient is God for a guardian. **133** If He so wills, He can take you, mankind, and replace you by others. This He surely has the power to do. **134** If anyone desires the rewards of this world, let him remember that with God are the rewards of this world and those of the life to come. God is indeed all-hearing, all-seeing.

135 Believers! Be ever steadfast in upholding equity, bearing witness to the truth for the sake of God, even though it be against yourselves, or your parents and kin. Whether the person concerned be rich or poor, God's claim takes precedence over [the claims of] either of them. Do not, then, follow your own desires, lest you swerve from justice. If you distort [the truth] or decline to do justice, then [know that] God is indeed aware of all that you do. **136** Believers! Believe in God and His Messenger, and in the Book which He has bestowed from on high upon His Messenger, and in the Book which He sent down in earlier times. Anyone who denies God, His angels, His revealed books, His messengers, and the Last Day has indeed gone far astray. **137** Those who come to believe, then reject faith, and again come to believe, and again reject the faith, and thereafter grow hardened in their disbelief, God will not forgive them, nor will He guide them in any way. **138** Happily announce to the hypocrites that painful suffering awaits them. **139** They are those who take unbelievers for their allies in preference to believers. Is it honour they seek among them? Indeed all honour belongs to God. **140** Already has He enjoined upon you in this Book that whenever you hear people deny the truth of God's revelations and mock at them, you shall avoid their company until they talk on some other theme; or else, you will indeed become like them. Indeed, God will gather both the hypocrites and the unbelievers together in Hell. **141** [Hypocrites are] those who wait and watch what happens to you: if triumph comes to you from God, they say: 'Were we not on your side?' But if the unbelievers gain a success, they say [to them]: 'Have we not earned your affection by defending you against those believers?' It is God who will judge between you all on the Day of Resurrection. Never will God allow the unbelievers a way [to win a complete triumph] over the believers. **142** The hypocrites seek to deceive God, the while it is He who causes them to be deceived [by themselves]. When they rise to pray, they rise reluctantly, only to be seen by people, remembering God but seldom, **143** wavering between this and that, [true] neither to these nor to those. For him whom God lets go astray you can never find any way. **144** Believers! Do not take the unbelievers for your allies in preference to the believers. Do you want to place before God a manifest proof against yourselves? **145** The hypocrites will be in the lowest depth of the Fire, and you will find none who can give them support. **146** Excepted shall be those who repent, live righteously, hold fast to God, and are more sincere in their faith in God. These shall be with the believers. God will in time grant a splendid reward for the believers. **147** What can God gain by your punishment, if you are grateful and you believe? God is always responsive to gratitude, all-knowing.

148 God does not love evil to be spoken openly unless it be by someone who has been truly wronged. God hears all and knows all. **149** Whether you do good openly or in private, or pardon others for evil [done against you], God indeed absolves sin and He is powerful. **150** Those who deny God and His messengers, and want to make a distinction between [belief in] God and [belief in] His messengers, and say: 'We believe in some but we deny others', and want to pursue a path in-between: **151** those, in truth, are unbelievers. We have prepared for unbelievers humiliating suffering. **152** As for those who believe in God and His messengers and make no distinction between any of them – to them He will give their reward. God is indeed much-forgiving, ever-merciful. **153** The people of earlier revelations ask you to have a book sent down to them from heaven. They asked Moses for something even greater than that, when they said: 'Make us see God with our own eyes'. The thunderbolt smote them for this their wrongdoing. After that, they took to worshipping the calf, even after clear evidence of the truth had come to them. Yet We pardoned them that, and We gave Moses clear authority. **154** We raised Mount Sinai high above them in witness of their solemn pledge. And We said to them: 'Enter the gate, prostrating yourselves'; and We also told them: 'Do not break the Sabbath-law'; and We received from them a most solemn pledge. **155** And so, [We punished them] for the breaking of their pledge, their disbelief in God's revelations, their killing of prophets against all right, and for their boast, 'Our hearts are closed'. Indeed God sealed their hearts on account of their disbelief. As a result they have no faith except for a few of them. **156** And for their disbelief and the monstrous calumny they utter against Mary, **157** and their boast: 'We have killed the Christ Jesus, son of Mary, God's messenger'. They did not kill him, and neither did they crucify him, but it only seemed to them [as if it had been] so. Those who hold conflicting views about him are indeed confused, having no real knowledge about it, and following mere conjecture. For, of a certainty, they did not kill him. **158** No! God raised him up to Himself. God is indeed almighty, wise. **159** There is not one of the people of earlier revelations but will, at the moment of his death, believe in him, and on the Day of Resurrection he will bear witness to the truth against them. **160** So, then, for the wrongdoing of the Jews did We forbid them some of the good things of life which had been formerly allowed to them; and, indeed for their turning away often from God's path, **161** and for their taking usury although it had been forbidden to them, and their wrongful devouring of other people's property. We have prepared for the unbelievers among them painful suffering. **162** Yet those of them who are versed in knowledge, and the believers, do believe in what is bestowed upon you from on high and that which was bestowed from on high before you. These are the ones who attend to their prayers and spend in charity, and who believe in God and the Last Day. To these We shall give a great reward. **163** We have sent revelations to you just as We did send revelations to Noah and the prophets after him; as We sent revelations to Abraham, Ishmael, Isaac, Jacob and their descendants, Jesus, Job, Jonah, Aaron and Solomon, and as We revealed to David a Book of divine wisdom, **164** and as [We inspired other] messengers whom We have mentioned to you previously, as well as other messengers whom We have not mentioned to you. And God has spoken His word directly to Moses. **165** [These] were messengers sent to bring good news and to give warning, so that people may have no argument against God once these messengers [had come]. God is almighty, wise. **166** However it be, God [Himself] bears witness to the truth of what He has bestowed from on high to you: with His knowledge He bestowed it from on high; and the angels also bear witness to that; although God is sufficient as a witness. **167** Those who disbelieve and debar others from the way of God have indeed gone far astray. **168** Those who disbelieve and persist in wrongdoing will find that God will never forgive them, nor will He guide them onto any road, **169** except the road to Hell, wherein they will abide beyond the count of time. That is indeed easy for God.

170 Mankind, the Messenger has now come to you with the truth from your Lord. Believe, then, for it is better for you. But if you disbelieve, know that to God belongs all that is in the heavens and all that is on earth. God is indeed all-knowing, wise. **171** People of earlier revelations! Do not overstep the bounds [of truth] in your religious beliefs, and do not say about God anything but the truth. The Christ Jesus, son of Mary, was no more than a messenger from God and His word which He gave to Mary and a soul from Him. So believe in God and His messengers and do not say, '[God is] a trinity!' Desist, for that will be better for you. God is only One God. Infinite He is in His Glory! [To imagine] that He may have a son! To Him belongs all that is in the heavens and all that is on earth. Sufficient is God for a guardian. **172** Never did the Christ feel too proud to be

God's servant, nor do the angels who are near to Him. Those who feel too proud to worship Him and glory in their arrogance will He gather all together before Himself; **173** then, to those who believe and do good deeds, He will grant their reward in full, and will give them yet more out of His bounty; while those who feel too proud and glory in their arrogance He will cause to suffer a painful punishment. They shall find none to protect them from God and none to bring them any help. **174** Mankind, a clear proof has now come to you from your Lord, and We have sent down to you a glorious light. **175** Those who believe in God and hold fast to Him, will He surely admit to His mercy and grace, and will guide them to Himself along a straight path. **176** They will ask you for a verdict. Say 'God Himself gives you His ruling concerning [inheritance from] a person who leaves no heir in the direct line. If a man dies childless and has a sister, she shall inherit one-half of what he has left, just as he shall inherit all her [property] if she dies childless. But if there are two sisters, they shall both together have two thirds of whatever he has left; and if there are brothers and sisters, then the male shall have the equal of two females' share. God makes all this clear to you, lest you go astray; and God knows everything'.

Surah 5   The Repast

This is another long surah revealed during the Madinan period. This was when the Qur'an was shaping the first Muslim society and giving it its distinctive character as a society based on clear belief in God's Oneness, and deriving its beliefs, concepts, laws and values from Him alone. It removes all deviant concepts of belief, whether introduced by the pagan Arabs or by followers of earlier divine religions, such as Christianity and Judaism. It makes it clear that all mankind are required to submit themselves to God alone.

The surah starts with a general address to all believers that they must be true to their contracts. As we go through the surah we realise that the term 'contract' transcends the idea of formal contract that specifies certain conditions applicable to a particular deal or transaction. Rather, it has a general application that starts with a contract made between God and human nature, requiring mankind to address all worship and obedience to God alone. Thus, the contract of faith is essential and must be fulfilled. Within this context the surah makes it clear that the Children of Israel were untrue to their contract, taking themselves outside the realm of belief in God's Oneness. Hence, they deserved God's punishment.

The surah lays strong emphasis on the need to address all worship to God alone. It relates all actions to worship, when they are undertaken with the intention of fulfilling the role God has assigned to man of building human life on earth on a sound basis. This is again a part of the contract mankind has to honour. It includes abstaining from what God has forbidden: types of food, ways of slaughtering animals for food, places of slaughter and hunting, as well as restricted times. All these come under a general title of setting proper controls for human life.

The last part of the surah (verses 109–120) gives an account of Jesus and his fulfilment of his message. It disassociates him from any claims of divinity, whether these be attached to him or to his mother.

The Repast

In the Name of God, the Lord of Grace, the Ever-Merciful

1 Believers, be true to your contracts. Lawful to you is the [flesh of the] beasts of cattle, other than that which is specifically prohibited. But

you are not allowed to hunt while you are in the state of consecration. God decrees what He will. **2** Believers, do not offend against the symbols set up by God, or against the sacred month, or the offerings or the garlands, or against those who repair to the Sacred House, seeking God's grace and pleasure. Only when you are clear of the Sacred Precincts and released from the state of consecration may you hunt. Do not let your hatred of people who would debar you from the Sacred Mosque lead you into aggression; but rather help one another in furthering righteousness and piety, and do not help one another in furthering evil and aggression. Have fear of God, for God is severe in retribution. **3** Forbidden to you are carrion, blood, the flesh of swine; and that over which any name other than God's has been invoked; and the animal that has been strangled, or beaten to death, or killed by a fall, or gored to death, or savaged by a beast of prey, except that which you may have slaughtered when it is still alive; and [forbidden to you are] animals that have been slaughtered on idolatrous altars. And [forbidden also] is the division [of meat] by raffling with arrows; for all this is sinful. Today, the unbelievers have lost all hope of your religion. Have no fear of them, then, but fear Me alone. This day I have perfected your religion for you and have bestowed on you the full measure of My blessings and have chosen Islam as a religion for you. He who is forced by hunger [to eat of what is forbidden], with no inclination to commit sin, [will find] God much-forgiving, ever-merciful. **4** They ask you what is lawful to them. Say: 'Lawful to you are all good things of life'. As for those hunting animals which you train by imparting to them something of the knowledge God has imparted to you, you may eat of what they catch for you. But mention God's name over it and have fear of God; indeed, God is swift in reckoning. **5** Today, all the good things of life have been made lawful to you. The food of those who were given revelations is lawful to you, and your food is lawful to them. And the virtuous women from among the believers and the virtuous women from among those who were given revelations before you [are also lawful to you] when you give them their dowries, taking them in honest wedlock, not in fornication, nor as mistresses. Anyone who rejects the faith [will find that] all his works will be in vain. In the life to come he shall be among the losers. **6** Believers, when you are about to pray, wash your faces, and your hands and arms up to the elbows, and pass your wet hands lightly over your heads, and wash your feet up to the ankles. If you are in a state of ceremonial impurity, purify yourselves. But If you are ill, or on a journey, or if one of you has come from the toilet, or if you have been in intimate contact with women and can find no water, then have recourse to pure dust, passing therewith lightly over your faces and your hands. God does not want to impose any hardship on you, but He wants to purify you, and to bestow on you the full measure of His blessings, so that you may be grateful. **7** Remember always the blessings God has bestowed on you and the covenant with which He has bound you when you said: 'we have heard and we obey'. Hence, remain God-fearing. Surely God has full knowledge of the secrets of people's hearts. **8** Believers, be steadfast in your devotion to God, bearing witness to the truth in all equity. Never allow your hatred of any people to lead you away from justice. Be just, this is closer to righteousness. And remain God-fearing. Surely, God is aware of all that you do. **9** God has promised those who believe and do righteous deeds that they shall have forgiveness of sins and a rich reward. **10** As for those who disbelieve and deny Our revelations, these are destined for the blazing Fire. **11** Believers, remember the blessings God has bestowed on you, when certain people designed to stretch against you their hands, but He stayed their hands from you. Remain, then, God-fearing. In God let the believers place their trust.

12 Indeed, God made a covenant with the Children of Israel and We appointed among them twelve captains. God said: 'I shall be with you. If you attend to your prayers, practise regular charity, believe in My messengers and support them and offer up to God a generous loan, I shall forgive you your sins and admit you into gardens through which running waters flow. But any of you who, after this, rejects the faith will indeed have strayed from the right path'. **13** Then for having broken their covenant, We rejected them and caused their hearts to harden. They now distort the meaning of [revealed] words, taking them out of their context. Moreover, they have forgotten much of what they have been told to bear in mind. From all but a few of them you will always experience treachery. But pardon them, and forbear. God loves those who do good. **14** Likewise, from those who said, 'We are Christians', We have accepted a firm covenant, but they, too, have forgotten much of what they had been told to bear in mind. Therefore, We have given rise among them to enmity and hatred to last until the Day of Resurrection. God will make clear to them what they have done. **15** People of earlier revelations, Our Messenger has come to you to make clear to you much of what you have been concealing of the Scriptures, and to forgive you much. There has come to you from God a light and a clear Book, **16** through which God guides those who seek His good pleasure to the paths of peace. By His grace, He leads them out of darkness into light and guides them to a straight way. **17** Unbelievers indeed are they who say: 'God is the Christ, son of Mary'. Say: 'Who could have prevailed with God in any way had it been His will to destroy the Christ, son of Mary, and his mother, and everyone on earth? To God belongs the kingdom of the heavens and the earth and all that is between them. He creates what He wills and God has power over all things'. **18** Both the Jews and the Christians say: 'We are God's children and His loved ones'. Say: 'Why then does He punish you for your sins? You are only human beings of His creation. He forgives whom He will and punishes whom He will. To God belongs the Kingdom of the heavens and the earth and all that is between them, and to Him all shall return'. **19** People of earlier revelations! Now after an interval during which no messengers have appeared, Our Messenger has come to you to make things plain to you, lest you say: 'No one has come to give us good news or to warn us'. Now there has come to you a bearer of good news and a warner. God has power over all things. **20** And so Moses said to his people: 'My people, remember the favours which God has bestowed upon you when He raised up prophets among you, made you kings and granted you what He has not granted to any other community. **21** My people, enter the holy land which God has assigned to you. Do not turn your backs, for then you will be lost'. **22** 'Moses', they answered, 'mighty people dwell in that land, and we will surely not enter it unless they depart from it. If they do depart, then we will enter'. **23** Thereupon two men who were God-fearing and on whom God had bestowed His grace said: 'Go in upon them through the gate. As soon as you enter it, you shall be victorious. In God you should place your trust, if you are true believers'. **24** They said, 'Moses, we will never go in so long as they are in it. Go forth, then, you and your Lord, and fight, both of you. We shall stay here'. **25** 'Lord', he said, 'I am master of none but myself and my brother. Do, then, draw a dividing line between us and these wrongdoing folk'. **26** He replied, 'This land shall, then, be forbidden to them for forty years, during which they will wander aimlessly on earth. Do not grieve for these wrongdoing folk'.

27 Relate to them in all truth the story of the two sons of Adam: how each offered a sacrifice, and it was accepted from one of them while it was not accepted from the other. [The latter] said: 'I will surely kill you'. [The other] replied: 'God accepts only from those who are God-fearing. **28** Even if you lay your hand on me to kill me, I shall not lay my hand on you to kill you; for I fear God, the Lord of all worlds. **29** I would rather you should add your sin against me to your other sins, and thus you will be destined to the Fire; since that is the just retribution of wrongdoers'. **30** His evil soul drove him to kill his brother; and he murdered him, and thus he became one of the lost. **31** God then sent forth a raven which scratched the earth, to show him how he might conceal the nakedness of his brother's body. He cried out: 'Woe to me! Am I then too weak to do what this raven has done, and to conceal the nakedness of my brother's body?' He was then overwhelmed by remorse. **32** Because of this did We ordain to the Children of Israel that if anyone slays a human being, for anything other than in punishment of murder or for spreading corruption on earth, it shall be as though he had slain all mankind; and that if anyone saves a human life, it shall be as though he had saved all mankind. Our messengers brought them clear evidence of the truth, but despite all this, many of them continue to commit all manner of excesses on earth. **33** It is but a just punishment of those who make war on God and His Messenger, and endeavour to spread corruption on earth, that they should be put to death, or be crucified, or have their hands and feet cut off on alternate sides or that they should be banished from the land. Such is their disgrace in this world, and more grievous suffering awaits them in the life to come; **34** except those who repent before you overpower them. For you must know that God is much-forgiving, ever-merciful. **35** Believers, fear God and seek the means to come closer to Him, and strive hard in His cause, so that you may be successful. **36** If those who disbelieve had all that is on earth and as much besides to offer as ransom from the suffering of the Day of Resurrection, it would not be accepted from them. Theirs shall be a painful suffering. **37** They will wish to come out of the Fire, but they shall not come out of it. Theirs shall be a long-lasting suffering. **38** As for the man or the woman who is guilty of stealing, cut off their hands in requital for what they have wrought, as an exemplary punishment ordained by God. God is almighty, wise. **39** But whoever repents after having thus done wrong, and makes amends, shall have his repentance accepted by God. God is much-forgiving, ever-merciful. **40** Do you not know that to God belongs the kingdom of the heavens and the earth? He punishes whom He wills and forgives whom He wills. God has power over all things.

41 Messenger, be not grieved by those who plunge headlong into unbelief; such as those who say with their mouths, 'We believe', while their hearts do not believe. Among the Jews are some who eagerly listen to falsehood, eagerly listen to other people who have not come to you. They tamper with words out of their context, and say, 'If such-and-such [a precept] is given you, accept it; but if you are not given it, then be on your guard'. If God wants to put anyone to test, you shall not be able to avail him anything against God. Such are the ones whose hearts God is not willing to purify. They will have disgrace in this world, and grievous suffering in the life to come. **42** They eagerly listen to falsehood and greedily devour what is unlawful. Hence, if they come to you [for judgement], you may either judge between them or decline to interfere. If you decline, they cannot harm you in any way. But if you do judge, then judge between them with fairness. God loves those who deal justly. **43** But how is it that they ask you for judgement when they have the Torah which contains God's judgement, and they still turn away? For certain, they are not true believers. **44** Indeed, it is We who revealed the Torah, containing guidance and light. By it did the prophets, who had surrendered themselves to God, judge among the Jews, and so did the devouts and the rabbis: [they gave judgement] in accordance with what had been entrusted to their care of God's Book and to which they themselves were witnesses. So, have no fear of men but fear Me; and do not barter away My revelations for a paltry price. Those who do not judge in accordance with what God has revealed are indeed unbelievers. **45** We decreed for them in it: a life for a life, an eye for an eye, a nose for a nose, an ear for an ear, a tooth for a tooth, and a similar retribution for wounds. But for him who forgoes it out of charity, it will atone for some of his sins. Those who do not judge in accordance with what God has revealed are indeed wrongdoers. **46** We caused Jesus, the son of Mary, to follow in the footsteps of those [earlier prophets], confirming what had already been revealed before him in the Torah; and We gave him the Gospel, containing guidance and light, confirming what had already been revealed before it in the Torah and giving guidance and admonition to the God-fearing. **47** Let, then, the followers of the Gospel judge in accordance with what God has revealed therein. Those who do not judge in accordance with what God has revealed are indeed transgressors. **48** And to you We have revealed the Book, setting forth the truth, confirming the Scriptures which had already been revealed before it and superseding them. Judge, then, between them in accordance with what God has revealed and do not follow their vain desires, forsaking thereby the truth that has come to you. To every one of you We have given a code of law and a way of life. Had God so willed, He could have made you all one community; but [it is His wish] to test you by means of that which He has bestowed on you. Vie, then, with one another in doing good works. To God you shall all return. He will then make you understand all that over which you now differ. **49** Hence, judge between them in accordance with what God has revealed, and do not follow their vain desires and beware of them lest they tempt you away from any part of what God has revealed to you. If they turn away, then know that it is God's will to afflict them for some of their sins. Indeed, a great many people are transgressors. **50** Do they desire to be ruled by the law of pagan ignorance? But for those who are firm in their faith, who can be a better law-giver than God?

51 Believers, do not take the Jews and the Christians for your allies. They are allies of one another. Whoever of you allies himself with them is indeed one of them. God does not bestow His guidance on the wrongdoers. **52** Yet you see those who are sick at heart rush to their defence, saying, 'We fear lest a change of fortune should befall us'. God may well bring about victory (for believers) or some other event of His own making, and those [waverers] will terribly regret the thought they had secretly harboured within themselves. **53** The believers will say: 'Are these the self-same people who swore by God their most solemn oaths that they were with you?' All their works are in vain and they will lose all. **54** Believers, if you renounce your faith, God will bring forth [in your stead] people whom He loves and who love Him, humble towards the believers, proud towards the unbelievers. They will strive hard for God's cause and will not fear to be censured by any critic. Such is God's favour which He grants to whom He wills. God encompasses all and knows all. **55** Your patron is only God, and His Messenger and those who believe – those who attend to their prayers, pay their zakat and bow down in worship. **56** Those who ally themselves with God and His Messenger and the believers [will find that] the party of God will be victorious. **57** Believers, do not take for your friends those among the people of earlier revelations who mock at your faith and make a jest of it or those who are unbelievers. Fear God, if you are truly believers. **58** For, when you call to prayer, they mock at it and make a jest of it. They do this because they are people who do not use their reason. **59** Say: 'People of earlier revelations! Do you find fault with us for any reason other than that we believe in God [alone], and in that which has been revealed to us as well as that which has been revealed previously, while most of you are transgressors?' **60** Say: 'Shall I tell you who, in God's sight, deserves an even worse retribution than these? They whom God has rejected and who have incurred His anger, and whom He has turned into apes and pigs, and who worship false gods. These are yet worse in station and they have gone farther astray from the right path'. **61** When they come to you, they say: 'We believe', whereas, in fact, they come unbelievers and depart unbelievers. God is fully aware of all that they would conceal. **62** You see many of them rushing into sin and transgression and in devouring the fruits of unlawful gain. Evil indeed is that which they do. **63** Why do not their devouts and their rabbis forbid them to make sinful assertions and to devour the fruits of unlawful gain? Evil indeed is that which they contrive. **64** The Jews say: 'God's hand is shackled!' It is their own hands that are shackled. Rejected [by God] are they for what they say. Indeed, both His hands are outstretched. He bestows [His bounty] as He wills. But that which has been revealed to you by your Lord is bound to make many of them more stubborn in their overweening arrogance and unbelief. We have cast enmity and hatred among them, [to last] until the Day of Resurrection. Every time they light a fire for war, God puts it out. They labour hard to spread corruption on earth; and God does not love those who spread corruption. **65** If only the people of earlier revelations would believe and be God-fearing, We should indeed efface their [past] bad deeds, and bring them into gardens of bliss. **66** If they would observe the Torah and the Gospel and all that has been revealed to them by their Lord, they would indeed be given abundance from above and from beneath. Some of them do pursue a right course, but many of them are of evil conduct.

67 Messenger, proclaim what has been revealed to you by your Lord. For, unless you do it fully, you will not have delivered His message. God will protect you from all men. God does not guide those who reject faith. **68** Say: 'People of earlier revelations, you have no ground to stand upon unless you observe the Torah and the Gospel and that which has been revealed to you by Your Lord'. That which is revealed to you by your Lord is bound to make many of them even more stubborn in their arrogance and disbelief. But do not grieve for unbelieving folk. **69** Those who believe, and those who are Jews, and the Sabians, and the Christians – anyone who believes in God and the Last Day and does what is right shall have no fear, nor shall they grieve. **70** Surely, We accepted a solemn pledge from the Children of Israel, and We sent to them messengers. But every time a messenger came to them with something that was not to their liking, [they rebelled:] some they denounced as liars and some they put to death. **71** They reckoned no harm would come to them, so they were wilfully blind and deaf [to the truth]. Thereafter, God accepted their repentance: still many of them acted blind and deaf. But God sees all that they do. **72** Unbelievers indeed are those who say: 'God is the Christ, son of Mary'. The Christ himself said: 'Children of Israel, worship God, my Lord and your Lord'. Whoever associates partners with God, God shall forbid him entrance into Paradise and his abode will be the Fire. Wrongdoers will have no helpers. **73** Unbelievers indeed are those who say: 'God is the third of a trinity'. Of certain, there is no god save the One God. Unless they desist from so saying, painful suffering will surely befall those of them who are unbelievers. **74** Will they not, then, turn to God in repentance and seek His forgiveness? God is much-forgiving, ever-merciful. **75** The Christ, son of Mary, was but a messenger: other messengers have passed away before him. His mother was a saintly woman. They both ate food [like other human beings]. Behold how clear We make [Our] revelations to them and behold how perverted they are. **76** Say: 'Would you worship in place of God anything that has no power to harm or to benefit you? It is God alone who hears all and knows all'. **77** Say: 'People of earlier revelations! Do not overstep the bounds of truth in your religious beliefs, and do not follow the vain desires of those who have gone astray in the past, and have led many others astray and are still straying from the right path'. **78** Those of the Children of Israel who disbelieved were cursed by David and Jesus, son of Mary. That was because they rebelled and persisted in their transgression. **79** They would never restrain one another from wrongdoing. Vile indeed were the things they did. **80** Now you can see many of them allying themselves with unbelievers. So evil is that which their souls make them do. They have incurred God's wrath and in suffering they shall abide. **81** Had they truly believed in God and the Prophet and all that which was revealed to them, they would not have taken them for allies, but many of them are evildoers.

82 You will certainly find that, of all people, the most hostile to those who believe are the Jews, and those who associate partners with God; and you will certainly find that the nearest of them in affection to the believers are those who say, 'We are Christians'. This is so because there are priests and monks among them and because they are not given to arrogance. **83** When they listen to what has been revealed to God's Messenger, you see their eyes overflow with tears because of the truth they recognise. They say: 'Our Lord, we do believe; so enrol us among those who bear witness to the truth'. **84** 'How could we fail to believe in God and the truth that has come to us when we dearly hope that our Lord will admit us among the righteous?'

85 And for this their prayer God will reward them with gardens through which running waters flow, where they will abide. Such is the reward of those who do good; **86** while those who disbelieve and deny Our revelations are destined for the blazing Fire.

87 Believers, do not forbid yourselves the good things God has made lawful to you. Do not exceed the bounds; God does not love those who exceed the bounds. **88** Eat of what God has provided for you of lawful and wholesome things, and have fear of God in whom you believe. **89** God will not take you to task for those of your oaths which you may utter without thought, but He will take you to task for oaths which you have sworn in earnest. The breaking of an oath must be atoned for by the feeding of ten needy people with more or less the same food as you normally give to your own families, or by clothing them, or by the freeing of one slave. He who cannot afford any of these shall fast three days instead. This shall be the atonement for your oaths when you have sworn [and broken them]. But be mindful of your oaths. Thus God makes clear to you His revelations, so that you may give thanks. **90** Believers, intoxicants, games of chance, idolatrous practices and divining arrows are abominations devised by Satan. Therefore, turn away from them so that you may be successful. **91** Satan seeks only to stir up enmity and hatred among you by means of intoxicants and games of chance, and to turn you away from the remembrance of God and from prayer. Will you not, then, desist? **92** Obey God, and obey the Messenger, and be ever on your guard. But if you turn away, then know that Our Messenger's only duty is a clear delivery of the message [entrusted to him]. **93** Those who believe and do righteous deeds shall have no blame attached to them for any food they may have eaten, so long as they fear God and truly believe and do righteous deeds, and continue to fear God and believe, and remain God-fearing and persevere in doing good. God loves those who do good. **94** Believers, God will certainly try you by means of game which may come within the reach of your hands or your spears, so that God may mark out those who truly fear Him in their hearts. Whoever transgresses after all this will have painful suffering. **95** Believers, kill no game while you are on pilgrimage. Whoever of you kills game by design shall make amends in cattle equivalent to what he has killed, adjudged by two people of probity among you, to be brought as an offering to the Ka'bah; or else he may atone for his sin by feeding some needy people, or by its equivalent in fasting, so that he may taste the evil consequences of his deeds. God has forgiven what is past; but whoever repeats his offence, God will inflict His retribution on him. God is almighty, and He exacts retribution. **96** Lawful to you is all water-game, and whatever food the sea brings forth, as a provision for you and for travellers. However, you are forbidden land-game as long as you are in the state of consecration [*ihram*]. Be conscious of God, to whom you shall all be gathered. **97** God has made the Ka'bah, the Inviolable House of Worship, a symbol for all mankind; and so too the sacred month and the garlanded sacrificial offerings. This, so that you may know that God is aware of all that is in the heavens and the earth, and that God has full knowledge of everything. **98** Know that God is severe in retribution and that God is much-forgiving, ever-merciful. **99** The Messenger's duty is but to deliver the message [entrusted to him]. God knows all that you reveal, and all that you conceal. **100** Say: 'Evil and good are not equal, even though the abundance of evil may be pleasing to you. Have fear of God, you who are endowed with understanding, so that you may be successful'. **101** Believers, do not ask about matters which, if made known to you, may cause you hardship. If you should ask about them while the Qur'an is being revealed, they shall be made plain to you. God will forgive you these; for God is much-forgiving, clement. **102** People before your time inquired about them, and on that account they came to deny the truth. **103** It was not God who instituted [superstitions like those of] a slit-ear she camel, or a she-camel let loose for free pasture, or idol sacrifices for twin-births in animals, or stallion-camels freed from work. It is unbelievers who attribute their own lying inventions to God. Most of them never use their reason. **104** When they are told, 'Come to that which God has revealed and to the Messenger', they reply, 'Sufficient for us are the ways we found our fathers following'. Why, even though their fathers knew nothing and were devoid of all guidance? **105** Believers, it is but for your own souls that you are accountable. Those who go astray can do you no harm if you [yourselves] are on the right path. To God you all must return. He will then make you understand all that you were doing [in life]. **106** Believers, let there be witnesses to what you do when death approaches you and you are about to make bequests: two people of probity from among your own people, or two others from outside, if the pangs of death come to you when you are travelling through the land. Detain them both after prayer, and if you have any doubt in mind, let them swear by God, 'We shall not sell this [our word] for any price, even though it were for a near kinsman; and neither shall we conceal anything of what we have witnessed before God; for then we should be among the sinful'. **107** But if afterwards it should come to light that the two [witnesses] have been guilty of [this very] sin, then two others should replace them from among those immediately concerned. Both shall swear by God, 'Our testimony is indeed truer than that of these two. We have not transgressed the bounds of what is right; for then we should be among the evil-doers'. **108** Thus it will be more likely that people will offer testimony in accordance with the truth; or else they will fear that the oaths of others may be taken after their oaths. Have fear of God and hearken [to Him]. God does not guide those who are iniquitous.

109 On the Day when God will gather all [His] messengers and ask them, 'What response did you receive?' – they will answer, 'We have no knowledge. Indeed, it is You alone who has full knowledge of all that lies beyond the reach of human perception'. **110** God will say: 'Jesus, son of Mary! Remember the blessings which I bestowed on you and your mother: how I strengthened you with the Holy Spirit, so that you could speak to people in your cradle, and as a grown man; how I instructed you in the Book and in wisdom, in the Torah and in the Gospel; how by My leave you fashioned from clay the figure of a bird and breathed into it so that, by My leave, it became a living bird; how, by My leave, you healed the blind man and the leper, and by My leave restored the dead to life; how I prevented the Children of Israel from harming you when you came to them with all evidence of the truth: when those of them who disbelieved declared: "This is plain sorcery". **111** And when I inspired the disciples to have faith in Me and in My messenger; they said: "We believe; and bear you witness that we have surrendered ourselves [to God]".' **112** The disciples said: 'Jesus, son of Mary! Can your Lord send down to us a repast from heaven?' He answered: 'Fear God, if you are truly believers'. **113** Said they: 'We desire to eat of it, so that our hearts are reassured and that we know that you have spoken the truth to us, and that we may be witness of it'. **114** 'God, our Lord', said Jesus, son of Mary, 'send down upon us a repast from heaven: it shall be an ever-recurring feast for us – for the first and the last of us – and a sign from You. And provide us our sustenance, for You are the best provider'. **115** God replied: 'I am sending it down to you. But whoever of you disbelieves after this, I shall inflict on him suffering the like of which I have not inflicted on anyone in the world'. **116** And God will say: 'Jesus, son of Mary! Did you say to people, "Worship me and my mother as deities beside God?"' [Jesus] answered: 'Limitless are You in Your glory! I could never have claimed what I have no right to [say]! Had I said this, You would certainly have known it. You know all that is within myself, whereas I do not know what is in Yourself. Most certainly, it is You alone who fully knows all that lies beyond the reach of human perception'. **117** 'Nothing did I tell them beyond what You bade me [to say]: "Worship God, who is my Lord and your Lord". I was witness to what they did as long as I lived in their midst. Then when You took me to Yourself, You have been watching over them. You are indeed a witness to all things.' **118** 'If You punish them, they are Your servants; and if You forgive them, You are indeed the Almighty, the Wise.' **119** God will say: 'This is the day when their truthfulness shall benefit all who have been truthful. Theirs shall be gardens through which running waters flow, where they will abide forever. God is well-pleased with them, and they are well-pleased with Him. That is the supreme triumph'. **120** To God belongs all sovereignty over the heavens and the earth and all they contain. He has power over all things.

Surah 6   Cattle

This surah of 165 verses was revealed complete on one occasion during the Makkan period. Apart from the first surah, this is the first Makkan revelation in the arrangement of the Qur'an, and as such we note the clear difference of style and subject matter between it and the previous surahs. Like all Makkan revelations, it focuses on the central issue of faith. It puts forward the concepts of God's Oneness, and His control of life and the universe very clearly, and spells out the status of man and his relationship with his Creator.

The fact that the Qur'an addressed this central issue over a period of 13 years, during which Prophet Muhammad (peace be upon him) advocated his message in Makkah gives us a clear idea of its importance. Indeed, more than half of the Qur'an is given over to this central issue, and on each occasion it is presented both newly and perfectly.

In Makkah, the Muslims had little contact with other divine religions, the society where the Islamic message began was essentially pagan. Hence, we see in this surah and in other parts of the Qur'an revealed in Makkah clear focus on refuting all arguments and claims presented by the Arab idolaters. Nevertheless, the Qur'anic argument against idolatry is clearly relevant to any form of belief which does not give to God His due status as the sole Creator and controller of the universe, human life and life generally.

The surah makes clear that all prophets, from Adam to Muhammad (peace be upon them all) preached the same central message of God's Oneness, even though divine religions may contain differences in matters of legislative detail. It gives us clear instructions about what God has forbidden and sums up what He has prohibited in three verses (151–153).

Cattle

In the Name of God, the Lord of Grace, the Ever-Merciful

1 All praise is due to God, who has created the heavens and the earth, and brought into being darkness and light; yet those who disbelieve regard other beings as equal to their Lord. 2 It is He who has created you out of clay, and then has decreed a term [for you], and there is another term known only to Him. Yet you are still in doubt. 3 He alone

is God in the heavens and on earth. He has full knowledge of all that you keep secret and all that you do openly. He knows what you earn.

4 Whenever a revelation comes to them from their Lord, they [who are unbelievers] turn their back upon it. **5** Thus they have denied the truth now that it has come to them. In time, they shall have full information about that which they used to deride. **6** Do they not see how many a generation We have destroyed before them – people whom We had made more powerful in the land than We have made you, and for whom We sent down abundant water from the sky, and made rivers flow at their feet? Yet We destroyed them for their sins, and raised up another generation in their place. **7** Even if We had sent down to you a book written on paper, and they had touched it with their own hands, surely the unbelievers would still say: 'This is nothing but plain sorcery'. **8** They say: 'Why has not an angel been sent down to him?' If We had sent down an angel, all would have been decided, and they would have been allowed no further respite. **9** And even if We had appointed an angel as Our messenger, We would certainly have made him [appear as] a man, and thus We would have confused them just as they are now confusing themselves. **10** Indeed other messengers have been derided before your time, but those who scoffed at them were eventually overwhelmed by the very thing they derided. **11** Say: 'Go all over the earth and see what was the fate of those who denied the truth'.

12 Say: 'To whom belongs all that is in the heavens and on earth?' Say: 'To God. He has committed Himself to bestow grace and mercy. He will certainly gather you all together on the Day of Resurrection, about which there is no doubt. Those who squandered their own souls will not believe. **13** To Him belongs whatever takes its rest in the night or in the day. He alone hears all and knows all'. **14** Say: 'Am I to take for my master anyone but God, the Originator of the heavens and the earth, who gives nourishment to all and Himself needs none?' Say: 'I am commanded to be the first of those who surrender themselves to God, and not to be among those who associate partners with Him'. **15** Say: 'Indeed I would dread, were I to disobey my Lord, the suffering of an awesome Day. **16** He who is spared that shall have received His grace. This will be a manifest triumph'. **17** If God were to expose you to affliction, none can remove it but He. And if He were to bless you with good fortune – well, He has power over all things. **18** He alone holds sway over all His servants, and He alone is truly wise, all-aware. **19** Say: 'What is weightiest in testimony?' Say: 'God is witness between me and you. This Qur'an has been revealed to me that I may thereby warn you and all whom it may reach. Will you in truth bear witness that there are other deities beside God?' Say: 'I bear no such witness'. Say: 'He is but one God. I disown all that you associate with Him'.

20 Those to whom We had given revelations know this as they know their own sons. But those who have squandered their own souls will never have faith. **21** Who is more wicked than one who invents a falsehood about God or denies His revelations? The wrongdoers shall never achieve success. **22** One day We shall gather them all together, then We shall say to those who associate partners with God: 'Where, now, are those partners which you have been claiming'. **23** They will have no contention then other than to say, 'By God, our Lord, we have never associated partners with Him'. **24** Behold how they have lied to themselves and how they have been forsaken by whatever they have fabricated. **25** Some of them listen to you. But over their hearts We have laid veils which prevent them from understanding what you say, and into their ears, deafness. Were they to see every sign, they would still not believe in it. When they come to you to contend with you, the unbelievers say: 'This is nothing but fables of the ancients'. **26** They forbid [others] to listen to it and go far away from it. They ruin none but themselves, though they do not perceive it. **27** If you could but see them when they will be made to stand before the Fire! They will say: 'Would that we could return! Then we would not deny our Lord's revelations, but would be among the believers'. **28** Indeed, that which in the past they used to conceal will manifest itself to them; and if they were to return to life they would go back to that which they have been forbidden. They are indeed liars. **29** They say: 'There is nothing beyond our life in this world, and we shall never be raised to life again'. **30** If you could but see them when they are made to stand before their Lord! He will say: 'Is this not the truth?' They will say: 'Yes, indeed, by our Lord!' He will then say, 'Taste, then, the suffering in consequence of your having refused to believe'. **31** Lost indeed are they who deny that they will have to meet God. When the Last Hour comes suddenly upon them, they cry, 'Alas for us! We have neglected much in our lifetime!' And they will be carrying their burdens on their backs. Evil indeed is that with which they are burdened. **32** The life of this world is nothing but a sport and a passing delight. Surely the life in the Hereafter is by far the better for those who are God-fearing. Will you not, then, use your reason?

33 We know too well that what they say grieves you. Yet it is not you that they charge with falsehood; but it is God's revelations that the wrongdoers deny. **34** Other messengers were charged with falsehood before your time, but they patiently endured all those charges and abuse, until Our help came to them. There is no power that can alter God's words. You have already received some of the history of those messengers. **35** If you find it so distressing that they turn their backs on you, seek, if you can, a chasm to go deep into the earth or a ladder to the sky by which you may bring them a sign. Had God so willed, He would have gathered them all to [His] guidance. Do not, therefore, allow yourself to be one of the ignorant. **36** Only those that can hear will surely answer. As for the dead, God will bring them back to life, then to Him shall they return. **37** They say: 'Why has no sign been sent down to him from his Lord?' Say: 'God is well able to send down any sign, but most of them are devoid of knowledge'. **38** There is not an animal that walks on earth and no bird that flies on its wings but are communities like your own. No single thing have We left out of the Book. Then to their Lord shall they all be gathered. **39** Those who deny Our revelations are deaf and dumb, groping along in darkness. Whomever God wills, He lets go astray; and whomever He wills, He guides along a straight path.

40 Say: 'If God's punishment befalls you or the Hour comes upon you, can you see yourselves calling upon anyone other than God? [Answer me] if you are truthful! **41** No, on Him alone you will call, whereupon He will, if He so wills, remove the ill which caused you to call on Him; and you will have forgotten all those you associate as partners with Him'. **42** Indeed We sent messengers before your time to other nations, and visited them with misfortune and hardship so that they might humble themselves. **43** If only, when the misfortune decreed by Us befell them, they humbled themselves! Rather, their hearts were hardened and Satan made their deeds seem goodly to them. **44** Then, when they had clean forgotten what they had been reminded of, We threw open to them the gates of all good things, until just when they were rejoicing in what they had been granted, We suddenly took them to task; and they were plunged into utter despair. **45** Thus the last remnant of the wrongdoing people was wiped out. All praise is due to God, the Lord of all worlds. **46** Say: 'Do but consider: if God should take away your hearing and your sight and seal your hearts, what deity but God is there to restore them to you'. See how varied and multifaceted We make Our signs, and yet they turn away! **47** Say: 'Do but consider, if God's punishment befalls you suddenly or in a perceptible manner, would any but the wrongdoing folk be destroyed?' **48** We send Our messengers only as bearers of good news and as warners. Those who believe and act righteously shall have nothing to fear, nor shall they grieve. **49** But those that deny Our revelations shall be afflicted with suffering as a result of their sinful deeds.

50 Say: 'I do not say to you that God's treasures are with me; nor do I know what is beyond the reach of human perception; nor do I say to you that I am an angel. I only follow what is revealed to me'. Say: 'Can the blind and the seeing be deemed equal? Will you not reflect?' **51** Warn with this [Qur'an] those who fear that they will be gathered to their Lord, when they shall have none to protect them from Him or to intercede with Him, so that they may be God-fearing. **52** Do not drive away those who call on their Lord morning and evening, seeking only to win His pleasure. You are in no way accountable for them, just as they are in no way accountable for you. Should you drive them away, you would be among the wrongdoers. **53** It is in this way that We try some of them by means of others, so that they may say: 'Are these the ones upon whom God has bestowed His favour from among us?' Does not God know best as to who is truly grateful? **54** When those who believe in God's revelations come to you, say: 'Peace be upon you. Your Lord has committed Himself to bestow grace and mercy: if any of you does a bad deed out of ignorance, and then repents and mends his ways, He will be much-forgiving, ever-merciful'. **55** Thus do We make plain Our revelations; so that the path of the guilty ones may be clearly distinct.

56 Say: 'I am forbidden to worship those beings whom you invoke instead of God'. Say: 'I do not follow your whims, for then I would have gone astray, and would not be on the right path'. **57** Say: 'I take my stand on a clear evidence from my Lord, yet you deny Him. It is not in my power [to produce] that which you so hastily demand. Judgement rests with God alone. He declares the truth and He is the best of arbiters'. **58** Say: 'If that which you so hastily demand were in my power, the case between me and you would have been decided. But God knows best as to who are the wrongdoers'. **59** With Him are the keys to what lies beyond the reach of human perception: none knows them but He. He knows all that the land and sea contain; not a leaf falls but He knows it; and neither is there a grain in the earth's deep darkness, nor anything fresh or dry but is recorded in a clear book. **60** It is He who causes you to be like the dead at night, and knows what you do in the daytime. He raises you again to life each day in order that a term set by Him be fulfilled. In the end, to Him you must return; and then He will tell you all that you have done. **61** He alone holds sway over His servants. He sends forth guardians to watch over you until, when death approaches any one of you,

Our messengers cause him to die. They leave no part of their duty unfulfilled. **62** They are then brought back to God, their true Lord Supreme. Indeed, His alone is all judgement; and He is most swift in reckoning. **63** Say: 'Who is it that saves you from the dark dangers of land and sea, when you call out to Him humbly and in secret: "If He will but save us from this peril, we will most certainly be grateful?"' **64** Say: 'God alone saves you from these and from every distress; and still you associate partners with Him'. **65** Say: 'It is He alone who has the power to let loose upon you suffering from above you and from beneath your feet, or to divide you into disputing groups, causing the one to suffer at the hands of the other. See how We make plain Our revelations so that they may understand'.

66 Your people have rejected this [the Qur'an], although it is the very truth. Say: 'I am not responsible for you'. **67** Every piece of news has a time set for its fulfilment, as you will come to know. **68** Whenever you see those who indulge in vain discourse about Our revelations, turn away from them until they talk of other things. Should Satan ever cause you to forget, do not, once you remember, stay with such wrongdoing folk. **69** Those who are God-fearing are in no way accountable for them. It is their duty, however, to admonish them, so that they may become God-fearing. **70** Stay away from those who, beguiled by the life of this world, take their religion for a pastime and a sport; but remind them with this [Qur'an], lest every human being should be held in pledge for whatever he has done, when he shall have none to protect him from God, and none to intercede for him. If he were to offer any conceivable ransom, it shall not be accepted from him. Those are the ones who are held in pledge for what they have done. Scalding water shall they drink, and grievous suffering awaits them because they were unbelievers.

71 Say: 'Shall we invoke, instead of God, something that can neither benefit nor harm us, and shall we turn back on our heels after God has given us guidance, like one whom the satans have lured away in the land, blunders along perplexed. Yet he has companions who call out to him, "Come to us for guidance".' Say: 'In truth, God's guidance is the only guidance. We are commanded to surrender ourselves to the Lord of all the worlds'. **72** And to attend regularly to prayers and to fear Him. It is to Him you all shall be gathered. **73** He it is who has created the heavens and the earth in truth. Whenever He says, 'Be', it shall be. His word is the truth. All sovereignty shall be His on the Day when the Trumpet is blown. He knows all that is beyond the reach of human perception, and all that anyone may witness. He alone is truly wise, all-aware.

74 Thus Abraham said to his father Azar: Do you take idols for gods? I see that you and your people have obviously gone astray. **75** Thus did we give Abraham an insight into [God's] mighty dominion over the heavens and the earth; so that he may become a firm believer. **76** When the night drew its shadow over him, he saw a star; and he exclaimed: 'This is my Lord!' But when it set, he said: 'I do not love things that set'. **77** Then when he beheld the rising moon, he said: 'This is my Lord!' But when it set, he said: 'If my Lord does not guide me, I will most certainly be one of those who go astray'. **78** Then when he beheld the sun rising, he said: 'This is my Lord! This is the greatest of all!' But when it also set, he said: 'My people, I disown all that you associate with God'. **79** 'I have turned my face with pure and complete devotion to Him who brought the heavens and the earth into being. I am not one of those who associate partners with God.' **80** His people argued with him. He said: 'Do you argue with me about God, when it is He who has given me guidance? I do not fear those beings you associate with Him, [for no evil can befall me] unless my Lord so wills. My Lord embraces all things within His knowledge; will you not, then, reflect?' **81** 'And why should I fear anything you worship side by side with Him, when you are not afraid of associating with God partners without His ever giving you any warrant? Which of the two parties has a better right to feel secure, if you happen to know?' **82** Those who believe and do not taint their faith with wrongdoing are the ones who will feel secure, as they follow right guidance. **83** This was Our argument with which We furnished Abraham against his people. We raise whom We will, degree after degree. Your Lord is wise, all-knowing. **84** We bestowed on him Isaac and Jacob, and We guided each of them as We had guided Noah before them. Among his offspring were [the Prophets] David, Solomon, Job, Joseph, Moses and Aaron. Thus do We reward those who do good. **85** And Zachariah, John, Jesus and Elijah; who were all righteous. **86** And Ishmael, Elisha, Jonah and Lot. Every one of them did We favour above all people. **87** And [We exalted likewise] some of their forefathers, their offspring and their brethren. We chose them and guided them to a straight path. **88** Such is God's guidance; He bestows it on whomever He wills of His servants. Had they associated partners with Him, in vain would certainly have been all that they ever did. **89** On these did We bestow revelation, wisdom and prophethood. If this generation were to deny this truth, We have certainly entrusted it to others who will never deny it; **90** Those are the ones whom God has guided. Follow, then, their guidance, [and] say: 'No reward do I ask of you for this. It is but an admonition to all mankind'. **91** No true understanding of God have they when they say: 'God has never revealed anything to any human being'. Say: 'Who, then, revealed the Book which Moses brought to people as a light and a guidance? You transcribe it on sheets to show around, while you suppress much. You have been taught [by it] what neither you nor your forefathers had ever known'. Say: 'God', and leave them to their play and foolish chatter. **92** This is a blessed[16] Book which We have revealed, confirming what came before it, that you may warn the Mother City and all who dwell around it. Those who believe in the life to come do believe in it, and they are ever-mindful of their prayers. **93** Who could be more wicked than one who invents a falsehood about God, or says: 'This has been revealed to me', when nothing has been revealed to him? – Or one who says, 'I can reveal the like of what God has revealed'? If you could but see the wrongdoers when they are in the throes of death and the angels stretch out their hands [and say]: 'Give up your souls!' Today you shall be rewarded with a humiliating punishment for having attributed to God something that is untrue and, in your arrogance, scorned His revelations. **94** 'And now, indeed, you have come to Us individually, just as We created you in the first instance; and you have left behind all that We conferred on you. Nor do We see with you those intercessors of yours whom you had claimed to be partners in your affairs. Broken are the ties which bound you, and that which you have been asserting has failed you.'

95 It is God who splits the grain and the fruit-stone. He brings forth the living out of that which is dead and the dead out of that which

---

16   The Qur'an is certainly a blessed book: it is blessed in its origin and destination, as it is a revelation from God to Muhammad (peace be upon him), His final messenger. 'It is also blessed in its size and contents. Compared to voluminous works written by human beings, it comprises a small number of pages, but its inspiration, impact, directives and meanings are far superior to those contained in scores of those books, each one of which is several times each size… It is impossible that human beings could express all the meanings, concepts and inspirations of the Qur'an in a work which is a great many times its size. Many a single verse includes meanings, facts and concepts that make it quotable in a variety of situations and for numerous purposes… The Qur'an is also blessed in its effect. It addresses human nature, and man as a whole, in a way which is remarkable, direct and gentle'. (Sayyid Qutb, *In the Shade of the Qur'an*, The Islamic Foundation, Markfield, 2002, vol. 5, p. 235)

is alive. Such is God. How, then, are you deluded away from the truth? **96** He is the One who causes the day to break. He has made the night to be [a source of] stillness, and the sun and the moon for reckoning. All this is laid down by the will of the Almighty, the All-Knowing. **97** It is He that has set up for you the stars, so that you may be guided by them in the deep darkness of land and sea. We have made Our revelations plain indeed to people who have knowledge. **98** He it is who has brought you all into being from a single soul and has given you a dwelling and a place of sojourn. We have made Our revelations plain indeed to people of understanding. **99** And He it is who sends down water from the sky with which We bring forth plants of every type and out of these We bring forth verdure from which We bring forth grain piled tight, packed on one another; and out of the spathe of the palm tree, dates in thick clusters; and gardens of vines; and the olive tree, and the pomegranate: all so alike, and yet so different. Behold their fruit when they come to fruition and ripen. Surely in these there are clear signs for people who truly believe. **100** Yet they make the jinn equals with God, although He created them; and in their ignorance they invent for Him sons and daughters. Limitless is He in His glory, and sublimely exalted above all that which they attribute to Him. **101** He is the Originator of the heavens and the earth. How can He have a child when He has never had a consort? He has created everything and has full knowledge of all things. **102** Such is God, your Lord; there is no deity other than Him, the Creator of all things, so worship Him alone. He is the Guardian of everything. **103** No power of vision can encompass Him, whereas He encompasses all vision; He is above all comprehension, yet is all-aware. **104** Means of insight have come to you from your Lord. Therefore, whoever chooses to see does so for his own good, and whoever chooses to remain blind only himself does he hurt. I am not your keeper. **105** Thus do We spell out Our revelations in diverse ways, that they may say, 'You have studied this', and that We may make it clear to people of knowledge. **106** Follow what has been revealed to you by your Lord, other than whom there is no deity, and turn your back on those who associate partners with God. **107** Had God so willed, they would not have associated partners with Him. We have not made you responsible for them, nor are you their guardian. **108** Do not revile those whom they invoke instead of God, lest they revile God out of spite, and in ignorance. Thus have We made the actions of every community seem goodly to them. Then to their Lord shall they all return, and He will explain to them all that they have been doing. **109** They swear by God most solemnly that if a miracle be shown to them they would believe in it. Say: 'Miracles are in God's power'. For all you know, even if one is shown to them, they may still not believe? **110** We will turn their hearts and eyes away since they did not believe in it the first time. We shall leave them to blunder about in their overweening arrogance. **111** Even if We were to send down angels to them, and if the dead were to speak to them, and even if We were to range all things before them, they would still not believe unless God so willed. Yet most of them are ignorant.

112 Thus have We set up against every prophet enemies: the evil ones among human beings and the jinn, who inspire each other with varnished and deluding falsehood. Had your Lord willed otherwise, they would not have done it. Therefore, leave them to their own inventions, **113** so that the hearts of those who do not believe in the life to come may be inclined to what they say and, being pleased with it, persist in their erring ways. **114** Am I to seek for judge anyone other than God, when it is He who has revealed the Book to you, clearly spelling out the truth. Those to whom We previously gave revelations know that it is the truth revealed by your Lord. So, do not be among the doubters. **115** Perfected are the words of your Lord in truth and justice. No one can change His words. He hears all and knows all. **116** If you were to pay heed to the greater part of those on earth, they would lead you away from God's path. They follow nothing but conjecture and they do nothing but guess. **117** Your Lord surely knows best who strays from His path, and best knows He those who are right-guided. **118** Eat, then, of that over which God's name has been pronounced, if you truly believe in His revelations. **119** And why should you not eat of that over which God's name has been pronounced when He has clearly spelled out to you what He has forbidden you [to eat] unless you are driven to do so by sheer necessity? Many people lead others astray by their errant views and lack of knowledge. Your Lord is fully aware of those who transgress. **120** Abstain from all sin, be it open or secret. Those who commit sins will be requited for what they have committed. **121** Hence, do not eat of that over which God's name has not been pronounced; for that is sinful. The evil ones do whisper to their friends to argue with you. Should you pay heed to them, you will end up associating partners with God. **122** Is he who was dead and whom We have raised to life, and for whom We set up a light to see his way among men, to be compared to one who is in deep darkness out of which he cannot emerge? Thus do their deeds seem goodly to the unbelievers. **123** And thus in every city have We placed arch-criminals so that they weave their schemes there. But it is only against themselves that they scheme, though they do not perceive it. **124** When a sign comes to them, they say: 'We shall not believe unless we are given the same as God's messengers were given'. But God knows best whom to entrust with His message. Humiliation before God and severe suffering will befall those guilty of evildoing for all their scheming. **125** Whomever God wills to guide, He makes his bosom open wide with willingness towards self-surrender [to Him]; and whomever He wills to let go astray, He causes his bosom to be tight and constricted, as if he were climbing up into the skies. Thus does God lay the scourge on the unbelievers. **126** Such is the path of your Lord, a straight path. We have made Our revelations plain for people who reflect. **127** Theirs shall be an abode of peace with their Lord. He will be their patron in reward for what they have been doing.

128 On the Day when He shall gather them all together, [He will say]: 'O you company of jinn! A great many human beings have you deluded'. Those who were their close friends among human beings will say: 'Our Lord, we have enjoyed each other's fellowship, and we have now reached the end of our term which You have appointed for us'. He will say: 'The Fire shall be your abode, where you shall remain, unless God wills it otherwise. Indeed, your Lord is wise, all-knowing'. **129** In this manner do We cause the wrongdoers to be close allies of one another, because of that which they do. **130** 'O you company of jinn and humans! Have there not come to you messengers from among yourselves who related to you My revelations and warned you of the coming of this your Day?' They will reply: 'We bear witness against ourselves'. The life of this world has beguiled them. So they will bear witness against themselves that they were unbelievers. **131** And so it is that your Lord would never destroy a community for its wrongdoing, while they remain unaware. **132** They all shall have their grades in accordance with their deeds. Your Lord is not unaware of what they do. **133** Your Lord is the self-sufficient One, the Merciful. If He so wills, He may remove you altogether and cause whom He wills to succeed you, just as He brought you into being out of other people's seed. **134** That which you are promised will inevitably come, and you cannot elude it. **135** Say: 'My people! Do all that may be in your power, and I will do what I can. You shall come to know to whom the future belongs. Never will the wrongdoers attain success'.

136 Out of the produce and the cattle He has created, they assign a portion to God, saying: 'This is for God' – or so they pretend – 'and this is for the partners we associate [with Him]'. Whatever they assign to their partners never reaches God, but that which is assigned to God does reach their partners. How ill they judge! **137** Thus have the partners they associate [with God] made the killing of their own children seem goodly to many idolaters, seeking to bring them to ruin and to confuse them in their faith. Had God willed otherwise, they would not have done so. Leave them, then, to their false inventions. **138** They say: 'Such cattle and crops are forbidden. None may eat of them save those whom we permit' – so they falsely claim. Other cattle they declare to be forbidden to burden their backs; and there are cattle over which they do not pronounce God's name, inventing [in all this] a lie against Him. He will surely requite them for their inventions. **139** They also say: 'That which is in the wombs of these cattle is reserved to our males and forbidden to our women'. But if it be stillborn, they all partake of it. He will requite them for all their false assertions. He is wise, all-knowing. **140** Losers indeed are those who, in their ignorance, foolishly kill their children and declare as forbidden what God has provided for them as sustenance, falsely attributing such prohibitions to God. They have gone astray and they have no guidance. **141** It is He who has brought into being gardens – both of the cultivated type and those growing wild – and the date-palm, and fields bearing different produce, and the olive tree, and the pomegranates, all resembling one another and yet so different. Eat of their fruit when they come to fruition, and give [to the poor] what is due to them on harvest day. But do not waste, for He does not love the wasteful. **142** And of the cattle some are reared for work and others for food. Eat of that which God has provided for you as sustenance and do not follow Satan's footsteps; he is your open foe. **143** Of cattle you have eight in [four] pairs: a pair of sheep and a pair of goats. Say: 'Is it the two males that He has forbidden, or the two females, or that which the wombs of the two females may contain? Tell me plainly if you are men of truth'. **144** And, likewise, a pair of camels and a pair of oxen. Say: 'Is it the two males that He has forbidden, or the two females, or that which the wombs of the two females may contain? Is it, perchance, that you were witnesses when God gave you these commandments?' Who could be more wicked than one who, without any real knowledge, invents lies about God in order to lead people astray? God does not guide the wrongdoers. **145** Say: 'In all that has been revealed to me, I do not find anything forbidden to eat, if one wishes to eat thereof, unless it be carrion, or blood poured forth, or the flesh of swine – for all that is unclean – or a sinful offering over which any name other than God's has been invoked'. But if one is driven by necessity, neither intending disobedience nor exceeding his bare need, then know that your Lord is much-forgiving, ever-merciful. **146** To those who followed the Jewish faith did We forbid all animals that have claws; and We forbade them the fat of both oxen and sheep, except that which is in their backs and entrails and what is mixed with their bones. Thus did We requite them for their wrongdoing. We are certainly true to Our word. **147** If they accuse you of lying, then say: 'Limitless is your Lord in His grace; but His punishment shall not be warded off from the guilty folk'. **148** Those who associate partners with God will say: 'Had God so willed, neither we nor our fathers would have associated any partners with Him; nor would we have declared anything as forbidden'. In like manner did those who have lived before them deny the truth, until they came to taste Our punishment. Say: 'Have you any certain knowledge which you can put before us? You follow nothing but conjecture, and you do nothing but guess'. **149** Say: 'With God alone rests the final evidence. Had He so willed, He would have guided you all aright'. **150** Say: 'Bring forward your witnesses who will testify that God has forbidden this'. If they so testify, do not you testify with them; and do not follow the wishes of those who deny Our revelations, and those who do not believe in the life to come and who consider others as equal to their Lord. **151** Say: 'Come, let me tell you what your Lord has forbidden to you: Do not associate partners with Him; [do not offend against but, rather,] be kind to your parents; do not kill your children because of your poverty – We provide for you and for them; do not commit any shameful deed, whether open or secret; do not take any human being's life – which God has made sacred, except in the course of justice. This He has enjoined upon you so that you may use your reason'. **152** 'Do not touch the property of an orphan before he comes of age, except to improve it.' Give just weight and full measure. We do not charge a soul with more than it can bear. When you speak, be just, even though it be against one of your close relatives. Be true to your covenant with God. This He has enjoined upon you so that you may bear it in mind. **153** Know that this is the way leading to Me, a straight path. Follow it, then, and do not follow other ways, for they cause you to deviate from His way. All this He has enjoined upon you so that you may remain God-fearing.

154 Moreover, We gave Moses the Book in fulfilment [of Our favour] upon him who would do right, clearly spelling out everything, and providing guidance and grace, so that they might believe in the meeting with their Lord. **155** And this is a Book which

We have bestowed from on high, a blessed one. Follow it, then, and be conscious of God, so that you might be graced with His mercy. **156** [It has been given to you] lest you say, 'Only two groups of people before our time have received revelations from on high; and we were unaware of what they learned'. **157** Or lest you say, 'If a book had been revealed to us, we would surely have followed its guidance better than they did'. Now then a clear evidence of the truth has come to you from your Lord, and guidance, and grace. Who could be more wicked than he who denies God's revelations and turns away from them in disdain? We shall punish those who turn away from our revelations in disdain with grave suffering for so turning away. **158** Are they waiting for the angels to come to them, or for your Lord [Himself], or are they certain of your Lord's signs to appear? On the Day when certain of your Lord's signs do appear, believing will be of no avail to any human being who did not believe before, or who did not put its faith to good uses. Say: 'Wait if you will; we too are waiting'. **159** As for those who have broken the unity of their faith and have become sects, you certainly have nothing to do with them. Their case rests with God. In time He will tell them the truth of what they were doing. **160** Whoever does a good deed shall be credited with ten times as much; and whoever does an evil deed will be requited with no more than its like. None shall be wronged. **161** Say: 'My Lord has guided me to a straight way, to an ever-true faith; the way of Abraham, who turned away from all that is false, and was not of those who associate partners with God'. **162** Say: 'My prayers, my worship, my living and my dying are for God alone, the Lord of all worlds. **163** He has no partner. Thus have I been commanded, and I shall be the first of those who surrender themselves to Him'. **164** Say: 'Am I, then, to seek a lord other than God, when He is the Lord of all things?' Whatever wrong any human being commits rests upon himself alone. No one shall be made to bear the burden of another. In time, to your Lord you all must return; and then He will tell you the truth of all that over which you were in dispute. **165** He it is who has made you inherit the earth and has raised some of you by degrees above others, so that He might try you by means of what He has bestowed upon you. For certain, your Lord is swift in retribution; yet, He is indeed much-forgiving, ever-merciful.

Surah 7   The Heights

Like the previous surah, this one was revealed in Makkah. As such, both concentrate on the main issue of faith, God's Oneness and the relationship between Him and man. Yet the two surahs cannot be more dissimilar in their methods of presentation and the way they discuss their common theme.

This surah concentrates on human history in relation to the divine faith. After an introductory passage, it gives us an account of the creation of man, Iblis's [Satan] disobedience of God's order to prostrate himself, like the angels, to Adam, and the ensuing war between man and evil which will continue throughout human history. The surah gives us accounts of different communities which disobeyed God's messengers, refused to believe and suffered God's punishment. It then gives us a very detailed account of Moses and the Children of Israel. This serves as a warning to the Muslim community against abandoning, or deviating from, the divine message.

The surah does not present these accounts of past communities as stories to be told and enjoyed, but instead as examples to derive lessons from. The issue of faith is central to human life and applicable to man across all generations and environments. Therefore, it must be presented in a way that remains valid for all people at all times. This is done through every account given in this surah.

The Heights

In the Name of God, the Lord of Grace, the Ever-Merciful

1 *Alif. Lam. Mim. Sad.* **2** This is a Book that has been bestowed on you from on high – so do not entertain any doubt about it – in order that you may warn people with its message, and admonish the believers. **3** Follow, [all of you], what has been sent down to you by your Lord, and follow no masters other than Him. How seldom do you keep this in mind. **4** How many a community have We destroyed, with Our punishment falling upon them by night, or at midday while they were resting. **5** And when Our punishment fell upon them, all they could say was: 'We have indeed been wrongdoers'. **6** We shall most certainly question those to whom a message was sent, and We shall most certainly question the messengers themselves. **7** And most certainly We shall reveal to them Our knowledge [of what they have done]; for never have We been absent. **8** On that Day, the weighing will be true and accurate: and those whose weight [of good deeds] is heavy in the balance are the ones who are successful; **9** whereas those whose weight is light in the balance are the ones who have lost their own souls because of their wilful rejection of Our revelations.

10 We have established you firmly on earth and We have provided you there with means of livelihood. How seldom are you grateful. **11** We have indeed created you, and then formed you. We then said to the angels: 'Prostrate yourselves before Adam!' They all prostrated themselves, except for Iblis: he was not one of those who prostrated themselves. **12** And [God] said: 'What has prevented you from prostrating yourself when I commanded you?' Answered [Iblis]: 'I am nobler than he: You created me out of fire, while you created him out of clay'. **13** [God] said: 'Off with you hence! It is not for you to show your arrogance here. Get out, then; you will always be among the humiliated'. **14** Said he: 'Grant me a respite until the Day when all will be raised [from the dead]'. **15** God replied: 'You shall indeed be among these granted respite'. **17** [Iblis] said: 'Since you let me fall in error, I shall indeed lurk in ambush for them all along Your straight path, and I shall most certainly fall upon them from the front and from the rear, and from their right and from their left; and You will find most of them ungrateful'. **18** [God] said: 'Get out of here, despised, disgraced. As for those of them that follow you, I shall fill Hell with you all. **19** And [as for you], Adam: dwell you and your wife in this Garden, and eat, both of you, whatever you may desire; but do not come near this tree, lest you become wrongdoers'. **20** But Satan whispered to them both, so that he might show them their nakedness, of which they had previously been unaware. He said to them: 'Your Lord has only forbidden you this tree lest you two become angels or immortals'. **21** And he swore to them: 'I am indeed giving you sound advice'. **22** Thus he cunningly deluded them. And when they both had tasted the fruit of the tree, their nakedness became apparent to them, and they began to cover themselves with leaves from the Garden. Their Lord called out to them: 'Did I not forbid you that tree and tell you both that Satan is your open enemy?' **23** Said they: 'Our Lord! We have wronged ourselves; and unless You grant us forgiveness and bestow Your mercy upon us, we shall certainly be lost'. **24** Said He: 'Get you down hence, [and be henceforth] enemies to one another, having on earth your abode and livelihood for a while'. **25** 'There shall you live', He added, 'and there shall you die, and from there shall you be brought forth [on the Day of Resurrection]'.

26 Children of Adam, We have sent down to you clothing to cover your nakedness, and garments pleasing to the eye; but the robe of God-fearingness is the finest of all. In this there is a sign from God, so that they may reflect. **27** Children of Adam, do not allow Satan to seduce you in the same way as he caused your [first] parents to be turned out of the Garden. He stripped them of their garment in order to make them aware of their nakedness. Surely, he and his tribe watch you from where you cannot perceive them. We have made the devils as patrons for those who do not believe. **28** When they commit a shameful deed, they say, 'We found our fathers doing it', and, 'God has enjoined it upon us'. Say: 'Never does God enjoin what is indecent. Would you attribute to God something of which you have no knowledge?' **29** Say: 'My Lord has enjoined justice, and that you set your whole selves [to Him] at every time and place of prayer, and call on Him, sincere in your faith in Him alone. As it was He who brought you into being in the first instance, so also [to Him] you will return: **30** some [of you] He will have graced with His guidance, whereas for some a straying from the right path will have become unavoidable. For, they will have taken satans for their protectors in preference to God, thinking all the while that they have found the right path'. **31** Children of Adam, dress well when you attend any place of worship. Eat and drink but do not be wasteful. Surely He does not love the wasteful. **32** Say, 'Who is there to forbid the beauty which God has produced for His servants, and the wholesome means of sustenance?' Say, 'They are [lawful] in the life of this world, to all who believe – to be theirs alone on the Day of Resurrection'. Thus do We make Our revelations clear to people of knowledge. **33** Say, 'My Lord has only forbidden shameful deeds, be they open or secret, and all types of sin, and wrongful oppression, and that you should associate with God anything for which He has given no authority, and that you attribute to God anything of which you have no knowledge'. **34** For every community a term has been set. When [the end of] their term approaches, they can neither delay nor hasten it by a single moment.

35 Children of Adam! Whenever there come to you messengers from among yourselves to relate to you My revelations, then those who are God-fearing and live righteously shall have nothing to fear, nor shall they grieve. **36** But those who deny and scorn Our revelations are the ones destined for the Fire, where they shall abide. **37** Who is more wicked than one who invents lies about God or denies His revelations? These shall have whatever has been decreed to be their lot [in life]. When Our messengers come to carry off their souls, they will say: 'Where, now, are those whom you used to invoke besides God?' They will reply: 'They are oblivious of us!' Thus, they will bear witness against themselves that they had been unbelievers. **38** [God] will say: 'Enter into the Fire to join the hosts of the jinn and humans who have gone before you'. Every time a host enters [the Fire], it will curse its fellow host. When all are gathered there, the last of them will say of the first: 'Our Lord, these are the ones who have led us astray, so give them double suffering in the Fire'. He will answer: 'Every one of you shall have double suffering, although you may not know it'. **39** And the first of them will say to the last: 'In no wise were you superior to us. Taste, then, this suffering on account of what you have been doing'. **40** For those who deny Our revelations and scorn them the gates of Heaven shall not be opened; nor shall they enter Paradise any more than a thick, twisted rope can pass through a needle's eye. Thus do We reward the evil-doers. **41** Hell shall be their resting place, and sheets of fire shall cover them. Thus do We reward the wrongdoers. **42** As for those who believe and do righteous deeds, We never burden a soul with more than it can bear. They are destined for Paradise, where they will abide. **43** We shall remove any rancour that may be lingering in their hearts. Running waters will flow at their feet; and they will say: 'All praise is due to God who has guided us to this. Had He not given us guidance, we would certainly have not found the right path. Our Lord's messengers have certainly brought us the truth'. [A voice] will call out to them: 'This is the Paradise you have inherited by virtue of what you used to do'. **44** The dwellers of Paradise will call out to the inmates of the Fire: 'We have found what our Lord promised to be true. Have you, too, found the promise of your Lord to be true?' They will answer: 'Yes', whereupon someone from their midst will proclaim: 'Cursed indeed are the wrongdoers **45** who turn others away from God's path and try to make it appear crooked, and who reject the truth of the life to come'. **46** Between the two parties there will be a barrier, and on the Heights there will be men who recognise everyone by their looks. They will call out to the dwellers of Paradise: 'Peace be upon you', – not having entered it themselves, but longing still [to be there]. **47** And whenever their eyes are turned towards the inmates of the Fire, they will say: 'Our Lord, do not place us alongside such wrongdoing people'. **48** Then those on the Heights will call out to certain people whom they recognise by their looks, saying: 'What have your great throngs and your false pride availed you? **49** Are these the self-same people whom you swore that God would never show them mercy?' [These are told,]

'Enter Paradise. You have nothing to fear, nor will you grieve'. **50** And the inmates of the Fire will cry out to the dwellers of Paradise: 'Pour some water on us, or give us some of the sustenance God has provided for you'. They will reply: 'God has forbidden both to the unbelievers, **51** who have taken their religion for a pastime and an idle sport, and who have been beguiled by the life of this world'. Today We shall be oblivious of them as they were oblivious of the meeting on this Day of theirs, and as they used to deny Our revelations. **52** We have indeed given them a Book which We have clearly and wisely spelled out, a guidance and a grace for people who have faith. **53** Are they waiting for its final meaning to unfold? On this Day when its final meaning unfolds, those who previously were oblivious of it will say: 'Our Lord's messengers have surely told us the truth. Have we, then, any intercessors who could plead on our behalf? Or could we live our lives again, so that we may act differently from the way we used to act'. They have lost their souls and all that which they invented has failed them.

54 Your Lord is God who has created the heavens and the earth in six aeons, and is established on the throne. He covers the day with the night in swift pursuit. The sun, the moon and the stars are subservient to His command. Surely all creation and all authority belong to Him. Blessed is God, the Lord of the worlds. **55** Call upon your Lord with humility, and in the secrecy of your hearts. He does not love those who transgress the bounds of what is right. **56** Do not spread corruption on earth after it has been so well ordered. Call on Him with fear and hope. Truly, God's grace is ever near to the righteous. **57** He it is who sends forth the winds heralding His coming mercy, and when they have gathered up heavy clouds, We may drive them towards dead land and cause the water to fall upon it, and thus We cause all manner of fruit to come forth. Thus shall We cause the dead to come to life, so that you may keep this in mind. **58** Good land brings forth its vegetation in abundance, by its Lord's leave, but from the bad land only poor and scant vegetation comes forth. Thus do We expound Our revelations in various ways for the benefit of those who are grateful.

59 We sent Noah to his people, and he said: 'My people, worship God alone: you have no deity other than Him. I fear lest suffering befall you on an awesome Day'. **60** The notables among his people replied: 'We certainly see that you are in obvious error'. **61** Said he: 'My people, I am not in error, but I am a messenger from the Lord of all the worlds. **62** I am delivering to you my Lord's messages and giving you sincere counsel, for I know [through revelation] from God what you do not know. **63** Do you think it strange that a reminder from your Lord should come to you through a man from among yourselves, so that he might warn you, and that you may keep away from evil and be graced with His mercy?' **64** But they accused him of lying, so We saved him together with all those who stood by him, in the ark, and caused those who rejected Our revelations to drown. Surely they were blind people. **65** And to 'Ad [We sent] their brother Hud. He said: 'My people, worship God alone, you have no deity other than Him. Will you not, then, be God-fearing'. **66** Said the notables among his people who disbelieved: 'We clearly see that you are weak-minded, and, truly, we think that you are a liar'. **67** Said [Hud]: 'Weak-minded I am not, my people', he said: 'I am a messenger from the Lord of all the worlds. **68** 'I am delivering to you my Lord's messages and giving you sincere and honest counsel. **69** Do you think it strange that a reminder from your Lord should come to you through a man from among yourselves, so that he might warn you? Do but remember that He has made you successors of Noah's people, and given you a larger stature than other people. Remember, then, God's favours so that you may attain success'. **70** They answered: 'Have you come to tell us to worship God alone, and give up what our forefathers used to worship? Bring about, then, whatever you are threatening us with, if you are a man of truth.' **71** Said [Hud]: 'You are already beset by loathsome evil and by your Lord's condemnation. Are you arguing with me about some names you and your forefathers have invented, and for which God has given no warrant? Wait, then, if you will. I too am waiting'. **72** So, by Our grace, We saved him together with all those who stood by him, and We wiped out the last remnant of those who denied Our revelations and would not believe. **73** And to Thamud [We sent] their brother Salih. He said: 'My people, worship God alone: you have no deity other than Him. Clear evidence of the truth has come to you from your Lord. This she-camel belonging to God is a token for you, so leave her alone to pasture on God's earth and do her no harm, lest grievous punishment befall you'. **74** 'Remember that He has made you the successors of 'Ad and settled you firmly in the land. You build for yourselves palaces on its plains and carve out houses on the mountains. Remember, then, God's favours and do not go about spreading corruption in the land'. **75** The notables among his people who gloried in their arrogance towards all who were deemed weak, said to the believers among them: 'Do you really know that Salih is a messenger sent by his Lord? They answered: 'We do believe in the message he has been sent with'.

76 The arrogant ones said: 'For our part, we reject what you believe in'. **77** They cruelly slaughtered the she-camel, and insolently defied the commandment of their Lord, and said: 'Salih, bring about the (punishment) with which you have threatened us, if you are truly one of (God's) messengers'. **78** Thereupon an earthquake overtook them and the morning found them lying lifeless on the ground in their very homes. **79** He turned away from them, and said: 'My people, I delivered to you my Lord's message and counselled you sincerely, but you do not like those who give sincere counsel'. **80** And Lot said to his people: 'Will you persist in the indecencies none in all the world had ever committed before you? **81** With lust you approach men instead of women. Indeed, you are given to excesses'. **82** His people's only answer was: 'Drive them out of your land; for they are indeed people who would keep chaste'. **83** We saved him together with his household, except his wife: she was one of those who stayed behind. **84** We let loose a heavy rain upon them. Behold what happened in the end to those criminal people. **85** And to Madyan [We sent] their brother Shuʿayb. He said: 'My people, worship God alone: you have no deity other than Him. Clear evidence of the truth has come to you from your Lord. Give full measure and weight [in your dealings], and do not deprive people of what rightfully belongs to them. Do not spread corruption on earth after it has been so well ordered. That is best for you, if you are true believers. **86** Do not squat on every road, threatening and turning away from God's path anyone who believes in Him, and trying to make it appear crooked. Remember when you were few and how He caused you to rapidly increase in number. Behold what happened in the end to those who spread corruption. **87** If there be some among you who believe in the message with which I am sent, and others who do not believe, then be patient until God shall judge between us. He is the best of all judges'. **88** Said the notables among his people, who gloried in their arrogance: 'We shall indeed expel you, Shuʿayb, and your fellow believers from our land unless you return to our fold'. He said: 'Even though we are unwilling? **89** We should be guilty of fabricating lies against God, if we were to return to your ways after God has saved us from them. It is not conceivable that we should return to them, unless God, our Lord, so wills. Our Lord has full knowledge of everything. In God we place our trust. Our Lord, lay open the truth between us and our people; for You are the best to lay open the truth'. **90** The notables who disbelieved among his people said: 'If you follow Shuʿayb, you shall indeed be losers'. **91** Thereupon an earthquake overtook them and

the morning found them lying lifeless on the ground in their homes,
92 as if those that rejected Shu'ayb had never prospered there. Those
that rejected Shu'ayb were indeed the losers. **93** He turned away from
them and said: 'My people, I delivered to you my Lord's messages
and counselled you sincerely. How, then, could I grieve for people
who persist in unbelief'.

94 Never have We sent a prophet to any city without trying its
people with tribulations and hardship that they may supplicate with
humility. **95** We then replaced the affliction with good fortune till they
throve and said, 'Hardship and good fortune befell our forefathers as
well'. We then smote them, all of a sudden, while they were totally
unaware. **96** Yet had the people of those cities believed and been God-
fearing, We would indeed have opened up for them blessings out of
heaven and earth. But they disbelieved, so We smote them on account
of what they had been doing. **97** Do the people of these cities feel
secure that Our might would not strike them at dead of night when
they are asleep? **98** Or do the people of these cities feel secure that Our
might would not strike them in broad daylight when they are playing
around? **99** Do they feel themselves secure from God's designs? None
feels secure from God's designs except those who are losers. **100** Is it
not plain to those who have inherited the earth in succession of former
generations that, if We so willed, We can punish them for their sins
and seal their hearts, leaving them bereft of hearing. **101** We have
related to you parts of the history of those communities. Messengers
from among themselves came to them with clear evidence of the
truth; but they would not believe in what they had formerly rejected.
Thus does God seal the hearts of the unbelievers. **102** We found that
most of them were untrue to their commitments; indeed We found
most of them to be transgressors.

103 Then after those We sent Moses with Our signs to Pharaoh
and his people, but they wilfully rejected them. Behold what happened
in the end to those spreaders of corruption. **104** Moses said: 'Pharaoh, I
am a messenger from the Lord of all the worlds, **105** and may say about
God nothing but the truth. I have come to you with a clear evidence
from your Lord. So, let the Children of Israel go with me'. **106** He
answered: 'If you have come with a sign, produce it then if you are so
truthful'. **107** Moses threw down his staff, and it immediately became
a plainly visible serpent. **108** And he drew forth his hand, and it was
[shining] white to the beholders. **109** The notables among Pharaoh's
people said: 'This man is indeed a sorcerer of great skill, **110** who
wants to drive you out of your land!' [Said Pharaoh] 'What, then, do

you advise?' **111** They said: 'Let him and his brother wait a while, and send heralds to all cities **112** to bring before you every sorcerer of great skill'. **113** The sorcerers came to Pharaoh and said: 'Surely there will be a handsome reward for us if it is we who prevail'. **114** Answered [Pharaoh]: 'Yes; and you will certainly be among those who are close to me'. **115** They said: 'Moses! Either you shall throw [first], or we shall be the first to throw?' **116** He answered: 'You throw [first]'. And when they threw [their staffs], they cast a spell upon people's eyes and struck them with awe, making a display of great sorcery. **117** We then inspired Moses: 'Throw your staff'. And it swallowed up their false devices. **118** Thus the truth prevailed and all their doings were proved to be vain. **119** They were defeated there and then, and became utterly humiliated. **120** The sorcerers fell down prostrating themselves, **121** and said: 'We believe in the Lord of all the worlds, **122** the Lord of Moses and Aaron'. **123** Pharaoh said: 'You believe in Him even before I have given you permission! This is indeed a plot you have contrived in this city in order to drive out its people, but you shall soon come to know [the consequences]. **124** I shall have your hands and feet cut off on alternate sides, and then I shall crucify you all'. **125** They replied: 'To our Lord we shall indeed return. **126** You want to take vengeance on us only because we have believed in the signs of our Lord when they were shown to us. Our Lord, grant us abundance of patience in adversity, and let us die as people who have surrendered themselves to You'. **127** The notables among Pharaoh's people said: 'Will you allow Moses and his people to spread corruption in the land and to forsake you and your gods?' He replied: 'We shall put their sons to death and shall spare only their women. We shall certainly overpower them'. **128** Moses said to his people: 'Turn to God (alone) for help and remain steadfast. The whole earth belongs to God. He allows it to be inherited by whomever He wills of His servants. The future belongs to those who are God-fearing'. **129** They said: 'We have been oppressed before you came to us and since you have come to us'. He replied: 'It may well be that your Lord will destroy your enemy and leave you to inherit the earth. He will then see how you conduct yourselves'. **130** We afflicted Pharaoh's people with drought and poor harvests, so that they might take heed. **131** Whenever something fine came their way, they would say: 'This is our due', but whenever affliction befell them, they attributed their ill omen to Moses and those who followed him. Surely, whatever befalls them has been decreed by God, though most of them do not know it. **132** They said [to Moses]: 'Whatever sign you may produce before us in order to cast a spell on us, we shall not believe in you'. **133** So we plagued them with floods, and locusts, and lice, and frogs, and blood: clear signs all; but they gloried in their arrogance, for they were evil-doing folk. **134** Whenever a plague struck them, they would cry: 'Moses, pray to your Lord for us on the strength of the covenant He has made with you. If you lift the plague from us, we will truly believe in you, and we will let the Children of Israel go with you'. **135** But when We had lifted the plague from them, for a term they were sure to reach, they broke their promise. **136** So We inflicted Our retribution on them, and caused them to drown in the sea, because they denied Our signs and were heedless of them. **137** We caused the people who were persecuted and deemed utterly low to inherit the eastern and western parts of the land which We had blessed. Thus your Lord's gracious promise to the Children of Israel was fulfilled, because they were patient in adversity; and We destroyed all that Pharaoh and his people had wrought, and all that they had built.

138 We led the Children of Israel across the sea; and thereupon they came upon people who were dedicated to the worship of some idols of theirs. Said [the Children of Israel]: 'Moses, set up a god for us like the gods they have'. He replied: 'You are indeed an ignorant people. **139** As for these people: their method will inevitably lead to destruction, and worthless is all that they have been doing'. **140** [And] he said: 'Am I to seek for you a deity other than God, although He has favoured you above all other people?' **141** We have indeed saved you from Pharaoh's people, who oppressed you cruelly: they slew your sons and spared your women. Surely that was an awesome trial from your Lord. **142** We appointed for Moses thirty nights, to which We added ten, whereby the term of forty nights set by His Lord was complete. Moses said to his brother Aaron: 'Take my place among my people and act righteously. Do not follow the path of those who spread corruption'. **143** When Moses came for Our appointment and his Lord spoke to him, he said: 'My Lord, show Yourself to me, so that I may look at You'. Said [God]: 'You shall not see Me. But look upon the mountain; if it remains firm in its place, then, only then, you shall see Me'. When his Lord revealed His glory to the mountain, He sent it crashing down. Moses fell down senseless. When he came to himself, he said: 'Limitless You are in Your glory. To You I turn in repentance. I am the first to truly believe in You'. **144** He said: 'Moses, I have chosen you of all mankind and favoured you by entrusting My messages to you and by my speaking to you. Take then what I have given you and be thankful'. **145** We wrote for him on the tablets all manner of admonition, clearly spelling out everything, and (said to him): 'Implement them with strength and determination, and bid your people to observe what is best in them. I shall show you the abode of the transgressors. **146** I will turn away from My revelations those who, without any right, behave arrogantly on earth: for, though they may see every sign, they do not believe in it. If they see the path of righteousness, they do not choose to follow it, but if they see the path of error, they choose it for their path; because they disbelieve in Our revelations and pay no heed to them. **147** Those who deny Our revelations and the certainty of the meeting in the Hereafter will see all their works collapse. Are they to be rewarded for anything other than what they have done?' **148** In his absence, the people of Moses took to the worship of the effigy of a calf made of their ornaments, which gave a lowing sound. Did they not see that it could neither speak to them nor give them any guidance? Yet they took to worshipping it, for they were wrongdoers. **149** When they were later afflicted with remorse, having realised that they had gone astray, they said: 'If our Lord does not have mercy on us and forgive us, we shall certainly be losers'. **150** When Moses returned to his people, full of wrath and sorrow, he said: 'What an evil thing you have done in my absence! Have you tried to hurry up your Lord's command?' He put down the tablets and, seizing his brother by the head, he pulled him to himself. Cried Aaron, 'Son of my mother, the people felt I was weak and they almost killed me. Do not let our enemies rejoice over my affliction, and do not count me among the wrongdoing folk'. **151** Said [Moses]: 'My Lord, forgive me and my brother, and admit us to Your grace: for You are indeed the most merciful of those who are merciful'. **152** Those who took to worshipping the calf have surely incurred their Lord's wrath, and disgrace [will be their lot] in this life. Thus do We reward those who invent falsehood. **153** But those who do evil deeds and later repent and truly believe will surely, after such repentance, find your Lord to be much-forgiving, ever-merciful. **154** Then when his wrath had subsided, Moses took up the tablets, upon which was inscribed a text of guidance and grace to those who stood in awe of their Lord. **155** Moses chose out of his people seventy men to come at a time set by Us. Then, when they were seized by violent trembling, he said: 'My Lord, had it been Your will, You could have destroyed them, and myself too, long ago. Would you destroy us because of what the weak-minded among us have done? This is only a trial You have ordained, whereby You allow to go astray whom You will, and You guide aright whom You will. You alone are our guardian: grant us, then, forgiveness and bestow mercy on us. You are the best of all those who do forgive. **156** Ordain for us what is good, both in this world and in the life to come. To You alone we turn'. [God] answered: 'I afflict anyone I wish with My torment while My grace encompasses all things; so I will confer it on those who steer away from evil, and spend in charity, and who believe in Our signs – **157** those who follow the Messenger, the unlettered Prophet whom they shall find described in the Torah and the Gospel that are with them. He commands them to do what is right and forbids them to do what is wrong, and makes lawful to them the good things of life and forbids them all that is foul. He lifts from them their burdens and the shackles that weigh upon them. Those, therefore, who believe in him, honour and support him, and follow the light that has been bestowed from on high through him shall indeed be successful'. **158** Say: 'Mankind, I am indeed God's Messenger to you all. It is to Him that sovereignty over the heavens and the earth belongs. There is no deity other than Him. He alone grants life and causes death. Believe, then, in God and His Messenger, the unlettered Prophet, who believes in God and His words. And follow him, so that you may be rightly guided'. **159** Yet among the folk of Moses there are some who guide (others) by means of the truth and act justly in its light. **160** We divided them into twelve tribes, each a community. And when his people asked Moses for water to drink, we inspired him: 'Strike the rock with your staff'. Twelve springs gushed forth from it, and each tribe knew its drinking-place. We caused the clouds to draw their shadow over them and sent down for them manna and quails, [saying]: 'Eat of the good things We have given you as sustenance'. Yet they could do Us no wrong, but they certainly wronged themselves. **161** It was said to them: 'Dwell in this city and eat of its food whatever you may wish, and say: "Lord, relieve us of our burden", and enter the gate in humility. We will forgive you your sins, and We will richly reward those who do good'. **162** But the wrongdoers among them substituted other words for those which they had been given. Therefore We let loose against them a scourge from heaven in requital for their wrongdoing. **163** Ask them about the town which stood by the sea: how its people profaned the Sabbath. Each Sabbath their fish appeared before them breaking the water's surface, but they would not come near them on other than Sabbath days. Thus did We try them because of their disobedience. **164** When some among them asked: 'Why do you preach to people whom God is certain to destroy, or at least to punish severely?' [Others] replied: 'So that we may be free from blame in the sight of your Lord, and that they may become

God-fearing'. **165** When they had forgotten all the warnings they had been given, We saved those who had tried to prevent evil, and overwhelmed the transgressors with dreadful suffering for their disobedience. **166** And when they insolently persisted in doing what they had been forbidden to do, We said to them: 'Turn into despicable apes'. **167** Then your Lord declared that He would most certainly raise against them people who would cruelly oppress them till the Day of Resurrection. Your Lord is swift indeed in His retribution, yet He is certainly much-forgiving, ever-merciful. **168** We dispersed them all over the earth as separate communities; some of them were righteous, and some far from that, and We tried them with blessings and misfortunes, so that they might mend their ways. **169** They were succeeded by generations who inherited the Book. Yet these are keen to enjoy the fleeting pleasures of this lower world and say, 'We shall be forgiven'. Should some similar pleasures come their way, they would certainly indulge them. Have they not solemnly pledged through their Scriptures to say nothing but the truth about God? And have they not studied well what is in [the Scriptures]? Surely the life in the Hereafter is better for all who are God-fearing. Will you not use your reason? **170** As for those who hold fast to the Scriptures and attend regularly to their prayers, We shall not fail to reward those who enjoin the doing of what is right. **171** We suspended the mountain over them as if it were a shadow, and they thought that it would fall down on them. [We said]: 'Hold fast with all your strength to what We have given you and bear in mind all that it contains, so that you may remain God-fearing'.

172 Your Lord brought forth their offspring from the loins of the children of Adam, and called them to bear witness about themselves. [He said]: 'Am I not your Lord?' They replied: 'Yes, indeed, we bear witness to that'. [This He did] lest you should say on the Day of Resurrection, 'We were truly unaware of this'; **173** or lest you say, 'It was our forefathers who, in times gone by, associated partners with God, and we were only their late offspring. Will You destroy us on account of what those inventors of falsehood did?' **174** Thus We make plain Our revelations so that they may return [to the right path]. **175** Tell them of the man to whom We give Our revelations, and who then discards them. Satan catches up with him and he strays, like many others, into error. **176** Had We so willed, We would have exalted him by means of those [revelations], but he clings to the earth and succumbs to his desires. He may be compared to a dog: no matter how you drive him off, he pants on away, and if you leave him alone, he still pants on. That is what the people who reject Our revelations are like. Tell them, then, such stories, so that they may take heed. **177** A dismal example is that provided by those who reject Our revelations; for it is against their own selves that they are sinning. **178** He whom God guides is on the right path; whereas those whom He lets go astray are indeed losers. **179** We have destined for Hell many of the jinn and many human beings; they have hearts they cannot understand with, and they have eyes with which they fail to see, and ears with which they fail to hear. They are like cattle; indeed, they are even further away from the right way. They are the truly heedless. **180** God has the finest names, so appeal to Him by these and stay away from those who blaspheme against His names. They shall be requited for all they do. **181** Among those whom We have created there is a community who guide others by means of the truth and with it establish justice. **182** As for those who deny Our revelations, We will lead them on, step by step, from whence they cannot tell; **183** for although I may give them respite, My subtle scheme is mighty. **184** Have they not thought things over? Their companion is no madman; he is only a plain warner. **185** Have they not considered [God's] dominion over the heavens and the earth, and all that God has created, and [reflected] that it may well be that their own term is drawing near? In what other message after this will they, then, believe? **186** Those whom God lets go astray will have no guide; and He leaves them in their overweening arrogance to stumble along blindly. **187** They ask you about the Last Hour: 'When will it come to pass?' Say: 'Knowledge of it rests with my Lord alone. None but He will reveal it at its appointed time. It will weigh heavily on the heavens and the earth; and it will not fall on you except suddenly'. They will ask you further as if you yourself persistently enquire about it. Say: 'Knowledge of it rests with God alone, though most people remain unaware'. **188** Say: 'It is not within my power to bring benefit to, or avert evil from, myself, except as God may please. Had I possessed knowledge of what lies beyond the reach of human perception, I would have availed myself of much that is good and no evil would have ever touched me. I am no more than one who gives warning, and a herald of good news to people who believe'. **189** It is He who has created you all from a single soul, and out of it brought into being its mate, so that he might incline with love towards her. When he has consorted with her, she conceives a light burden, which she carries with ease. Then, when she grows heavy, they both appeal to God, their Lord: 'Grant us a goodly child and we will be truly grateful'.

190 Yet when He had granted them a goodly child, they associate with Him partners, particularly in respect of what He has granted them. Exalted is God above anything people may associate with Him as partners. **191** Do they associate with Him those that can create nothing, while they themselves have been created, **192** and neither can they give them any support nor can they even help themselves. **193** If you call them to guidance they will not follow you. It is all the same whether you call them or keep silent. **194** Those whom you invoke beside God are God's servants, just like you. Invoke them, then, and let them answer you, if what you claim is true. **195** Have they, perchance, feet on which they could walk, or hands with which to grasp things, or eyes with which to see, or ears with which to hear? Say: 'Appeal to those you claim to be partners with God, and scheme against me, and give me no respite. **196** My guardian is God who has bestowed this Book from on high. It is He who is the guardian of the righteous. **197** Those whom you invoke beside Him cannot give you any support, nor can they even help themselves. **198** If you pray to them for guidance, they will not hear you. You may see them looking at you but they do not see'.

199 Make due allowance for man's nature, and enjoin the doing of what is right; and turn away from those who choose to remain ignorant. **200** If a prompting from Satan stirs you up, seek refuge with God; He hears all and knows all. **201** If those who are God-fearing experience a tempting thought from Satan, they bethink themselves [of God]; and they begin to see things clearly. **202** Their [evil] brethren try to draw them into error with unceasing determination. **203** When you do not bring them a sign, they say: 'Why do you not seek to have one?' Say: 'I only follow what is revealed to me by my Lord: this [revelation] is a means of clear insight from your Lord, and a guidance and grace for people who will believe'. **204** When the Qur'an is recited, hearken to it, and listen in silence, so that you may be graced with God's mercy. **205** And bethink yourself of your Lord humbly and with awe, and without raising your voice, in the morning and evening; and do not be negligent. **206** Those who are near to your Lord are never too proud to worship Him. They extol His limitless glory, and before Him alone prostrate themselves.

Surah 8   Spoils of War

This surah was revealed towards the end of the second year after the Prophet's migration to Madinah. It comments on the Battle of Badr, the first major battle during the Prophet's lifetime, when the Muslims achieved a remarkable victory against an army that outnumbered them by three to one.

The surah tells the Muslim community that whenever they fight their enemies, they must remain steadfast and be sure of their objectives. They must have no motive other than supporting the truth of the divine message. They must not seek power for themselves or for their national interests, as such. They are advocates of the truth and must remain so if they are to be certain of God's support as was clearly demonstrated in the Battle of Badr.

The surah deals with the question of spoils of war, because after victory, the Muslims who had been struggling with straitened circumstances, now looked forward to some gain and benefit. This surah, therefore, lays down a principle for the division of such spoils of war.

The surah concludes with a delineation of relations between the Muslim community and other groups. It makes it clear that the Muslims form one community and their relations with others must be based on the attitude these others take towards Islam.

Spoils of War

In the Name of God, the Lord of Grace, the Ever-Merciful

1 They ask you about the spoils of war. Say: 'The spoils of war belong to God and the Messenger. So, have fear of God and set to right your internal relations. Obey God and His Messenger, if you are true believers'. 2 True believers are only those whose hearts are filled with awe whenever God is mentioned, and whose faith is strengthened whenever His revelations are recited to them. In their Lord do they place their trust. 3 They attend regularly to their prayers and spend in charity some of what We have provided them with. 4 It is those who are truly believers. They shall be given high ranks with their Lord, and forgiveness of sins and generous provisions. 5 Just as your Lord brought you forth from your home for the truth, even though some of the believers were averse to it. 6 They would argue with

you about the truth even after it had become manifest, just as if they were being driven to certain death and saw it with their very eyes. **7** God promised you that one of the two hosts would fall to you. It was your wish that the one which was not powerful to be yours, but it was God's will to establish the truth in accordance with His words and to wipe out the unbelievers. **8** Thus He would certainly establish the truth firmly and show falsehood to be false, however hateful this might be to the ones who are guilty. **9** When you implored your Lord for help, He answered: 'I will reinforce you with a thousand angels advancing in ranks'. **10** God made this only as good news with which to reassure your hearts, for victory comes only from God. Indeed, God is almighty, wise. **11** He made slumber fall upon you, as an assurance from Him, and He sent down water from the sky to cleanse you and to remove from you Satan's filth, to strengthen your hearts and steady your footsteps. **12** Your Lord inspired the angels, saying: 'I am with you. So, give courage to the believers. I shall cast terror into the hearts of the unbelievers. Strike, then, their necks and strike off their every fingertip'. **13** This is because they have defied God and His Messenger. Whoever defies God and His Messenger [will find out that] God is severe in retribution. **14** This is for you, [enemies of God]! Taste it, then. The unbelievers shall be made to suffer the torment of fire. **15** Believers, when you meet in battle those who disbelieve, do not turn your backs to them in flight. **16** Anyone who turns his back to them on that day, except when manoeuvring for battle or in an endeavour to join another troop, shall incur God's wrath, and Hell shall be his abode: how vile a journey's end. **17** It was not you who slew them, but it was God who slew them. When you threw [a handful of dust], it was not your act, but God's, so that He might put the believers through a fair test of His own making. Indeed, God hears all and knows all. **18** That is so; it is God who shall make feeble the schemes of the unbelievers. **19** If you were seeking a judgement, then a judgement has come to you. If you desist, it will be best for you; and if you revert to your erring ways, We will also be back [with Our punishment]. Your host, numerous as it may be, shall avail you nothing; for God is with the believers. **20** Believers, obey God and His Messenger, and do not turn away from him now that you have heard [his message]. **21** Do not be like those who say: 'We have heard', the while they do not listen. **22** Indeed, the worst of all creatures, in God's sight, are the deaf and dumb who are devoid of reason. **23** If God had known of any good in them, He would certainly have made them hear. But even if He were to make them hear, they would have turned away and refused to listen. **24** Believers, respond to the call of God and the Messenger when he calls you to that which will give you life, and know that God comes in between a man and his heart, and that to Him you shall all be gathered. **25** Beware of temptation that does not lure only those among you who are wrongdoers. Know that God is severe in retribution. **26** Remember when you were few and helpless in the land, fearful lest people do away with you: how He sheltered you, strengthened you with His support and provided you with many good things so that you might be grateful. **27** Believers, do not betray God and the Messenger, nor knowingly betray the trust that has been reposed in you. **28** Know that your worldly goods and your children are but a trial, and that with God there is a great reward. **29** Believers, if you remain God-fearing, He will give you a standard by which to discern the true from the false, and will wipe off your bad deeds, and forgive you. God's bounty is great indeed.

30 Remember how the unbelievers were scheming against you, seeking to keep you in chains or have you slain or banished. Thus they plot and plan, but God also plans. God is above all schemers. **31** Whenever Our revelations are recited to them, they would say: 'We have heard them. If we wanted, we could certainly compose the like of this. This is nothing but fables of the ancients'. **32** They would also say: 'God, if this be indeed Your revealed truth, then rain down upon us stones from the skies, or inflict grievous suffering on us'. **33** But God would not punish them while you were present in their midst, nor would God punish them when they may yet ask for forgiveness. **34** What [plea] have they now that God should not punish them, when they debar other people from the Sacred Mosque, although they are not its rightful guardians? Its only guardians are those that fear God; but of this most of these [evildoers] are unaware. **35** Their prayers at the House are nothing but whistling and clapping of hands. Taste then this punishment in consequence of your disbelief. **36** The unbelievers spend their riches in order to turn people away from the path of God. They will go on spending them, and then this will become a source of intense regret for them; and then they shall be defeated. The unbelievers shall into Hell be driven. **37** God will separate the bad from the good. The bad He will place one upon another, so He may heap them all up together, and then cast them into Hell. Those indeed are the losers. **38** Say to the unbelievers that if they desist, all that is past shall be forgiven them; but if they persist [in their erring ways], let them remember what happened to the like of them in former times. **39** Fight them until there is no more oppression, and all submission is made to God alone. If they desist, God is certainly aware of all they do. **40** But if they turn away, know that God is your Lord Supreme. How splendid is this Lord Supreme, and how splendid is this giver of support.

41 Know that one-fifth of whatever booty you may acquire in war is for God and the Messenger, and for the near of kin, the orphans, the needy and the traveller in need. [This you must observe] if you believe in God and what We revealed to Our servant on the day when the true was distinguished from the false, the day when the two hosts met in battle. God has power over all things. **42** [Remember the day] when you were at the near end of the valley and they were at the farthest end, with the caravan down below you. If you had made prior arrangements to meet there, you would have differed on the exact timing and location. But it was all brought about so that God might accomplish something He willed to be done, and so that anyone who was destined to perish might perish in clear evidence of the truth and anyone destined to live might live in clear evidence of the truth. God certainly hears all and knows all. **43** God made them appear to you in your dream as few in number. Had He shown them to you as a large force, you would have lost heart and would surely have been in dispute about what to do. But this God has spared you. He has full knowledge of what is in people's hearts. **44** When you actually met, He made them appear few in your eyes, just as He made you appear as a small band in their eyes, so that God might accomplish something He willed to be done. To God shall all things return. **45** Believers, when you meet an enemy force, be firm, and remember God often, so that you may be successful. **46** Obey God and His Messenger and do not dispute with one another, lest you lose heart and your moral strength. Be patient in adversity, for God is with those who are patient in adversity. **47** Do not be like those who left their homes full of self-conceit, seeking to be seen and praised by others. They debar others from the path of God; but God has knowledge of all that they do. **48** Satan made their deeds seem fair to them, and said: 'No one can overcome you today, and I will stand firm by you'. But when the two hosts came within sight of each other, he turned on his heels and said: 'I am done with you, for I can see what you cannot. I fear God, for God is severe in retribution'. **49** The hypocrites and those in whose hearts there was disease said: 'Their faith has deluded these people'. But he who puts his trust in God knows that God is almighty, wise. **50** If you could but see how the angels gather up the souls of the unbelievers. They strike them on their faces and their backs and

[say]: 'Taste the punishment of burning, **51** in return for what your own hands have committed. Never does God do any injustice to His servants'. **52** Like Pharaoh's people and those who lived before them, they denied God's revelations; so God took them to task for their sins. God is mighty, severe in retribution. **53** This is because God would never alter the favours He bestows on a community unless they change what is in their hearts. God hears all and knows all. **54** Like Pharaoh's people and those who lived before them, they disbelieved in their Lord's revelations; so We destroyed them for their sins, as We caused Pharaoh's people to drown. They were wrongdoers all.

55 Indeed, the worst of all creatures in God's sight are the ones who have denied the truth, and therefore will not believe; **56** those with whom you have concluded a treaty, and then they break their treaty at every occasion, entertaining no sense of fearing God. **57** Should you meet them in battle, make of them a fearsome example for those who follow them, so that they may reflect and take it to heart. **58** And if you fear treachery from any folk, cast [your treaty with them] back to them in a fair manner. God does not love the treacherous. **59** Let not those who disbelieve reckon that they shall escape. They can never be beyond [God's] grasp. **60** Make ready against them whatever force and war mounts you can muster, so that you may strike terror into the enemies of God who are also your own enemies, and others besides them of whom you may be unaware, but of whom God is well aware. Whatever you may spend in God's cause shall be repaid to you in full, and you shall not be wronged. **61** If they incline to peace, then incline you to it as well, and place your trust in God. He alone hears all and knows all. **62** Should they seek to deceive you, God is all-sufficient for you. He it is who has strengthened you with His help and rallied the believers round you, **63** uniting their hearts. If you were to spend all that is on earth you could not have so united their hearts, but God has united them. He is mighty and wise. **64** Prophet, God is enough for you and those of the believers who follow you. **65** Prophet, urge the believers to fight. If there are twenty steadfast men among you, they will overcome two hundred, and if there are a hundred of you, they will defeat a thousand of those who disbelieve, for those are devoid of understanding. **66** Now God has lightened your burden, for He knows that you are weak. So, if there are a hundred steadfast men among you, they will overcome two hundred, and if there are a thousand of you they will, by God's will, defeat two thousand. God is with those who are steadfast. **67** It does not behove a prophet to have captives unless he has battled strenuously in the land. You may desire the fleeting gains of this world, but God desires for you the good of the life to come. God is almighty, wise. **68** Had it not been for a decree from God that had already gone forth, you would have been severely punished for what you have taken. **69** Enjoy, then, what you have gained, as lawful and good, and remain God-fearing; indeed God is much-forgiving, ever-merciful. **70** Prophet, say to the captives who are in your hands: 'If God finds goodness in your hearts, He will give you something better than all that has been taken from you, and He will forgive you your sins. God is much-forgiving, ever-merciful'. **71** Should they seek to play false with you, they were previously false to God Himself, but He gave [you] mastery over them. God is all-knowing, wise. **72** Those who believe and have migrated and striven hard, with their possessions and their lives, for God's cause, as well as those who give them shelter and support – these are friends and protectors of one another. As for those who believe but have not migrated [to join you], you owe no duty of protection to them until they have migrated. Yet, should they appeal to you for support, on grounds of faith, it is your duty to support them, except against a people with whom you have a treaty. God sees all that you do. **73** The unbelievers are allies of one another. Unless you do likewise, there will be oppression on earth and much corruption. **74** Those who believe and have migrated and striven hard for God's cause, as well as those who give them shelter and support are indeed the true believers. Forgiveness of sins, and most generous provisions await them. **75** And those who subsequently come to believe, and migrate and strive hard with you [for God's cause] shall also belong to you. Those who are bound by ties of blood have the first claim on one another in accordance with God's decree. God has full knowledge of everything.

Surah 9   Repentance

This surah was revealed in the ninth year of the Madinah period when the Muslim state had become well established, with most Arabian tribes flocking towards Islam. It begins with a declaration giving a four-month notice of termination for all indefinite treaties the Muslim state held with Arabian tribes, during which people had to define their attitude towards Islam, either accepting it or leaving to live somewhere else. All treaties made for specified periods of time were to be honoured until the end of their terms, provided that the other party to any such treaty fulfilled its commitments under it.

The surah establishes certain rules about dealing with unbelievers who seek refuge with the Muslim community. It reclaims the Sacred Mosque in Makkah as a place where God alone may be worshipped, placing it out of bounds for unbelievers. It states the main rule that defines the beneficiaries of zakat, the charity which Islam makes obligatory.

However, the main theme of this surah, which is the last of the seven longest surahs of the Qur'an, is to expose the reality of the hypocrites who pretend to be Muslims but who instead do their best to undermine the Muslim community and cause trouble. It launches a long and sustained campaign showing the hypocrites to be the worst kind of unbelievers. Unlike those who take an openly hostile attitude to Islam and the Muslim community, hypocrites pretend to be Muslims, trying their best to assure the Muslims that they belong to them and wish them well. In reality, however, they are hostile to them and their faith. Therefore, the surah clearly shows that there can be no compromise with such hypocrisy. Indeed, this is the only surah in the Qur'an that does not start with asserting God's attribute of mercy because God does not show mercy to hypocrites who mock at His revelations and who make them a subject of sarcasm and ridicule.

The surah concludes with a description of the Prophet's attitude towards Muslims and to mankind in general. It speaks of his kindness and compassion, as well as his eager desire that people should follow divine guidance that brings them happiness in both this life and the life to come.

Repentance

1 Disavowal by God and His Messenger [is hereby announced] to those of the idolaters with whom you have made a treaty. **2** [Announce to them:] You may go freely in the land for four months, but you must realise that you can never escape God's judgement, and that God shall bring disgrace upon the unbelievers. **3** And a proclamation from God and His Messenger is hereby made to all mankind on this day of the greater pilgrimage: God is free from obligation to the idolaters, and so is His Messenger. If you repent, it shall be for your own good; and if you turn away, then know that you can never escape God's judgement. Give the unbelievers the news of painful suffering, **4** except for those idolaters with whom you have made a treaty and who have honoured their obligations [under the treaty] in every detail, and have not aided anyone against you. To these fulfil your obligations until their treaties have run their term. God loves those who are God-fearing. **5** When these months of grace are over, slay the idolaters wherever you find them, and take them captive, besiege them, and lie in wait for them at every conceivable place. Yet if they should repent, take to prayer and pay the zakat, let them go their way. For God is much-forgiving, ever-merciful. **6** If any of the idolaters seeks asylum with you, grant him protection, so that he may hear the word of God, and then convey him to his place of safety. That is because the idolaters are people who lack knowledge. **7** How can there be a treaty with God and His Messenger for the idolaters, unless it be those of them with whom you have made a treaty at the Sacred Mosque? So long as they are true to you, be true to them; for God loves those who are God-fearing. **8** How [else could it be] when, should they prevail over you, they will respect neither agreement made with you, nor obligation of honour towards you? They try to please you with what they say, while at heart they remain adamantly hostile. Most of them are transgressors. **9** They barter away God's revelations for a paltry price and debar others from His path. Evil indeed is what they do. **10** They respect neither agreement nor obligation of honour with regard to any believer. Those indeed are the aggressors. **11** Yet, if they repent, take to prayers and pay the zakat, they are your brethren in faith. Clear do We make Our revelations to people of knowledge. **12** But if they break their pledges after having concluded a treaty with you, and revile your religion, then fight these archetypes of faithlessness who have no [respect for a] binding pledge, so that they may desist. **13** Will you not fight against people who have broken their solemn pledges and set out to drive out the Messenger, and who were the first to attack you? Do you fear them? It is God alone whom you should fear, if you are true believers. **14** Fight them: God will punish them at your hands, and will bring disgrace upon them; and will grant you victory over them and will grant heart-felt satisfaction to those who are believers, **15** removing all angry feelings from their hearts. God will turn in His mercy to whom He wills. God is all-knowing and wise. **16** Do you think that you will be left alone, unless God takes cognisance of those of you who strive hard for His cause and establish close association with none other than God, His Messenger and the believers? God is well aware of what you do. **17** It is not for the idolaters to visit or tend God's houses of worship; for they are self-confessed unbelievers. Vain shall be their actions and they shall abide in the Fire. **18** God's houses of worship may be tended only by those who believe in God and the Last Day, are constant in prayers, pay zakat (the obligatory charity) and fear none other than God. It is those who are likely to be rightly guided. **19** Do you, perchance, consider that the provision of drinking water to pilgrims and tending the Sacred Mosque equal to believing in God and the Last Day and striving for God's cause? These are not equal in God's sight. God does not provide guidance for people who are wrongdoers. **20** Those who believe, and leave their homes and strive hard for God's cause with their property and their lives stand higher in rank with God. It is they who shall triumph. **21** Their Lord gives them the happy news of bestowing on them His grace, and acceptance, and of the gardens of eternal bliss **22** where they shall reside forever. God's reward is great indeed. **23** Believers, do not take your fathers and brothers for allies if they choose unbelief in preference to faith. Those of you who take them for allies are indeed wrongdoers. **24** Say: 'If your fathers, your sons, your brothers, your spouses, your clan, and the property you have acquired, and the business in which you fear a decline, and the dwellings in which you take pleasure, are dearer to you than God and His Messenger and the struggle in His cause, then wait until God shall make manifest His will. God does not provide guidance to the transgressors. **25** God has granted you His support on many a battlefield, and also in the Battle of Hunayn, when you took pride in your numerical strength, but it availed you nothing. For all its vastness, the earth seemed too narrow for you, and you turned back in flight. **26** God then bestowed from on high an air of inner peace on His Messenger and on the believers, and He sent down forces whom you could not see, and punished those who disbelieved. Such is the reward for the unbelievers. **27** God will then turn in His mercy to whom He wills, for God is much-forgiving, ever-merciful'. **28** Believers, know that the idolaters are certainly impure. So, let them not come near to the Sacred Mosque after this year is ended. If you fear poverty, then in time God will enrich you with His own bounty, if He so wills. Truly, God is all-knowing, wise.

29 Fight against those who – despite having been given Scriptures – do not truly believe in God and the Last Day, and do not treat as forbidden that which God and His Messenger have forbidden, and do not follow the religion of truth, till they [agree to] pay the submission tax with a willing hand, after they have been humbled. **30** The Jews say: 'Ezra is the son of God', while the Christians say: 'The Christ is the son of God'. Such are the assertions they utter with their mouths, echoing assertions made by the unbelievers of old. May God destroy them! How perverse they are! **31** They make of their rabbis and their monks, and of the Christ, son of Mary, lords besides God. Yet they have been ordered to worship none but the One God, other than whom there is no deity. Exalted be He above those to whom they ascribe divinity. **32** They want to extinguish God's light with their mouths, but God will not allow anything [to interfere with His will] to spread His light in its fullness, however hateful this may be to the unbelievers. **33** It is He who has sent His Messenger with guidance and the religion of truth, so that He may cause it to prevail over all [other] religions, however hateful this may be to the idolaters. **34** Believers, some of the rabbis and monks wrongfully devour people's property and turn people away from God's path. To those who hoard up gold and silver and do not spend them in God's cause, give the news of a painful suffering, **35** on the day when it will all be heated in the fire of Hell, and their foreheads, sides and backs will be branded with them. [They will be told]: 'This is what you have hoarded up for yourselves. Taste, then, what you have been hoarding'.

36 The number of months, in God's sight, is twelve as set by God's decree on the day when He created the heavens and the earth. Of these, four are sacred, according to the ever-true law [of God]. Therefore, do not wrong yourselves by violating them. But fight against the idolaters all together as they fight against you all together, and know that God is with those who are God-fearing. **37** The postponement [of sacred months] is only an excess of unbelief, in which the unbelievers are led astray. They declare it permissible one year and forbidden another year, so that they may make up the number of the months which God has sanctified, and thus they make lawful what God has forbidden. The evil of their deeds thus seems fair to them. God does not guide those who are unbelievers.

38 Believers, what is amiss with you that, when it is said to you: 'Go forth to fight in God's cause', you cling heavily to the earth? Are you content with the comforts of this world in preference to the life to come? Paltry indeed are the enjoyments of life in this world when compared with those of the life to come. **39** If you do not go forth to fight [in God's cause], He will punish you severely and replace you by other people. You will not harm Him in any way, for God has power over all things. **40** If you do not help him [the Prophet]; God [will, as He] supported him at the time when the unbelievers drove him away. He was only one of two. When these two were alone in the cave, he said to his companion: 'Do not grieve, for God is with us'. Thereupon God bestowed on Him the gift of inner peace, and sent to his aid forces which you did not see. He brought the word of the unbelievers utterly low, while the word of God remained supreme. God is mighty, wise. **41** Go forth, whether you be lightly or heavily armed, and strive in God's cause with your wealth and your lives. This will be best for you if you but knew it.

42 Had there been [a prospect of] an immediate gain, and a short journey, they would certainly have followed you; but the distance was too far for them. Yet they will swear by God: 'Had we been able, we would surely have joined you'. They bring ruin upon themselves. God knows indeed that they are liars. **43** May God forgive you [Prophet]! Why did you grant them permission [to stay behind] before you had come to know who were speaking the truth and who were the liars. **44** Those who believe in God and the Last Day will not ask you to exempt them from striving with their property and with their lives. God has full knowledge as to who are the God-fearing. **45** Only those who do not truly believe in God and the Last Day ask you for exemption. Their hearts are filled with doubt; and troubled by doubt, they do waver. **46** Had they really intended to set out [with you], they would surely have made some preparations for that. But God was averse to their going, so He caused them to hold back; and it was said to them: 'Stay behind with those who stay'. **47** Had they set out with you, they would have added nothing to you but trouble, and would have scurried to and fro in your midst, seeking to sow discord among you. There are among you some who would have lent them ear. Certainly God has full knowledge of the wrongdoers. **48** They had, even before this time, tried to sow discord, and devised plots against you, until the truth was revealed and the will of God prevailed, no matter how hateful it is to them. **49** There is among them [many a] one who may say: 'Give me leave to stay behind, and do not expose me to temptation'. Surely they have succumbed to temptation. Hell is certain to engulf the unbelievers. **50** Your good fortune grieves them; but if a disaster befalls you, they will say: 'We are lucky to have taken our precautions'. Thus they turn away rejoicing. **51** Say: 'Nothing will befall us except what God has decreed. He is our guardian. In God alone should the believers place their trust'. **52** Say: 'Are you waiting for something [bad] to happen to us; but [nothing may happen to us except] one of the two best things. On our part we are waiting for God to inflict upon you a scourge, either directly from Himself or by our hands. Wait, then, if you will; we shall also be waiting'. **53** Say: 'Whether you spend willingly or unwillingly, it will not be accepted from you; for you are indeed wicked people'. **54** What prevents their offerings from being accepted from them is that they have disbelieved in God and His Messenger, and they only come to prayer with reluctance, and never donate anything [for a righteous cause] without being resentful. **55** Let neither their riches nor their children rouse your admiration. God only wishes to punish them by means of these in this worldly life, and that their souls perish while they are unbelievers. **56** They swear by God that they belong to you, when certainly they do not belong to you, but are people overwhelmed by fear. **57** If only they could find a place of shelter, a cavern, or any hiding place, they would rush headlong into it. **58** Among them there are those who speak ill of you concerning the distribution of charity. If they are given a share of it, they are pleased, but if no share is given to them, they are enraged. **59** Yet [how much better it would have been for them] had they contented themselves with what God and His Messenger have given them, and said: 'God is sufficient for us. God will give us out of His bounty, and so too will His Messenger. To God alone do we turn in hope'. **60** Charitable donations are only for the poor and the needy, and those who work in the administration of such donations, and those whose hearts are to be won over, for the freeing of people in bondage and debtors, and to further God's cause, and for the traveller in need. This is a duty ordained by God, and God is all-knowing, wise. **61** And among them are others who hurt the Prophet and say: 'He is all ear'. Say: 'He is an ear listening to what is good for you. He believes in God, trusts the believers and he is a mercy to those of you who are true believers. Those who hurt God's Messenger shall have painful suffering'. **62** They swear to you by God in order to please you. Yet it is God and His Messenger that they should strive to please, if indeed they are believers. **63** Do they not know that anyone who defies God and His Messenger shall have the fire of Hell, therein to abide? That is the ultimate disgrace. **64** The hypocrites dread lest a surah be revealed about them, making clear to them what is really in their hearts. Say: 'Scoff, if you will; God will surely bring to light the very thing you are dreading'. **65** Should you question them, they will say: 'We have only been indulging in idle talk and jesting'. Say: 'Was it, then, at God, His revelations and His Messenger that you have been mocking? **66** Make no excuses. You have disbelieved after you have professed to be believers'. Though We may pardon some of you, We shall punish others, on account of their guilt. **67** The hypocrites, both men and women, are all of a kind. They enjoin what is wrong and forbid what is right, and tighten their fists. They have forgotten God and so He has chosen to forget them. Surely the hypocrites are the transgressors. **68** God has promised the hypocrites, both men and women, and the unbelievers the fire of Hell, where they shall abide. It shall be sufficient for them. God has rejected them, and theirs is a lasting torment. **69** Yours is just like the case of those before you. They were more powerful than you and had greater wealth and more children. They enjoyed their share. And you have been enjoying your share, just as those who preceded you enjoyed their share; and you have been indulging in idle talk just like they did. Their works have come to nothing in this world and shall come to nothing in the life to come. They are indeed the losers. **70** Have they not heard the histories of those who preceded them, such as Noah's people, 'Ad and Thamud, and Abraham's people, and the folk of Madyan and the ruined cities? Their messengers came to them with clear evidence of the truth. It was not God who wronged them; it was they who wronged themselves. **71** The believers, men and women, are friends to one another: They enjoin what is right and forbid what is wrong; they attend to their prayers, and pay their zakat, and obey God and His Messenger. It is on these that God will have mercy. Surely, God is almighty, wise. **72** God has promised the believers, men and women, gardens through which running waters flow, where they will abide, and goodly dwellings in the Garden of Eden. Yet God's acceptance is the greatest blessing of all. This is indeed the supreme triumph. **73** Prophet, strive hard against the unbelievers and the hypocrites, and press hard on them. Their ultimate abode is Hell, and how vile a journey's end. **75** Some of them have pledged to God: 'If He gives us of His bounty, we will certainly spend in charity, and we will be among the righteous'. **76** But when He has given them of His bounty they grew miserly and turned away, heedless [of their pledges]. **77** In consequence, He caused hypocrisy to take root in their hearts till the Day on which they will meet Him, because they have been untrue to the pledges they made to God, and because of the lies they used to tell. **78** Do they not realise that God knows both their secret thoughts and what they talk about in private, and that God has full knowledge of all things that are hidden away? **79** It is those hypocrites that taunt the believers who donate freely, as well as those who have nothing to give except what they earn through their toil, and deride them all. God derides them, and painful suffering awaits them. **80** You may pray for their forgiveness or may not pray for them, [for it will all be the same]. Even if you were to pray seventy times for their forgiveness, God will not forgive them, for they have denied God and His Messenger. God does not guide those who are transgressors. **81** Those who were left behind rejoiced at having stayed at home after [the departure of] God's Messenger, for they were averse to striving with their property and their lives in God's cause. They said [to one another]: 'Do not go to war in this heat'. Say: 'The fire of Hell is far hotter'. Would that they understood. **82** They shall laugh but a little, and they will weep much, in return for what they have earned. **83** If God brings you back and you meet some of them, and then they ask leave to go forth with you, say: 'Never shall you go forth with me, nor shall you fight an enemy with me. You were happy to stay behind on the first occasion, so you stay now with those who remain behind'. **84** You shall not pray for any of them who dies, and you shall not stand by his grave. For they have denied God and His Messenger and died as hardened transgressors. **85** Let not their riches and their children excite your admiration. God only wishes to punish them by means of these in the life of this world, and that their souls perish while they are unbelievers. **86** When a surah was revealed from on high calling on them to believe in God and to strive alongside His Messenger, those of them who were well able to do so asked you to give them leave and said to you: 'Allow us to stay with those who remain behind'. **87** They are well-pleased to remain with those who are left behind. And their hearts are sealed, so that they are unable to understand [the truth]. **88** But the Messenger and those who have believed with him strive hard in God's cause with their property and their lives. These shall have all the good things. These shall certainly prosper. **89** God has prepared for them gardens through which running waters flow, where they shall abide. That is the supreme triumph. **90** Some of the bedouins who had excuses to offer turned up, begging to be granted exemption; while those who denied God and His Messenger stayed behind.

Grievous suffering shall befall those of them that disbelieved. **91** No blame shall be attached to the weak, the sick or those who do not have the means, if they are sincere towards God and His Messenger. There is no cause to reproach those who do good. God is much-forgiving, ever-merciful. **92** Nor shall those be blamed who, when they came to request you for transport and you said: 'I have no means of transporting you', turned away with their eyes overflowing with tears, sad that they did not have the means to cover their expenses. **93** But blame shall certainly attach only to those who ask you for exemption even though they are rich. They are well pleased to be with those who are left behind. God has sealed their hearts, so that they have no knowledge. **94** They shall come to you with their excuses when you return to them. Say: 'Do not offer any excuses, for we shall not believe you. God has already enlightened us about you. God will see how you act, and so will His Messenger; and in the end you shall be brought before Him who knows all that is beyond the reach of human perception and all that is manifest when He will tell you what you used to do'. **95** When you return to them they will swear to you by God so that you may let them be. Let them be, then: they are unclean. Hell shall be their abode in recompense for what they used to do. **96** They swear to you trying to make you pleased with them. Should you be pleased with them, God shall never be pleased with such transgressing folk.

97 The desert Arabs are more tenacious in unbelief and hypocrisy, and more likely to be ignorant of the ordinances which God has revealed to His Messenger. But God is all-knowing, wise. **98** Some desert Arabs regard what they may spend [for God's cause] as a loss, and wait for some misfortune to befall you. The evil turn of fortune will be theirs. God hears all and knows all. **99** Still other desert Arabs believe in God and the Last Day, and regard what they spend [for God's cause] as a means to bring them closer to God and of [their being remembered] in the Messenger's prayers. It shall certainly be for them a means of drawing near to God. God will admit them to His grace, for God is much-forgiving, ever-merciful. **100** As for the first to lead the way, of the Muhajirin and the Ansar, as well as those who follow them in [the way of] righteousness, God is well-pleased with them, and well-pleased are they with Him. He has prepared for them gardens through which running waters flow, where they shall abide forever. That is the supreme triumph. **101** Some desert Arabs around you are hypocrites, and so are some of the people from Madinah, who are indeed persistent in their hypocrisy. You do not know them, but We know them. Twice shall We punish them, and then they will be given over to a grievous suffering. **102** There are others who have acknowledged their sins, after having mixed righteous deeds with evil ones. It may well be that God will accept their repentance. God is much-forgiving, ever-merciful. **103** Take a portion of their money as charity, so that you may cleanse and purify them thereby; and pray for them: for your prayers are a source of comfort for them. God hears all and knows all. **104** Do they not know that it is God alone who accepts repentance from His servants, and He is truly the One who takes charitable offerings, and that God is the only One to accept repentance and bestow mercy? **105** Say to them: 'Do as you will. God will see your deeds, and so will His Messenger, and the believers; and in the end you shall be brought before Him who knows all that is beyond the reach of human perception and all that is manifest when He will tell you what you used to do'. **106** And yet there are others who must await God's judgement. He will either punish them or turn to them in His mercy. God is all-knowing, wise. **107** And there are those who have established a house of worship out of mischievous motives, to promote unbelief and disunity among the believers, and to provide an outpost for those who have already been warring against God and His Messenger. They will certainly swear: 'We have only the best of intentions'. God bears witness that they certainly are liars. **108** Never set a foot there. Only a house of worship that from the very first day has been founded on piety is worthy of you standing to pray there. In it are men who love to grow in purity, for God loves those who purify themselves. **109** Who is better: a man who founds his building [motivated by a sense of] being God-fearing and seeking His goodly acceptance, or one who founds his building on the edge of a crumbling precipice, so that it tumbles with him in to the fire of Hell? God does not guide the wrongdoers. **110** The structure which they have built will continue to be a source of disquiet in their hearts, until their hearts are torn to pieces. God is all-knowing, wise.

111 God has bought of the believers their lives and their property, promising them heaven in return: they fight for the cause of God, kill and be killed. This is a true promise which He has made binding on Himself in the Torah, the Gospel and the Qur'an. Who is more true to his promise than God? Rejoice, then, in the bargain you have made with Him. That is the supreme triumph. **112** [It is a triumph for] those who turn to God in repentance, who worship and praise Him, who contemplate [God and His creation], who bow down and prostrate themselves, who enjoin the doing of what is right and forbid the doing of what is wrong, and keep within the limits set out by God. Give you

[Prophet] glad tidings to the believers. **113** It is not for the Prophet and the believers to pray for the forgiveness of those who associate partners with God, even though they may be their close relatives, after it has become clear that they are destined for the blazing Fire. **114** Abraham prayed for the forgiveness of his father only because of a promise he had made to him. But when it became clear to him that he was God's enemy, he disowned him; Abraham was most tender-hearted, clement. **115** Never will God let people go astray after He has given them guidance until He has made plain to them all that they should avoid. God has perfect knowledge of all things. **116** To God belongs the kingdom of the heavens and the earth; He alone gives life and causes death. Besides God, you have none to protect or support you. **117** God has assuredly turned in His mercy to the Prophet, the Muhajirin and the Ansar, who followed him in the hour of hardship, when the hearts of a group of them had almost faltered. Then again He turned to them in mercy; for He is compassionate towards them, ever-merciful. **118** And [so too] to the three who were left behind: when the earth, vast as it is, seemed to close in upon them, and their own souls had become too constricted, they realised that there was no refuge from God except by returning to Him. He then turned to them in mercy, so that they might repent. God is indeed the One who accepts repentance, the ever-merciful. **119** Believers, have fear of God and be among those who are truthful. **120** It does not behove the people of Madinah and the desert Arabs who live around them to hold back from following God's Messenger, or to care for themselves more than for him; for, whenever they endure thirst, stress, or hunger for the sake of God, or take any step which would irritate the unbelievers, or inflict any loss on the enemy, a good deed is recorded in their favour. God does not suffer the reward of those who do good to be lost. **121** And whenever they spend anything for the sake of God, be it little or much, or traverse a valley [in support of God's cause], it is recorded for them, so that God will give them the best reward for what they do. **122** It is not desirable that all the believers should go out to fight. From every section of them some should go forth, so that they may acquire a deeper knowledge of the faith and warn their people when they return to them, so that they may take heed. **123** Believers, fight those of the unbelievers who are near you, and let them find you tough; and know that God is with those who are God-fearing. **124** Whenever a surah is revealed, some of them say: 'Which of you has this strengthened in faith?' It certainly strengthens the believers in their faith, and so they rejoice. **125** But as for those whose hearts are diseased, it only adds wickedness to their wickedness, and so they die unbelievers. **126** Do they not see that they are tested once or twice every year? Yet they do not repent, and they do not take warning. **127** Whenever a surah is revealed, they look at one another [as if to say]: 'Is anyone watching?' Then they turn away. God has turned their hearts away, for they are people devoid of understanding. **128** Indeed, there has come to you a Messenger from among yourselves: one who grieves much that you should suffer; one who is full of concern for you; and who is tender and full of compassion towards the believers. **129** Should they turn away, then say to them: 'God is enough for me! There is no deity other than Him. In Him have I placed my trust. He is the Lord of the Mighty Throne'.

Surah 10   Jonah

The surah derives its name from Prophet Jonah who is mentioned in Verse 98. It is a Makkan surah tackling the same theme as all Qur'anic revelation of the same period, focusing on faith and its central issue of God's Oneness. It is similar in its presentation to Surah 6, Cattle, but it spreads a more relaxed atmosphere and has a quieter rhythm. The similarity between the two surahs does not detract from the fact that each surah has its own character and distinctive features.

The surah shows the unbelievers in Makkah that their attitude is without solid foundation. There is nothing strange about God's choice of a man to be given revelations so that people should have divine guidance. Guidance that enables them to conduct their lives on the basis of the truth. In this way, the surah states the right concepts of Godhead and man's servitude to Him and calls on the people to believe. Their demand for a miracle to prove the truth of revelation is discussed and shown to be no more than a hollow excuse. The surah shows that the proof of revelation is there for them to see. It is the Qur'an itself which is unlike anything human beings can produce. The Arab idolaters were themselves adept linguists, had many fine poets, but even they had to acknowledge that the Qur'an was unlike anything they knew. Yet still they refused to accept its divine origin.

The surah reminds them of God's presence and His being a witness of everything they do, think of or intend. He is in control of the universe and everything that occurs in it. It also reminds them that His punishment may overwhelm them at any moment. Yet, His grace is granted all the time. People will do well to reflect on this and take heed. It concludes with instructions to the Prophet to declare to them that they have received the message of the truth and they will be accountable for the attitude they take towards it. The Prophet, meanwhile, should follow what is revealed to him and remain patient awaiting God's judgement.

Jonah

In the Name of God, the Lord of Grace, the Ever-Merciful

1 *Alif. Lam. Ra.* These are verses of the divine Book, full of wisdom.
2 Does it seem strange to people that We have inspired a man from their own midst: 'Warn all mankind, and give those who believe the

glad tidings that they are on a sound footing with their Lord?' The unbelievers say: 'This is plainly a skilled enchanter'. **3** Your Lord is God who created the heavens and the earth in six aeons, and established Himself on the Throne, regulating and governing all that exists. There is none who may intercede with Him unless He first grants leave for that. That is God, your Lord: so worship Him alone. Will you not then keep this in mind? **4** To Him you shall all return. This is, in truth, God's promise. He originates all His creation, and then brings them all back to life so that He may reward, with equity, those who have believed and done good deeds. As for the unbelievers, they shall have a scalding drink and a painful suffering for their unbelief. **5** He it is who made the sun a source of radiant light and the moon a light [reflected], and determined her phases so that you may know how to compute the years and measure [time]. God has not created this otherwise than in accordance with the truth. He makes plain His revelations to people of knowledge. **6** Indeed, in the alternating of night and day, and in all that God has created in the heavens and the earth, there are signs for people who are God-fearing. **7** Those who entertain no hope of meeting Us, but are content with the life of this world, and feel well at ease about it, and those who pay no heed to Our revelation, **8** shall have the Fire as their abode in requital for what they used to do. **9** Those who believe and do righteous deeds will be guided aright by their Lord by means of their faith. Running waters will flow at their feet in gardens of bliss. **10** There they will call out: 'Limitless are You in Your glory, God', and their greeting will be, 'Peace!' Their call will conclude with the words: 'All praise is due to God, the Lord of all the worlds!' **11** If God were to hasten for mankind the ill [they have earned] as they would hasten the good, their end would indeed come forthwith. But We leave those who have no hope of meeting Us in their overweening arrogance, blindly stumbling to and fro. **12** When affliction befalls man, he appeals to Us, whether he be lying on his side, sitting, or standing, but as soon as We relieve his affliction, he goes on as though he had never appealed to Us to save him from the affliction that befell him. Thus do their deeds seem fair to those who are given to excesses. **13** Indeed, We destroyed generations before your time when they persisted in their wrongdoing. The messengers sent to them brought them veritable evidence of the truth, but they would not believe. Thus do We reward the guilty. **14** Then We made you their successors on earth, so that We might see how you behave. **15** When Our revelations are recited to them in all their clarity, those who have no hope of meeting Us say:

'Bring us a discourse other than this Qur'an, or else alter it'. Say: 'It is not for me to alter it of my own accord. I only follow what is revealed to me. I dread the torment of an awesome Day if I should disobey my Lord!' **16** Say: 'Had God so willed, I would not have recited it to you, nor would He have brought it to your knowledge. I spent a whole lifetime among you before it [was revealed to me]. Will you not, then, use your reason?' **17** Who is more wicked than one who attributes his lying inventions to God or denies His revelations? Indeed those who are guilty shall not be successful. **18** They worship, side by side with God, what can neither harm nor benefit them, and say: 'These will intercede for us with God'. Say: 'Do you presume to inform God of something in the heavens or on earth that He does not know? Limitless is He in His glory, and exalted above whatever they may associate with Him'. **19** All mankind were once but one single community, and then they disagreed among themselves. Had it not been for a decree from your Lord that had already gone forth, all their differences would have been resolved. **20** They ask: 'Why has no sign been sent down to him by his Lord?' Say: 'God's alone is the knowledge of what is beyond the reach of human perception. Wait, then, if you will: I too am waiting'. **21** Whenever We let people taste grace after some hardship has afflicted them, they turn to scheme against Our revelations. Say: 'More swift is God's scheming. Our messengers are recording all that you may devise'. **22** He it is who enables you to travel on land and sea. Then when you are on board ships, and sailing along in a favourable wind, they feel happy with it, a stormy wind comes upon them and waves surge towards them from all sides, so that they believe they are encompassed [by death]. [At that point] they appeal to God, in complete sincerity of faith in Him alone: 'If You will save us from this, we shall certainly be most grateful'. **23** Yet when He has saved them, they transgress in the land, offending against all right. Mankind, it is against your own souls that your offences rebound. [You care only for] the enjoyment of this present life, but in the end you will return to Us when We will tell you the truth of what you were doing [in this life]. **24** This present life may be compared to rain which We send down from the sky, and which is then absorbed by the plants of the earth from which men and animals eat. Then, when the earth has been clad with its fine adornments and well embellished, and its people believe that they have full mastery over it, Our command comes down upon it, by night or by day, and We make it like a field that has been mowed down, as if it did not blossom but yesterday. Thus do We spell out Our revelations to people who think. **25** God calls to the abode of peace, and guides him that wills to a straight path.

26 For those who do good there is a good reward, and more besides. Neither darkness nor any disgrace will overcast their faces. These are destined for Paradise, where they will abide. **27** As for those who have done evil, an evil deed is rewarded with its like. Ignominy will overshadow them – for they will have none to protect them from God – as if their faces have been covered with patches of the night's own darkness. Such are destined for the Fire, where they will abide. **28** One day we shall gather them all together, and then We shall say to those who associated partners with God: 'Keep to your places, you and those you associated with God as partners'. We will then separate them from one another. Then those whom they associated as partners with God will say: 'It was not us that you worshipped'. **29** 'God is sufficient as a witness between us and you. We were, for certain, unaware of your worshipping us.' **30** There and then every soul will realise what it had done in the past; and all will be brought back to God, their true Lord Supreme. All their invented falsehood will have forsaken them. **31** Say: 'Who is it that provides for you from heaven and earth? Or, who is it that has power over hearing and sight? Who brings forth the living out of that which is dead, and brings forth the dead out of that which is alive? Who regulates all affairs?' They will say: 'God'. Say, then: 'Will you not, then, fear Him?' **32** 'Such is God, your true Lord. Apart from the truth, what is left but error? How is it, then, that you turn away?' **33** Thus is the word of your Lord proved true with regard to those who do evil: they will not believe. **34** Say: 'Can any of your partners [whom you associate with God] originate creation, and then bring it back [to life] again?' Say: 'It is God alone who originates creation and then brings it back [to life] again. How is it, then, that you are so misled?' **35** Say: 'Does any of your partners [whom you associate with God] guide to the truth?' Say: 'God alone guides to the truth. Who is more worthy to be followed: He that guides to the truth, or he who cannot find the right way unless he is guided? What is then amiss with you? How do you judge?' **36** Most of them follow nothing but mere conjecture. But conjecture can in no way be a substitute for truth. God has full knowledge of all that they do. **37** This Qur'an could not have been devised by anyone other than God. It is a confirmation of [revelations] that went before it, and a full explanation of God's Book, about which there is no doubt. It certainly comes from the Lord of all the worlds. **38** If they say: 'He has invented it', say: 'Produce, then, one surah like it, and

call for help on all you can other than God, if what you say is true'.
39 Indeed they disbelieve what they cannot grasp, particularly since
its inner meaning has not become clear to them. Likewise did those
who lived before them disbelieve. But see what happened in the end
to those wrongdoers. **40** Some of them do believe in it, while others
do not. But your Lord is fully aware of those who spread corruption.
41 If they disbelieve you, then say: 'I shall bear the consequences
of my deeds, and you your deeds. You are not accountable for what
I do and I am not accountable for your doings'. **42** Yet some of
them [pretend to] listen to you; but can you make the deaf hear you,
incapable as they are of using their reason? **43** And some of them
[pretend to] look towards you; but can you show the way to the blind,
bereft of sight as they are? **44** Indeed, God does not do the least wrong
to mankind, but it is men who wrong themselves. **45** On the Day when
He will gather them together, [it will seem to them] as though they
had not sojourned in this world more than an hour of a day, getting to
know one another. Lost indeed will be those who [in their lifetime]
disbelieved in meeting God and did not follow the right guidance.
46 Whether We show you some of what We have promised them or
We cause you to die, it is to Us that they shall return. God is witness
of all that they do. **47** To every community was sent a messenger. It is
when their messenger had come to them that judgement is passed on
them in all fairness; and never are they wronged. **48** They say: 'When
will this promise be fulfilled, if you are truthful?' **49** Say: 'I have
no control over any harm or benefit to myself, except as God may
please. For every community a term has been appointed. When their
time arrives, they can neither delay it by a single moment, nor indeed
hasten it'. **50** Say: 'Do but consider. Should His punishment befall
you by night or by day, what could there be in it that the guilty ones
should wish to hasten?' **51** 'Is it, then, when it has come to pass that
you will believe in it? Is it now, while so far you have been asking for
it to come speedily?' **52** Then it will be said to the wrongdoers: 'Taste
the long lasting torment. Is this requital anything other than the just
due for what you used to do?' **53** They will ask you: 'Is all this true?'
Say: 'Yes, by my Lord. It is most certainly true, and you will never
be beyond God's reach'. **54** Should every wrongdoer possess all that
the earth contains, he will gladly offer it all as ransom. They will
harbour feelings of remorse when they see the suffering. Judgement
will be passed on them in all fairness; and they will not be wronged.
55 Indeed, to God belongs all that is in the heavens and earth. God's
promise always comes true, but most of them do not know it. **56** He

alone gives life and causes death, and to Him you shall all return. **57** Mankind, there has come to you an admonition from your Lord, a cure for all that may be in your hearts, and guidance and grace for all believers. **58** Say: 'In God's bounty and grace, in this let them rejoice; for this is better than all that they may amass'. **59** Say: 'Do but consider all the means of sustenance that God has bestowed on you! Some of it you then made unlawful, and some lawful'. Say: 'Has God given you leave to do so, or do you fabricate lies against God?' **60** But what will they think, those who invent lies against God, on the Day of Resurrection? God is truly bountiful to mankind, but most of them are ungrateful. **61** In whatever business you may be engaged, and whatever part you may recite of the Qur'an, and whatever deed you [mankind] may do, We will be your witnesses from the moment you are engaged with it. Not even an atom's weight [of anything whatsoever] on earth or in heaven escapes your Lord, nor is there anything smaller or larger than that, but is recorded in a clear book. **62** For certain, those who are close to God have nothing to fear, nor shall they grieve; **63** for they do believe and remain God-fearing. **64** Theirs are the glad tidings in the life of this world and in the life to come: there is no changing the word of God. This is the supreme triumph. **65** Be not grieved by what they say. All might and glory belong to God alone. He alone hears all and knows all. **66** Indeed, to God belongs all those who are in the heavens and earth. Those who invoke other beings beside God do not follow any real partners with Him. They follow mere conjecture, and they utter nothing but falsehood. **67** It is He who has made the night for you, so that you may have rest, and the day, so that you may see. In this there are certainly signs for those who listen. **68** They say: 'God has taken unto Himself a son.' Limitless is He in His glory. Self-sufficient is He. To Him belongs all that is in the heavens and earth. No evidence whatever have you for this. Would you say about God something which you do not know? **69** Say: 'Those who invent falsehood about God shall not be successful. **70** They may have a brief enjoyment in this world, but then to Us they must return, and We will then make them suffer severe torment for their unbelief'.

71 Relate to them the story of Noah. He said to his people: 'My people! If my presence among you and my reminders to you of God's revelations are repugnant to you – well, in God have I placed my trust. Decide, then, what you are going to do, and [seek the help of] those whom you associate as partners with God. Be clear about your course of action, leaving no room for uncertainty, then carry out against me whatever you may have decided and give me no respite. **72** But if you turn away, [remember that] I have asked of you no reward whatsoever. My reward rests with none but God. I have been commanded to be one of those who surrender themselves to Him'. **73** But they disbelieved him. So we saved him and all those who joined him in the ark, and made them inherit the earth. And we drowned the others who denied Our revelations. Reflect on the fate of those who were forewarned. **74** Then after him We sent forth other messengers to their respective peoples, and they brought them clear evidence of the truth, but they would not believe in what they had once denied. Thus it is that We seal the hearts of those who transgress. **75** Then after those [prophets] We sent Moses and Aaron with Our signs to Pharaoh and his nobles, but they persisted in their arrogance, for they were hardened offenders. **76** When the truth came to them from Us, they said: 'This is clearly nothing but sorcery'. **77** Moses replied: 'Do you say this to the truth when it has come to you? Can this be sorcery? But sorcerers will never be successful'. **78** They said: 'Have you come to turn us away from what we found our forefathers believing in, so that the two of you might become supreme in the land? We will never believe in you'. **79** Then Pharaoh commanded: 'Bring before me every learned sorcerer'. **80** And when the sorcerers came, Moses said to them: 'Throw whatever you may wish to throw'. **81** And when they had thrown, Moses said to them: 'What you have contrived is mere sorcery which God will certainly bring to nothing. God does not further the work of those who spread corruption. **82** By His words, God proves the truth to be true, much as the guilty may dislike it'. **83** None except a few of his people believed in Moses, for they feared Pharaoh and their nobles, lest they persecute them. Surely Pharaoh was mighty on earth and was indeed given to excesses. **84** Moses said: 'My people, if you believe in God, then place your trust in Him – if you have truly surrendered yourselves to Him'. **85** They replied: 'In God have we placed our trust. Our Lord, do not let us suffer at the hands of evildoing people. Save us, by Your grace, from the people who disbelieve'. **86** And thus did We inspire Moses and his brother: 'Take for your people some houses in Egypt, and make your houses places of worship, and be constant in prayer'. And give glad tidings to all believers. **88** Moses said, 'Our Lord! You have bestowed on Pharaoh and his nobles splendour and riches in this life, with the result that they have been leading people astray from Your path. Our Lord! Wipe out their riches and harden their hearts, so that they do not believe until they face the grievous suffering'. **89** He replied: 'Your prayer is accepted. Continue, both of you, steadfastly on the right path, and do not follow the path of those who are devoid of knowledge'. **90** And We brought the Children of Israel across the sea; but Pharaoh and his legions pursued them with tyranny and aggression. But as he was about to drown, Pharaoh said: 'I have come to believe that there is no deity other than Him in whom the Children of Israel believe, and to Him I surrender myself'. **91** [But God said:] 'Only now? But before this you were rebelling [against Us], and you spread corruption in the land. **92** But today We shall save only your body, so that you may become a sign to those who will come after you; for a great many people do not heed Our signs'. **93** We settled the Children of Israel in a most goodly abode and We provided for them sustenance out of the good things of life. It was not until knowledge was given them that they began to disagree among themselves. Your Lord will judge between them on the Day of Resurrection regarding that on which they differed. **94** If you are in doubt concerning what We have bestowed on you from on high, ask those who read the Scriptures [revealed] before you. It is surely the truth that has come to you from your Lord. Do not, then, be among the doubters. **95** And do not be among those who deny God's revelations, for then you shall be among those who are lost. **96** Surely, those against whom your Lord's word [of judgement] has come true will not believe, **97** even though every sign should come to their knowledge, until they are faced with the grievous suffering. **98** Had it believed, every community would have profited by its faith. It was so only with Jonah's people. When they believed, We lifted from them the suffering of disgrace in this life, and allowed them to enjoy things for a while. **99** Had your Lord so willed, all people on earth, in their entirety, would have believed. Do you, then, try to compel people to believe? **100** No human being can believe, except by God's leave. It is He who lays abomination on those who will not use their reason. **101** Say: 'Consider all that there is in the heavens and the earth'. But of what benefit could all signs and warnings be to people who will not believe? **102** What are they waiting for except a repetition of the days [of calamity] experienced by those who have gone before them? Say: 'Wait, then, if you will. I am also waiting'. **103** Thereupon, We save Our messengers and those who believe. Thus have We willed it upon Ourselves: We save those who believe.

104 Say: 'Mankind, if you are still in doubt as to what my faith is, then [know that] I do not worship those whom you worship beside God, but I worship God alone who will cause all of you to die.

I have been commanded to be one of those who believe. **105** And adhere exclusively and sincerely to the true faith, and do not be one of those who associate partners with God. **106** Do not invoke, instead of God, anything that can neither benefit nor harm you. For if you do, you will surely be among the wrongdoers'. **107** Should God afflict you with any hardship, none other than He can remove it; and if He wills any good for you, none can withhold His bounty. He bestows it on whomsoever He wills. He is the One who is much-forgiving, ever-merciful. **108** Say: 'Mankind, the truth has come to you from your Lord. Whoever chooses to follow the true guidance does so for his own good; and whoever chooses to go astray, does so at his own peril. I am not responsible for your conduct'. **109** Follow whatever is revealed to you, and be patient in adversity, until God shall give His judgement. He is the best of all judges.

Surah 11   Hud

This surah was revealed in Makkah, focusing on the main issue of God's Oneness and man's duty to submit himself to Him. It is similar to Surah 7 in the way it tackles its theme and presentation. It starts by stating the Islamic concept of God and that the universe and all it contains are God's creation. All submit to Him. It refutes the unbelievers' argument that the Prophet might have fabricated the Qur'an and attributed it to God, challenging them to produce anything like it.

The surah then moves on to show the history of the divine faith, as preached by successive prophets and messengers. It gives us a detailed account of Noah and his people, and the punishment that overwhelmed them. The account stresses the concept of every human being's individual responsibility. Prophet Noah could not save his own son from God's punishment, because his son chose to turn away from the truth.

The surah gives us accounts of several of God's messengers and how their peoples rejected the truth and suffered God's punishment. Every messenger reminded his people of God's favours and promised them an increase of such favours, only to be met with hostility, ridicule and outright rejection. The shortest account of past communities given in this surah is that of Moses and his people. Its message, however, is very clear. It is people who wrong themselves and incur God's punishment. It is they who can avoid all this, as well as punishment in the life to come, if they give the right response to God's message and believe in Him. This is the only way to achieve happiness both in this life and in the life to come.

Hud

In the Name of God, the Lord of Grace, the Ever-Merciful

1 *Alif. Lam. Ra.* This is a Book, with verses which have been perfected and distinctly spelled out, bestowed on you by One who is wise, all-aware. **2** Worship none but God. I come to you from Him as a warner and a bearer of glad tidings. **3** Seek the forgiveness of your Lord, and then turn towards Him in repentance, and He will grant you a goodly enjoyment of life for an appointed term. He will grant everyone with merit a full reward for his merit. But if you turn away, I dread for you the suffering of an awesome Day. **4** To God you shall all return, and He has power over all things. **5** They cover up their chests in order to hide from Him. Surely, when they cover themselves with their garments, He knows all that they keep secret as well as all that they bring into the open. He has full knowledge of what is in people's hearts. **6** There is no living creature on earth but depends for its sustenance on God; and He knows its habitation and its resting-place. All this is in a clear record. **7** He it is who has created the heavens and the earth in six aeons, whereas His throne has rested upon water, so that He may test you [to make manifest] which of you is best in conduct. Yet if you say to them: 'You shall be raised again after death', those who disbelieve are sure to say: 'This is nothing but plain sorcery'. **8** If we defer their suffering for a definite term, they are sure to say: 'What is holding it back?' On the Day when it befalls them there will be nothing to avert it from them; and they shall be overwhelmed by that which they used to deride. **9** And thus it is: if We let man taste some of Our grace, and then take it away from him, he becomes utterly in despair, totally ungrateful. **10** And if We let him taste ease and plenty after hardship has visited him, he is sure to say: 'Gone is all affliction from me', and he grows jubilant and boastful. **11** Not so the ones who are patient in adversity and do righteous deeds. They shall have forgiveness and a great reward. **12** Is it, then, conceivable that you may omit any part of what is being revealed to you and feel distressed in your heart at their saying: 'Why has not a treasure been bestowed on him from on high?' – or, 'Why has not an angel come with him?' You are only a warner, whereas God has everything in His care. **13** If they say: 'He has invented it', say: 'Produce, then, ten invented surahs like it, and call for help on all you can other than God, if what you say is true'. **14** If they do not respond to you, know that it [the Qur'an] has been bestowed from on high with God's knowledge, and that there is no deity other than Him. Will you then submit yourselves to Him? **15** As for those who desire only the life of this world and its bounties, We shall fully repay them in this life for all they do, and they shall suffer no diminution of their just dues. **16** It is they who, in the life to come, shall have nothing but the Fire. In vain shall be all that they have done in this world, and worthless shall be all their actions. **17** Have you considered him who takes his stand on clear evidence from his Lord, followed by a testimony from Him, which is preceded by the Book of Moses [revealed as] a guide and a mercy [to people]? These believe in it. As for those, of any groups, who deny its truth, the Fire is their appointed place. So, be not in doubt concerning it; it is the truth from your Lord, even though most people do not believe. **18** Who could be more wicked than one who invents lies against God? These shall be brought before their Lord, and witnesses shall say: 'These are they who lied against their Lord'. God's curse is on the wrongdoers, **19** who debar others from the path of God and seek to make it crooked, and who deny the life to come. **20** Never can they be immune [from punishment] on earth, nor have they any friends to protect them from God. Their suffering shall be doubled. They could not bear to hear, and they used not to see. **21** These are the ones who have lost their own souls, and that which they used to invent shall fail them. **22** Most certainly, it is they who in the life to come shall be the greatest losers. **23** Those who believe and do righteous deeds and humble themselves before their Lord are destined for Paradise, and there shall they abide. **24** The case of the two parties is like that of the one who is blind and deaf and the one who sees and hears. Can the two be deemed equal? Will you not take heed?

25 We sent forth Noah to his people: 'I have come to you with a plain warning. **26** Worship none but God. I certainly fear that suffering should befall you on a grievous Day'. **27** The notables of his people who disbelieved said: 'We see you but a mortal man like ourselves. Nor can we see anyone following you except the most abject among us; those who are rash and undiscerning. We do not consider that you are in any way superior to us: indeed we think you are liars'. **28** Noah said: 'Think, my people! If I take my stand on clear evidence from my Lord, and He has favoured me with grace from Himself, to which you have remained blind, can we force it upon you when you are averse to it? **29** And, my people, I ask of you no money in return; my reward rests with none but God. Nor will I drive away those who believe; they will surely meet their Lord, whereas in you I see people with no awareness [of right and wrong]. **30** And, my people, who would protect me from God were I to drive them away? Will you not reflect? **31** I do not say to you that God's treasures are with me, or that I know what lies beyond the reach of human perception. Nor do I say: I am an angel. Nor do I say of those whom you eye with contempt that God will never grant them any good. God knows best what is in their hearts – for then I would indeed be a wrongdoer'. **32** 'Noah', they replied, 'you have argued with us, and argued to excess. Bring upon us that with which you have been threatening us, if you are a man of truth'. **33** He said: 'Only God can bring it upon you, if He so wills. You cannot be immune. **34** Nor will my counsel benefit you, much as I desire to give you good counsel, if it is God's will to let you remain in error. He is your Lord and to Him you shall return'. **35** Do they claim that he [Muhammad] has invented it? Say: 'If I have invented it, upon me be this crime of mine, but I am innocent of the crimes you perpetrate'. **36** Noah received this revelation: 'None of your people will believe now apart from those who have already accepted the faith. Be not in distress over anything they may do. **37** 'Build the ark under Our eyes, and according to Our inspiration. Do not appeal to Me on behalf of the wrongdoers. They shall be drowned'. **38** So he set himself on building the ark. And whenever a group of his people passed by him they scoffed at him. He said: 'If you are scoffing at us, we are indeed scoffing at you, just as you are scoffing at us'. **39** You will surely come to know who it is that will be visited by suffering that will cover him with ignominy, and who will be afflicted by long-lasting suffering. **40** Until, when Our will came to pass and the fountains of the earth gushed forth, We said [to Noah]: 'Take into it a pair of every species, as well as your family, except those against whom Our word has passed, and all those who have accepted the faith'. None believed with him except a few. **41** He said to them: 'Embark on it. In the name of God be its course and its riding at anchor. Indeed is my Lord much-forgiving, ever-merciful'. **42** And it sailed with them amid waves towering like mountains. Noah cried out to a son of his who stood apart [from the rest]: 'Embark with us, my child, and do not stay with the unbelievers'. **43** He answered: 'I shall seek refuge in a mountain, which will afford me protection from the water'. Said (Noah): 'Today there is no protection for anyone from God's judgement, except those who shall enjoy His mercy'. Thereupon waves rose up between them and he was among those who were drowned. **44** And the word was spoken: 'Earth, swallow up your waters. Heaven, cease [your rain]'. Thus the waters sank into the earth, and God's will was done, and the ark came to rest on Mount Judi. The word was spoken: 'Away with these wrongdoing folk'. **45** Noah called out to his Lord, saying: 'Lord, my son is of my family. Surely Your promise always comes true, and You are the most just of judges'. **46** 'Noah', He answered, 'he was not of your family; his was unrighteous conduct. Do not question me about matters of which you have no knowledge. I admonish you lest you become one of the ignorant'. **47** Said (Noah): 'My Lord, I do indeed seek refuge with You from ever questioning you about anything of which I have no knowledge. Unless you grant me forgiveness and have mercy on me I shall be among the losers'. **48** The word was spoken: Noah, disembark in peace from Us, and with Our blessings upon you as well as upon generations from those who are with you. As for other folk, We shall let them have enjoyment, and then there will befall them grievous suffering from Us. **49** These accounts of things that have passed We now reveal to you. Neither you nor your people knew them before this. Be, then, patient in adversity; for the future belongs to those who are God-fearing.

50 To the 'Ad We sent their brother Hud. He said: 'My people! Worship God alone; you have no deity other than Him. You are indeed inventors of falsehood. **51** No reward do I ask of you, my people, for this [message]. My reward rests with Him who brought me into being. Will you not, then, use your reason? **52** My people! Seek your Lord's forgiveness, and then turn to Him in repentance. He will cause the sky to rain abundance on you, and will add strength to your strength. Do not turn away as guilty criminals'. **53** They replied: 'Hud, you have brought us no clear evidence. We are not forsaking our gods on your mere word, nor will we believe in you. **54** All we can say is that one of our gods may have smitten you with something evil'. He said: 'I call God to witness, and you, too, bear witness, that I disassociate myself from all those you claim to be partners with God. **55** Scheme against me, all of you, if you will, and give me no respite. **56** Indeed I have placed my trust in God, my Lord and your Lord. There is no living creature which He does not hold by its forelock. Straight indeed is my Lord's way. **57** But if you turn away, I have delivered to you the message with which I was sent to you. My Lord may replace you with another people. You can do Him no harm. My Lord watches over all things'. **58** And so, when Our judgement came to pass, by Our grace We saved Hud and those who shared his faith. We have indeed saved them from severe suffering. **59** Such were the 'Ad. They denied their Lord's revelations, disobeyed His messengers, and followed the bidding of every arrogant, unrestrained tyrant. **60** They were pursued by a curse in this world and on the Day of Judgement. Indeed, the 'Ad denied their Lord. Oh, away with the 'Ad, the people of Hud. **61** To the Thamud We sent their brother Salih. He said 'My people! Worship God alone. You have no deity other than Him. He it is who brought you into being out of the earth and settled you therein. Seek His forgiveness and then turn to Him in repentance. My Lord is ever-near. He answers all'. **62** They answered: 'Salih, great hopes did we place in you before this. Would you now forbid us to worship what our forefathers worshipped? We are indeed in grave doubt about that to which you call us'. **63** He said: 'Think, my people! If I take my stand on clear evidence from my Lord who has bestowed on me His grace, who will save me from God were I to disobey Him? You are, in such a case, only aggravating my ruin. **64** And, my people, here is God's she-camel, a clear sign for you. Leave her to graze at will in God's land, and do her no harm, lest speedy punishment befall you'. **65** Yet they cruelly slaughtered her. He said: 'You have just three more days to enjoy life in your homes. This is a promise which will not be belied'. **66** When Our judgement came to pass, by Our grace We saved Salih and those who shared his faith from the ignominy of that day. Indeed, your Lord is the One who is powerful, almighty. **67** The blast overtook the wrongdoers, and when morning came, they lay lifeless on the ground, in their very homes, **68** as though they had never prospered there. The Thamud denied their Lord! Oh, away with the Thamud.

69 Our messengers came to Abraham with good news. They bade him peace, and he answered: 'Peace [be to you]'. He then hastened to bring them a roasted calf. **70** But when he saw that their hands did not reach out to it, he felt their conduct strange and became apprehensive of them. They said: 'Do not be alarmed. We are sent to the people of Lot'. **71** His wife, standing nearby, laughed; whereupon We gave her the happy news of [her giving birth to] Isaac and after Isaac, Jacob. **72** Said she: 'Woe is me! Shall I bear a child, now that I am an old woman and this my husband is well-advanced in years? This is a strange thing indeed'. **73** They said: 'Do you marvel at God's decree? May God's mercy and blessings be on you, people of this house. He is indeed ever to be praised, glorious'. **74** When his fear had left Abraham, and he received the happy news, he began to plead with Us for Lot's people. **75** Abraham was indeed most clement, tender-hearted, and devout. **76** Abraham! Leave off all this [pleading]. Your Lord's judgement must come to pass. They shall be afflicted by an irrevocable torment. **77** When Our messengers came to Lot he was troubled on their account, for he was powerless to offer them protection. He said: 'This is a woeful day'. **78** His people came running towards him, for they had been long keen on abominable practices. He said: 'My people! Here are my daughters: they are purer for you. Have fear of God and do not disgrace me by wronging my guests. Is there not one right-minded man among you?' **79** They answered: 'You know we have no need of your daughters; and indeed you well know what we want'. **80** He said: 'Would that I had the strength to defeat you, or that I could lean on some mighty support'. **81** [The angels] said: 'Lot, we are messengers from your Lord. They shall not touch you. Depart with your household, during the night, and let none of you look back, except for your wife. She shall suffer the same fate which is to befall them. Their appointed time is the morning. Is not the morning near?' **82** When Our judgement came to pass We turned those [towns] upside down, and rained on them stones of clay, ranged one upon another, **83** marked out as from Your Lord. Nor is such [punishment] far from the wrongdoers.

84 And to Madyan We sent their brother Shuʿayb. He said: 'My people! Worship God alone. You have no deity other than Him. Do not give short measure and weight. I see you now in a happy state, yet I dread lest suffering befall you on a fateful Day which will encompass all. **85** 'My people, always give full measure and weight, in all fairness, and do not deprive people of what is rightfully theirs, and do not spread corruption on earth by wicked actions. **86** That which rests with God is better for you, if you truly believe. I am not your keeper'. **87** They said: 'Shuʿayb, do your prayers compel you to demand of us that we should renounce all that our forefathers worshipped, or that we refrain from doing what we please with our property? You are indeed the one who is clement and right-minded!' **88** He said: 'Think, my people! If I take my stand on clear evidence from my Lord and He has provided me with goodly sustenance which He alone can give? I have no desire to do, in opposition to you, what I ask you not to do. All that I desire is to set things to rights in so far as it lies within my power. My success depends on God alone. In Him have I placed my trust, and to Him I always turn. **89** My people, let not your disagreement with me bring upon you a fate similar to those that befell the peoples of Noah, Hud or Salih; nor were Lot's people far away from you. **90** Hence, pray to your Lord to forgive you your sins, and then turn towards Him in repentance. My Lord is indeed ever-merciful and all-loving'. **91** They said: 'Shuʿayb, we cannot understand much of what you say. But we do see clearly how weak you are in our midst. Were it not for your family, we would have stoned you. You do not command a position of great respect among us'. **92** Said he: 'My people, do you hold my family in greater esteem than God? You have turned your backs on Him. My Lord encompasses [with His might] all that you do'. **93** Do what you will, my people, and so will I. You shall come to know who shall be visited by suffering that will cover him with ignominy, and who is a liar. Watch, then [for what is coming], and I shall watch with you. **94** When Our judgement came to pass, by Our grace We saved Shuʿayb and those who shared his faith. The blast overtook the wrongdoers, and when morning came, they lay lifeless on the ground, in their very homes, **95** as though they had never prospered there. Oh, away with the people of Madyan, even as the Thamud have been done away with! **96** Indeed, We sent Moses with Our signs and a manifest authority **97** to Pharaoh and his noble men. They, however, followed only Pharaoh's bidding. Pharaoh's bidding led by no means to what is right. **98** He will come at the head of his people on the Day of Resurrection, leading them to the Fire. Vile was the destination towards which they were led. **99** A curse is made to follow them in this world and on the Day of Resurrection. Vile was the renewable gift which they were given.

100 These are some of the accounts of past communities which We relate to you. Some still remain while others are extinct, like a field mowndown. **101** No wrong did We do to them, but it was they who wronged themselves. Those deities of theirs which they were keen to invoke instead of God availed them nothing when your Lord's judgement came to pass; they only added to their ruin. **102** Such is your Lord's punishment whenever He takes to task any community which is bent on wrongdoing; His punishment is indeed painful, severe. **103** In this there is surely a sign for those who fear the suffering in the life to come. That is a Day when all mankind shall be gathered together, and that is a Day which will be witnessed [by all]. **104** We shall not delay it beyond an appointed term. **105** When that Day comes, not a soul will speak except by His leave. Some among them will be wretched, and some happy. **106** Those who will have brought wretchedness upon themselves, they will be in the Fire where, moaning and sobbing, **107** they will abide as long as the heavens and the earth endure, unless your Lord wills it otherwise. Your Lord always does whatever He wills. **108** And those who are blessed with happiness will be in Paradise, abiding there as long as the heavens and the earth endure, unless your Lord wills it otherwise: an unceasing gift. **109** So be not in doubt about anything which these people worship. They worship only as their fathers worshipped before them. We shall most certainly give them their full due, without any reduction. **110** Indeed, We gave the Scriptures to Moses, and there was strife over them. Had it not been for a decree that had already gone forth from your Lord, judgement would have been passed on them. Yet, they are in grave doubt concerning that. **111** To each and all your Lord will surely give their full due for whatever they may have done. He is indeed aware of all that they do. **112** Follow, then, the right course as you are bidden, together with those who, with you, have turned to Him; and let none of you transgress. Surely, He sees all that you do. **113** Put no trust in those who do wrong, lest the Fire engulf you.

You would, then, have none to protect you from God, nor would you find any help. **114** Attend to your prayers at both ends of the day and in the early watches of the night. Surely, good deeds erase evil ones. This is a reminder for those who are thoughtful. **115** And be patient in adversity; God does not fail to reward those who do good. **116** If only there had been among the generations that have gone before you some people of virtue to speak out against the spread of corruption on earth, as did the few whom We saved from among them! The wrongdoers pursued what ensured for them a life of comfort and plenty; they were indeed guilty. **117** In truth, your Lord would have not destroyed those cities, without just cause, had their people been righteous. **118** Had your Lord so willed, He would have made all mankind one single community. As it is, they continue to differ, **119** except those upon whom your Lord has bestowed His grace. And to this end He created them. The word of your Lord shall be fulfilled: 'I shall certainly fill Hell with jinn and humans all'. **120** All that We relate to you of the histories of earlier messengers is a means by which We strengthen your heart. Through these [accounts] there has come to you the truth, as well as an admonition and a reminder for all believers. **121** Say to those who will not believe: 'Do whatever lies within your power, and so shall we. **122** Wait if you will; we too are waiting'. **123** God alone knows whatever is hidden in the heavens and the earth. All authority over all matters belongs to Him alone. Worship Him, then, and place your trust in Him alone. Your Lord is not unaware of what you do.

Surah 12   Joseph

This is a Makkan revelation, giving in detail the history of Prophet Joseph from childhood to establishment in high position in Egypt and reunion with his parents and brothers. Accounts of other prophets are given in several surahs with varying emphasis as suits each surah. Joseph's story is given in full in this surah, taking up its entirety except for an introduction in three verses and a conclusion in ten verses.

There is much emphasis in the surah on knowledge and wisdom, as these are important factors in the events that unfold with each episode of the story. The surah also reflects the attitude of firm believers as they are met with different types of adversity. In prison, wrongly accused as he was, Joseph does not hesitate to call on his fellow prisoners to believe in God alone and to abandon the false deities upheld by his community. When he is in charge of the country's provisions, he discharges his responsibilities on the basis of fair dealing, preservation of the harvest and fair distribution to all. The surah also highlights the virtue of forgiveness as Joseph forgives his brothers.

In its conclusion, the surah refers to the adversity that is met by believers and advocates of the truth, stating that even prophets and messengers of God may almost reach the point of despair.

Joseph

In the Name of God, the Lord of Grace, the Ever-Merciful

1 *Alif. Lam. Ra.* These are the verses of the Book that clearly shows [the truth]. **2** We have revealed it as a discourse in Arabic so that you may understand. **3** In revealing this Qur'an We relate to you the best of narratives. Before it you were among those who are unaware [of revelation]. **4** Joseph said to his father: 'Father, I saw in a dream eleven stars, as well as the sun and the moon; I saw them prostrate themselves before me'. **5** 'My son', he replied, 'do not relate your dream to your brothers, lest they plot some evil against you. Satan is indeed man's open enemy. **6** Even thus will your Lord make you His chosen one, and will impart to you some understanding of the real meaning of statements. He will perfect His favour to you and to the House of Jacob, as He perfected it to your forefathers, Abraham and Isaac. Your Lord is certainly all-knowing, wise'. **7** Surely in

Joseph and his brothers there are signs for those who inquire. **8** They said [to one another]: 'Truly, Joseph and his brother are dearer to our father than we, even though we are many. Surely our father is in manifest error. **9** Kill Joseph, or cast him away in some faraway land, so that you have your father's attention turned to you alone. After that you will [repent and] be righteous people.' **10** One of them said: 'Do not kill Joseph, but rather – if you must do something – cast him into the dark depth of this well. Some caravan may pick him up'. **11** [Thereupon] they said [to their father]: 'Father, Why do you not trust us with Joseph, when we are indeed his well-wishers? **12** Send him with us tomorrow, that he may enjoy himself and play. We will certainly take good care of him'. **13** He answered: 'It certainly grieves me that you should take him with you; and I dread that the wolf may eat him when you are heedless of him'. **14** They said: 'If the wolf were to eat him when we are so many, then we should surely be lost'. **15** And when they went away with him, they resolved to cast him into the depth of the well. We revealed [this] to him: 'You will tell them of this their deed at a time when they shall not know you'. **16** At nightfall they came to their father weeping, **17** and said: 'Father, we went off racing and left Joseph behind with our belongings, and the wolf devoured him. But you will not believe us even though we are saying the truth'. **18** And they produced his shirt stained with false blood. He said: 'No, but your minds have tempted you to evil. Sweet patience! It is to God alone that I turn for support in this misfortune that you have described'. **19** And there came a caravan; and they sent their water-drawer, and he let down his bucket into the well – [and when he saw Joseph] he cried: 'What good luck. Here is a boy!' They concealed him with a view to selling him; but God had full knowledge of what they were doing. **20** And they sold him for a paltry price, a few silver coins. Thus low did they value him.

21 The man from Egypt who bought him said to his wife: 'Be kind to him. He may well be of use to us, or we may adopt him as our son'. Thus We established Joseph in the land, and We imparted to him some understanding of the real meaning of statements. God always prevails in whatever be His purpose; though most people may not know it. **22** And when he attained his full manhood, We bestowed on him wisdom and knowledge. Thus do We reward those who do good. **23** She in whose house he was living tried to seduce him. She bolted the doors and said, 'Come'. He said: 'God protect me. Goodly has my master made my stay here. Those who do wrong come to no good'. **24** She truly desired him, and he desired her. [He would have succumbed] had he not seen a clear sign of his Lord. Thus We averted from him evil and indecency. He was truly one of Our faithful servants. **25** And they both rushed to the door. She tore his shirt from behind. And at the door they met her husband. She said: 'What ought to be the punishment of someone who had evil designs on your wife other than that he should be thrown in prison or some painful punishment'. **26** [Joseph] said: 'It was she who sought to seduce me'. One of her own household testified: 'If his shirt has been torn from the front, then she is speaking the truth and he is lying. **27** But if it has been torn from behind, then she is lying, and he is speaking the truth.' **28** When [her husband] saw that Joseph's shirt was torn from behind, he said to her: 'This is indeed [an instance] of the guile of you, women. Your guile is awesome indeed!' **29** 'Joseph, let this pass! And you, woman, ask forgiveness for your sin. You have been seriously at fault'. **30** In the city, women were saying: 'This minister's wife is trying to seduce her slave boy, as she is passionately in love with him. We see that she is clearly going astray'. **31** When she heard of their malicious talk, she sent for them, and prepared for them a sumptuous feast, and handed each one of them a knife and said [to Joseph]: 'Come out and present yourself to them'. When they saw him, they were amazed at him, and they cut their hands, exclaiming: 'God preserve us! This is no mortal man! This is none other than a noble angel'. **32** Said she: 'This is he on whose account you have been blaming me! Indeed I have tried to seduce him, but he guarded his chastity. Now, however, if he does not do what I bid him, he shall certainly be thrown in prison, and shall indeed be humiliated'. **33** [Joseph] said: 'My Lord, I would sooner be put in prison than comply with what they are inviting me to do. Unless You turn away their guile from me, I may yield to them and lapse into folly'. **34** His Lord answered his prayer and warded off their guile from him. It is He alone who hears all and knows all.

35 Yet for all the evidence they had seen, they felt it right to put him in jail for a time. **36** Two young men went to prison with him. One of them said: 'I saw myself [in a dream] pressing wine'. The other said: 'And I saw myself [in a dream] carrying bread on my head, and birds were eating of it'. 'Tell us the meaning of these dreams, for we can see that you are a man of virtue'. **37** [Joseph] answered: 'Your food which is provided for you will not have come to you before I have informed you of the real meaning of [your dreams]. That is part of the knowledge which my Lord has imparted to me. I have left the faith of people who do not believe in God, and who deny the truth of the life to come. **38** I follow the faith of my forefathers,

Abraham, Isaac and Jacob. It is not for us to associate any partners with God. This is part of God's grace which He has bestowed on us and on all mankind, but most people do not give thanks. **39** My two prison companions! Which is better: [to believe] in diverse lords, or to believe in God, the One who holds sway over all that exists? **40** Those you worship instead of Him are nothing but names you and your fathers have invented, and for which God has given no sanction from on high. All judgement rests with God alone. He has ordained that you should worship none but Him. This is the true faith, but most people do not know it. **41** My two prison companions! One of you will give his lord wine to drink. The other will be crucified, and the birds will eat from his head. The matter on which you have sought to be enlightened has thus been decided'. **42** And [Joseph] said to the one whom he believed would be released: 'Remember me in the presence of your lord'. But Satan caused him to forget to mention Joseph to his lord, and so he remained in prison for several years. **43** And the King said: 'I saw [in a dream] seven fat cows being devoured by seven emaciated ones, and seven green ears of wheat next to seven others dry and withered. Tell me the meaning of my vision, my nobles, if you are able to interpret dreams'. **44** They replied: 'This is but a medley of dreams, and we have no deep knowledge of the real meaning of dreams'. **45** At that point, the man who had been released from prison suddenly remembered [Joseph] after all that time and said: 'I will tell you the real meaning of this dream, so give me leave to go'. **46** 'Joseph, man of truth, tell us of the seven fat cows being devoured by seven emaciated ones, and seven green ears of wheat next to seven others dry and withered, so that I may return to the people [of the court], and that they would come to know.' **47** He replied: 'You shall sow for seven consecutive years, but let the grain you harvest remain in its ear, except for the little which you may eat. **48** Then after that there will come seven hard years which will devour all that you have laid up for them, except a little of what you have kept in store. **49** Then after that there will come a year of abundant rain, in which the people will be able to press [oil and wine]'. **50** The King said: 'Bring this man before me'. But when the [King's] envoy came to him, Joseph said: 'Go back to your lord and ask him about the women who cut their hands. My Lord has full knowledge of their guile'. **51** The King asked [the women]: 'What was the matter with you when you tried to seduce Joseph?' The women said: 'God save us! We did not perceive the least evil on his part'. The nobleman's wife said: 'Now has the truth come to light. It was I who tried to seduce him. He has indeed told the truth'. **52** From this he will know that I did not betray him behind his back, and that God does not bless with His guidance the schemes of those who betray their trust. **53** And yet, I am not trying to claim to be free of sin. Indeed man's soul does incite him to evil, except for those upon whom God has bestowed His mercy. My Lord is much-forgiving, ever-merciful. **54** And the King said: 'Bring him before me. I will choose him for my own'. And when he had spoken to him, the King said: 'You shall henceforth be in a position of high standing with us, invested with all trust'. **55** Joseph replied: 'Give me charge of the store-houses of the land. I am able to look after them with wisdom'. **56** Thus did We establish Joseph in the land, free to do what he willed. We bestow Our mercy on whom We will, and We never fail to give their reward to those who do good. **57** But as for those who believe in God and keep away from evil, the reward of the life to come is much better indeed.

58 Joseph's brothers arrived and presented themselves before him. He immediately knew them, but they did not recognise him. **59** And when he had given them their provisions, he said: 'Bring me that brother of yours from your father's side. Do you not see that I give just measure and that I am the best of hosts? **60** But if you do not bring him, you shall never again receive from me a single measure [of provisions], nor shall you come near me'. **61** They said: 'We shall endeavour to persuade his father to let him come. We will make sure to do so'. **62** Joseph said to his servants: 'Place their merchandise in their camel-packs, so that they may discover it when they return to their people. Perchance they will come back'. **63** When they returned to their father, they said: 'Father, any [further] grain is henceforth denied us. Therefore, send our brother with us so that we may obtain our full measure [of grain]. We will take good care of him'. **64** He replied: 'Am I to trust you with him in the same way as I trusted you with his brother in the past? But God is the best of guardians; and of all those who show mercy He is the most-merciful'. **65** When they opened their camel-packs, they discovered that their merchandise had been returned to them. 'Father', they said, 'what more could we desire? Here is our merchandise: it has been returned to us. We will buy provisions for our people, and we will take good care of our brother. We will receive an extra camel-load: that should be an easy load'. **66** He said: 'I will not send him with you until you give me a solemn pledge before God that you will indeed bring him back to me, unless the worst befall you'. When they had given him their solemn pledge, [Jacob] said: 'God is witness to all that we say'.

67 And he added: 'My sons, do not enter [the city] by one gate, but enter by different gates. In no way can I be of help to you against God. Judgement rests with none but God. In Him have I placed my trust, and Him alone should trust all those who need to place their trust'. **68** And when they entered as their father had bidden them, it did not profit them in the least against God. It was but a wish in Jacob's soul which he had thus fulfilled. He was endowed with knowledge which We had given him. But most people do not know it. **69** And when they presented themselves before Joseph, he drew his brother to himself, and said: 'I am your brother. Do not grieve over their past deeds'. **70** And when he had given them their provisions, he placed the [King's] drinking-cup in his brother's camel-pack. Then an announcer called out: 'You people of the caravan! You are surely thieves'. **71** Turning back towards them, they said: 'What is it that you have lost?' **72** 'We have lost the King's goblet', they answered. 'Whoever brings it shall have a camel-load [of grain as a reward]. I pledge my word for it'. **73** They said: 'By God, you know that we have not come to commit any evil deed in this land, and that we are no thieves'. **74** [The Egyptians] said: 'But what shall be the punishment for this deed, if you are proved to be lying?' **75** They replied: 'He in whose camel-pack it is found shall be enslaved in punishment for it. Thus do we punish the wrongdoers'. **76** Thereupon, [Joseph] began by searching their bags before the bag of his brother, and then took out the drinking-cup from his brother's bag. Thus did We contrive for Joseph. He had no right under the King's law to detain his brother, had God not so willed. We do exalt [in knowledge] whom We will, but above everyone who is endowed with knowledge there is One who knows all. **77** [Joseph's brothers] said: 'If he has stolen – well, a brother of his had stolen previously'. Joseph kept his secret to himself and revealed nothing to them, saying [within himself]: 'You are in a far worse position, and God knows best what you are speaking of'. **78** They said: 'High minister! This boy has a father who is very old. Take one of us instead of him. We see that you are indeed a generous man'. **79** He answered: 'God forbid that we should take any other than the man with whom we found our property; for then we would be wrongdoers'.

80 When they despaired of [moving] him, they withdrew to begin earnest consultations among themselves. The eldest of them said: 'Do you not recall that your father took from you a pledge in God's name, and that previously you were at fault with respect to Joseph? I shall not depart from this land until my father gives me leave or God judges for me. He is certainly the best of judges'. **81** Go back to your father and say: 'Father, your son has stolen. We testify only to that which we know. We cannot guard against the unforeseen. **82** You may ask the [people of the] town where we were, and the caravan with which we travelled. We are certainly telling the truth'. **83** He said: 'No, but your minds have tempted you to evil. Sweet patience! God may well bring them all back to me. He is the One who is all-knowing, wise'. **84** He then turned away from them and said: 'Oh, woe is me for Joseph!' His eyes became white with grief, and he was burdened with silent sorrow. **85** They said: 'By God, you will continue to remember Joseph until you wither away or until you are dead'. **86** He said: 'It is only to God that I complain and express my grief. For I know of God what you do not know'. **87** 'My sons, go and seek news of Joseph and his brother; and do not despair of God's mercy; for none but unbelievers can ever despair of God's mercy.' **88** When they presented themselves before [Joseph] again, they said: 'High minister! Hardship has befallen us and our people, and so we have brought but little merchandise. Give us our full measure [of grains], and be charitable to us. Indeed God rewards those who are charitable'. **89** He said: 'Do you know what you did to Joseph and his brother, when you were still unaware?' **90** They said: 'Why – is it indeed you who are Joseph?' He replied: 'I am Joseph, and this is my brother. God has indeed been gracious to us. If one remains God-fearing and patient in adversity, God will not fail to reward those who do good'. **91** They said: 'By God! Most certainly has God raised you high above us, and we were indeed sinners'. **92** He replied: 'None shall reproach you today. May God forgive you. He is indeed the most-merciful of those who show mercy'. **93** 'Now go and take this shirt of mine and lay it over my father's face, and he will recover his sight. Then come back to me with all your family.' **94** As the caravan set out, their father said [to the people around him]: 'I feel the breath of Joseph, though you will not believe me'. **95** They replied: 'By God! You are still lost in your old illusions'. **96** But when the bearer of good news arrived [with Joseph's shirt], he laid it over his face; and he regained his sight. He said: 'Did I not say to you that I know from God something that you do not know?' **97** [His sons] said: 'Father, pray to God to forgive us our sins, for we were sinners indeed'. **98** He said: 'I shall pray to God to forgive you. He is certainly the Most-Forgiving, the Ever-Merciful'. **99** When they all presented themselves before Joseph, he drew his parents to himself, saying: 'Enter Egypt in peace, if it so pleases God'. **100** And he raised his parents to the highest place of honour, and they fell down on their knees, prostrating themselves before him. He said: 'Father, this is the real meaning of my dream of long ago. My Lord has made it come true. He has been gracious to me, releasing me from prison, and bringing you all from the desert after Satan had sown discord between me and my brothers. My Lord is gracious in whatever way He wishes. He is the One who is all-knowing, wise'. **101** 'My Lord, You have given me power and imparted to me some understanding of the real meaning of statements. Originator of the heavens and the earth! You are my guardian in this world and in the life to come. Let me die as one who has surrendered himself to You, and admit me among the righteous.'

102 That is an account which We have now revealed to you, speaking of things that have been beyond your perception. You were not present when they [Joseph's brothers] resolved upon their plans and completed their schemes. **103** Yet however strongly you may desire it, most people will not believe. **104** You ask no recompense from them for it. It is but God's reminder to all mankind. **105** Yet many are the signs in the heavens and the earth which they pass by, paying no heed to them. **106** And most of them do not even believe in God without also associating partners with Him. **107** Do they feel confident that the overwhelming scourge of God's punishment will not fall upon them, or that the Last Hour will not come upon them all of a sudden, taking them unaware. **108** Say: 'This is my way. I call [all mankind] to God on the basis of sure knowledge, I and all those who follow me. Limitless is God in His glory. I am not one of those who associate partners with Him'. **109** Even before your time, We only sent [as messengers] men to whom We gave Our revelations, choosing them from among their people. Have they not travelled the land and seen what was the end of those [unbelievers] who lived before them? Better indeed is the life to come for those who remain God-fearing. Will you not, then, use your reason? **110** When at length [Our] messengers lost all hope and thought that they were denied, Our help came to them, saving those whom We willed [to be saved]. Never can Our [mighty] punishment be averted from people who are guilty. **111** Indeed their stories give a lesson to those who are endowed with understanding. This [revelation] could not possibly be an invented discourse. It is a confirmation of earlier revelations, an explanation of all things, as well as guidance and mercy for people who believe.

Surah 13   Thunder

This is a Makkan surah that derives its name from the mention of thunder as it extols the praises of God, glorifying Him. Thus, it gives a clear impression that all that is in the universe of creation, natural phenomena and operative laws are part of a complete system of creation that submits to God and is governed by His will.

The surah tackles the central theme of Makkan revelations, concentrating on the issues of God's Oneness, His message that provides guidance for human life, life after death and man's accountability for whatever he does in this present life.

The surah maintains the same rhythm and provides a consistent atmosphere, giving a wealth of contrasting images that leave us with the clear impression of a harmonious universe, shaped by the hand of God.

Thunder

In the Name of God, the Lord of Grace, the Ever-Merciful

1 *Alif. Lam. Mim. Ra.* These are verses of the Book. That which is revealed to you by your Lord is the truth, yet most people will not believe. 2 It is God who raised the heavens without any support that you could see, and established Himself on the Throne. And He it is who has made the sun and the moon subservient [to His laws], each pursuing its course for a set term. He ordains all things. He makes plain His revelations so that you may firmly believe that you will certainly be meeting your Lord. 3 It is He who has spread out the earth and placed upon it firm mountains and rivers, and created on it two sexes of every type of fruit, and caused the night to cover the day. In all these there are signs for people who think. 4 And there are on earth adjoining tracts of land; and vineyards, and fields of grains and date-palms, growing in clusters or non-clustered. [All] are irrigated by the same water; yet some of them are favoured above others with regard to the food [they provide]. In all this there are signs for people who use their reason. 5 But if you are amazed, amazing, too, is their saying: 'What! After we have become dust, shall we be raised [to life] in a new act of creation?' These are the ones who deny their Lord. They are the ones who carry their own shackles around their necks; and they are the ones who are destined for the Fire wherein

they will abide. **6** They ask you to hasten evil rather than good, although exemplary punishments have indeed come to pass before their time. Your Lord always extends forgiveness to people despite their wrongdoing. Yet your Lord is certainly severe in retribution. **7** The unbelievers say: 'Why has no miraculous sign been bestowed on him by his Lord?' But you are only a warner. Every community has [its] guide. **8** God knows what every female bears, and by how much the wombs may fall short [in gestation], and by how much they may increase. With Him everything has its definite measure. **9** He knows all that lies beyond the reach of human perception and all that anyone may witness. He is the Great One, the Most High. **10** It is all alike [to Him] whether any of you speaks in secret or aloud, whether he seeks to hide under the cover of the night or walks openly in the light of day. **11** Each has guardian angels before him and behind him, who watch him by God's command. Indeed God does not change a people's conditions unless they first change what is in their hearts. When God wills people to suffer some misfortune, none can avert it. Besides Him, they have none to protect them. **12** It is He who displays before you the lightning, giving rise to both fear and hope, and who originates the heavy clouds. **13** And the thunder extols His limitless glory and praises Him, and so do the angels, in awe of Him. He hurls the thunderbolts to smite with them whom He wills. Yet they stubbornly argue about God. His might is both stern and wise. **14** To Him is due the prayer aiming at the truth. Those whom people invoke beside God cannot respond to them in any way. They are just like a man who stretches his open hands towards water, [hoping] that it will come to his mouth; but it will never reach it. The prayer of those without faith is nothing but wandering in grievous error. **15** To God prostrate themselves, willingly or unwillingly, all those who are in the heavens and on earth, as do their very shadows, morning and evening. **16** Say: 'Who is the Lord of the heavens and the earth?' Say: '[It is] God'. Say: 'Why, then, do you take for your protectors, instead of Him, others who have no power to cause either benefit or harm even to themselves?' Say: 'Can the blind and the seeing be deemed equal? Or is the depth of darkness equal to light?' Or do they assign to God partners that have created the like of His creation, so that both creations appear to them to be similar? Say: 'God is the Creator of all things. He is the One who has power over all things'. **17** He sends down water from the sky, so that riverbeds flow according to their measure, and the torrent bears a swelling foam. Likewise, from what people smelt in the fire to make ornaments or utensils rises similar foam. Thus does God illustrate truth and falsehood. The scum is cast away, while that which is of benefit to mankind abides on earth. Thus does God set forth His parables. **18** For those who respond to their Lord is a rich reward. As for those who do not respond to Him, should they have all that the earth contains, and twice as much, they would gladly offer it for their ransom. Theirs shall be an awful reckoning, and Hell shall be their abode, an evil resting-place!

19 Is, then, he who knows that what has been revealed to you by your Lord is the truth like one who is blind? Only those who are endowed with understanding keep this in mind: **20** those who are true to their bond with God and never break their covenant; **21** and who keep together what God has bidden to be joined; who fear their Lord and dread the terrors of the reckoning; **22** who remain patient in adversity seeking the countenance of their Lord, and attend to their prayers, and spend in charity, secretly and openly, out of what We provide for them, and who repel evil with good. Such will have the attainment of the [ultimate] abode: **23** gardens of perpetual bliss, which they will enter together with the righteous from among their parents, their spouses and their offspring. The angels will come in to them from every gate, **24** [saying]: 'Peace be upon you, because you have persevered'. Blessed indeed is the attainment of the [ultimate] abode. **25** As for those who break their bond with God after it has been established, and cut asunder what God has bidden to be joined, and spread corruption on earth, the curse will be laid upon them; and theirs shall be an evil abode. **26** God grants abundant sustenance, or gives it in scant measure, to whomever He wills. They [the unbelievers] rejoice in the life of this world, even though, compared to the life to come, the life of this world is nought but a fleeting pleasure. **27** The unbelievers say: 'Why has no miraculous sign been bestowed on him by his Lord?' Say: 'God lets go astray anyone who wills [to go astray] and guides to Himself those who turn to Him; **28** those who believe and whose hearts find comfort in the remembrance of God. It is indeed in the remembrance of God that people's hearts find their comfort. **29** Those who believe and do righteous deeds shall have happiness and a most beautiful final goal'. **30** Thus have We sent you to a community before whom other communities had passed away, so that you might recite to them what We have revealed to you. Yet they deny the Lord of Grace. Say: 'He is my Lord. There is no deity other than Him. In Him have I placed my trust, and to Him shall I return'. **31** Even if there should be a Qur'an by which mountains could be moved, or the earth cleft asunder, or the dead made to speak! For certain, God's alone is the command in all things. Have they who believe not come to realise that, had God so willed, He would indeed have guided all mankind? As for the unbelievers, because of their misdeeds, calamity will always befall them or will fall close to their homes, until God's promise is fulfilled. God never fails to fulfil His promise. **32** Before your time, other messengers were derided, but for a while I gave rein to the unbelievers; but then I took them to task, and how [terrible] was My retribution. **33** Is, then, He who stands over every soul [and knows] all that it does [like any other]? Yet they ascribe partners to God. Say: 'Name them. Would you tell Him of anything on earth which He does not know; or are these merely empty words?' Indeed their own cunning devices seem fair to the unbelievers, and they are turned away from the right path. Whoever God lets go astray can never find any guide. **34** They shall endure suffering in the life of this world, but, truly, their suffering in the life to come will be harder still, and they will have none to shield them from God. **35** Such is the Paradise which the God-fearing have been promised: through it running waters flow. Its fruits will be everlasting, and so will be its shade. Such will be the destiny of those who fear God, while the destiny of the unbelievers is the Fire. **36** Those to whom We have given revelations rejoice at what has been bestowed on you from on high, but among different factions there are some who deny part of it. Say: 'I have only been bidden to worship God, and not to associate any partners with Him. To Him I pray, and to Him do I return'. **37** Thus have We revealed it, a code of judgement in the Arabic tongue. If you should follow their desires after all the knowledge you have been given, you shall have none to protect or shield you from God. **38** We have indeed sent messengers before you and given them wives and offspring. Yet no messenger could produce a miracle except by God's permission. Every age has had its revelation. **39** God annuls or confirms what He pleases. With Him is the source of all revelation. **40** Whether We let you see some of what We have promised them, or cause you to die [before its fulfilment], your duty is only to deliver your message: it is for Us to do the reckoning. **41** Do they not see how We gradually reduce the land from its outlying borders? When God judges, there is no power that could repel His judgement. He is swift in reckoning. **42** Those who lived before them also schemed, but God is the master of all scheming. He knows what is earned by every soul. The unbelievers will in time come to know who will attain the ultimate abode. **43** The unbelievers say: 'You are no messenger of God'. Say: 'God is sufficient as a witness between me and you, and so are those who have true knowledge of the Book'.

Surah 14   Abraham

This surah was revealed in Makkah and deals with the central issue of faith. It commences with a statement that the Qur'an is revealed so that it will bring mankind out of darkness into the light. It derives its name from its reference to Prophet Abraham and his supplication to God to make Makkah a secure city. It also refers to Abraham's request that God protect him and his offspring from worshipping anyone other than Him. The surah makes clear that its import is general and that worship of 'idols' not only means addressing worship to statues which are claimed to be deities. Instead, it has a more general import that includes whatever is given priority ahead of the divine message and its laws.

The surah focuses on two main facts relating to the divine faith: the first is that the message given to all prophets throughout human history is the same. All God's messengers advocated the same message and resisted disbelief in whatever form it took. No change in the message ever took place, despite the fact that God's messengers lived in widely different times and addressed greatly different communities. The second fact is that God bestows abundant grace on mankind, and His grace and favours will always be increased when people give due thanks for what He gives them.

Abraham

In the Name of God, the Lord of Grace, the Ever-Merciful

1 *Alif. Lam. Ra.* This is a Book which We have bestowed on you from on high so that you might bring forth all mankind, by their Lord's leave, from darkness into the light, to the path of the Almighty, the One to whom all praise is due, **2** to God, to whom all that is in the heavens and all that is on earth belongs. Woe to the unbelievers; for theirs will be a severe suffering. **3** These are the ones who love the life of this world preferring it to the life to come, and who turn others away from God's path and try to make it appear crooked. They have gone far astray. **4** Never have We sent a messenger otherwise than speaking the language of his own people, so that he might make [the truth] clear to them. But God lets go astray whomever He wills, and guides whomever He wills. He is almighty, wise. **5** We have sent forth Moses with Our revelations, saying, 'Lead your people out of darkness into the light, and remind them of the Days of God'. Surely in this there are signs for every one who is patient in adversity and deeply grateful [to God]. **6** Moses said to his people: 'Remember the blessings God bestowed on you when He saved you from Pharaoh's people who afflicted you with grievous torment, slaughtered your sons and spared [only] your women. That was indeed an awesome trial from your Lord'. **7** For your Lord had declared: 'If you are grateful, I shall certainly give you more; but if you are ungrateful, then My punishment shall be severe indeed'. **8** And Moses said: 'If you and whoever lives on earth were to deny God, [know that] God is indeed self-sufficient, worthy of all praise'. **9** Have you not received accounts of what befell those who lived before you? The people of Noah, the 'Ad, and Thamud, and those who came after them? None knows them all but God. Their messengers came to them with clear evidence of the truth, but they put their hands to their mouths, and said: 'We disbelieve in that with which you have been sent, and we are in grave doubt about that to which you call us'. **10** Said the messengers sent to them: 'Can there be any doubt about God, the Originator of the heavens and the earth? He calls you, so that He may forgive you your sins and grant you respite for an appointed term'. They replied: 'You are only human like ourselves. You want to turn us away from what our forefathers used to worship. Bring us, then, a clear proof'. **11** Their messengers replied: 'We are indeed only human like yourselves. But God bestows His grace on whomever He wills of His servants. It is not within our power to bring you any proof, except by God's leave. It is in God that all believers must place their trust. **12** And why should we not place our trust in God, when He has guided us on our paths? Hence we will bear with patience all your persecution. In God alone let all those who trust place their trust'. **13** The unbelievers said to their messengers: 'We shall most certainly expel you from our land, unless you return to our ways'. Their Lord revealed this to His messengers: 'Most certainly shall We destroy the wrongdoers, **14** and most certainly shall We cause you to dwell in the land long after they are gone. This [I promise] to all who stand in awe of My presence, and stand in awe of My warnings'. **15** 'And they prayed for God's help and victory [for the truth]. And every powerful, obstinate enemy of the truth shall come to grief. **16** Behind him stretches Hell where he shall be made to drink putrefied water, **17** gulping it little by little, and yet hardly able to swallow it. Death will beset him from every side, yet he shall not die. More severe suffering still awaits him. **18** The works of those who disbelieve in their Lord are like ashes which the wind blows about fiercely on a stormy day. They cannot achieve any benefit from all that they might have earned. This [disbelief] is indeed going very far astray. **19** Do you not see that God has created the heavens and the earth in accordance with the truth? If He so wills, He can do away with you and bring into being a new creation. **20** This is no difficult thing for God. **21** They will all appear before God, and then the weak will say to those who acted with arrogance: 'We were your followers: can you relieve us of something of God's punishment?' [And the others] will reply: 'Had God given us guidance, we would have guided you. It is now all one for us whether we grieve impatiently or endure with patience. There is no escape for us now'. **22** And when everything will have been decided, Satan will say: 'God has made you a true promise. I, too, made promises to you, but I did not keep them. Yet I had no power at all over you, except that I called you and you responded to me. Hence, do not now blame me, but blame yourselves. It is not for me to respond to your cries, nor for you to respond to mine. I have already disclaimed your associating me with God'. Indeed, for all wrongdoers there is painful suffering in store. **23** Those who believe and do righteous deeds will be admitted to gardens through which running waters flow, wherein they will abide, by their Lord's leave. Their greeting shall be: 'Peace'. **24** Do you not see how God compares a good word to a good tree? Its roots are firm and its branches reach to the sky. **25** It yields its fruits at all times by its Lord's leave. Thus does God set parables for people so that they may reflect. **26** And an evil word is like a corrupt tree, torn up onto the face of the earth. It cannot have a stable position. **27** God will strengthen the believers through the true, unshakeable word in both this life and the life to come; but the wrongdoers God lets go astray. God does whatever He wills.

28 Have you not seen those who have exchanged God's blessings for unbelief, and landed their people in the House of Perdition, **29** Hell, which they will have to endure? How vile a place to settle in! **30** They set up false deities as equal to God, and so they lead people to stray from His path. Say: 'Enjoy yourselves [in this life], for you will surely end up in Hell'. **31** Tell My servants who have attained to faith that they should attend regularly to their prayers and spend [in My way], secretly and openly, out of the sustenance We provide for them, before a Day shall come when there will be no trading and no friendship. **32** It is God who has created the heavens and the earth, and who sends down water from the sky with which He brings forth fruits for your sustenance. He has placed under your service ships which by His leave sail through the sea, and He has made the rivers subservient to [His law] for your benefit. **33** And for your benefit He has made the sun and the moon, both diligently pursuing their courses, subservient to [His law]; and has made the night and the day subservient to [His law]. **34** And He gives you of everything you ask of Him. Should you try to count God's blessings, you will never be able to compute them. Yet man is persistent in wrongdoing, stubbornly ungrateful. **35** Abraham said: 'My Lord! Make this land secure, and preserve me and my children from ever worshipping idols. **36** My Lord, they have indeed led many people astray. Hence, he who follows me belongs to me. As for him who disobeys me, well, You are truly much-forgiving, ever-merciful. **37** Our Lord, I have settled some of my offspring in a valley without cultivation, by Your Sacred House, so that they may establish regular prayers. So, cause You people's hearts to incline towards them, and provide them with fruits, so that they may give thanks. **38** Our Lord, You certainly know all that we conceal and all that we bring into the open: for nothing whatever, on earth or in heaven, can be hidden from God. **39** All praise is due to God who has given me, in my old age, Ishmael and Isaac. Surely my Lord hears all prayers. **40** My Lord, cause me and [some of] my offspring to establish regular prayers. My Lord, accept my prayer. **41** Our Lord, grant Your forgiveness to me and my parents, and all the believers on the Day when the reckoning will come to pass'. **42** Never think that God is unaware of what the wrongdoers are doing. He only grants them respite till the Day when eyes will stare fixedly in horror, **43** when they will be dashing in confusion, with their heads lifted up, unable to turn their eyes from what they behold, and their hearts an utter void. Hence, warn mankind of the Day when suffering may befall them; when those who do wrong will say: 'Our Lord, grant us respite for a short while, so that we may respond to Your call and follow Your messengers'. **44** 'Why? Did you not in time past swear that you would suffer no decline? **45** And you dwelt in the dwellings of those who wronged their own souls before you. Yet you knew for certain how We had dealt with them, and We placed many examples before you'. **46** They devised their plots, but their plots are all within God's grasp, even though their plots are so powerful as to move mountains. **47** Never think that God may ever fail to fulfil the promise which He has given to His messengers. Indeed God is almighty, avenger of evil! **48** On the Day when the earth shall be changed into another earth, as shall be the heavens, and when all people stand before God, the One who holds sway over all that exists. **49** On that Day you will see the guilty chained together in fetters, **50** wearing garments of black pitch, and their faces covered with flames. **51** God will requit each soul according to what it has done. God is indeed swift in reckoning. **52** This is a message to all mankind. Let them be warned thereby, and let them know that He is the One and Only God. Let those who are endowed with insight take heed.

Surah 15   Al-Hijr

This surah belongs to the last couple of years of the Makkan period, the same period during which Surahs 10, 11 and 12 were revealed. It was a period of extreme tension between the small Muslim community and the unbelievers who had physical and economic power. Therefore, the surah highlights the nature of those who reject these divine faiths, exposing their real motives. It starts with a stern warning to the stubborn rejecters, so that they should understand that they face a fearful outcome. Yet it makes clear that God has no wish to punish anyone. He is much-forgiving, ever-merciful. People should heed the lessons of past communities, such as the peoples who were addressed by the Prophets Lot, Shu'ayb and Salih. The surah presents various images of the world around us and the universe at large to drive home to people that God is the Creator of all and that believing in Him is the only way people should choose to ensure their happiness both in this life and the next.

Al-Hijr

In the Name of God, the Lord of Grace, the Ever-Merciful

1 *Alif. Lam. Ra.* These are the verses of the Book, a clear discourse. 2 Little do those who disbelieve wish that they were Muslims. 3 Let them eat and enjoy themselves, and let their hopes beguile them. For they will surely come to know [the truth]. 4 Never have We destroyed any community unless divine revelations have been made known to it. 5 No community can ever forestall its term, nor can they delay it. 6 They say: 'You to whom this reminder has been bestowed from on high! You are truly mad. 7 Why do you not bring the angels before us, if you are truthful?' 8 We never send down angels except in accordance with the truth. And then, [the unbelievers] would be given no further respite. 9 It is We Ourselves who have bestowed this reminder from on high, and it is We who shall preserve it intact. 10 Indeed We have sent before you messengers to communities of old, 11 but whenever a messenger came to any of them they mocked at him. 12 Thus do We cause it [this scorn of revelation] to slip into the hearts of the guilty, 13 who do not believe in it, although the ways of ancient communities have gone before them. 14 If We opened for the unbelievers a gateway to heaven and they had ascended higher

160   Surah 15   Al-Hijr

and higher, **15** still they would surely say: 'It is only our eyes that are spellbound! Indeed, we must have been bewitched'.

16 We have indeed set up in the heavens constellations, and endowed them with beauty for all to behold, **17** and We have guarded them from every cursed devil, **18** so that anyone who tries to eavesdrop is pursued by a flame clear to see. **19** We have spread out the earth, and placed on it firm mountains, and caused [life] of every kind to grow on it in a balanced manner. **20** We have placed various means of livelihood on it for you, as well as for those whom you do not have to provide for. **21** There is not a thing but with Us are its storehouses; and We send it down only in accordance with a defined measure. **22** We send forth winds heavily loaded, then We send down water from the skies for you to drink. You are not the ones who store it up. **23** It is We who give life and cause death, and it is We who are the inheritors [of all things]. **24** Well do We know those who lived before you and those who will come after you. **25** Your Lord will gather them all together. He is indeed wise, all-knowing.

26 Indeed We have created man out of sounding clay, out of black mud moulded into shape, **27** whereas the jinn We had created before him out of the fire of scorching winds. **28** Your Lord said to the angels: 'I am creating a human being out of sounding clay, out of black mud moulded into shape. **29** When I have fashioned him and breathed of My spirit into him, fall down in prostration before him'. **30** Thereupon, the angels, one and all, prostrated themselves. **31** Not so Iblis, who refused to be among those who prostrated themselves. **32** God said: 'Iblis! What is your reason for not being among those who have prostrated themselves?' **33** [Iblis] replied: 'I am not one to prostrate myself to a human being whom You have created out of sounding clay, out of mud moulded into shape'. **34** God said: 'Then get out of here, for you are accursed, **35** and the curse shall be on you till the Day of Judgement'. **36** Said [Iblis]: 'My Lord, grant me a respite till the Day when all shall be resurrected'. **37** [God] said: 'You are among those who are granted respite **38** till the Day of the appointed time'. **39** [Iblis] said: 'My Lord, since You have let me fall in error, I shall make [evil] seem fair to them on earth, and I shall most certainly beguile them all into grievous error, **40** except for those of them who are truly Your faithful servants'. **41** Said He: 'This is, with Me, a straight way. **42** You shall have no power over My servants, except for those who, having fallen into error, choose to follow you'. **43** 'For all such, Hell is the promised destiny. **44** It has seven gates, with each gate having its allotted share of them'. **45** The

God-fearing shall dwell amidst gardens and fountains. **46** [They are received with the greeting]: 'Enter here in peace and security'. **47** We shall have removed from their hearts any lurking feelings of malice, [and they shall rest] as brothers, facing one another, on couches. **48** No weariness shall ever touch them there, nor shall they ever be made to depart.

49 Tell My servants that I alone am much-forgiving, ever-merciful; **50** and also, My punishment is indeed the most grievous suffering. **51** Tell them about Abraham's guests, **52** when they went in to him and said: 'Peace'. But he replied: 'We feel afraid of you'. **53** They said: 'Do not be alarmed. We bring you the happy news of the birth of a son to you who will be endowed with knowledge'. **54** Said he: 'Do you give me this happy news when I have been overtaken by old age? Of what, then, is your good news?' **55** They replied: 'That good news we have given you is the truth. So do not abandon hope'. **56** He said: 'Who but a person going far astray abandons hope of His Lord's grace?' **57** [Abraham] said: 'What is your business, you [heavenly] messengers?' **58** They replied: 'We are sent to a guilty nation, **59** except for Lot's household, all of whom we shall save, **60** except for his wife'. We have decreed that she should remain with those who stay behind. **61** And when the messengers [of God] came to the house of Lot, **62** he said: 'You are unknown here'. **63** They answered: 'No, but we bring you news of that over which they have been disputing. **64** We are bringing you the certainty [of its fulfilment], for we are speaking the truth indeed. **65** Depart with your household in the dead of night, with yourself following them in the rear. Let none of you look back, but proceed to where you are commanded'. **66** And We made plain the case to him, that the last remnant of those [wrongdoers] will be wiped out by the morning. **67** The people of the city came [to Lot] rejoicing [at the news of the young people]. **68** Said he: 'These are my guests: so do not put me to shame. **69** Fear God and do not bring disgrace on me'. **70** They replied: 'Have we not forbidden you to entertain any people?' **71** He said: 'Here are these daughters of mine [to marry], if you must do [what you intend to do]'. **72** By your life, they were reeling in their drunkenness, **73** when the blast [of punishment] overtook them at sunrise, **73** and We turned those [towns] upside down, and rained on them stones of clay. **75** Surely in this there are messages for those who read the signs. **76** Those [towns] stood on a road that is trodden still. **77** In all this there is a sign for true believers. **78** The dwellers of the wooded dales [of Madyan] were also wrongdoers, **79** and so We punished them. Both these [communities] lived by an open highway, plain to see. **80** Likewise, the people of al-Hijr also denied [God's] messengers. **81** We have given them Our signs, but they turned their backs on them. **82** Out of the mountains did they hew their dwellings, leading a life of security. **83** But the blast [of punishment] overtook them at early morning. **84** Of no avail to them was all that they had acquired.

85 It was only with the truth that We have created the heavens and the earth and all that is between them. The appointed Hour will certainly come. Hence overlook their faults in fair forbearance. **86** Your Lord is the All-Knowing Creator. **87** We have given you seven oft-repeated verses and this sublime Qur'an. **88** Do not turn your eyes longingly to the good things We have granted to some among them, and do not grieve on their account, but spread the wings of your tenderness over the believers, **89** and say: 'I am indeed the plain warner'. **90** Just as We have bestowed from on high on those who later broke it into parts, **91** and declared the Qur'an to be a confused medley. **92** But, by your Lord, We will call them all to account **93** for whatever they have done. **94** Therefore, proclaim what you are bidden and turn away from those who associate partners with God. **95** We shall suffice you against all who deride [this message – all] **96** who claim that there are other deities beside God. They shall certainly come to know. **97** We know that you are distressed by what they say. **98** But extol your Lord's limitless glory and praise Him, and be among those who prostrate themselves before Him, **99** and worship your Lord till the certainty [of death] comes to you.

Surah 16   The Bees

This surah concentrates on the major issues of faith: Godhead, revelation, resurrection and individual accountability. It chooses a mild and calm rhythm, but its background is the great expanse of the universe: its heavens and earth, the pouring rain, the growing trees, the succession of day and night, the sun, the moon, the stars, the oceans, the mountains, the great events of this life and the different destiny in the life to come. All these are God's creation, and He tells us that He creates what we do not know.

Very early in the surah we are reminded of the great many blessings God has placed in the universe for mankind. They are all around us in land, sea and air, but they also come from the world beyond us. We are then reminded that the One who creates is unlike any other. His blessings are countless and He continues to give them because he is much-forgiving, ever-merciful.

Towards its end, the surah mentions Prophet Abraham and tells us that he was grateful for God's favours. We will do well to follow his lead and show our gratitude to God for all His favours that He continues to bestow on us all.

The Bees

In the Name of God, the Lord of Grace, the Ever-Merciful

1 God's judgement is bound to come; so do not seek to hurry it on. Limitless is He in His glory and sublimely exalted above anything people may associate with Him. 2 He sends down angels with this divine inspiration, [bestowed] by His will on such of His servants as He pleases: 'Warn [mankind] that there is no deity other than Me: so fear Me'. 3 He has created the heavens and the earth in truth; sublimely exalted is He above anything people may associate with Him. 4 He creates man out of a drop of sperm; yet this same man is openly contentious. 5 He creates cattle which give you warmth and other benefits; and from them you obtain food. 6 And you find beauty in them when you drive them home in the evening and when you take them out to pasture in the morning. 7 And they carry your loads to distant lands, which you could not otherwise reach without much hardship to yourselves. Your Lord is certainly most-compassionate, ever-merciful. 8 And [He creates] horses, mules and asses for you to

ride or put on show. And He creates other things of which you have no knowledge. **9** It is God alone who points to the right path. Yet many may swerve from it. Had He so willed, He would have guided you all aright. **10** It is He who sends down water from the skies. From it you drink, and with it grow the plants on which you pasture your cattle. **11** And with it He causes crops to grow for you, and olive trees, and date-palms, and grapes, and all other kinds of fruit. Surely in this there is a sign for people who think. **12** And He has made the night and the day and the sun and the moon to be subservient to you; and all the stars are subservient to His command. In this there are signs for people who use their reason. **13** On the earth He has fashioned for you objects of various hues; surely in this there is a sign for people who take heed. **14** It is He who has made the sea subservient to [His laws], so that you may eat fresh meat from it, and take from it gems which you may wear. You see the ships ploughing through the waves, so that you may be able to go forth in quest of His bounty, and that you may be grateful. **15** He has placed firm mountains on earth lest it should sway with you; and rivers and paths so that you may find your way, **16** as well as landmarks. By the stars, too, are people guided. **17** Is He, then, who creates like one that cannot create? Will you not think? **18** Should you try to count God's blessings, you will never be able to compute them. God is indeed much-forgiving, ever-merciful. **19** God knows all that you keep secret and all that you bring into the open. **20** Those beings that some people invoke beside God cannot create anything; they themselves are created. **21** They are dead, not living, and they do not know when they will be raised back to life.

22 Your God is the One God. Those who deny the life to come have hearts that persist in denying the truth. They are full of arrogance. **23** God surely knows what they keep secret and all that they bring into the open. He does not love those who are arrogant. **24** Whenever they are asked, 'What has your Lord bestowed from on high?' they say: 'Fables of the ancients!' **25** On the Day of Resurrection they shall bear the full weight of their burdens, as well as some of the burdens of those ignorant ones whom they have led astray. Evil is the burden they shall bear. **26** Those who lived before them also schemed. But God struck their edifice at its foundation, and its roof fell in upon them from above, and suffering befell them from where they did not perceive. **27** Then, on the Day of Resurrection He will cover them with ignominy, and say: 'Where are those alleged partners of Mine concerning whom you have engaged in dispute?' Those who are endowed with knowledge will say: 'Ignominy and misery shall this day befall the unbelievers, **28** those whom the angels have gathered in death while they are still wronging themselves'. These will then offer their submission, saying: 'We have done no wrong!' [They will be answered]: 'Yes, indeed. God has full knowledge of all that you were doing! **29** Enter the gates of Hell, where you shall abide'. Evil indeed is the abode of the arrogant! **30** But when the God-fearing are asked: 'What has your Lord revealed?' they say: 'All that is good'. For those who do good in this world, good reward [is assured]; but far better is their abode in the Hereafter. Blessed is the dwelling place of the God-fearing. **31** The Gardens of Eden they will enter; through which running waters flow. There they shall have everything they desire. Thus shall God reward the God-fearing; **32** those whom the angels gather in death while they are in a state of purity, saying: 'Peace be upon you! Enter Paradise by virtue of what you were doing [in life]'. **33** Are they [who disbelieve] awaiting anything but for the angels to appear before them, or for your Lord's command to come? Those before them did the same. It was not God who wronged them, but it was they who wronged themselves. **34** The evil consequences of their misdeeds overtook them, and they were overwhelmed by the very thing they used to deride. **35** Those who associate partners with God say, 'Had God so willed, neither we nor our forefathers would have worshipped any other than Him, nor would we have declared anything forbidden without a commandment from Him'. Those before them said the same. Are the messengers bound to do anything other than to clearly deliver the message? **36** Indeed, We have raised a messenger in every community, [who said to them]: 'Worship God and shun the Evil One'. Among them were some whom God graced with His guidance, while others were inevitably doomed by their error. Go, then, about the earth and observe what was the end of those who denied the truth. **37** However eager you may be to show them the right way, [know that] God does not bestow His guidance upon any whom He judges to have gone astray. They shall have none to support them. **38** They most solemnly swear by God that God never raises the dead to life. Yes indeed! That is a promise to which He has bound Himself, even though most people do not know it. **39** [Thus] He will make clear to them the reality of matters over which they differ, and the unbelievers will know that they were liars. **40** Whenever We will anything to be, We need only say, 'Be' – and it is. **41** As for those who forsake their homes for the sake of God after having suffered injustice, We shall most certainly give them a fine abode in this life; yet better still is their reward in the life to come, if they but knew it. **42** [Such reward is granted to] those who, having been patient in adversity, place their trust in their Lord. **43** The messengers We sent before you were but men whom We inspired. So, if you have not realised this, ask those who are endowed with knowledge. **44** [We sent such messengers] with clear proofs and divine books, and We have now bestowed on you the reminder so that you may elucidate to mankind all that has been bestowed on them, and that they may take thought. **45** Do those who devise evil schemes feel secure that God will not cause the earth to swallow them, or that suffering will not befall them whence they do not perceive? **46** – Or that He will not suddenly take them to task in the midst of their comings and goings; for they can never frustrate His design? **47** – Or that He will seize them when they are alert and apprehensive? Surely your Lord is most-compassionate, ever-merciful. **48** Do people not see how every object God has created casts its shadow right and left, prostrating itself before God in complete submission? **49** For, before God prostrates itself every living thing in the heavens and the earth, as do the angels. They do not behave in arrogant defiance. **50** They fear their Lord, who is high above them, and do as they are bidden.

51 God has said: 'Do not take [for worship] two deities, for He is but one God. Hence, of Me alone stand in awe'. **52** His is all that is in the heavens and the earth, and to Him alone submission is always due. Will you then fear anyone but God? **53** Whatever blessing you have comes from God; and whenever harm befalls you, it is to Him that you cry out for help. **54** Yet no sooner does He remove the harm from you than some among you associate partners with their Lord, **55** [as if] to show their ingratitude for what We have given them. Enjoy, then, your life [as you may]; before long you will come to know [the truth]. **56** They assign a share of the sustenance We provide for them to what they know nothing of. By God, you shall certainly be called to account for your false inventions. **57** And they assign daughters to God, who is limitless in His glory, whereas for themselves they choose what they desire. **58** And when any of them is given the happy news of the birth of a girl, his face darkens and he is filled with gloom. **59** He tries to avoid all people on account of the [allegedly] bad news he has received, [debating within himself:] shall he keep the child despite the shame he feels, or shall he bury it in the dust? Evil indeed is their judgement. **60** To those who do not believe in the life to come applies the attribute of evil, whereas to God applies the attribute of all that is most sublime, for He is almighty, wise. **61** If God were to take people to task for their wrongdoing, He would not leave a single living creature on the face [of the earth]. But He gives them respite for a set term. When their time arrives, they cannot delay it by an hour, nor can they hasten it. **62** They attribute to God what they hate [for themselves]. And their tongues assert the lie that theirs is the supreme reward. Without doubt, it is the Fire that awaits them, and they will be hastened on into it. **63** By God, We have sent messengers to various communities before your time, but Satan made their foul deeds seem fair to them. He is also their patron today. A grievous suffering awaits them. **64** We have bestowed upon you from on high this Book for no other reason than that you may make clear to them those issues on which they differ, and [to serve] as guidance and grace to people who believe. **65** And God sends down water from the skies, giving life to the earth after it has been lifeless. In this there is surely a sign for people who listen. **66** In cattle too you have a worthy lesson: We give you to drink of that [fluid] which is in their bellies, produced alongside excretions and blood: pure milk, pleasant to those who drink it. **67** And from the fruit of the date-palms and vines you derive intoxicants and wholesome food. Surely in this there is a sign for people who use their reason. **68** Your Lord has inspired the bee: 'Take up homes in the mountains, in the trees and in structures people may put up. **69** Then eat of all manner of fruit, and follow humbly the paths your Lord has made smooth for you'. There issues from its inside a drink of different colours, a cure for people. Surely in this there is a sign for people who think. **70** It is God who has created you; and in time will cause you to die. Some of you are left to the most feeble stage of life, so that they no longer know what they had previously known. God is indeed all-knowing, infinite in His power. **71** To some of you God has given more than He has given to others. Those who are so favoured are unwilling to share their provisions with those whom their right hands possess, so that they are all equal in this respect. Will they, then, deny God's favours? **72** And God has given you spouses of your own kind and has given you, through your spouses, children and grandchildren, and provided you with wholesome sustenance. Will they, then, believe in falsehood and deny God's grace and blessings? **73** Instead of God, they worship something that can provide them with no sustenance from the heavens or the earth. Never can they have such power. **74** Do not, then, compare anything with God. Indeed, God knows all, whereas you have no knowledge. **75** God makes this comparison between a man enslaved, unable to do anything of his own accord, and a [free] man on whom We have bestowed goodly favours, and he gives of it both in private and in public. Can these two be equal? All praise is to God alone, but most people have no knowledge. **76** And God makes another comparison between two men, one of whom is dumb and can do nothing of his own accord. He is a sheer burden to his master: wherever he sends him, he accomplishes no good. Can he be considered equal to one who enjoins justice and follows a straight path?

77 To God belong the hidden secrets of the heavens and the earth. The advent of the Last Hour will be accomplished in a twinkling of an eye, or closer still. God has power over all things. **78** God has brought you forth from your mothers' wombs devoid of all knowledge, but He has given you hearing, and sight, and minds, so that you may be grateful. **79** Do they not see the birds and how they are enabled to fly in mid-air? None but God holds them aloft. In this there are signs for people who will believe. **80** And God has made your homes as places of rest, and has given you dwellings out of the skins of animals, which are easy for you to handle when you travel and when you camp. Out of their wool, fur and hair, He has given you furnishings and articles of convenience for temporary use. **81** And God has made for you, out of the many things He has created, shelter and shade, and has given you places of refuge in the mountains, and has furnished you with garments to protect you from the heat and other garments to protect you from your [mutual] violence. Thus does He perfect His favours to you, so that you may submit to Him. **82** But if they turn away [from you, remember that] your only duty is to deliver [your message] clearly. **83** They are certainly aware of God's favours, but they nevertheless refuse to acknowledge them. Most of them are unbelievers. **84** One day We will raise up a witness from every community, but then the unbelievers will not be allowed to make pleas, nor will they be allowed to make amends. **85** And when the wrongdoers actually see the suffering [that awaits them], it will in no way be mitigated for them, nor will they be granted respite. **86** And when those who associate partners with God will see their [alleged] partners, they will say: 'Our Lord, these are our partners whom we used to invoke instead of You'. But they will throw their word back at them, saying: 'You are indeed liars'. **87** On that Day, they shall proffer submission to God; and all their inventions will have forsaken them. **88** Upon those who disbelieve and debar others from the path of God We will heap suffering upon suffering in punishment for all the corruption they wrought. **89** One day We will raise up within every nation a witness from among themselves to testify against

them. And We will bring you, [Prophet] as a witness against these
[your people]. We have bestowed from on high upon you the Book to
make everything clear, and to provide guidance and grace, and to give
good news to those who submit themselves to God.

90 God enjoins justice, kindness [to all], and generosity to one's
kindred; and He forbids all that is shameful, all reprehensible conduct
and aggression. He admonishes you so that you may take heed.
91 Fulfil your covenant with God whenever you make a pledge. Do
not break your oaths after you have confirmed them, and have made
God your surety. God certainly knows all that you do. **92** Be not like
her who untwists the yarn which she has firmly spun, using your
oaths as a means to deceive one another, simply because a particular
group may be more powerful than another. By this, God puts you
to the test. On the Day of Resurrection He will make clear to you
all that on which you now differ. **93** Had God so willed, He would
have surely made you all one single community. But He lets go astray
him that wills [to go astray] and guides aright him that wills [to be
guided]. You shall certainly be called to account for all that you do.
94 Do not use your oaths as a means to deceive one another, lest your
foot should slip after it has been firm, and lest you should be made
to suffer the evil [consequences] of your having debarred others from
the path of God, with tremendous suffering awaiting you. **95** Do not
barter away your covenant with God for a trifling price. Surely, that
which is with God is far better for you, if you but knew it. **96** Whatever
you have is certain to come to an end, but that which is with God is
everlasting. We will certainly grant those who are patient in adversity
their reward according to the best that they ever did. **97** Whoever
does righteous deeds, whether man or woman, and is a believer, We
shall most certainly give a good life. And We shall indeed reward
these according to the best that they ever did. **98** Whenever you read
the Qur'an, seek refuge with God from Satan, the accursed. **99** He
certainly has no power over those who believe and place their trust
in their Lord. **100** He has power only over those who are willing
to follow him, and thus ascribe to him a share in God's divinity.
101 When We replace one verse by another – and God knows best
what He reveals – they say: 'You are but a fabricator'. Indeed most
of them have no knowledge. **102** Say: 'The Holy Spirit has brought it
down from your Lord in truth, so as to strengthen the believers, and to
provide guidance and good news to those who surrender themselves
to God'. **103** We know fully well that they say: 'It is but a man that
teaches him [all] this'. But the man to whom they so maliciously

allude speaks a foreign tongue, while this is Arabic speech, pure and clear. **104** Those who do not believe in God's revelations shall not be granted guidance by God. Painful suffering awaits them. **105** It is only those who do not believe in God's revelations that invent falsehood. It is they indeed who are liars. **106** As for anyone who denies God after having accepted the faith – and this certainly does not apply to one who does it under duress, while his heart remains true to his faith, but applies to him who willingly opens his heart to unbelief – upon all such falls God's wrath, and theirs will be a tremendous suffering. **107** This is because they love the life of this world better than the life to come. God does not bestow His guidance on those who reject the truth. **108** Such are those whose hearts and ears and eyes are sealed by God; such are the heedless. **109** Without doubt, in the life to come they will be the losers. **110** But then, your Lord [grants forgiveness] to those who forsake their homes after enduring trials and persecution, and strive hard [in God's cause] and remain patient in adversity. After all this, your Lord is certainly much-forgiving, ever-merciful. **111** One day every soul will come pleading for itself. Every soul will be repaid in full for all its actions, and none shall be wronged.

112 God cites the case of a town living in security and ease. Its sustenance comes to it in abundance from all quarters. Yet it was ungrateful for God's favours. Therefore, God caused it to experience the misery of hunger and fear for what its people used to do. **113** There had come to them a messenger from among themselves, but they denied him. Therefore, suffering overwhelmed them as they were wrongdoers. **114** So eat of all the lawful and good things God has provided for you, and be grateful to God for His favours, if it is truly him that you worship. **115** He has forbidden you only carrion, blood, the flesh of swine and anything over which any name other than God's has been invoked. But if anyone is driven to it by necessity, neither desiring it nor exceeding his immediate need, then God is much-forgiving, ever-merciful. **116** Do not say – for any false thing you may utter with your tongues – that 'This is lawful and this is forbidden', so as to attribute your lying inventions to God. Indeed those who attribute their lying inventions to God will never be successful. **117** Brief is their enjoyment [of this life], and grievous suffering awaits them [in the life to come]. **118** To the Jews We have made unlawful such things as We have mentioned to you earlier. We did them no wrong, but they were the ones who persistently wronged themselves. **119** But indeed your Lord [grants forgiveness] to those who do evil out of ignorance, and then repent and mend their ways.

After all this, your Lord is certainly much-forgiving, ever-merciful. **120** In truth Abraham was a model, devoutly obedient to God, and true in faith. He was not one of those who associated partners with God. **121** He showed his gratitude for the blessings bestowed by Him who had chosen him and guided him to a straight path. **122** We bestowed on him good in this world; and truly, in the life to come he will be among the righteous. **123** And now We have inspired you with [this message]: 'Follow the creed of Abraham, who was true in faith, and who was not one of those who associated partners with God'. **124** [The observance of] the Sabbath was ordained only to those who differed about him. Your Lord will judge between them on the Day of Resurrection with regard to all that on which they dispute. **125** Call people to the path of your Lord with wisdom and goodly exhortation, and argue with them in the most kindly manner. Your Lord knows best who strays from His path and who are rightly guided. **126** If you should punish, then let your punishment be commensurate with the wrong done to you. But to endure patiently is far better for those who are patient in adversity. **127** Endure, then, with patience, remembering always that it is only God who helps you to be patient; and do not grieve over them, nor be distressed by their intrigues. **128** God is indeed with those who remain God-fearing and those who do good.

Surah 17   The Night Journey

This surah takes its name from the Prophet's night journey, when he was taken by the Angel Gabriel from Makkah to Jerusalem, and from there to heaven, before returning to Makkah. All this took place on the same night, shortly after the death of his first wife, Khadijah and his uncle Abu Talib.

The surah starts with a reference to this night journey. Its main theme is the Prophet himself, the unbelievers' attitude towards him and to the Qur'an given to him, the nature of the Qur'an and the guidance it provides. It also speaks of the nature of the divine message and the messengers who delivered it to their peoples at different times. It makes clear that as delivered to Muhammad (peace be upon him), the divine message does not provide material miracles aimed to show the unbelievers God's limitless power. It was a divine law that when God gave people any such miracle and they continued to deny His message, refusing to believe in Him, they were destroyed totally, as happened to the peoples of Prophets Hud and Salih. In its treatment of its main theme, the surah establishes the Islamic concept of God's Oneness in perfect clarity. It is this concept that should be the basis of human society. The surah also shows the absurdity of pagan beliefs and calls on believers to continue along their way, paying no heed to their enemies' attempts to divert them from their course.

The Night Journey

In the Name of God, the Lord of Grace, the Ever-Merciful

1 Limitless in His glory is He who transported His servant by night from the Sacred Mosque [in Makkah] to the Aqsa Mosque [in Jerusalem] – the environs of which We have blessed – so that We might show him some of Our signs. Indeed He alone is the One who hears all and sees all. 2 We gave Moses the Book and made it a [source of] guidance for the Children of Israel, saying: 'Do not take anyone for a guardian other than Me. 3 You are the descendants of those whom We carried [in the ark] with Noah. He was a truly grateful servant of Ours'. 4 We made it clear to the Children of Israel in the Book: 'Twice will you spread corruption on earth and will indeed become grossly overbearing'. 5 When the prediction of the first of these came true, We sent against you some of Our servants of great

might who wrought havoc throughout the land. Thus [Our] warning came to be fulfilled. **6** Then We let you prevail against them once more, and We gave you wealth and offspring, and made you more numerous [than ever. And We said:] **7** 'If you do good, you will be but doing good to yourselves; and if you do evil, it will be also against yourselves'. And when the second prediction came true, [We allowed your enemies] to disgrace you utterly, and to enter the Mosque just like [their predecessors] had entered it the first time, and to visit with destruction all that fell into their power. **8** It may be that your Lord will have mercy on you; but if you revert [to your old ways], We shall revert [to punishing you]. Indeed We have made Hell a place of confinement for the unbelievers. **9** Surely this Qur'an shows the way to that which is most upright. It gives the believers who do good deeds the happy news that theirs will be a rich reward; **10** and [declares] that We have prepared a grievous suffering for those who do not believe in the life to come. **11** Yet man prays for evil as eagerly as he prays for good. Truly man is ever hasty. **12** We have made the night and the day as two [of Our] signs. Then We have effaced the sign of the night while the sign of the day We have left enlightened, so that you may seek bounty from your Lord, and you may learn to compute the years and be able to reckon. Most clearly have We spelled out everything. **13** Every human being's action have We tied around his own neck. On the Day of Resurrection We shall produce for him a record which he will find wide open. **14** [And We will say:] 'Read this your record! Sufficient it is for you today that your own soul should make out your account'. **15** Whoever chooses to follow guidance does so for his own good, and whoever goes astray does so to his own loss. No soul shall be made to bear the burden of another. We would never inflict punishment [on anyone] until We have sent a Messenger [to give warning]. **16** When it is Our will to destroy a community, We convey Our command to those of its people who live a life of affluence. If they persist in sin, judgement is irrevocably passed, and We utterly destroy them. **17** Many generations have We destroyed since Noah's time. Suffice it that your Lord is well aware of His servants' sins, and observes them all. **18** As for those who care only for [the pleasures of] this fleeting life, We readily grant of it whatever We may please to whomever We will. In the end We consign any such person to Hell, where he will burn disgraced and rejected. **19** But those who care only for the life to come, strive for it as it should be striven for, and are true believers, are indeed the ones who will have their endeavours well rewarded. **20** On all – these as well as those – do We bestow the bounty of your Lord. Indeed your Lord's bounty is not denied [to anyone]. **21** See how We have bestowed more bounty on some than on others. But the life to come will be higher in rank and greater in merit.

22 Do not set up any deity side by side with God, lest you find yourself disgraced, forsaken. **23** Your Lord has ordained that you shall worship none but Him, and that you must be kind to your parents. Should one of them, or both, attain to old age in your care, never say 'Ugh' to them or chide them, but always speak gently and kindly to them, **24** and spread over them humbly the wings of your tenderness, and say, 'My Lord, bestow on them Your grace, even as they reared and nurtured me when I was a child'. **25** Your Lord knows best what is in your hearts. If you are righteous, He is certainly most-forgiving to those who turn repeatedly to Him [seeking His mercy]. **26** Give to the near of kin their due, and also to the needy and the traveller in need. Do not squander your substance wastefully, **27** for the wasteful squanderers are Satan's brothers, and Satan has always been ungrateful to His Lord. **28** But if you must turn aside from them in pursuit of an act of kindness you hope to receive from your Lord, then at least speak to them kindly. **29** Do not be miserly, allowing your hand to remain shackled to your neck, nor stretch it out fully to the utmost limit, lest you find yourself being blamed or reduced to destitution. **30** Your Lord gives in abundance, or in scant measure, to whom He wills. He is indeed fully aware of all His servants, and sees them all. **31** Do not kill your children for fear of want. It is We who shall provide for them and for you. To kill them is indeed a great sin. **32** Do not come near adultery. It is indeed an abomination and an evil way. **33** Do not kill any one, for God has forbidden killing, except in [the pursuit of] justice. If anyone is slain wrongfully, We have given his heir authority [to seek just retribution]. He [the heir] must not exceed the bounds of equity in [retributive] killing. He is given help. **34** Do not come near the property of an orphan before he comes of age, except with the best of intentions. Be true to all your promises, for you will be called to account for all that you promise. **35** And give full measure whenever you measure, and weigh with accurate scales. That is fair, and best in the end. **36** Do not pursue that of which you have no knowledge. Man's ears, eyes and heart shall all be called to account. **37** Do not walk on earth with an air of self conceit; for you cannot rend the earth asunder, nor can you rival the mountains in height. **38** All this is evil; odious in your Lord's sight. **39** These [injunctions] are but a part of the wisdom with which your Lord has inspired you. Do not set up any deity alongside God, lest you should be cast into Hell, blamed and rejected.

40 Has your Lord distinguished you by [giving you] sons and taken for Himself daughters from among the angels? That which you utter is indeed an enormity. **41** We have certainly explained things in various ways in this Qur'an, so that they may take it to heart, but it only increases their aversion. **42** Say: 'If there were other deities alongside Him, as some people assert, they would have to seek a way to the Lord of the Throne. **43** Limitless is He in His glory and sublimely exalted is He above everything they may say [about Him]'. **44** The seven heavens extol His limitless glory, as does the earth, and all who dwell in them. Indeed every single thing extols His glory and praise, but you cannot understand their praises. He is indeed clement, much-forgiving. **45** When you read the Qur'an, We place an invisible barrier between you and those who do not believe in the life to come. **46** We cast a veil over their hearts which makes them unable to grasp its meaning, and their ears We make deaf. And so, when you mention your Lord in the Qur'an as the One and only God, they turn their backs in aversion. **47** We are fully aware of what they are listening for when they listen to you, and what they say when they speak to each other in private. The wrongdoers say: 'The man you follow is certainly bewitched'. **48** See to what they liken you. They have certainly gone astray and are unable to find a way back [to the truth]. **49** They say: 'When we are bones and dust, shall we be raised to life again as a new creation?' **50** Say: 'Be you stones or iron, **51** or some other form of creation which, to your minds, appears even harder [to bring to life]'. They will say: 'Who is it that will bring us back [to life]?' Say: 'He who created you the first time'. Thereupon they shake their heads [in disbelief] and ask: 'When will this be?' Say: 'It may very well be near at hand. **52** On that Day He will call you, and you will answer by praising Him, thinking that you stayed on earth but a very short while'. **53** Tell My servants that they should always say that which is best. Satan tries to sow discord between them. Satan is indeed man's open foe. **54** Your Lord is fully aware of what you are. If He so wills, He will bestow His grace on you; and if He so wills, He will inflict punishment on you. We have not sent you, Prophet, to be their guardian. **55** Your Lord is fully aware of all beings that are in the heavens and earth. Indeed We have exalted some of the prophets above others, just as We gave the Psalms to David. **56** Say: 'Call on those whom you claim [to be gods] besides Him, but they have no power to remove any affliction from you, nor can they shift it'. **57** Those whom they invoke strive to obtain their Lord's favour, vying with each other to be near Him. They hope for His grace and dread His punishment. Indeed your Lord's punishment is something to beware of.

58 There is no community but We shall destroy or severely punish before the Day of Resurrection. That is laid down in Our decree. **59** Nothing hinders us from sending miraculous signs except that the people of former times treated them as false. To the Thamud We gave the she-camel as a sign to open their eyes, but they did wrong in respect of her. We never send signs for any purpose other than to give warning. **60** We said to you that your Lord encompasses all mankind. We have made the vision which We have shown you, as also the tree cursed in this Qur'an, only a trial for people. We seek to put fear in their hearts, but it only increases their gross transgression. **61** When We said to the angels, 'Prostrate yourselves before Adam', they all prostrated themselves; but not so Iblis. He said, 'Am I to bow down before one whom You have created out of clay?' **62** And he added: 'You see this being whom You have exalted above me! Indeed, if You will give me respite until the Day of Resurrection, I shall bring his descendants, all but a few, under my sway'. **63** [God] said: 'Begone! As for those of them who follow you, Hell will be the recompense of you all, a most ample recompense. **64** Entice with your voice such of them as you can. Muster against them all your cavalry and your infantry, and share with them wealth and offspring, and promise them [what you will] – indeed, whatever Satan promises them is nothing but a means of deception. **65** But over My servants you shall have no power. Your Lord is sufficient as a guardian'. **66** Your Lord is He who makes ships go smoothly through the sea, so that you may go about in quest of His bounty. He is indeed most-merciful to you. **67** And when you are in distress at sea, all those you may call upon to help you will forsake you, except Him. Yet when He has brought you safe to dry land, you turn away. Indeed, bereft of all gratitude is man! **68** Can you feel so sure that He will not let a tract of the land cave in beneath you, or let loose against you a deadly stormwind? You will not find then anyone to protect you. **69** Or can you feel so sure that He will not let you go back to sea again, and then let loose against you a violent tempest to drown you for your ingratitude? You shall not find then anyone to help you against Us. **70** We have indeed honoured the children of Adam, and borne them over land and sea, and provided for them sustenance out of the good things of life, and favoured them far above many of Our creatures. **71** One Day We shall summon every community by their leaders. Those who are given their records in their right hands will read their records. None shall be wronged by as much as a hair's breadth. **72** But whoever is blind in this world will be even more blind in the life to come, and still further astray from the path of truth.

73 They endeavour to tempt you away from that which We have revealed to you, hoping that you would invent something else in Our name, in which case they would have made you their trusted friend. **74** Indeed, had We not given you strength, you might have inclined to them a little. **75** And in that case We would have made you taste a double punishment in life and a double punishment after death, and you would have none to support you against Us. **76** And they endeavour to scare you off the land with a view to driving you away. But, then, after you have gone, they will not remain there except for a short while. **77** Such was the way with all Our messengers whom We sent before you. No change shall you find in Our ways. **78** Keep up prayer when the sun is on its decline, in the darkness of the night, and recite the Qur'an at dawn, for the recitation of the Qur'an at dawn is indeed witnessed. **79** At night, rise from your sleep to recite it in prayer, as an additional offering from you. Your Lord may thus raise you to an honourable station. **80** Say, 'My Lord, cause me to enter in a true and sincere manner and to leave in a true and sincere manner, and grant me, by Your grace, sustaining strength'. **81** And say, 'The truth has now come about while falsehood has withered away. For falsehood is always bound to wither away'. **82** We bestow of the Qur'an from on high what serves as a healing and a blessing to true believers, while it only adds to the ruin of the evildoers. **83** Yet when We bestow Our blessings on man, he turns his back and draws arrogantly aside, and when he is afflicted by evil he gives himself up to despair. **84** Say, 'Everyone acts according to his own disposition. Your Lord is fully aware as to who has chosen the best path'. **85** They question you about the spirit. Say, 'The [knowledge of the nature of the] spirit belongs to my Lord alone. You, [mankind], have been granted but little knowledge. **86** Had We so willed, We would have taken away that which We have revealed to you. In that case, you would not find anyone to plead with Us on your behalf, except through the grace of your Lord. **87** His favour towards you has been great indeed'. **88** Say, 'If all mankind and the jinn were to gather together for the purpose of producing the like of this Qur'an, they would not produce anything like it, even though they pooled their resources together [for the purpose]'. **89** Indeed We have explained to mankind, in this Qur'an, every kind of lesson. Yet most people refuse to accept anything other than unbelief. **90** They say: 'We shall not believe in you till you cause a spring to gush forth for us from the earth, or you have a garden of date-palms and vines, **91** and you cause rivers to flow through it, **92** or you cause the sky to fall upon us in pieces, as you have threatened, or you bring God and the angels face to face before us, or you have a house of gold, or you ascend to heaven. Indeed we shall not believe in your ascent to heaven until you bring us a book for us to read'. **93** Say, 'Limitless in His glory is my Lord. Surely I am only a man and a Messenger'. **94** Nothing has ever prevented people from believing, whenever guidance came to them except that they would say: 'Can it be that God has sent a human being as His messenger?' **95** Say, 'Had there been angels walking about on earth as their natural abode, We would have sent them an angel messenger from heaven'. **96** Say, 'Sufficient is God for a witness between me and you. He is indeed fully aware of His servants, and He sees all things'. **97** He whom God guides is indeed rightly guided; whereas for those whom He leaves to go astray you cannot find anyone to protect them from Him. On the Day of Resurrection We shall gather them together, prone upon their faces, blind, dumb and deaf. Hell shall be their abode. Every time it abates We will increase for them its blazing flame. **98** That is their reward for having disbelieved in Our revelations and said, 'When we are bones and dust, shall we be raised to life again as a new creation?' **99** Do they not see that God, who has created the heavens and the earth, has power to create their like? He has beyond any doubt set a term for their resurrection. But the evildoers refuse to accept anything other than unbelief. **100** Say, 'Had you possessed the treasures of my Lord's mercy, you would have been tight-fisted for fear of spending them. For man has always been miserly'. **101** To Moses We gave nine clear signs. Ask the Children of Israel [about what happened]. When he came to them, Pharaoh said to him, 'Indeed, Moses, I think that you are bewitched'. **102** [Moses] said, 'You know full well that none other than the Lord of the heavens and the earth has revealed these eye-opening signs. Indeed, Pharaoh, I think that you are utterly lost'. **103** So he resolved to wipe them off the face of the earth, but We caused him and all those who were with him to drown. **104** Then We said to the Children of Israel, 'Dwell in the land. When the promise of the Last Day shall come to pass, We will bring you all together'. **105** We have bestowed [this Qur'an] from on high in truth, and in truth has it come down. We have sent you only as a herald of good news and a warner. **106** We have divided the Qur'an into parts so that you may recite it to people with deliberation. We have indeed bestowed it from on high step by step. **107** Say, 'You may believe in it or you may not'. Those who were given knowledge before it was revealed fall down on their faces in humble prostration when it is recited to them, and say, 'Limitless in His glory is our Lord. **108** Truly has the promise of our Lord been fulfilled'. **109** And upon their faces they fall down, weeping, and it increases their humility. **110** Say, 'Call upon God or call upon the Lord of Grace. By whichever name you invoke Him, His are the most gracious names'. Do not raise your voice too loud in prayer, nor say it in too low a voice, but follow a middle course in between. **111** And say, 'All praise is due to God who has never begotten a son; who has no partner in His dominion; who needs none to support Him against any difficulty'. And extol His greatness.

Surah 18   The Cave

The main theme of this surah is faith, its concepts, principles and values. It sets the proper code for evaluating beliefs, views and practices so that people can judge matters and adopt what is right. The surah portrays all this by relating several stories. It tells us first about the young men who defied their pagan society and believed in God's Oneness. When they feared persecution by their people, they sought refuge in a cave, where they were overtaken by sleep.

The surah then gives us the story of two friends and their debate on the main concept of God's Oneness and resurrection after death. The third story given in the surah is that of Moses and his association with a good man, who was given guidance by God and ordered to do certain actions that appeared totally against proper values. They are subsequently explained to show that God only commands what is good and proper. Finally the surah gives us the story of the good king who establishes justice and undertakes great tasks to ensure the welfare of people and who helps them to guard against the perpetrators of evil.

The Cave

In the Name of God, the Lord of Grace, the Ever-Merciful

1 All praise is due to God who has bestowed this Book from on high on His servant, and has ensured that it remains free of distortion, 2 unerringly straight, meant to warn people of a severe punishment from Himself, and to give the believers who do good works the happy news that they shall have a goodly reward 3 which continues to be theirs forever. 4 Furthermore, it warns those who assert, 'God has taken to Himself a son'. 5 No knowledge whatever have they of Him, and neither had their forefathers. Dreadful indeed is this saying that issues from their mouths. Nothing but falsehood do they utter. 6 Would you, perhaps, torment yourself to death with grief over them if they will not believe in this message? 7 We have made all that is on earth as an adornment in order to test people as to which of them are best in conduct; 8 and, in time, We shall indeed reduce all that is on it to barren dust. 9 Do you think that the People of the Cave and the Inscription were a wonder among Our signs? 10 When those youths took refuge in the cave, they said: 'Our Lord! Bestow on us Your grace, and provide for us right guidance in our affairs'. 11 So

We drew a veil over their ears in the cave, for a number of years, **12** and then We awakened them so that We might mark out which of the two parties managed to calculate the time they had remained in that state. **13** We shall relate to you their story in all truth. They were young men who believed in their Lord, so We increased them in guidance. **14** We put courage in their hearts, so that they stood up and said: 'Our Lord is the Lord of the heavens and the earth. Never shall we call upon any deity other than Him. If we did, we should indeed have uttered an enormity! **15** These people of ours have taken for worship deities other than Him, without being able to show any convincing proof of their beliefs. Who does more wrong than he who invents a lie about God?' **16** Hence, now that you have withdrawn from them and all that they worship instead of God, take refuge in the cave. God may well spread His grace over you and make fitting arrangements for you in your affairs. **17** You might have seen the sun, on its rising, incline away from their cave on the right, and, on its setting, turn away from them on the left, while they lay in a space within. That was one of God's signs. He whom God guides is indeed rightly guided, but for him whom He lets go astray you can never find any protector who would point out the right way. **18** You would have thought that they were awake, when they were certainly asleep. And We turned them over repeatedly, now to the right, now to the left; and their dog lay at the cave's entrance, with its forepaws outstretched. Had you come upon them, you would have certainly turned away from them in flight, and would surely have been filled with terror of them. **19** Such being their state, We awakened them; and they began to question one another. One of them asked: 'How long have you remained thus?' They answered: 'We have remained thus a day, or part of a day'. They said: 'Your Lord knows best how long you have remained thus. Let, then, one of you go with these silver coins to the town, and let him find out what food is purest there, and bring you some of it. But let him behave with great care and by no means make anyone aware of you. **20** For, indeed, if they should come to know of you, they might stone you to death or force you back to their faith, in which case you would never attain to any good!'[17]

---

17   The discussion between these people is expressed using second person pronouns, although some if not all, might have been given in the first person such as: 'How long have we remained thus?' and 'Our Lord knows best'. I considered putting it thus, but, on reflection, decided to retain the pronouns as they are given in the Arabic, even though it may give the impression that the speaker is not one of the group. In the original Arabic, there is absolutely no confusion.

21 In this way have We drawn people's attention to their case, so that they might know that God's promise is true and that there can be no doubt as to the Last Hour. The people disputed among themselves as to what happened to them. Some of them said: 'Erect a building in their memory. God knows their case best'. Those whose opinion prevailed in the end said: 'Indeed, we must surely raise a house of worship in their memory'. **22** Some will say, 'They were three, the fourth of them being their dog', while others will say, 'Five, with their dog being the sixth of them', idly guessing at the unknown. Yet others will say, 'They were seven, the eighth of them being their dog'. Say: 'My Lord knows best how many they were. None but a few have any real knowledge of them'. Hence, do not enter into argument about them, except on a matter that is clear, nor ask anyone of these people to enlighten you about them. **23** Never say about anything, 'I shall do this tomorrow', without adding, 'if God so wills'. **24** Should you forget, then call your Lord to mind and say, 'I pray that my Lord will guide me even closer than this to what is right'. **25** So they stayed in their cave three hundred years, and [some] add nine years more. Say: 'God knows best how long they remained there. His alone is the knowledge of the secrets of the heavens and earth. **26** How well does He see and hear! No guardian have they apart from Him; nor does He allot to anyone a share in His rule'. **27** Recite whatever has been revealed to you of your Lord's Book. There is nothing that could alter His words. You can find no refuge other than with Him.

28 And contain yourself in patience with those who call on their Lord morning and evening, seeking His countenance. Let not your eyes pass beyond them in quest of the beauties of the life of this world. Pay no heed to any whose heart We have left to be negligent of all remembrance of Us because he always followed his own desires, and whose case has gone beyond all bounds. **29** Say: 'The truth [has now come] from your Lord. Let him who wills, believe in it, and let him who wills, reject it'. For the wrongdoers We have prepared a Fire whose billowing folds will encompass them from all sides. If they beg for water, they will be given water [hot] like molten lead, which will scald their faces. Dreadful is the drink, and evil is the place to seek rest. **30** As for those who believe and do righteous deeds – We, for certain, do not fail to reward any who perseveres in doing good. **31** Theirs shall be gardens of perpetual bliss, with rivers rolling at their feet. There they will be adorned with bracelets of gold and will wear green garments of silk and brocade, and they will recline on couches. Excellent is the recompense, and comfortable is the place to rest. **32** Set forth to them the case of two men, to one of whom We gave two vineyards and surrounded them with date-palms, and placed a field of grain in between. **33** Each of the two gardens yielded its produce and never failed to do so in any way. In the midst of them We caused a stream to flow. **34** And so [the man] had fruit in abundance. This man said once to his friend, in the course of a discussion between them, 'More wealth have I than you, and more power and followers'. **35** And having thus wronged his soul, he went into his garden, saying: 'I do not think that this will ever perish! **36** Nor do I think that the Last Hour will ever come. But even if [it does and] I am brought before my Lord, I should surely find there something better than this in exchange'. **37** His friend replied in the course of their discussion: 'Do you deny Him who has created you out of dust, and then out of a drop of sperm, and in the end fashioned you into a man? **38** But for my part, I believe that He is God, my Lord, and none shall I associate with my Lord. **39** If only you said as you entered your garden, "Whatever God wills [shall come to pass, for] there is no power except with God!" Although, as you see, I have less wealth and offspring than you, **40** yet it may well be that my Lord will give me something better than your garden, just as He may let loose a calamity out of heaven upon this [your garden], so that it becomes a heap of barren dust **41** or its water sinks deep into the ground, so that you will never be able to find it'. **42** So his fruitful gardens were encompassed with ruin, and there he was, wringing his hands over all that he had spent on that which now lay waste, with its trellises caved in; and he could only say: 'Would that I had not associated partners with my Lord!' **43** He had none to support him against God, nor was he able to save himself. **44** For thus it is: all protection comes from God, the True One. He is the best to grant reward and the best to [determine] outcome. **45** Set forth to them a simile about the life of this world: [it is] like the water which We send down from the skies, and which is absorbed by the plants of the earth. In time they turn into dry stubble which the winds blow freely about. It is God alone who has power over all things. **46** Wealth and children are the adornment of the life of this world: but the things that endure, good deeds, are of far greater merit in your Lord's sight, and a far better source of hope.

47 One day We shall cause the mountains to move and you will see the earth void and bare. We will gather them all together, leaving out not a single one of them. **48** They will be lined up before your Lord, [and He will say]: 'Now you have come to Us as We created you in the first instance, although you claimed that We would never appoint for you a time [for your resurrection]!' **49** The record [of everyone's deeds] will be laid open; and you will see the guilty filled with dread at what it contains. They will say: 'Woe to us! What a record is this! It leaves out nothing, small or great, but takes everything into account'. They will find all that they ever wrought now facing them. Your Lord does not wrong anyone. **50** When We said to the angels: 'Prostrate yourselves before Adam', they all prostrated themselves. Not so Iblis, who belonged to the jinn and he disobeyed his Lord's command. Will you, then, take him and his progeny for your masters instead of Me, when they are enemies to you? Vile is the substitute for the wrongdoers! **51** I did not call them to witness the creation of the heavens and the earth, nor their own creation; nor do I seek aid from those who lead people astray. **52** One day He will say, 'Call now on those beings whom you alleged to be My partners!' They will invoke them, but those [beings] will not respond to them; for We shall have placed an unbridgeable gulf between them. **53** And when those who were lost in sin will see the Fire, they will realise that they are bound to fall in it, and will find no way to escape from it. **54** We have indeed given in this Qur'an many facets to every kind of lesson for mankind. But man is, above all else, always given to contention. **55** What is there to keep people from accepting the faith now that guidance has come to them, and from seeking forgiveness from their Lord, unless it be that they are waiting for the fate of the [sinful] people of ancient times to befall them as well, or for the suffering to be brought before their eyes? **56** We send Our messengers only as bearers of good news and as warners. But with false arguments the unbelievers seek to refute the truth. They make My revelations and warnings a target for their mockery. **57** Who could be more wicked than one who, when reminded of his Lord's revelations, turns away from them and forgets what his own hands have done? Over their hearts We have cast veils which prevent them from grasping the truth, and into their ears, deafness. Even if you call them to the right path, they shall never be guided. **58** Your Lord is most-forgiving, limitless in His grace. Were He to take them now to task for whatever they do, He would indeed bring about their speedy punishment. But they have an appointed time which they cannot evade. **59** The same applied to other communities which We destroyed when they persisted in wrongdoing. For We had set a time for their destruction.

60 Moses said to his servant: 'I shall journey on until I reach the point where the two seas meet, though I may march for ages'. **61** But when they reached the junction between the two seas, they forgot their fish, and it took its way into the sea and disappeared from sight. **62** And after they had marched on for some distance, Moses said to his servant: 'Bring us our mid-day meal; we are indeed worn out by this our journey'. **63** Said [the servant]: 'Do you recall when we stopped at that rock for a rest. There I forgot the fish – and none but Satan made me thus forget it! – and it took its way into the sea. How strange' **64** [Moses] said: 'That is [the place] we are seeking!' So they turned back, retracing their footsteps, **65** and found one of Our servants, on whom We had bestowed Our mercy and whom We had endowed with knowledge of Our own. **66** Moses said to him: 'May I follow you, on the understanding that you will teach me something of the wisdom you have been taught?' **67** The other answered: 'You will not be able to have patience with me, **68** for how can you be patient with something which you cannot fully comprehend?' **69** Moses replied: 'You will find me patient, if God so wills; and I shall not disobey you in anything'. **70** The other said: 'Well, then, if you are to follow me, do not question me about anything until I mention it to you myself'. **71** And so the two went on their way, and when they embarked, [the sage] made a hole in the boat. Moses exclaimed: 'Have you made a hole in it in order to drown the people in it? Strange indeed is that which you have done!' **72** He replied: 'Did I not say that you would not be able to have patience with me?' **73** Moses said: 'Do not take me to task for my having forgotten, and be not hard on me on account of what I have done'. **74** And so the two went on until they met a certain young man. [The sage] slew him, whereupon Moses exclaimed: 'Have you killed an innocent man with no cause of just retribution for murder? Foul indeed is that which you have perpetrated!' **75** He replied: 'Did I not make it clear to you that you would not be able to have patience with me?' **76** Moses said: 'If ever I question you again, do not keep me in your company; for then you would have had enough excuses from me'. **77** And so the two went on until they came to a town, where they asked its people for food, but they refused them all hospitality. There they found a wall on the point of falling down, and [the sage] rebuilt it. Moses said: 'Had you wished, you could have taken payment for what you did'. **78** [The sage] replied: 'This is the parting of ways between me and you. Now I shall explain to you the real meaning of all [those events] which you were unable to bear with patience. **79** As for the boat, it belonged to some needy people who toiled upon the sea – and I desired to slightly damage it because behind them there was a king who was taking every boat by force. **80** And as for the young man, his parents are true believers, and we feared lest he should cause them much grief by his overweening wickedness and unbelief. **81** And so we desired that their Lord grant them in his stead [a son] of greater purity than him, and closer in loving tenderness. **82** And as for the wall, it belonged to two orphan boys living in the town, and beneath it was buried a treasure belonging to them. Their father had been a righteous man. So your Lord has willed it that when they come of age they should dig up their treasure by your Lord's grace. I did not do any of this of my own accord. This is the real meaning of all [those events] which you were unable to bear with patience'.

83 They will ask you about Dhul-Qarnayn. Say: 'I will give you an account of him'. **84** We established his power on earth, and gave him means to achieve anything. **85** So he followed a certain way and [marched westwards] till, when he came to the setting of the sun, it appeared to him that it was setting in dark, turbid waters; and nearby he found a certain people. **86** 'Dhul-Qarnayn', We said, 'you may either punish them or treat them with kindness'. **87** He replied: 'The one who does wrong we shall punish. Then he will return to his Lord and be sternly punished by Him. **88** But the one who believes and does righteous deeds shall have a goodly reward, and we shall assign to him a task that is easy to fulfil'. **89** Then he followed another way **90** and [marched eastwards] till, when he came to the rising of the sun, he found that it was rising on a people for whom We had provided no coverings against it. **91** So he did; and We had full knowledge of all the means available to him. **92** Then he followed yet another way **93** and [marched on] till, when he reached a place between the two mountain-barriers he found beneath them a people who could scarcely understand a word. **94** 'Dhul-Qarnayn', they said, 'Gog and Magog are ravaging this land. May we pay you a tribute so that you erect a barrier between us and them?' **95** He answered: 'That with which my Lord has established me is better [than any tribute]. Hence, do but help me with strength, and I shall erect a rampart between you and them! **96** Bring me blocks of iron!' At length, when he had filled up the gap between the two mountain-sides, he said: 'Ply your bellows!' Then, when he made [the iron glow like] fire, he said: 'Bring me molten copper which I will pour over it'. **97** And thus their enemies were unable to scale [the rampart], nor could they dig their way through it. **98** He said: 'This is a mercy from my Lord. Yet when the time appointed by my Lord shall come, He will make this [rampart] level with the ground. My Lord's promise always comes true'. **99** On that Day We shall leave them to surge like waves dashing against one another. The Trumpet will be blown, and We shall gather them all together. **100** And We shall, on that Day, present Hell, all spread out, for the unbelievers, **101** who have turned a blind eye to My admonition and a deaf ear to My warning. **102** Do the unbelievers think that they could take My creatures for patrons against Me? We have indeed readied Hell as a dwelling place for the unbelievers. **103** Say: 'Shall we tell you who are the greatest losers in whatever they may do? **104** It is they whose labour in this world has been misguided, and who nonetheless think that what they do is right. **105** It is they who have chosen to disbelieve in their Lord's revelations and deny the truth that they will meet Him. Vain will be their works. No weight shall We assign to them on Resurrection Day. **106** That will be their reward, Hell, for having rejected the faith, and made My revelations and My messengers a target of their mockery'. **107** But those who have faith and do righteous deeds shall have the Gardens of Paradise as their dwelling place. **108** Therein they will abide, and never will they desire any change to befall them. **109** Say: 'If the sea were ink for my Lord's words, the sea would surely dry up before my Lord's words are exhausted, even though we were to add to it another sea to replenish it'. **110** Say: 'I am but a human being like yourselves. It has been revealed to me that your God is the One and only God. Hence, whoever expects to meet his Lord [on Judgement Day], let him do what is right, and in the worship due to his Lord admit no one as partner'.

Surah 19   Mary

The larger part of this surah is devoted to stories of earlier prophets, beginning with Zachariah and how he was given a son in his old age. This is followed by the story of the birth of Jesus to his virgin mother, Mary. It establishes the truth of Jesus, leaving no room for argument about his human status. A portion of Abraham's history is then told, concentrating on his call on his father to believe in God and to ascribe no aspect of Godhead to anyone else. These stories are then followed by brief references to several prophets, concluding with a statement outlining the nature of the prophethood.

The final third of the surah is devoted to a discussion of life after death. It mentions what happens when people are resurrected and how their fate is sealed. It presents particularly powerful descriptions of the universe as it denounces the very idea of associating partners with God.

Mary

In the Name of God, the Lord of Grace, the Ever-Merciful

1 *Kaf. Ha. Ya. 'Ayn. Sad.* **2** This is an account of the grace which your Lord bestowed on His servant Zachariah: **3** when he called out to his Lord in the secrecy of his heart, **4** he prayed: 'My Lord! Feeble have become my bones, and my head glistens with grey hair. But never, my Lord, has my prayer to You remained unanswered. **5** Now, I fear [what] my kinsmen [will do] after I am gone, for my wife is barren. Bestow, then, upon me, out of Your grace, a successor **6** who will be my heir as well as an heir of the House of Jacob; and make him, my Lord, one with whom You are pleased'. **7** 'Zachariah! We bring you the happy news of [the birth of] a son whose name shall be John. Never have We given this name to anyone before him.' **8** [Zachariah] said: 'My Lord! How can I have a son when my wife is barren, and I am well advanced in years?' **9** He said: 'Thus it is. Your Lord says, "This is easy for Me; even as I had earlier created you when you were nothing".' **10** [Zachariah] said: 'My Lord! Give me a sign'. He replied: 'Your sign will be that for three full nights [and days] you will not speak to people'. **11** He then came out to his people from the sanctuary and signified to them [by gesture] to extol God's limitless glory by day and by night. **12** [To his son We said]: 'John! Hold fast to the Book with [all your] strength'. **13** We granted him wisdom while he was still a youth, as well as, by Our grace, compassion and purity; and he was [always] God-fearing, and kind to his parents. **14** Never was he haughty or rebellious. **15** So peace was upon him on the day he was born, and on the day of his death, and will be on the day when he shall be raised to life again. **16** Relate in the Book [the story of] Mary and how she withdrew from her family to a place in the east, where she kept herself in seclusion from them. **17** We, then, sent to her Our Spirit, who appeared to her in the shape of a well-made human being. **18** She said: 'May the Lord of Grace protect me from you. [Do not come near me] if you fear God'. **19** 'I am but an emissary of your Lord', he said, '[and have come] to give you a son endowed with purity'. **20** She said: 'How shall I have a child when no man has ever touched me and I have never been a loose woman?' **21** He answered: 'Thus did your Lord speak: This is easy for Me. We will make him a sign for mankind and an act of grace from Us. It is a matter [We have] decreed'. **22** So she conceived him, and retired to a far-off place. **23** And the throes of childbirth drove her to the trunk of a palm-tree. [In her anguish] she cried: 'Would that I had died before this and passed into complete oblivion!' **24** But [a voice] from below called out to her: 'Do not give in to grief. **25** Your Lord has provided a brook running beneath you. Shake the trunk of the palm-tree towards you, and it will drop you fresh ripe dates. **26** So eat and drink and be happy. Should you see any human being, just convey this to him: "I have vowed a fast to the Lord of Grace and will not speak today to any human being".' **27** At length, she went to her people carrying the child. **28** They said: 'Mary, you have indeed done an amazing thing! Sister of Aaron, your father was not a wicked man, nor was your mother a loose woman!' **29** But she pointed to the child. They said: 'How can we talk to a babe in the cradle?' **30** Whereupon he said: 'I am a servant of God. He has revealed to me revelations and made me a prophet, and made me blessed wherever I may be. **31** He has enjoined on me prayer and charity as long as I live. **32** He has made me kind to my mother, not haughty or bereft of grace. **33** Peace was on me on the day when I was born, and [will be on me] on the day of my death and on the day when I shall be raised to life again'. **34** Such was, in the words of truth, Jesus the son of Mary, about whose nature they still dispute. **35** It is not conceivable that God should beget a son. Limitless is He in His glory! When He wills a thing to be, He only says to it, 'Be', and it is. **36** God is my Lord and your Lord; so worship Him alone. That is a straight path. **37** Yet are the sects at variance among themselves. Woe, then, to the unbelievers when a momentous Day arrives. **38** How well they will hear and see on the Day they will appear before Us. Truly the wrongdoers are today in evident error. **39** Hence, warn them of the Day of Distress, when everything will have been determined while they remain heedless, persisting in unbelief. **40** We alone shall remain after the earth and all who live on it have passed away. To Us they shall all return.

41 Mention in the Book Abraham. He certainly was a man of truth and a prophet. **42** He said to his father: 'My father! Why do you worship something that neither hears nor sees and can be of no avail whatever to you? **43** My father! There has come to me knowledge which you do not have. Follow me, and I shall guide you along a straight path. **44** My father! Do not worship Satan, for Satan has indeed rebelled against [God] the Lord of Grace. **45** My father! I dread lest a scourge will fall upon you from the Lord of Grace, and then you will become one of Satan's friends'. **46** He answered: 'Are you renouncing my gods, Abraham? If you do not desist, I shall most certainly have you stoned. Now begone from me for good!' **47** Abraham replied: 'Peace be on you. I shall pray to my Lord to forgive you; for He has always been very kind to me'. **48** 'But I shall withdraw from you all and from whatever you invoke instead of God, and I shall pray to my Lord alone. Perhaps, by my prayer to my Lord I shall not be unblest.' **49** When he had withdrawn from them and from all that they were worshipping instead of God, We bestowed on him Isaac and Jacob, each of whom We made a prophet. **50** We bestowed on them of Our mercy and We granted them the high honour of [conveying] the truth. **51** And mention in the Book Moses, who was a chosen one, a messenger of God and a prophet. **52** We called out to him from the right side of Mount Sinai and drew him near [to Us] in mystic communion. **53** We gave him, out of Our grace, his brother Aaron, to be a prophet. **54** And mention in the Book Ishmael who was always true to his promise, and was a messenger of God, a prophet. **55** He used to enjoin on his people prayer and charity, and his Lord was well pleased with him. **56** And mention in the Book Idris, who was a man of truth, a prophet. **57** We raised him to a lofty station. **58** These were some of the prophets upon whom God bestowed His blessings – of the seed of Adam, and of those whom We carried in the ark with Noah, and of the seed of Abraham and Israel, and of those whom We had guided and chosen. When the revelations of [God] the Lord of Grace were recited to them they fell down prostrating themselves [before Him] and weeping. **59** They were succeeded by generations who neglected their prayers and followed only their lusts; and these will, in time, meet with utter disillusion. **60** Excepted, however, shall be those who repent, believe and do righteous deeds. These will enter the Garden and will not be wronged in any way: the Gardens of Eden which [God] the Lord of Grace has promised to His servants, in the realm that lies beyond the reach of human perception. **61** Indeed, His promise is certain of fulfilment. **62** There they will hear no idle talk, but only the voice of peace. And their sustenance shall be given them there morning and evening. **63** Such is the Paradise which We shall give the righteous among Our servants to inherit. **64** We descend only by the command of your Lord. To Him belongs all that is before us and all that is hidden from us and all that is in between. Never does your Lord forget anything. **65** He is the Lord of the heavens and the earth and all that is between them. Worship Him alone, then, and remain steadfast in His worship. Do you know any whose name is worthy to be mentioned side by side with His?

66 'What!' says man, 'When I am once dead, shall I be raised up alive?' **67** Does not man remember that We earlier created him, when he was nothing? **68** By your Lord, We shall most certainly bring them forth together with the evil ones, and then We shall most certainly gather them, on their knees, around Hell; **69** and thereupon We shall drag out from every group those who had been most obstinate in their rebellion against the Lord of Grace. **70** For, indeed, We know best who most deserve to be burnt in the fire of Hell. **71** There is not one among you who shall not pass over it: this is, for your Lord, a decree that must be fulfilled. **72** But We shall save those who are God-fearing, and leave the wrongdoers there, on their knees. **73** When Our revelations are recited to them in all their clarity, the unbelievers say to those who believe: 'Which of the two sides has a better position and a superior community?' **74** How many a generation have We destroyed before their time, who were superior in material riches and in splendour. **75** Say: 'As for those who live in error, may the Lord of Grace lengthen their span of life!' But when they see the fulfilment of that of which they have been forewarned, be it suffering or the Last Hour, they will realise who is worst in position and weaker in forces. **76** God advances in guidance those who seek His guidance. Good deeds of lasting merit are, in your Lord's sight, worthy of greater recompense, and yield far better returns. **77** Have you ever considered [the case of] the one who denies Our signs and boasts: 'I shall surely be given wealth and children!' **78** Has he, perchance, attained to a realm which is beyond the reach of human perception? Or has he concluded a covenant with the Lord of Grace? **79** By no means! We shall record what he says, and We shall long extend his suffering, **80** and We shall divest him of all that he is now speaking of, and he shall appear before Us all alone. **81** They have taken to worshipping deities other than God, hoping that they will give them power and glory. **82** By no means! They will renounce their worship and turn against them. **83** Have you not seen how We let loose satanic forces upon the unbelievers to repeatedly incite them to evil? **84** So, be not in haste: We only allow them a fixed number of days. **85** The Day [will surely come] when We shall gather the God-fearing before [God] the Lord of Grace, as honoured guests, **86** and drive those who are lost in sin to Hell as a thirsty herd. **87** None will have power to intercede for them except one who has received permission from [God] the Lord of Grace. **88** They say: 'The Lord of Grace has taken to Himself a son!' **89** Indeed you have said a most monstrous falsehood, **90** at which the heavens might be rent into fragments, and the earth be split asunder, and the mountains fall down in ruins! **91** That people should ascribe a son to the Lord of Grace, **92** although it is inconceivable that the Lord of Grace should take to Himself a son. **93** Not one of all [the beings] that are in the heavens or on earth but shall appear before the Lord of Grace as a servant. **94** Indeed, He has full cognisance of them. He has kept a strict count of their numbers, **95** and, on the Day of Resurrection, every one of them will appear before Him all alone. **96** As for those who believe and do righteous deeds, God will certainly bestow love on them. **97** And so have We made [the Qur'an] easy to understand, in your own tongue, so that you may give good tidings to the God-fearing and give warning to those who are given to futile contention. **98** How many a generation have We destroyed before their time! Can you find a single one of them now, or hear so much as a whisper of them?

Surah 20   Ta Ha

The two separate letters that begin this surah give it its name. It starts and ends with an address to the Prophet defining his role. A large part of the surah is devoted to Moses' story, beginning at the start of his mission when God commands him to go and warn Pharaoh. Details of his meeting with Pharaoh and the latter's response are given before the episode with Pharaoh's sorcerers gathered to demonstrate tricks that might ensure that his people remain subservient to him. The drowning of Pharaoh and his troops is mentioned in the context of Moses and his people being saved. The story of Moses continues up to the time his people started to worship the calf.

The surah makes a brief reference to Adam and how God bestowed mercy on him after he sinned. He was given guidance and his descendants are given freedom of choice: either to follow divine guidance or to go astray. The surah also shows scenes of the Day of Judgement as it brings the end of human life which began with the creation of Adam, his fall and the message addressed to mankind.

Ta Ha

In the Name of God, the Lord of Grace, the Ever-Merciful

1 *Ta. Ha.* **2** We did not bestow this Qur'an on you from on high to cause you distress, **3** but only as an admonition to the God-fearing. **4** It is a revelation from Him who has created the earth and the high heavens, **5** the Lord of Grace, established on the throne of His almightiness. **6** To Him belongs all that is in the heavens and on earth, as well as all that is between them, and underneath the soil. **7** If you say anything aloud, then [know that] He knows all that is secret, as well as all that is yet more hidden. **8** [He is] God; there is no deity other than Him. His alone are all the attributes of perfection. **9** Have you learnt the story of Moses? **10** When he saw a fire, he said to his family: 'Wait here! I perceive a fire. Perhaps I can bring you a lighted torch, or find some guidance at the fire'. **11** But when he came close to it, a voice called out to him: 'Moses, **12** I am your Lord! Take off your sandals, for you are in the sacred Valley of Tuwa. **13** Know that I have chosen you. Listen, then, to what is being revealed. **14** Indeed, I alone am God; there is no deity other than Me. So, worship Me alone, and establish regular prayer to celebrate My praise.

15 Although I have chosen to keep it hidden, the Last Hour is bound to come, so that every soul may be rewarded in accordance with what it strove for. **16** Hence, let not anyone who does not believe in its coming and follows only his own desires turn your thoughts from it, lest you perish'. **17** 'Now, what is this in your right hand, Moses?' **18** He answered: 'It is my staff; upon it I lean, and with it I beat down the leaves for my sheep; and other uses have I for it'. **19** Said He: 'Throw it down, Moses'. **20** So he threw it down, and thereupon it was a snake, moving rapidly. **21** Said He: 'Take it up and have no fear. We shall restore it to its former state. **22** Now put your hand under your armpit. It will come out [shining] white, without blemish: another sign. **23** We shall show you some of Our most wondrous signs. **24** Go to Pharaoh; for he has indeed transgressed all bounds'. **25** Said [Moses]: 'My Lord, open up my heart [to Your light], **26** and make my mission easy for me, **27** and free my tongue from its impediment, **28** so that people may understand what I say. **29** Appoint for me a helper from among my kinsmen, **30** Aaron, my brother. **31** Grant me strength through him, **32** and let him share my task, **33** so that together we may extol Your limitless glory **34** and remember You always. **35** You are surely watching over us'. **36** Said He: 'You are granted all that you have asked for, Moses. **37** And indeed We bestowed Our favour upon you in time gone by, **38** when We inspired your mother, saying: **39** "Place [your child] in a chest and throw it into the river. The river will cast him ashore, and one who is an enemy to Me and an enemy to him will pick him up". I lavished My love on you, so that you may be reared under My watchful eye. Then your sister went forth and said [to Pharaoh's people]: "Shall I direct you to one who might take care of him?" Thus did We restore you to your mother, so that her mind might be set at ease and that she might not grieve. **40** And [when you came of age,] you killed a man; but We saved you from all grief, although We tested you with various trials. **41** You then stayed for years among the people of Madyan; and now you have come here, Moses, as ordained [by Me]; for I have chosen you for Myself. **42** Go forth, then, you and your brother, with My signs, and never slacken in remembering Me. **43** Go forth, both of you, to Pharaoh; for he has transgressed all bounds of equity! **44** But speak to him mildly, so that he may yet take heed, or may be filled with apprehension'. **45** They said: 'Our Lord! We fear lest he hasten with insolence or tyranny against us'. **46** Answered He: 'Have no fear. I shall be with you. I hear all and see all. **47** Go, then, you two to him and say, "We are the emissaries of your Lord. Let the Children of

Israel go with us, and oppress them no more. We have now come to you with a message from your Lord. Peace to all who follow [God's] guidance. **48** It has been revealed to us that the suffering shall befall those who deny the truth and turn away from it".' **49** [Pharaoh] said: 'Who, now, is this Lord of you two, Moses?' **50** He replied: 'Our Lord is He who gives everything its distinctive nature and form, and further guides them'. **51** Said [Pharaoh]: 'And what of all the past generations?' **52** [Moses] answered: 'Knowledge of that rests with my Lord alone, recorded in a book. My Lord does not err, and neither does He forget'. **53** He it is who has made the earth your cradle, and has traced on it paths for you to walk on, and who sends down waters from the sky with which We bring forth diverse pairs of plants. **54** Eat, then, and graze your cattle. In all this there are signs for those who are endowed with reason. **55** Out of this [earth] have We created you, and into it shall We return you, and out of it shall We bring you forth once again. **56** And, indeed, We showed Pharaoh all Our signs, but he denied them and refused [to take heed]. **57** He said: 'Have you, Moses, come to drive us out of our land with your magic? **58** In that case, we shall most certainly produce for you magic to match it. Set, then, for us an appointment which neither we nor you shall fail to keep, at a suitable, open place'. **59** Answered Moses: 'Your appointment shall be the day of the Festival; and let the people assemble when the sun is risen high'. **60** Thereupon Pharaoh withdrew and put together the artful scheme which he would pursue; and then turned up. **61** Moses said to them: 'Woe betide you! Do not invent any falsehood against God, lest He afflict you with most grievous suffering. He who contrives such a lie is sure to come to grief'. **62** So they debated among themselves as to what to do; but they kept their counsel secret. **63** They said: 'These two are surely sorcerers intent on driving you away from your land by their sorcery, and on doing away with your exemplary way of life. **64** Hence, decide on the scheme you will pursue, and then come forward in one single body. For, indeed, he who prevails today shall ever be successful'. **65** Said [the sorcerers]: 'Moses! Either you throw [first], or we shall be the first to throw'. **66** He answered: 'You throw first!' And by virtue of their sorcery, their ropes and staffs seemed to him to be moving rapidly. **67** And in his heart Moses became apprehensive. **68** But We said [to him]: 'Have no fear! It is you who shall certainly prevail. **69** Now throw that which is in your right hand and it shall swallow up all that they have wrought. For, they have wrought nothing but a sorcerer's deceitful trick; and sorcerers can never come to any good, whatever they may do'. **70** So down fell the sorcerers, prostrating themselves, and declared: 'We do believe in the Lord of Aaron and Moses'. **71** Said [Pharaoh]: 'Do you believe in him before I have given you permission? Surely, he must be your master who has taught you witchcraft! I shall most certainly cut off your hands and feet on opposite sides, and I shall most certainly crucify you on the trunks of the palm-trees. You will then come to know for certain which of us can inflict a more severe and longer lasting punishment'. **72** They answered: 'Never shall we prefer you to all the evidence of the truth that has come to us, nor to Him who has brought us into being! Decree, then, whatever you are going to decree. You can only decree on what pertains to this worldly life. **73** As for us, we have come to believe in our Lord, hoping that He may forgive us our faults and all that magic to which you have forced us. God is certainly the best and He is Everlasting'. **74** He who shall appear before his Lord [on Judgement Day] laden with sin shall be consigned to Hell, where he shall neither die nor live. **75** But he who shall appear before Him as a believer, having done righteous deeds, shall be exalted to the highest ranks, abiding in the Gardens of Eden, through which running waters flow. **76** Such shall be the recompense of those who keep themselves pure. **77** Then We thus inspired Moses: 'Go forth with My servants by night, and strike out for them a dry path through the sea. Have no fear of being overtaken, and dread nothing'. **78** Pharaoh pursued them with his hosts, but they were overwhelmed by the power of the sea. **79** For Pharaoh had led his people astray and had not guided them aright. **80** Children of Israel! We saved you from your enemy, and then We made a covenant with you on the right flank of Mount Sinai. We sent down manna and quails for you. **81** 'Eat of the wholesome things which We have provided for you and do not transgress, lest you should incur My wrath. He that incurs My wrath has indeed thrown himself into utter ruin; **82** but I certainly forgive all sins for anyone who repents, believes and does righteous deeds, and thereafter keeps to the right path'. **83** [And God said]: 'Now what has caused you, Moses, to leave your people behind in so great a haste?' **84** He answered: 'They are treading in my footsteps, while I have hastened to You, my Lord, so that You might be well-pleased with me'. **85** Said He: 'Then [know that] in your absence We have put your people to a test, and the Samiriy has led them astray'. **86** Thus Moses returned to his people full of wrath and sorrow: 'My people,' he said, 'Did not your Lord hold out a goodly promise to you? Did, then, [the fulfilment of] this promise seem to you too long in coming? Or are you determined to see your Lord's condemnation fall upon you, and so you broke your promise to me?' **87** They answered: 'We did not break our promise to you of our own free will, but we were loaded with the burdens of the [Egyptian] people's ornaments, and so we threw them [into the fire], and likewise this Samiriy threw'. **88** Thus he produced for them the effigy of a calf, which made a lowing sound. 'This', they said, 'is your deity and the deity of Moses; but he has forgotten'. **89** Why! Did they not see that it could not give them any response, and that it could neither harm nor benefit them? **90** And, indeed, Aaron had said to them earlier: 'My people! You are but being tempted to evil by this calf. Your only Lord is the Lord of Grace! Follow me, then, and do as I bid you'. **91** But they had replied: 'By no means shall we cease worshipping it until Moses comes back to us'. **92** [Moses] said: 'Aaron! What has prevented you, when you saw that they had gone astray, from following me? **93** Why have you disobeyed me?' **94** 'Son of my mother', he replied, 'do not seize me by my beard, or by my head! I was afraid that you might say: "You have caused a split among the Israelites and did not wait for my orders".' **95** Said [Moses]: 'What is then your case, Samiriy?' **96** He answered: 'I have gained insight into something which they were unable to see; and so I took a handful of dust from the trail of the messenger and flung it away; for thus has my mind prompted me to act'. **97** Said [Moses]: 'Begone, then! It shall be your lot to say throughout your life, "Do not touch me". But you shall be faced with a destiny from which you shall have no escape. Now look at this deity of yours to whose worship you have become so devoted: we shall most certainly burn it, and then scatter it far and wide over the sea'. **98** Your only deity is God, other than whom there is no deity. His knowledge encompasses all things.

99 Thus do We relate to you some of the history of past events; and thus have We given you, out of Our grace, a reminder. **100** All who shall turn away from it will certainly bear a heavy burden on the Day of Resurrection. **101** For ever shall they bear it; and grievous for them will be its weight on the Day of Resurrection, the Day when the Trumpet is blown. **102** For on that Day We shall assemble all the guilty ones, their eyes dimmed [by terror], **103** whispering to one another, 'You have spent but ten days on earth'. **104** We know best what they will be saying when the most perceptive of them shall say: 'You have spent there but one day!' **105** They ask you about the mountains. **106** Say: 'My Lord will scatter them far and wide, and leave the earth level and bare, **107** with no curves or ruggedness to be seen'. **108** On that Day, all will follow the summoning voice from which there will be no escape. All sounds will be hushed before the Lord of Grace, and you will hear nothing but a faint sough in the air. **109** On that Day, intercession will be of no avail to any except a person in whose case the Lord of Grace will have granted permission, and whose word He will have accepted. **110** He knows all that lies open before them and all that is hidden from them, whereas they cannot have thorough knowledge of Him. **111** All faces shall be humbled before the Ever-Living, the Self-Subsisting Lord; and undone shall be he who is burdened with evildoing; **112** but anyone who will have done righteous deeds, being a believer, need have no fear of being wronged or deprived. **113** And thus have We bestowed from on high the Qur'an in the Arabic tongue, and have given in it many facets to all manner of warnings, so that they may be God-fearing or that it may be for them a source of remembrance. **114** Sublimely exalted is God, the Ultimate Sovereign, the Ultimate Truth. Be not in haste with the Qur'an before it has been revealed to you in full, but always say: 'My Lord, increase my knowledge'. **115** Long ago, We made a covenant with Adam; but he forgot it, and We found him lacking in firmness of purpose. **116** And when We said to the angels, 'Prostrate yourselves before Adam', they all prostrated themselves; except Iblis, who refused. **117** 'Adam', We said, 'this is indeed a foe to you and your wife; so let him not drive the two of you out of the Garden, for then you will be plunged into affliction. **118** It is guaranteed that you shall not hunger here or feel naked, **119** and you shall not thirst here or suffer from the blazing sun'. **120** But Satan whispered to him, saying: 'Adam, shall I lead you to the tree of life eternal, and to a kingdom that will never decay?' **121** They both ate of its fruit; and thereupon their shameful parts became visible to them, and they began to cover themselves with pieced-together leaves from the Garden. Thus did Adam disobey his Lord, and thus did he stray into error. **122** Then his Lord elected him [for His grace], accepted his repentance, and bestowed His guidance upon him. **123** 'Get down, both of you, and be out of it'; He said, 'each of you shall be an enemy to the other. When guidance shall come to you from Me, he who follows My guidance will not go astray, nor will he suffer misery; **124** but he who turns away from My message shall have a straitened life and We shall raise him up blind on the Day of Resurrection'. **125** 'Lord', he will say, 'why have You raised me up blind, while I was endowed with sight?' **126** He will reply: 'Thus it is: Our revelations were brought to you, but you were oblivious to them. So today shall you be consigned to oblivion'. **127** For thus shall We reward him who transgresses and does not believe in his Lord's revelations. Indeed the suffering in the life to come shall be most severe and most enduring. **128** Can they not see how many generations We have destroyed before their time? They walk about in the very places where they dwelt. In this there are signs for people of wisdom. **129** Now, were it not for a decree from your Lord already gone forth, setting a term, their destruction would have been inescapable. **130** Hence, bear with patience whatever they may say, and extol your Lord's limitless glory and praise Him before the rising of the sun and before its setting; and extol His glory, too, during the hours of the night as well as during the hours of the day, so that you may attain a state of contentment. **131** Do not turn your eyes covetously towards whatever splendour of this world's life We have allowed many of them to enjoy in order that We may test them thereby. Whatever provisions your Lord may give are indeed better and longer lasting. **132** Enjoin prayer on your people, and be diligent in its observance. We do not ask you for any provisions. It is We who provide for you. The future belongs to the God-fearing. **133** They say: 'Why does he not bring us a sign from his Lord?' Has there not come to them a clear evidence of the truth in the earlier Scriptures? **134** Had We destroyed them with a calamity before his coming, they would have said, 'Our Lord, if only You had sent us a Messenger, we would have followed Your revelations rather than be humiliated and disgraced'. **135** Say: 'Everyone is hopefully waiting; so wait, if you will. You will certainly come to know who has followed the even path, and who has been rightly guided'.

Surah 21   The Prophets

The fact that this Makkan surah mentions many of the earlier prophets serves to emphasise that there is nothing new about God sending prophets and messengers to guide mankind to the true faith, so that they submit themselves to God alone. Prior to mentioning any of the prophets, the surah portrays scenes of the universe and the laws that operate in it, reminding people that the universe, its laws and all creatures living in it are God's creation.

The surah gives a detailed reference to Abraham and tells the story of how he dealt with the idols worshipped by his people. A short episode of David and Solomon is given, but the references to all other prophets, including Moses, are very brief, highlighting a single point each. However, we feel that the surah gives us a glimpse of a very long history of divine guidance being provided to human generations. The provision of such guidance is undoubtedly an aspect of divine mercy. It culminates with the statement that Prophet Muhammad (peace be upon him) has been sent as a manifestation of God's mercy which He bestows in abundance on all mankind, and indeed all worlds.

The Prophets

In the Name of God, the Lord of Grace, the Ever-Merciful

1 Closer to people draws their reckoning, yet they continue to blithely turn away. **2** Whenever there comes to them any new reminder from their Lord, they listen to it but take it in jest; their hearts set on pleasure. **3** Yet, concealing their inner thoughts, the wrongdoers say to one another: 'Is this man anything but a human being like yourselves? Will you, then, follow his sorcery with your eyes open?' **4** He says: 'My Lord knows whatever is spoken in heaven and earth. He is the One who hears all and knows all'. **5** 'Nay', they say, 'it is but a medley of dreams!' – 'Nay, he has invented it himself!' – 'Nay, he is only a poet!' – 'Let him, then, bring us some sign, as the prophets of old were sent with'. **6** Not one of the communities whom We destroyed in bygone days would ever believe. Will these, then, believe? **7** Before your time, We never sent [as Our messengers] any but men whom We inspired. Hence, ask the followers of earlier revelations if you do not know this. **8** Neither did We give them bodies that did not eat food, nor were they immortal. **9** In the end, We fulfilled Our promise to them, and We saved them and all whom We willed [to save], and We destroyed those who transgressed beyond bounds. **10** We have now revealed for you a Book bringing you respect. Will you not, then, use your reason? **11** How many a community that persisted in wrongdoing have We dashed into fragments, and raised another people in their stead. **12** And as soon as they began to feel Our might they took to their heels and fled. **13** Do not run away. Return to all your comforts and to your dwellings, so that you might be called to account. **14** They said: 'Woe betide us! We were indeed wrongdoers!' **15** And that cry of theirs did not cease until We caused them to become like a field mown down, still and silent as ashes. **16** We have not created the heavens and the earth and all that is between them in mere idle play. **17** Had We willed to indulge in a pastime, We would indeed have found one near at hand; if ever We were to do so! **18** Nay, but We hurl the truth against falsehood, and it crushes the latter, and behold, it withers away. But woe to you for all your false claims. **19** To Him belong all those who are in the heavens and the earth. Those that are with Him are never too proud to worship Him and never grow weary of that. **20** They extol His limitless glory by night and day, tirelessly. **21** Or have they taken for worship some earthly deities who can restore the dead to life? **22** Had there been in heaven or on earth any deities other than God, both would surely have fallen into ruin! But limitless in His glory is God, Lord of the Throne, and exalted is He above all that they attribute to Him! **23** He cannot be questioned about whatever He does, whereas they shall be questioned. **24** Or have they taken for worship some deities besides Him? Say: 'Produce your convincing proof. This is the message of those who are with me and the message of those before me'. But nay, most of them do not know the truth, and so they stubbornly turn away. **25** Before your time We never sent a messenger without having revealed to him that there is no deity other than Me. Therefore, you shall worship Me alone. **26** They say: 'The Lord of Grace has taken to Himself a son!' Limitless is He in His glory! No; they are but His honoured servants. **27** 'They do not speak until He has spoken, and they act at His behest. **28** He knows all that lies before them and all behind them. They do not intercede for any but those whom He has already graced with his goodly acceptance, since they themselves stand in reverent awe of Him'. **29** If any of them were to say, 'I am a deity beside Him', We shall requite him with Hell. Thus do We reward the wrongdoers. **30** Are the unbelievers unaware that the heaven and the earth were once one single entity, which We then parted asunder? We have made out of water every living thing. Will they not, then, believe? **31** We have also set firm mountains on earth, lest it sway with them, and We have cut out there broad paths, so that they might find their way, and We have set up the sky as a well-secured canopy. **32** Yet they stubbornly turn away from all its signs. **33** It is He who has created the night and the day and the sun and the moon: each moves swiftly in its own orbit. **34** Never have We granted life everlasting to any man before you. Should you yourself die, do they, perchance, hope to live forever? **35** Every soul shall taste death. We test you all with evil and good by way of trial. To Us you all must return.

36 When the unbelievers see you, they make you the target of their mockery, saying [to one another], 'Is this the one who speaks against your gods?' Yet they are the ones who, at the mention of the Lord of Grace, are quick to deny Him. **37** Man is a creature of haste. I shall show you My signs: do not, then, ask Me to hurry them on. **38** They say: 'When is this promise to be fulfilled, if what you say be true?' **39** If only the unbelievers knew [that there will come] a time when they will not be able to shield their faces and their backs from the Fire; a time when they will find no support. **40** Indeed, it will come upon them of a sudden, and will stupefy them. They will be unable to avert it, nor will they be allowed any respite. **41** Other messengers were derided before your time; but those who scoffed at them were [in the end] overwhelmed by the very thing that they derided. **42** Say: 'Who could protect you, by night or by day, from the Lord of Grace?' Yet, from the remembrance of their Lord do they stubbornly turn away. **43** Do they have gods other than Us to protect them? Those [alleged deities] are not even able to succour themselves, nor can they be given company by Us. **44** We have allowed these, and their fathers, to enjoy the good things of life until their lifespan grew too long. Can they not see that We gradually reduce the land from its outlying borders? Is it they, then, who will triumph? **45** Say: 'I do but warn you on the strength of divine revelation!' But the deaf cannot hear this call, however often they are warned. **46** Yet, if they were to experience but a breath of your Lord's punishment, they are sure to cry, 'Oh, woe betide us! We were wrongdoers indeed'. **47** We shall set up just scales on the Day of Resurrection, so that no soul shall be wronged in the least. If there be but the weight of a mustard seed, We shall bring it [to account]. Sufficient are We for reckoning.

48 Indeed We gave to Moses and Aaron the standard by which to distinguish right from wrong, a guiding light and a reminder for the God-conscious **49** who fear their Lord in their most secret thoughts, and are weary of the Last Hour. **50** And this one, too, is a blessed reminder which We have bestowed from on high: will you, then, reject it? **51** We formerly bestowed on Abraham his consciousness of what is right, and We were aware of him **52** when he said to his father and his people, 'What are these images to which you are so devoted?' **53** They answered: 'We found our forefathers worshipping them'. **54** Said he: 'Indeed, you and your forefathers have been in evident error'. **55** They asked: 'Is it the truth you are preaching to us? Or are you one who jests?' **56** He replied: 'Indeed, your Lord is the Lord of the heavens and the earth, who has brought them into being. And I am a witness to this [truth.] **57** By God, I shall most certainly bring about the downfall of your idols when you have turned your backs and gone away!' **58** So he broke the idols to pieces, [all] except for the biggest of them, so that they might turn back to him. **59** They said: 'Who has done this to our gods? He is definitely one of the wrongdoers'. **60** They said: 'We heard a youth speak of them; he is called Abraham'. **61** They said: 'Then bring him here in sight of all people, so that they may bear witness'. **62** They said: 'Abraham, was it you who did this to our gods?' **63** He answered: 'Nay, it was this one, the biggest of them, who did it. But ask them, if they can speak!' **64** So they turned to themselves, saying, 'Surely, it is you who are doing wrong'. **65** But then they relapsed into their old position and said, 'You know very well that these [idols] cannot speak!' **66** Said [Abraham]: 'Do you then worship, instead of God, something that cannot benefit or harm you in any way? **67** Fie upon you and upon all that you worship instead of God! Will you not, then, use your reason?' **68** They cried: 'Burn him, and succour your gods, if you are going to do [anything at all]!' **69** But We said: 'Fire, be cool to Abraham, and a source of inner peace [for him]'. **70** They sought to lay a snare for him, but We caused them to be the absolute losers. **71** We delivered him and Lot, [bringing them] to the land which We have blessed for all mankind. **72** And We gave him Isaac and, as an additional gift, Jacob, and caused all of them to be righteous men, and We made them leaders to give guidance at Our behest. **73** We inspired them to do good works, and to be constant in prayer, and to give regular charity. It is Us alone that they worshipped. **74** And to Lot, too, We gave sound judgement and knowledge. We saved him from that community which was given to deeds of abomination. They were people lost in evil, depraved. **75** Him We admitted to Our grace; for he was righteous. **76** And long before that, Noah called out [to Us], and We responded to him and saved him with his household from the great calamity, and helped him against the people who had denied Our revelations. **77** Lost in evil were they, and so We caused them all to drown. **78** And remember David and Solomon, when both gave judgement concerning the field into which some people's sheep had strayed and grazed by night. We were witness to their judgement. **79** We gave Solomon insight into the case. Yet We gave sound judgement and knowledge to both of them. And We caused the mountains to join David in extolling Our limitless glory, and likewise the birds. We are indeed able to do [all things]. **80** And We taught him how to make garments for you, so that they may fortify you against all that which may cause you fear. Will you, then, give thanks? **81** To Solomon We subjected the stormy wind, so that it sped at his behest towards the land which We had blessed. It is We who have knowledge of everything. **82** And of the evil ones, [We assigned him] some that dived for him into the sea and performed other works besides; but it was We who kept a watch over them. **83** And remember Job, when he cried out to his Lord: 'Affliction has befallen me, but of all those who show mercy You are the most merciful'. **84** We responded to him and removed the affliction he suffered. We restored to him his family and as many more with them, as an act of grace from Ourself, and as a reminder to all who worship Us. **85** And remember Ishmael, Idris and Dhul-Kifl: they all were men of constancy and patience. **86** We admitted them to Our grace, for they were among the righteous. **87** And remember Dhul-Nun, when he went away in anger, thinking that We would not force him into a tight situation! But then he cried out in the deep darkness: 'There is no deity other than You! Limitless are You in Your glory! I have done wrong indeed!' **88** So We responded to him and delivered him from his distress. Thus do We deliver those who have faith. **89** And remember Zachariah when he cried out to his Lord: 'My Lord! Do not leave me alone, although You are the best of inheritors'. **90** So We responded to him and gave him John, having cured his wife for him. They all would vie with one another in doing good works, and would call on Us in yearning and awe. They were always humble before Us. **91** And remember her who guarded her chastity, whereupon We breathed into her of Our spirit and caused her, together with her son, to become a sign to all mankind. **92** Surely, your community is but one community, and I am your only Lord. So, worship Me alone.

93 But people have divided themselves into factions. Yet to Us shall they all return. **94** Whoever does righteous deeds and is a believer withal, his endeavour shall not be lost: We shall record it in his favour. **95** It is forbidden that any community We have ever destroyed should not return [to Us]. **96** When Gog and Magog are let loose and swarm down from every corner, **97** when the true promise draws close [to its fulfilment], staring in horror shall be the eyes of the unbelievers, [and they will exclaim:] 'Oh, woe to us! Of this we were indeed heedless. We have assuredly done wrong'. **98** You and all that you were accustomed to worship instead of God are but the fuel of Hell: that is what you are destined for. **99** If those [objects of your worship] had truly been divine, they would not have been destined for it. But there all shall abide. **100** There they will be groaning with anguish, and bereft of hearing. **101** But those for whom [the promise of] ultimate good has already gone forth from Us will be kept far away from that Hell, hearing none of its hissing sound. **102** They will abide in all that their souls have ever desired. **103** The Supreme Terror will cause them no grief, since the angels will receive them with the greeting, 'This is your Day which you were promised'. **104** On that Day We shall roll up the heavens like a scroll of parchment. As We brought into being the first creation, so We shall bring it forth anew. That is a promise We willed upon Ourselves. We are indeed able to do all things. **105** We wrote in the Psalms, after the Reminder [given to Moses] that 'the righteous among My servants shall inherit the earth'. **106** In this, there is a message for people who worship God. **107** We have sent you as a [manifestation of Our] grace towards all the worlds. **108** Say: 'It has been revealed to me that your God is the One and only God: will you, then, surrender yourselves to Him?' **109** If they turn away, say: 'I have proclaimed this in equity to all of you alike; but I do not know whether that which you are promised is imminent or far off. **110** He certainly knows all that is said openly, just as He knows all that you would conceal. **111** For all I know, this may be but a trial for you, and a short reprieve'. **112** Say: 'My Lord, judge You in truth!' and [say]: 'Our Lord is the Lord of Grace whose help is ever to be sought against all that you claim'.

Surah 22   Pilgrimage

Some passages of this surah were revealed in Makkah while the verses that give the Muslim community permission to fight and the passage that mentions pilgrimage and its rites were definitely revealed in Madinah. However, it is mostly concerned with the themes addressed in Makkan surahs. It begins with a fearful scene of the Day of Judgement when all mankind are gathered to account for their deeds and to be shown their fate. It calls on all mankind to be God-fearing and warns them against disobedience. A long passage in the surah is devoted to the pilgrimage, reminding us that the Ka'bah, where many of the pilgrimage duties are performed, was built by the Prophets Abraham and Ishmael, who called on people to believe in God's Oneness.

The surah describes the calamities that befell earlier communities which denied the truth of God's Oneness and rejected their prophets. As it draws to its end, the surah shows the hollowness of erring beliefs. It tells the unbelievers that those whom they associate with God as partners cannot create a fly, even though they might pool all their resources for such purpose. It concludes with calling on the believers to continue to follow the guidance given to them and to strive for God's cause as best they can.

Pilgrimage

In the Name of God, the Lord of Grace, the Ever-Merciful

1 Mankind! Have fear of your Lord. The violent convulsion at the Last Hour will be awesome indeed. 2 On the Day when it comes, every suckling mother will utterly forget her nursling, and every woman heavy with child will cast her burden; and it will seem to you that all mankind are drunk, although they are not drunk. But severe indeed will be God's punishment. 3 Yet some people argue about God without having any knowledge, and follow every rebellious devil. 4 It is decreed for whoever entrusts himself to any [such devil] that he will lead him astray and guide him towards the suffering of the blazing flame. 5 Mankind! If you are in doubt as to the resurrection, remember that We have created you out of dust, then out of a gamete, then out of a clinging cell mass, then out of an organised and unorganised embryo, so that We might make things clear to you. We cause to rest in the [mothers'] wombs whatever We please for an appointed term, and then

We bring you forth as infants, that you may grow up and attain your prime. Some of you die young, and some live on to abject old age when all that they once knew they know no more. You can see the earth dry and barren; and [suddenly,] when We send down water upon it, it stirs and swells and puts forth every kind of radiant bloom. **6** That is because God alone is the Ultimate Truth; and He alone brings the dead to life; and He has the power to will anything. **7** And that the Last Hour is certain to come, beyond any doubt; and that God will certainly resurrect all who are in their graves. **8** Yet some people argue about God without having any knowledge, without guidance, and without any light-giving revelations. **9** They turn away in scorn so as to lead others astray from the path of God. Disgrace is in store for them in this world, and on the Day of Resurrection We shall make them taste suffering through fire. **10** [They shall be told:] 'This is the outcome of what your own hands have wrought. Never does God do the least wrong to His creatures'. **11** Some people worship God on the border-line [of faith]. If good befalls such a person, he is content; but if a trial assails him, he turns away utterly; thus losing this world and the life to come. This is, indeed, a loss beyond compare. **12** He invokes, instead of God, something that can neither harm nor benefit him. This is the utmost that one can go astray. **13** Indeed he invokes one that is far more likely to cause harm than benefit. Vile indeed is such a patron, and vile the friend. **14** God will certainly admit those who believe and do righteous deeds into gardens through which running waters flow. God certainly does whatever He wills. **15** If anyone thinks that God will not succour him in this world and in the life to come, let him stretch out a rope to the sky and then cut himself off; and then let him see whether his scheme will remove that which has enraged him. **16** Thus have we bestowed from on high this [Qur'an] in clear verses. God guides him who wills [to be guided]. **17** As for the believers, the Jews, the Sabians, the Christians, the Magians, and those who associate partners with God, God will decide between them on the Day of Judgement. God is witness to everything. **18** Are you not aware that to God bow down in worship all those who are in the heavens and on earth, the sun, the moon, the stars, the mountains, the trees and the beasts, and a great number of human beings? But a great number also will inevitably have to suffer punishment. He whom God shall disgrace will have none who could bestow honour on him. God certainly does what He wills. **19** These two adversaries have become engrossed in contention about their Lord. **20** For the unbelievers garments of fire shall be cut out; and scalding water will be poured over their heads, melting all that is in their bellies and their skin. **21** In addition, there will be grips of iron for them. **22** Whenever, in their anguish, they try to get out, they are returned there, and will be told: 'Taste the torment of fire'. **23** God will certainly admit those who believe and do righteous deeds into gardens through which running waters flow, wherein they will be adorned with bracelets of gold and pearls, and where silk will be their raiment. **24** For they were guided to the best of words; and so they were guided to the way that leads to the One to whom all praise is due.

25 The unbelievers who debar others from the path of God and the Sacred Mosque which We have set up for all people alike, both those who dwell there and those who come from abroad... Anyone who seeks to profane it by wrongdoing We shall cause to taste painful suffering. **26** When We assigned to Abraham the site of the [Sacred] House, [We said], 'Do not associate anything as partner with Me. Purify My House for those who will walk around it, and those who will stand before it, and those who will bow down and prostrate themselves in prayer'. **27** 'Proclaim to all people the duty of pilgrimage. They will come to you on foot and on every kind of fast mount. They will come from every far-away quarter, **28** so that they might experience much that shall be of benefit to them, and that they might extol the name of God on the days appointed [for sacrifice], over whatever heads of cattle He may have provided for them. Eat, then, of such [sacrificed cattle] and feed the unfortunate poor. **29** Thereafter let them complete the rites prescribed for them, fulfil their vows, and again walk around the Ancient House'. **30** All this [is ordained by God]. Whoever honours God's sanctities, it will be better for him with his Lord. All kinds of cattle have been made lawful to you, except for what is specified to you [as forbidden]. Turn away, then, from the loathsome evil of idolatrous beliefs and practices; and turn away from every word that is untrue. **31** Be absolutely true to God, associating no partners with Him. For he who associates partners with God is like one who is hurling down from the skies; whereupon he is snatched by the birds, or blown away by the wind to a far-off place. **32** This is [to be borne in mind]. Anyone who honours the symbols set up by God [shows evidence of] God-fearingness in people's hearts. **33** You have benefit in them for a term appointed; and in the end their place of sacrifice is near the Ancient House. **34** For every community We have appointed [sacrifice as] an act of worship, so that they might extol the name of God over whatever heads of cattle He may have provided for them. Your God is the One and Only God. Hence, surrender yourselves to Him. **35** Give good news to those who are humble, whose hearts tremble with awe whenever God is mentioned, and who patiently bear whatever befalls them, attend regularly to their prayer and spend in charity out of what We provide for them. **36** The sacrifice of camels We have ordained for you as one of the symbols set up by God, in which there is much good for you. Hence, extol the name of God over them when they are lined up [for sacrifice]; and after they have fallen lifeless to the ground, eat of their meat, and feed the poor who is contented with his lot, as well as the one who is forced to beg. It is to this end that We have made them subservient to your needs, so that you might have cause to be grateful. **37** Never does their meat or their blood reach God; it is your piety that reaches Him. It is to this end that He has made them subservient to your needs, so that you might glorify God for all the guidance with which He has graced you. Give good news to those who do good. **38** God will certainly defend those who believe. For certain, God does not love anyone who betrays his trust and is bereft of gratitude. **39** Permission to fight is given to those against whom war is waged, because they have been wronged. Most certainly, God has the power to grant them victory. **40** These are the ones who have been driven from their homelands against all right for no other reason than their saying, 'Our Lord is God!' Were it not that God repels some people by means of others, monasteries, churches, synagogues and mosques – in all of which God's name is abundantly extolled – would surely have been destroyed. God will most certainly succour him who succours God's cause. God is certainly most-powerful, almighty. **41** They are those who, if We firmly establish them on earth, attend regularly to their prayers, give in charity, enjoin the doing of what is right and forbid the doing of what is wrong. With God rests the final outcome of all events.

42 If they accuse you of falsehood, before their time, the people of Noah, 'Ad and Thamud similarly accused [their prophets] of falsehood, **43** as did the people of Abraham and the people of Lot, and the dwellers of Madyan; and so too was Moses accused of falsehood. **44** [In every case] I gave rein, for a while, to the unbelievers, but then I took them to task. How awesome was the way I rejected them. **45** How many a township have We destroyed because it had been immersed in wrongdoing. Now they lie in desolate ruin. How many a well lies abandoned, and how many a proud palace lies empty. **46** Have they never journeyed through the lands, letting their hearts gain wisdom, and their ears hear? It is not eyes that go blind; but blind indeed become the hearts that are in people's breasts. **47** They challenge you to hasten the coming upon them of God's punishment;

but God never fails to fulfil His promise. Well, in your Lord's sight a day is like a thousand years of your reckoning. **48** To how many a township that was immersed in wrongdoing have I given rein for a while! But then I took it to task. With Me is the end of all journeys. **49** Say: 'Mankind, I am but a plain warner, sent to you!' **50** Those who believe and do righteous deeds shall be granted forgiveness of sins and a most excellent sustenance; **51** whereas those who strive against Our revelations, seeking to defeat their purpose, are destined for the blazing Fire. **52** Whenever We sent forth a messenger or a prophet before you, and he was hoping for something, Satan would throw some aspersion on his wishes. But God renders null and void whatever aspersion Satan may cast; and God makes His messages clear in and by themselves. God is all-knowing, wise. **53** He may cause whatever aspersion Satan may cast to become a trial for all in whose hearts is disease and all whose hearts are hardened. Indeed, all who are thus sinning are most deeply in the wrong. **54** And those who are endowed with knowledge may realise that this [Qur'an] is the truth from your Lord, and thus they may believe in it, and their hearts may humbly submit to Him. God will surely guide those who believe to a straight path. **55** Yet the unbelievers will not cease to be in doubt about Him until the Last Hour comes suddenly upon them, or suffering befalls them on a Day with no more [days] to follow. **56** On that Day, all dominion shall belong to God. He shall judge between them. Thus, all who believe and do righteous deeds shall find themselves in gardens of bliss, **57** whereas for the unbelievers who have denied Our revelations there shall be shameful suffering in store.

58 As for those who leave their homes to serve God's cause, and are then slain or die, God will most certainly grant them a goodly provision. God is indeed the most munificent provider. **59** He will most certainly admit them to a place with which they shall be well pleased. God is surely all-knowing, clement. **60** Thus shall it be. If one retaliates only to the extent of the injury he has received, and then is wronged again, God will certainly succour him. God is certainly the One who absolves sin, who is much-forgiving. **61** Thus it is, because God causes the night to pass into the day, and the day to pass into the night; and because God hears all and sees all. **62** Thus it is, because God alone is the Ultimate Truth, and all that people invoke beside Him is sheer falsehood, and because God alone is the One Most High, Great. **63** Are you not aware that God sends down water from the skies, whereupon the earth becomes green? God is unfathomable in His wisdom, all aware. **64** To Him belongs all that is in the heavens and on earth. God alone is indeed free of all want, worthy of all praise. **65** Do you not see that God has made subservient to you all that is on earth, and the ships that sail the sea at His bidding? He it is who holds the celestial bodies, so that they may not fall upon the earth except by His leave. Most compassionate is God, and ever-merciful to mankind. **66** It is He who gave you life, and then will cause you to die, and then will bring you back to life. Bereft of all gratitude is man. **67** To every community We have appointed ways of worship, which they should observe. Let them not draw you into disputes on this score, but call [them all] to your Lord. You are indeed on the right way. **68** Should they argue with you, say: 'God knows best what you are doing'. **69** God will judge between you on the Day of Resurrection with regard to all on which you dispute. **70** Do you not know that God knows all that occurs in heaven as well as on earth? Indeed it is all in a record. All this is easy for God. **71** And yet they worship beside God something for which He has never bestowed any warrant from on high, and of which they cannot have any knowledge. The wrongdoers shall have none to help them. **72** As it is, whenever Our revelations are recited to them in all their clarity, you can perceive utter repugnance in the faces of unbelievers. They would almost assault those who recite Our revelations to them. Say: 'Shall I tell you of something worse than that? It is the Fire which God has promised to those who deny Him. How vile an end!' **73** Mankind! An aphorism is set forth; hearken, then, to it. Those beings whom you invoke instead of God cannot create a fly, even though they were to join all their forces to that end. If a fly robs them of anything, they cannot rescue it from him! Weak indeed is the seeker, and weak the sought! **74** No true understanding of God have they. God is certainly most-powerful, almighty. **75** God chooses message bearers from among the angels and from among men. God hears all and sees all. **76** He knows all that lies open before them and all that is hidden from them. To God all things shall return. **77** Believers! Bow down and prostrate yourselves, and worship your Lord alone, and do good, so that you might be successful. **78** And strive hard in God's cause as you ought to strive. It is He who has chosen you, and has laid no hardship on you in [anything that pertains to] religion; the creed of your forefather Abraham. It is He who has named you Muslims, in bygone times and in this [Book], so that the Messenger might bear witness for you, and that you might bear witness for all mankind. Thus, attend regularly to your prayer, and pay out your zakat, and hold fast to God. He is your Guardian: the best of guardians and the best to give support.

Surah 23   The Believers

This Makkan surah begins with an outline of the qualities of the believers and their community which is united by its faith, looking after its poor and upholding high moral standards. It makes clear that they are the ones who will achieve success in the life to come. The surah then speaks of the start of human life from conception to birth. It is a great miracle that people ignore because of overfamiliarity. The surah relates this to other aspects of life in the world around us and to the universe at large, before it speaks of God's messengers beginning with Noah. They all preached the message of God's Oneness and they each received stiff opposition. We learn that people in all generations objected to God's messenger being human like them. They thought that a messenger from God should be an angel. Despite the succession of God's messengers, people moved away from the path of faith, following a multitude of directions.

As it draws to its end, the surah speaks to Prophet Muhammad (peace be upon him), directing him to repel evil with what is good. He should not trouble himself much over what the unbelievers say. Their attitude only betrays their ignorance and there will come a time when they realise the truth. By then, however, it will be too late for them to benefit by it.

The Believers

In the Name of God, the Lord of Grace, the Ever-Merciful

1 Truly, successful shall be the believers, **2** who humble themselves in their prayer, **3** who turn away from all that is frivolous, **4** who are active in deeds of charity, **5** who refrain from sex except with those joined to them in marriage, **6** or those whom they rightfully possess – for then, they are free of all blame, **7** whereas those who seek to go beyond that [limit] are indeed transgressors, **8** who are faithful to their trusts and to their pledges, **9** and who are diligent in their prayers. **10** These shall be the heirs **11** who will inherit Paradise; therein shall they abide. **12** Indeed, We create man out of the essence of clay, **13** then We place him, a gamete, in a safe place of rest. **14** Then We create out of the gamete a clinging cell mass, and out of the clinging cell mass We create an embryo. Then We create within the embryo bones, then We clothe the bones with flesh. We then bring this into being as another creation. Exalted be God, the best of creators. **15** And then, after all this, you are destined to die; **16** and then, you shall be restored to life on the Day of Resurrection. **17** We have created above you seven [celestial] orbits; and never are We unmindful of [Our] creation. **18** We send down water from the skies in accordance with a set measure, and We cause it to lodge in the earth; and We are most certainly able to take it all away. **19** And by means of this water We bring forth for you gardens of date-palms and vines, yielding abundant fruit, and from which you eat, **20** as well as a tree that grows on Mount Sinai yielding oil and relish for all to eat. **21** In the cattle too there is a lesson for you: We give you to drink of that which is in their bellies, and you gain many other benefits from them, and you eat of their flesh. **22** By them, as by the ships you are carried.

23 We sent forth Noah to his people, and he said: 'My people! Worship God alone, for you have no deity other than Him. Will you not be God-fearing?' **24** The unbelieving elders of his people said: 'This man is but a mortal like yourselves who wants to make himself superior to you. Had God willed, He would surely have sent down angels. We have never heard anything like this ever happening to our forefathers. **25** He is but a madman; so bear with him for a while'. **26** He said: 'My Lord, help me against their accusation of lying'. **27** We revealed to him to 'build the ark, under Our eyes, and according to Our inspiration. When Our judgement comes to pass, and water gushes forth over the face of the earth, place on board this ark one pair of every species, as well as your family, except those on whom sentence has already been passed. Do not plead with Me for the wrongdoers; for they shall be drowned. **28** When you and those who are with you are settled in the ark, say: "All praise is due to God who has saved us from those wrongdoing folk". **29** And also say: "My Lord! Let my landing be blessed. You are the best to bring us to safe landing".' **30** Surely, in that there are signs. Indeed, We always put [people] to a test. **31** Then after these people We raised a new generation. **32** And We sent forth to them a messenger from among themselves, and he said: 'My people! Worship God alone, for you have no deity other than Him. Will you not be God-fearing?' **33** The unbelieving elders of his people, who denied the life to come and to whom We granted ease and plenty in this worldly life, said: 'This man is but a mortal like yourselves, eating of what you eat and drinking of what you drink. **34** Indeed, if you pay heed to a man like yourselves, you will certainly be the losers. **35** Does he promise you that, after you have died and become dust and bones, you shall be brought forth to life? **36** Improbable, improbable indeed is what you are promised! **37** There is no life beyond this, our present life; we die and we live, and we shall never be restored to life. **38** He is nothing but a man who attributes his lies to God. Never will we believe in him'. **39** He said: 'My Lord, help me against their accusation of lying'. **40** Said [God]: 'Before long they shall certainly come to rue it'. **41** Then the blast overtook them in all justice, and We caused them to be like dead leaves. And so – away with those wrongdoing folk! **42** Then after them We raised new generations. **43** No community can forestall the end of its term nor delay it. **44** And We sent forth Our messengers, one after another. Every time their messenger came to a community, they accused him of lying. So, We caused them to follow one another, and let them become mere tales. And so – away with the folk who would not believe. **45** And then We sent forth Moses and his brother Aaron, with Our signs and with clear authority, **46** to Pharaoh and his nobles; but these behaved with arrogance, for they were haughty people. **47** And so they said: 'Are we to believe two men like ourselves, even though their people are our slaves?' **48** Thus, they accused them of lying, and earned their place among the doomed. **49** We had indeed given Moses the Book, so that they might be guided. **50** And We made the son of Mary and his mother a symbol, and provided them with an abode in a lofty place of lasting restfulness and a fresh spring. **51** Messengers! Eat of that which is wholesome, and do good deeds: I certainly have full knowledge of all that you do. **52** This community of yours is one single community, and I am your only Lord. Therefore, fear Me alone.

53 But people have divided themselves into factions, each delighting in what they have. **54** So, leave them alone, lost in their ignorance, till a time appointed. **55** Do they think that by all the wealth and offspring We provide for them **56** We hasten to them all that is good? By no means! But they are devoid of perception. **57** Truly, those who stand in reverent awe of their Lord, **58** and who believe in their Lord's revelations, **59** and who do not associate any partners with their Lord, **60** and who give away whatever they have to give with their hearts filled with awe, knowing that to their Lord they shall certainly return: **61** these vie with one another in doing good works, and they are the ones who are foremost in them. **62** We do not charge a soul with more than it can bear. We have a record that speaks the truth. None shall be wronged. **63** Nay, their hearts are blind to all this. But apart from all that, they have deeds which they will continue to commit. **64** Then, when We shall have overwhelmed with suffering those of them that live in luxury, they cry out in belated supplication. **65** [But they will be told:] 'Do not cry out this day, for from Us you shall receive no help. **66** Time and again were My revelations recited to you, but every time you would turn about on your heels, **67** revelling in your arrogance, and talking senselessly far into the night'. **68** Have they, then, never tried to understand this word [of God]? Or has there come to them something that never came to their forefathers of old? **69** Or do they not recognise their Messenger, and so they deny him? **70** Or do they say that there is in him a touch of madness? Nay, he has brought them the truth; and the truth do most of them detest. **71** Had the truth been in accord with their desires, the heavens and the earth, together with all that lives in them, would surely have been in utter corruption. Nay, We have given them all that brings them glory. Yet from this their glory they turn away. **72** Or do you ask of them any recompense? But the recompense given by your Lord is best, since He is the best of providers. **73** Most certainly, you call them to a straight path. **74** But those who will not believe in the life to come are bound to deviate from the right path. **75** Even were We to show them mercy and remove whatever distress might afflict them, they would still persist in their overweening arrogance, blindly stumbling to and fro. **76** Indeed, We took them to task, but they neither humbled themselves before their Lord, nor do they submissively implore [Him]. **77** Yet when We open before them a gate of truly severe suffering, they will plunge in despair. **78** It is He who has endowed you with hearing, and sight, and minds. How seldom are you grateful. **79** And He it is who caused you to multiply on earth; and to Him you shall be gathered. **80** And He it is who grants life and causes death; and to Him is due the alternation of night and day. Will you not, then, use your reason? **81** But they say like the people of old times used to say. **82** They say: 'What! After we have died and become dust and bones, shall we be raised to life? **83** This we have been promised before, we and our forefathers! This is nothing but fables of the ancients'. **84** Say: 'To whom belongs the earth and all that lives therein? [Tell me] if you know'. **85** They will reply: 'To God'. Say: 'Will you not, then, reflect?' **86** Say: 'Who is the Lord of the seven heavens, and the Lord of the Supreme Throne?' **87** They will reply: '[They all belong] to God'. Say: 'Will you not, then, fear Him?' **88** Say: 'In whose hand rests the sovereignty of all things, protecting all, while against Him there is no protection? [Tell me] if you know'. **89** They will reply: '[They all belong] to God'.

Say: 'How, then, can you be so deluded?' **90** Nay, We have revealed to them the truth; and yet, they are certainly lying. **91** Never did God take to Himself any offspring, nor has there ever been any deity alongside Him. Had there been any, each deity would surely have taken away his own creation, and they would surely have tried to establish superiority over one another. Limitless in His glory is God, far above all that which they attribute to Him. **92** He knows all that is beyond the reach of human perception, and all that can be witnessed. Sublimely exalted is He above anything they associate as partner with Him. **93** Say: 'My Lord! If it be your will to show me that which they are warned against, **94** then, my Lord, do not let me be one of those wrongdoing folk'. **95** We are most certainly able to show you that which We promise them. **96** Repel evil with that which is best. We are fully aware of all that they say. **97** And say: 'My Lord! I seek refuge with You from the promptings of the evil ones; **98** and I seek refuge with You, my Lord, lest they come near me'.

99 When death approaches any of them, he says: 'My Lord! Let me return [to life], so that I may act righteously in whatever I have failed to do'. **100** By no means! It is but a word he says. Behind them there stands a barrier till the Day when all will be raised from the dead. **101** Then, when the Trumpet is sounded, there will be no ties of kinship between them on that Day, nor will they ask about one another. **102** Those whose weight [of good deeds] is heavy in the scales will be successful; **103** but those whose weight is light will have lost their souls and will abide in Hell. **104** The Fire will scorch their faces, and therein they will look gloomy. **105** 'Were not My revelations read out to you, and did you not consider them as lies?' **106** They will reply: 'Our Lord! Our misfortune has overwhelmed us, and so we went astray. **107** Our Lord! Bring us out of this [suffering]. If ever We relapse, then we shall be wrongdoers indeed'. **108** He will say: 'Away with you into this ignominy! And do not plead with Me. **109** Among My servants there were those who said: "Our Lord! We believe in You. Forgive us and have mercy on us; for You are the best of those who show mercy". **110** But you made them the target of your derision to the point where it made you forget all remembrance of Me; and you went on laughing at them. **111** Today I have rewarded them for their patience in adversity. Indeed it is they who have achieved triumph.' **112** And He will ask: 'How many years have you spent on earth?' **113** They will answer: 'We have spent there a day, or part of a day; but ask those who keep count'. **114** He will say: 'Brief indeed was your sojourn, if you but knew it. **115** Did you think that

We created you in mere idle play, and that to Us you would not have to return?' **116** Sublimely exalted is God, the Ultimate Sovereign, the Ultimate Truth. There is no deity other than Him, the Lord of the Glorious Throne. **117** He that invokes besides God any other deity – a deity for whose existence he has no evidence – shall be brought to account before his Lord. Most certainly, the unbelievers shall never be successful. **118** Say: 'My Lord! Forgive and have mercy. You are the best of those who show mercy'.

Surah 24   Light

This Madinan surah includes a wealth of legislation for the Muslim community and the human society Islam builds. It derives its name from the verse that attaches light to God, stating that God is the light of the heavens and the earth.

The surah begins with a denunciation of adultery as a sinful practice that is forbidden by Islam, and indeed by all divine religions. It states the mandatory punishment for adultery and the requirements for its enforcement. It then speaks of the moral standards that should be implemented in Muslim society and relates them to God's light. The surah gives a fascinating and breathtaking image of God's light. This description comes in the middle of passages that outline the standards of morality and good manners that every Muslim community should implement.

The surah concludes with a statement that the heavens and the earth, and indeed the entire universe, belong to God alone. He knows the secret thoughts of every individual. His knowledge is perfect and complete. Nothing is withheld from Him.

Light

In the Name of God, the Lord of Grace, the Ever-Merciful

1 [This is] a surah which We have bestowed from on high and which We have ordained; and in it have We revealed clear verses, so that you may keep them in mind. **2** As for the adulteress and the adulterer, flog each of them with a hundred stripes, and let not compassion for them keep you from [carrying out] this law of God, if you truly believe in God and the Last Day; and let a number of believers witness their punishment. **3** The adulterer couples with none other than an adulteress or an idolatress; and with the adulteress couples none other than an adulterer or an idolater. This is forbidden to the believers. **4** As for those who accuse chaste women [of adultery], and cannot produce four witnesses, flog them with eighty stripes; and do not accept their testimony ever after; for they are indeed transgressors. **5** Excepted are those who afterwards repent and make amends; for God is much-forgiving, ever-merciful. **6** And as for those who accuse their own wives [of adultery], but have no witnesses except themselves, let each of them call God four times to witness that he is indeed telling the truth; **7** and the fifth time, that God's curse be upon him if he is telling a lie. **8** However, punishment is averted from her if she calls God four times to witness that he is indeed telling a lie; **9** and the fifth time, that God's wrath be upon her if he is telling the truth. **10** Were it not for God's favour upon you and His grace, and that God is the One who accepts repentance, the Wise…! **11** Those who concocted the falsehood were a band from among you. Do not regard it as bad for you; indeed it is good for you. Each one of them shall bear what he has earned of sin; and grievous suffering awaits the one who took on himself the lead among them. **12** When you heard it, why did not the believers, men and women, think the best of themselves, and say: 'This is a blatant falsehood'. **13** Why did they not produce four witnesses to prove it? Since they have not produced witnesses, then in the sight of God, they are certainly liars. **14** Were it not for God's favour upon you and His grace, in this world and in the life to come, grievous suffering would indeed have afflicted you on account of what you indulged in. **15** You took it up with your tongues and uttered with your mouths something of which you have no knowledge, thinking it a light matter whereas in God's sight it is grave indeed. **16** If only when you heard it you said: 'It is not right for us to speak of this! All glory belongs to You. This is a monstrous slander'. **17** God admonishes you lest you ever revert to the like of this, if you are truly believers. **18** And God makes plain to you His revelations. God is all-knowing, wise. **19** Those who love that gross indecency should spread among the believers shall be visited with painful suffering both in this world and in the life to come. God knows, but you do not know. **20** Were it not for God's favour upon you and His grace, and that God is compassionate, ever-merciful…! **21** Believers! Do not follow Satan's footsteps, for he who follows Satan's footsteps will only enjoin what is shameful and wrong. Were it not for God's favour upon you and His grace, none of you would have ever been pure. It is God who causes whomever He wills to grow in purity. God hears all and knows all. **22** Let not those of you who have been graced with God's favour and ample means resolve by oath not to help those who are near of kin, the needy and those who have left their homes for the sake of God. But let them pardon and forbear. Do you not desire that God should forgive you your sins? God is indeed much-forgiving, ever-merciful. **23** Those who accuse chaste women who may have been unthinkingly careless but remained true believers, shall be rejected by God in this world as well as in the life to come. **24** They shall endure grievous suffering; on the

Day when their own tongues, hands and feet will testify to what they did. **25** On that Day God will pay them in full their just due, and they will come to know that God alone is the Ultimate Truth, absolutely manifest. **26** Corrupt women are for corrupt men, and corrupt men for corrupt women, just as good women are for good men, and good men for good women. These are innocent of all that people may impute to them. Forgiveness and excellent sustenance are in store for them.

27 Believers, do not enter houses other than your own unless you have obtained permission and greeted their inmates. This is best for you, so that you may take heed. **28** If you find no one in the house, do not enter it until you are given leave; and if you are told to go back, then go back, as it is most proper for you. God has full knowledge of all that you do. **29** You will incur no sin if you enter uninhabited houses in which you have something of use. God knows all that you do openly, and all that you would conceal. **30** Tell believing men to lower their gaze and to be mindful of their chastity. This is most conducive to their purity. God is certainly aware of all that they do. **31** And tell believing women to lower their gaze and to be mindful of their chastity, and not to display their charms except what may ordinarily appear thereof. Let them draw their head-coverings over their bosoms and not display their charms to any but their husbands, or their fathers, or their husbands' fathers, or their sons, or their husbands' sons, or their brothers, or their brothers' sons, or their sisters' sons, or their womenfolk, or those whom they rightfully possess, or such male attendants as are free of physical desire, or children that are as yet unaware of women's nakedness. Let them not swing their legs in walking so as to draw attention to their hidden charms. Believers, turn to God in repentance, so that you may achieve success. **32** Marry the single from among you as well as such of your male and female slaves as are virtuous. If they are poor, God will grant them sufficiency out of His bounty. God is munificent, all-knowing. **33** As for those who are unable to marry, let them live in continence until God grants them sufficiency out of His bounty. And if any of your slaves desire to obtain a deed of freedom, write it out for them if you are aware of any good in them; and give them something of the wealth God has given you. Do not force your maids to prostitution when they desire to preserve their chastity, in order to make some worldly gain. If anyone should force them, then after they have been compelled, God will be much-forgiving, ever-merciful. **34** We have bestowed upon you from on high revelations clearly showing the truth, and lessons from [the stories of] those who have passed away before you, and admonition for the God-fearing.

35 God is the light of the heavens and the earth. His light may be compared to a niche containing a lamp; the lamp within a glass, the glass like a radiant star; lit from a blessed tree – an olive tree that is neither of the east nor of the west. Its very oil would almost give light even though no fire had touched it. Light upon light! God guides to His light him that wills [to be guided]. God propounds parables for all people, since God alone has full knowledge of all things. **36** In houses which God has sanctioned to be raised so that His name be remembered in them, there are [such as] extol His limitless glory, morning and evening **37** – people whom neither commerce nor profit can divert from the remembrance of God, and from attending regularly to prayer, and from paying their zakat; who are filled with fear of the day when all hearts and eyes will be convulsed; **38** who [only hope] that God may reward them in accordance with the best that they ever did, and lavish His grace upon them. God gives to whom He wills beyond all reckoning. **39** As for the unbelievers, their deeds are like a mirage in the desert, which the thirsty traveller supposes to be water, but when he comes near to it, he finds that it is nothing. But he finds that God [has always been present] with him, and that He will pay him his account in full; for God is swift in reckoning. **40** Or else, like the depths of darkness in a vast deep ocean, covered by waves above which are waves, with clouds above it all: depths of darkness, layer upon layer, [so that] when one holds up his hand, he can hardly see it. Indeed the one from whom God withholds light shall find no light at all. **41** Are you not aware that it is God whose limitless glory all creatures that are in the heavens and earth extol, even the birds as they spread out their wings? Each of them knows how to pray to Him and to glorify Him; and God has full knowledge of all that they do. **42** To God belongs the dominion over the heavens and the earth, and to God shall all return. **43** Are you not aware that it is God who causes the clouds to move onwards, then joins them together, then piles them up in masses, until you can see rain come forth from their midst. He it is who sends down from the skies mountainous masses charged with hail, striking with it whom He wills and averting it from whom He wills. The flash of His lightning well-nigh deprives people of their sight. **44** It is God who causes night and day to alternate. In this too there is surely a lesson for all who have eyes to see. **45** God has created every animal from water; and among them are such as creep on their bellies, and such as walk on two legs, and others yet on four. God creates what He wills. Surely God has power over all things.

46 We have sent down revelations that make things manifest; and God guides onto a straight way him who wills [to be guided]. **47** They say: 'We believe in God and in the Messenger, and we obey'. But then some of them turn away after this [assertion]. Surely these are not believers. **48** Whenever they are summoned to God and His Messenger in order that he might judge between them, some of them turn away; **49** but if the right is on their side, they come to him with all submission. **50** Is there disease in their hearts? Or are they full of doubt? Or do they fear that God and His Messenger might deal unjustly with them? Nay, it is they who are the wrongdoers. **51** The response of believers, whenever they are summoned to God and His Messenger in order that he may judge between them, is none other than, 'We have heard, and we obey'. It is they that shall be successful. **52** Those who obey God and His Messenger, stand in awe of God and remain truly God-fearing are the ones who shall certainly triumph. **53** They swear their most solemn oaths by God that if you [God's Messenger] should ever bid them to do so, they would most certainly march forth. Say: 'Do not swear. Your [sort of] obedience is well known. God is certainly well aware of all that you do'. **54** Say: 'Obey God, and obey the Messenger'. But if you turn away, he will have to answer only for whatever he has been charged with, and you, for what you have been charged with. If you obey him, you shall be rightly guided. The Messenger is not bound to do more than clearly deliver his message. **55** God has promised those of you who believe and do good deeds that, of a certainty, He will cause them to accede to power on earth, in the same way as He caused those who lived before them to accede to it; and that, of a certainty, He will firmly establish for them the religion which He has chosen for them; and that, of a certainty, He will cause their erstwhile state of fear to be replaced by a state of security. They will thus worship Me alone and associate with Me no partners whatsoever. Those who, after this, choose to disbelieve are indeed wicked. **56** Attend regularly to your prayers and pay your zakat, and obey the Messenger, so that you might be graced with God's mercy. **57** Do not think that the unbelievers can frustrate [God's plan] on earth. The Fire is their abode, and vile indeed is such a journey's end.

58 Believers! Let those whom you rightfully possess, and those of you who have not yet attained to puberty, ask leave of you at three times of day: before the prayer of daybreak, and whenever you lay aside your garments in the middle of the day, and after the prayer of nightfall. These are three occasions on which you may happen to be undressed. Beyond these occasions, neither you nor they will incur any sin if they move freely about you, attending to one another. Thus God makes clear to you His revelations. God is all-knowing, wise. **59** Yet when your children attain to puberty, let them ask leave of you, as do those senior to them [in age]. Thus does God make revelations clear to you. God is all-knowing, wise. **60** Such elderly women as are past the prospect of marriage incur no sin if they lay aside their [outer] garments, provided they do not make a showy display of their charms. But it is better for them to be modest. God hears all and knows all. **61** No blame attaches to the blind, nor does blame attach to the lame, nor does blame attach to the sick; and neither to yourselves for eating from your houses, or your fathers' houses, or your mothers' houses, or your brothers' houses, or your sisters' houses, or your paternal uncles' houses, or your paternal aunts' houses, or your maternal uncles' houses, or your maternal aunts' houses, or in houses of which the keys are in your possession, or in the houses of your friends. You will incur no sin by eating in company or separately. But when you enter houses, greet one another with a blessed, goodly greeting, as enjoined by God. Thus does God make His revelations clear to you, so that you may use your reason. **62** They only are true believers who believe in God and His Messenger, and who, whenever they are with him upon a matter requiring collective action, do not depart unless they have obtained his leave. Those who ask leave of you are indeed the ones who believe in God and His Messenger. Hence, when they ask your leave to attend to some business of theirs, grant you this leave to whomever of them you choose, and pray to God to forgive them. God is indeed much-forgiving, ever-merciful. **63** Do not address God's Messenger in the manner you address one another. God certainly knows those of you who would slip away surreptitiously. So, let those who would go against His bidding beware, lest some affliction or painful suffering befall them. **64** To God belongs all that is in the heavens and on earth. Well does He know what you are intent upon. One day, all will be brought back to Him, and then He will tell them all that they have done. God has full knowledge of everything.

Surah 25   The Criterion

This surah discusses what the divine message faces of opposition from unbelievers. Rather than looking at the message and the Qur'an that presents it, the unbelievers objected to the Messenger himself, and to the method of revelation, essentially ridiculing what the Qur'an said. The surah comforts the Prophet as he faced such entrenched hostility and also refutes the unbelievers' arguments.

The surah starts by glorifying God, who revealed the Qur'an as a warning for mankind. The Qur'an, which is the Criterion that distinguishes truth from falsehood, provides guidance and ensures that those who follow it will live in peace with themselves, their community and the world at large. They will be happy even when they face stiff opposition and rejection.

Scenes of the universe are portrayed to bring home to people that even very familiar natural criteria, such as the succession of day and night, rainfall, the growth of vegetation, etc. could not have come about without God's will.

It concludes with a calm description of the believers to whom the surah refers to as 'the servants of the Lord of Grace'. They are the ones who observe the highest moral standards in public and private. They are the ones who will receive God's rich reward.

The Criterion

In the Name of God, the Lord of Grace, the Ever-Merciful

1 Blessed is He who from on high bestowed upon His servant the Standard to discern the true from the false, so that it might be a warning to all the worlds: **2** He to whom belongs the dominion over the heavens and the earth, and who begets no offspring, and has no partner in His dominion. It is He who has created all things and ordained them in due proportions. **3** Yet, some choose to worship, instead of Him, deities that cannot create anything but are themselves created, and do not have it in their power to avert harm from, or bring benefit to, themselves, and have no power over death, life or resurrection. **4** The unbelievers say: 'This [Qur'an] is nothing but a lie which he has devised with the help of other people'. In truth, it is they who have perpetrated an inequity and a falsehood. **5** And they say: 'Fables of ancient times which he has caused to be written down, so that they might be read out to him morning and evening'. **6** Say: 'This [Qur'an] is bestowed from on high by Him who knows the secrets of the heavens and the earth. He is indeed much-forgiving, ever-merciful'. **7** They also say: 'What sort of messenger is this, who eats food and goes about in the market-places? Why has not an angel been sent down to him to give warning alongside him? **8** Or why has not a treasure been granted to him? Or he should have a garden to provide his sustenance'. The wrongdoers say: 'The man you follow is certainly bewitched'. **9** See to what they liken you. They have certainly gone astray and are unable to find a way back [to the truth]. **10** Blessed is He who, if it be His will, shall give you better things than these; gardens through which running waters flow, and shall give you palaces too. **11** Nay! It is the Last Hour that they deny. For those who deny the Last Hour We have prepared a blazing fire. **12** When it sees them from a far-off place, they will hear its fury and its raging sigh. **13** And when, chained together, they are flung into a tight space within, they will pray for extinction there and then. **14** [But they will be told]: 'Do not pray today for one single extinction, but pray for many extinctions!' **15** Say: 'Which is better: that, or the Paradise of eternity which the God-fearing have been promised as their reward and their ultimate abode?' **16** There they will have all they wish for, abiding there forever. It is a promise given by your Lord, always to be prayed for. **17** On the Day He gathers them with all those they worship instead of God, He will ask: 'Was it you who led these My servants astray, or did they by themselves stray from the right path?' **18** They will say: 'Limitless are You in Your glory! It was never proper for us to take for our masters anyone but Yourself. But You allowed them and their fathers to enjoy [the pleasures of] life, until they forgot the Reminder. For they were people devoid of all good'. **19** [Then God will say]: 'Now have they denied all your assertions, and you can neither avert [your punishment] nor obtain help. Whoever of you does wrong, him shall We cause to taste grievous suffering. **20** Even before you, We never sent messengers other than [men] who indeed ate food and went about in the marketplaces. We have made some of you a means of testing others. Are you able to endure with patience? Surely your Lord sees all'.

21 Those who entertain no hope of meeting Us say: 'Why have no angels been sent down to us?' – or, 'Why do we not see our Lord?' Indeed, they are far too proud of themselves and they have been insolently overbearing. **22** On the Day when they shall see the angels, the sinners will receive no happy news then, and they will say:

'A forbidding ban!' **23** We shall turn to whatever deeds they have done, and We shall transform it all into scattered dust. **24** On that Day, those destined for Paradise will be graced with the best of abodes and the fairest place of repose. **25** On the Day when the skies shall be rent asunder with clouds, and the angels shall be sent down [in ranks]. **26** On that Day, true sovereignty belongs to the Lord of Grace [alone]. It will be a day of dire distress for the unbelievers. **27** On that Day the wrongdoer will bite his two hands and say: 'Would that I had followed the path shown to me by the Messenger. **28** Oh, woe is me! Would that I had never taken so-and-so for a friend! **29** He surely led me astray from the Reminder after it had come to me!' Satan is ever treacherous to man. **30** And the Messenger will say: 'My Lord! My people have regarded this Qur'an as something to be discarded!' **31** Thus against every prophet We have set up enemies from among the wicked. Sufficient is your Lord to provide guidance and support. **32** The unbelievers ask: 'Why has not the Qur'an been revealed to him all at once?' Thus [it has been revealed] so that We might strengthen your heart with it, and We have imparted it to you by gradual revelation. **33** Whenever they come to you with an argument, We shall reveal to you the truth and the best explanation. **34** Those who will be gathered to Hell on their faces – they will be worst in station and still farther away from the [right] path. **35** Indeed, We gave the Book to Moses, and appointed his brother Aaron to help him to bear his burden. **36** And We said: 'Go you both to the people who denied Our signs', and then We utterly destroyed those people. **37** When the people of Noah rejected their messengers, We caused them to drown, and made of them an example for mankind. For the wrongdoers We have prepared painful suffering. **38** And also the 'Ad and Thamud, and the people of al-Rass, and many generations in between. **39** To each of them did We proffer lessons, and each of them did We utterly annihilate. **40** They must have surely passed by the town which was rained upon with a shower of evil. Have they, then, never seen it? But nay, they would not believe in resurrection. **41** When they see you, they make you a target of their mockery, [saying]: 'Is this the one whom God has sent as His emissary? **42** He could almost have led us astray from our deities, had we not been steadfastly attached to them!' But in time, when they see the suffering, they will come to know who it was that went farthest astray. **43** Have you considered the one who makes his desires his deity? Could you, then, be held responsible for him? **44** Or do you think that most of them listen and use their reason? They are but like cattle. Nay, they are even far worse astray.

45 Do you not see how your Lord causes the shadow to lengthen when, had He so willed, He could have indeed made it stand still? But then We have made the sun its guide. **46** And then, little by little, We draw it in towards Ourselves. **47** He it is who makes the night a garment for you, and sleep a repose. He makes every day a resurrection. **48** And He it is who sends forth the winds as heralds of His coming grace. And We cause pure water to descend from the skies, **49** so that with it We may bring dead land to life and give drink to a countless number of Our creation, beast as well as human. **50** Many times have We explained this [in the] Qur'an to them, so that they may take it to heart, but most people refuse to be anything but unbelievers. **51** Had We so willed, We could have sent a warner to every city. **52** Do not obey the unbelievers, but strive most vigorously against them with this Qur'an. **53** He it is who has brought the two bodies of water to a meeting point; the one sweet and thirst-quenching, and the other salty and bitter. Yet between them He has made a barrier and a forbidding ban. **54** And He it is who has created man from water and established for him bonds of lineage and marriage. All-powerful is your Lord. **55** Yet people worship, instead of God, things that can neither benefit nor harm them. An unbeliever always gives support against his Lord. **56** We have sent you only as a herald of good news and a warner. **57** Say: 'No reward do I ask of you for this. All I ask is that he who so wills may find a way leading to his Lord. **58** Hence, place your trust in the Living One who does not die, and extol His limitless glory and praise. Sufficient is it that He is well aware of His servants' sins. **59** He it is who has created the heavens and the earth and all that is between them in six days, and is established on the throne of His almightiness, the Lord of Grace. Ask, then, about Him, the One who knows everything'. **60** Yet when they are told, 'Prostrate yourselves before the Lord of Grace,' they ask, 'What is the Lord of Grace? Are we to prostrate ourselves before whatever you bid us?' And they grow more rebellious. **61** Blessed is He who has set up in the skies great constellations, and has placed among them a lamp and a light-giving moon. **62** And He it is who causes the night and the day to succeed one another; [a clear sign] for him who would take heed or would show gratitude.

63 The true servants of the Lord of Grace are those who walk gently on earth, and who, whenever the ignorant address them, say: 'Peace'; **64** who stay up far into the night in adoration of their Lord, prostrating themselves and standing; **65** who pray: 'Our Lord, avert from us the suffering of Hell, for the suffering it causes is indeed a dire torment; **66** it is indeed an evil abode and a terrible station; **67** and who, whenever they put their money to use, are neither wasteful nor miserly, but always maintain a just mean between the two; **68** and who never invoke any deity side by side with God, and do not take any human being's life – [the life] which God has willed to be sacred – except for a just cause, and do not commit adultery. **69** Whoever does any of this will face punishment, and on the Day of Resurrection his suffering will be doubled, and he will abide therein in ignominy. **70** Excepted, however, shall be they who repent, attain to faith and do righteous deeds, for God will transform their bad deeds into good ones. God is indeed much-forgiving, ever-merciful. **71** Whoever repents and does what is right has truly turned to God by [his act of] repentance. **72** [And the true servants of God are] those who never bear witness to what is false, and whenever they pass by [people engaged in] frivolity, pass on with dignity; **73** and who, whenever they are reminded of their Lord's signs, do not fall deaf and blind to them; **74** and who pray: 'Our Lord! Grant us spouses and offspring who will be a joy to our eyes, and cause us to be foremost among the God-fearing'. **75** These will be rewarded for all their patient endurance [in life] with a high station in heaven, and will be met there with a greeting of welcome and peace, **76** and there they shall abide; how goodly an abode and how high a station; **77** say: 'No weight or value would my Lord attach to you were it not for you calling out [to Him]. You have indeed denied [His message], and in time this [sin] will cleave unto you'.

Surah 26   The Poets

This surah starts with a short introduction that comforts the Prophet as he faced determined rejection of his message. This is followed by several stories of earlier prophets and what they had faced of rejection by their peoples. Accounts of no less than seven prophets are given in succession. The common feature of their stories, with the exception of Moses, is the heedless opposition to the divine message by their communities and its acceptance by only a small group. The surah concludes by clearly stating the truth that the Qur'an is God's Book which He revealed to the Prophet so as to warn people and provide them with guidance.

The surah derives its name from the mention of poets right at its end. Poets are described as letting their imagination roam in different directions, bent on exaggeration that leaves a wide gap between what they say and what they do.

The Poets

In the Name of God, the Lord of Grace, the Ever-Merciful

1 *Ta. Sin. Mim.* **2** These are verses of the Book that makes things clear. **3** Would you, perhaps, torment yourself to death [with grief] because they would not believe? **4** If We will, We can send down to them from the skies a sign before which their necks will remain bent in submission. **5** Yet whenever any fresh reminder comes to them from the Lord of Grace, they always turn their backs on it. **6** They have indeed denied [the truth of revelation]; and they will in time come to understand what it was they used to deride. **7** Do they not see the earth, how much of every noble kind We have caused to grow on it. **8** Indeed, there is in this a sure sign; yet most of them will not believe. **9** And indeed it is your Lord who is the Mighty One, the Ever-Merciful.

10 Your Lord called Moses: 'Go to the wrongdoing people, the people of Pharaoh. **11** Will they have no fear of God?' **12** He said: 'My Lord, I fear that they will charge me with falsehood, and then my breast will be straitened and my tongue will not be fluent. **13** So send as well for Aaron. **14** Moreover, they have a charge of crime against me, and I fear that they will kill me'. **15** Said He: 'By no means! Go forth, then, both of you, with Our signs; We are with you, listening to all. **16** Go, both of you, to Pharaoh, and say: "We are messengers from the Lord of all the worlds: **17** let the Children of Israel go with us".' **18** [Pharaoh] said [to Moses]: 'Did we not bring you up when you were an infant? And did you not stay with us many years of your life? **19** Yet you have done that deed of yours while being an unbeliever'. **20** Replied [Moses]: 'I committed it while I was still going astray; and I fled from you because I feared you. **21** Then my Lord granted me sound judgement and made me one of [His] messengers. **22** And what sort of favour is this you are taunting me with: was it not because you had enslaved the Children of Israel?' **23** Pharaoh said: 'And what is that "Lord of all the worlds"?' **24** [Moses] answered: 'He is the Lord of the heavens and the earth and all that is between them, if you want to be sure'. **25** [Pharaoh] said to those around him: 'Do you hear?' **26** [Moses] said: 'He is your Lord as well as the Lord of your forefathers of old'. **27** [Pharaoh] said: 'For certain, the messenger who has been sent to you is indeed a madman'. **28** [Moses] went on: 'He is indeed the Lord of the East and the West and of all that is between them, if you would but use your reason'. **29** [Pharaoh] said: 'If you ever serve a god other than me, I will most certainly have you imprisoned'. **30** Said [Moses]: 'Even if I bring before you a clear proof?' **31** [Pharaoh] said: 'Produce it, then, if you are a man of truth'. **32** So he threw down his staff and behold, it was a serpent, plain for all to see. **33** And he drew out his hand, and behold, it was white to the onlookers. **34** [Pharaoh] said to the noble ones around him: 'This is indeed a sorcerer of great knowledge who wants to drive you out of your land by his sorcery. **35** What, then, do you advise?' **36** They said: 'Let him and his brother wait a while, **37** and send heralds to all cities to bring before you every sorcerer of great skill'. **38** So the sorcerers were assembled at a set time on an appointed day, **39** and the people were asked: 'Will you all be present, **40** so that we may follow the sorcerers if they emerge triumphant?' **41** When the sorcerers arrived they said to Pharaoh: 'Will there be a [handsome] reward for us if we are the ones to prevail?' **42** Said he: 'Yes, indeed! And in that case you will be among those who are close to me'. **43** Moses said to them: 'Throw whatever you are going to throw!' **44** So they threw their ropes and staffs, and said: 'By Pharaoh's might, it is we indeed who will prevail'. **45** Then Moses threw his staff, and it swallowed up their false devices. **46** The sorcerers fell down prostrating themselves, **47** and said: 'We believe in the Lord of all the worlds, **48** the Lord of Moses and Aaron'. **49** [Pharaoh] said: 'You believe in Him even before I have given you permission! Surely, this one must be your master who has taught you witchcraft! But in time you shall come to know. I shall most certainly have your hands and feet cut off on alternate sides, and I shall most certainly crucify you all'. **50** They said: 'No harm [can you cause us]. To our Lord we shall indeed return. **51** We certainly hope that our Lord will forgive us our sins, since we are the first who have believed'. **52** Then We revealed to Moses: 'Set forth with My servants by night, for you will be pursued'. **53** Pharaoh sent heralds to all cities, **54** [saying]: 'These are but a small band, **55** and most certainly they have enraged us; **56** but we are all united, and well prepared'. **57** Thus We drove them out of their gardens, springs, **58** treasures and honourable positions. **59** And We bequeathed it all to the Children of Israel. **60** And so they [Pharaoh's army] pursued them at sunrise. **61** When the two hosts came in sight of each other, the followers of Moses said: 'We shall certainly be overtaken'. **62** He replied: 'No indeed! My Lord is with me and He will guide me'. **63** And We revealed to Moses: 'Strike the sea with your staff'. So it divided, and each part was like a massive mountain. **64** And We caused the others to draw near, **65** and We saved Moses and all who were with him, **66** while We caused the others to drown. **67** Indeed, there is in this a sure sign; yet most of them will not believe. **68** And indeed it is your Lord who is the Mighty One, the Ever-Merciful.

69 Relate to them the story of Abraham, **70** when he said to his father and his people: 'What is that you worship?' **71** They answered: 'We worship idols, and we remain devoted to them'. **72** Said he: 'Do they hear you when you call on them, **73** or benefit you or do you harm?' **74** They said: 'But we found our forefathers doing the same'. **75** He said: 'Do you see those which you have been worshipping – **76** you and your forefathers of old? **77** They are my enemies, except for the Lord of all the worlds. **78** It is He who has created me, and is the One who guides me. **79** He is the One who gives me to eat and to drink. **80** When I fall ill, He is the One who restores me to health, **81** and will cause me to die and then will bring me back to life. **82** It is He also who, I hope, will forgive me my faults on the Day of Judgement'. **83** 'My Lord! Grant me sound judgement, and join me with the righteous; **84** and grant me the advocacy of the truth in later generations; **85** place me among those who will inherit the garden of bliss! **86** Forgive my father; for he is among the ones who have gone astray. **87** Let me not suffer disgrace on the Day when all shall be raised from the dead; **88** the Day when neither wealth nor children will be of any benefit; **89** but only the one who comes to God with a sound heart [will be happy].' **90** Paradise will be brought within sight of the God-fearing; **91** whereas the blazing Fire will be placed in full view of the ones lost in error. **92** It shall be said to them: 'Where is now all that you used to worship instead of God? **93** Can they help you or even help themselves?' **94** They will be hurled into Hell, as also those who are lost in error, **95** and Iblis's hosts, all together. **96** And there, quarrelling with one another, they will say: **97** 'By God, we were obviously in error, **98** when we deemed you equal to the Lord of all the worlds. **99** It was only the truly guilty ones who led us astray. **100** And now we have none to intercede for us **101** nor any loving friend. **102** Would that we had a second chance [in life], so that we could be believers'. **103** Indeed, there is in this a sure sign; yet most of them will not believe. **104** And indeed it is your Lord who is the Mighty One, the Ever-Merciful.

105 The people of Noah, too, denied God's messengers. **106** Their brother Noah said to them: 'Will you have no fear of God? **107** I am a messenger [sent by Him] to you, worthy of all trust. **108** So, fear God and pay heed to me. **109** No reward whatever do I ask of you for it: my reward is only from the Lord of all the worlds. **110** So, fear God and pay heed to me'. **111** They said: 'Are we to believe in you, even though only the lowest of the low follow you?' **112** Said he: 'What knowledge do I have as to what they used to do in the past? **113** Their reckoning rests with none other than my Lord, if you could but understand. **114** I am not one to drive away the believers. **115** I am only a plain warner'. **116** Said they: 'Noah! If you will not desist, you will surely be stoned to death'. **117** He prayed: 'My Lord! My people have denied me. **118** So, judge decisively between me and them, and save me and those of the believers who are with me'. **119** So We saved him, and those with him, in the laden ark, **120** and We caused the others who stayed behind to drown. **121** Indeed, there is in this a sure sign; yet most of them will not believe. **122** And indeed it is your Lord who is the Mighty One, the Ever-Merciful.

123 The 'Ad, too, denied God's messengers. **124** Their brother Hud said to them: 'Will you have no fear of God? **125** I am a messenger [sent by Him] to you, worthy of all trust. **126** So, fear God and pay heed to me. **127** No reward whatever do I ask of you for it: my reward is only from the Lord of all the worlds. **128** Do you build a landmark on every high place, in vain endeavour, **129** and make for yourselves strong structures, hoping to be immortal? **130** When you exercise your power, you do so like cruel tyrants. **131** So, fear God and pay heed to me. **132** Fear Him who has provided you with all that you know. **133** He has provided you with cattle and children,

134 and gardens and springs. **135** Indeed, I fear lest suffering befall you on an awesome day'. **136** They answered: 'It is all one to us whether you admonish us or you never give admonition. **137** This is none but the practice of the ancients. **138** Never are we going to be punished'. **139** Thus they denied him. So We destroyed them. Indeed, there is in this a sure sign; yet most of them will not believe. **140** And indeed it is your Lord who is the Mighty One, the Ever-Merciful.

141 The Thamud, too, denied God's messengers. **142** Their brother Salih said to them: 'Will you have no fear of God? **143** I am a messenger [sent by Him] to you, worthy of all trust. **144** So, fear God and pay heed to me. **145** No reward whatever do I ask of you for it: my reward is only from the Lord of all the worlds. **146** Will you be left secure [forever] in the midst of what you have here, **147** among gardens and springs **148** and plantations and palm-trees laden with ripe fruit? **149** You carve dwellings out of the mountains with great skill. **150** So, fear God and pay heed to me. **151** And pay no heed to the counsel of those who are given to excesses – **152** who spread corruption on earth instead of setting things to rights'. **153** They said: 'You are but one who has been bewitched. **154** You are only a human being like us. So bring us a sign if you are a man of truth'. **155** He said: 'Here is a she-camel: she shall have her drinking share, and you shall have your drinking share, each on an appointed day. **156** Do not harm her, lest suffering befall you on an awesome day'. **157** But they cruelly slew her; then they became regretful. **158** So the suffering befell them. Indeed, there is in this a sure sign; yet most of them will not believe. **159** And indeed it is your Lord who is the Mighty One, the Ever-Merciful.

160 The people of Lot, too, denied God's messengers. **161** Their brother Lot said to them: 'Will you have no fear of God? **162** I am a messenger [sent by Him] to you, worthy of all trust. **163** So, fear God and obey me. **164** No reward whatever do I ask of you for it: my reward is only from the Lord of all the worlds. **165** Of all the creatures in the world, will you lustfully approach males, **166** and reject the wives God has created for you? You are indeed people who transgress all bounds'. **167** Said they: 'Lot! If you will not desist, you will most certainly be expelled'. **168** He said: 'I am one who utterly abhors your doings. **169** My Lord! Save me and my family from what they do'. **170** So We saved him and all his family **171** except an old woman, who was among those who stayed behind. **172** Then We utterly destroyed the others, **173** and rained down upon them a [devastating] rain. Dire indeed was the rain that fell on those who were forewarned. **174** Indeed, there is in this a sure sign; yet most of them will not believe. **175** And indeed it is your Lord who is the Mighty One, the Ever-Merciful.

176 The dwellers of the wooded dales, too, denied God's messengers. **177** Their brother Shuʿayb said to them: 'Will you have no fear of God? **178** I am a messenger [sent by Him] to you, worthy of all trust. **179** So, fear God and obey me. **180** No reward whatever do I ask of you for it: my reward is only from the Lord of all the worlds. **181** Give full measure, and be not of those who give others less [than their due], **182** and weigh with even scales, **183** and do not deprive others of what rightfully belongs to them, and do not act wickedly on earth spreading corruption, **184** and fear Him who has created you as well as the countless generations of old'. **185** They said: 'You are but one who has been bewitched. **186** You are only a human being like us! And, indeed, we believe that you are lying. **187** Cause, then, fragments of the sky to fall down on us, if you are a man of truth'. **188** Answered he: 'My Lord knows fully well all that you do'. **189** But they denied him. Thus suffering overtook them on the day of the darkening cloud. It was truly the suffering of an awesome day. **190** Indeed, there is in this a sure sign; yet most of them will not believe. **191** And indeed it is your Lord who is the Mighty One, the Ever-Merciful.

192 Most certainly, this [Qur'an] has been bestowed from on high by the Lord of all the worlds. **193** The trustworthy Spirit has brought it down **194** into your heart – so that you may give warning, **195** in the clear Arabic tongue. **196** It was surely foretold in the revealed books of former peoples. **197** Is it not sufficient proof for them that the learned ones among the Children of Israel have recognised it [as true]? **198** Had We revealed it to any non-Arab, **199** and had he recited it to them, they would not have believed in it. **200** Thus have We caused it to pass through the hearts of the guilty: **201** they shall not believe in it until they see the grievous suffering. **202** It will come to them all of a sudden, without their being aware of it. **203** And then they will say: 'Could we have a respite?' **204** Do they, then, wish that Our punishment be hurried on? **205** But consider this: If We allow them to enjoy themselves for several years, **206** and then the promised [punishment] befalls them – **207** of what avail to them will be all their past enjoyment? **208** Never have We destroyed any community unless it had received warnings, **209** and reminders. Never do We wrong anyone. **210** No evil spirits have brought down [this Qur'an]. **211** It is not for them [to do so], nor can they. **212** Indeed they are debarred even from hearing it. **213** Hence, do not invoke any other deity side by side with God, lest you find yourself among those suffering punishment. **214** And warn your nearest kindred, **215** and spread the wing of your tenderness over all of the believers who follow you. **216** But if they disobey you, say: 'I am not accountable for what you do'. **217** Place your trust in the Mighty One, the Ever-Merciful **218** who sees you when you stand, **219** and [sees] your movement among those who prostrate themselves [before Him]. **220** It is He alone who hears all and knows all. **221** Shall I tell you upon whom it is that the satans descend? **222** They descend upon every lying sinner. **223** They eagerly listen, but most of them are liars. **224** As for the poets, only those who are lost in error follow them. **225** Are you not aware that they roam confusedly through all valleys, **226** and that they say what they do not do? **227** Excepted are those who believe, and do righteous deeds, and remember God often, and strive to be triumphant after they have been wronged. Those who are bent on wrongdoing will in time know what an evil turn their destiny will surely take.

Surah 27   The Ants

This surah starts with a short introduction followed by stories and a conclusion. The stories begin with a quick episode about when Moses first received his message. We then have a long account of Prophet Solomon and an episode from Prophet Salih's history. There is no other reference in the Qur'an to either of these episodes. Solomon's story relates to his correspondence with the Queen of Sheba culminating in her visit to him and her acceptance of the divine faith. The surah then tells us about the people of Thamud and how they conspired to assassinate Prophet Salih in the middle of the night. Their scheme was foiled by God and their community destroyed as a result. The stories the surah relates are concluded with a brief account of Prophet Lot and his people.

The surah then portrays scenes of the universe and speaks of human nature. In both, it shows that it is all the creation of the One God. It is He who brings it into existence, sustains life, gives provision, knows everything and to whom all shall return. This is followed by some indicators of the approach of the Last Hour and the Day of Judgement.

The Ants

In the Name of God, the Lord of Grace, the Ever-Merciful

1 *Ta. Sin.* These are verses of the Qur'an, a clear, elucidating Book; **2** a guidance and joyful tidings to the believers **3** who attend regularly to prayers and pay their zakat, and who firmly believe in the life to come. **4** As for those who will not believe in the life to come, We make their deeds seem fair to them, and so they wander about in distraction. **5** These are the ones for whom grievous suffering is in store, and who in the life to come shall be the worst losers. **6** Most certainly, you receive the Qur'an out of the grace of One who is wise, all-knowing.

7 Moses said to his family: 'I perceive a fire. I will bring you from there some information, or else, I will bring you a burning brand so that you may warm yourselves'. **8** But when he came close to it, he was addressed: 'Blessed are those in the fire and those around it! And limitless in His glory is God, the Lord of all the worlds'. **9** 'Moses! Truly, I am alone God, the Almighty, the Wise! **10** Now throw down your staff!' But when he saw it moving, as if it were a serpent, he turned and fled, with no thought of turning back. 'Moses, have no fear!' [Said God]: 'Messengers have nothing to fear in My presence. **11** If anyone has done wrong and then replaced the wrong with good; well, I am much-forgiving, ever-merciful. **12** Now place your hand inside your garment, and it will come out [shining] white without blemish. [This is one of] the nine signs for Pharaoh and his people. They are wicked people'. **13** But when Our light-giving signs came to them, they said: 'This is plain sorcery'. **14** Within their souls they knew them to be true, yet they, in their wickedness and arrogance, rejected them. Consider, then, what happened in the end to the evildoers.

15 For sure, We granted knowledge to David and Solomon, and both of them said: 'All praise is due to God who has favoured us above many of His believing servants'. **16** Solomon inherited David. He said: 'O people! We have been taught the speech of birds, and have been given of all good things. This is indeed a manifest favour [from God]'. **17** Before Solomon were marshalled his troops of jinn and men and birds; and they were all lined in orderly ranks. **18** At length, when they came to a valley of ants, one ant said: 'Go into your dwellings, ants, lest Solomon and his troops inadvertently crush you'. **19** He smiled joyously at her words, and said: 'My Lord! Grant me that I will always be grateful for the blessings which You have bestowed on me and on my parents, and that I may do righteous deeds that will meet with Your goodly acceptance; and include me, by Your grace, among Your righteous servants'. **20** He inspected the birds and said: 'Why is it that I do not see the hoopoe? Is he among the absentees? **21** I will certainly punish him severely, or I will kill him, unless He brings me a clear warrant [for his absence]'. **22** But the hoopoe did not take long in coming. He said: 'I have just learnt things that are unknown to you, and I come to you from Sheba with accurate information. **23** I found there a woman ruling over them; and she has been given of all good things, and hers is a magnificent throne. **24** I found her and her people prostrating themselves to the sun instead of God; and Satan has made their deeds seem goodly to them, thus turning them away from the path [of God], so that they cannot find the right way. **25** That they should not prostrate themselves in worship of God who brings forth all that is hidden in the heavens and the earth, and knows what you conceal and what you reveal. **26** God, other than whom there is no deity, the Lord of the [truly] magnificent Throne'. **27** Said [Solomon]: 'We shall see whether you have told the truth or you are a liar. **28** Go with this my letter and deliver it to them;

and then draw back from them, and see what answer they return'. **29** [The Queen of Sheba] said: 'Know, my nobles, that a worthy letter has been delivered to me. **30** It is from Solomon, and it reads, "In the name of God, the Lord of Grace, the Ever-Merciful: **31** Do not exalt yourselves against me, but come to me in submission [to God]". **32** Nobles, counsel me in this my affair; no decision on any matter do I take unless you are present'. **33** They said: 'We are endowed with power and with mighty prowess in war; but the command is yours. Consider, then, what you would command'. **34** Said she: 'When kings enter a country, they despoil it, and make the noble ones of its people the most abject. Thus do they behave. **35** Hence, I am going to send these people a gift and wait to see what the envoys bring back'. **36** When [the Queen's envoy] came to Solomon, he said: 'Is it gold that you would give me? What God has given me is much better than all that He has given you. Yet you rejoice with your own gift. **37** Go back to them, for we shall certainly come to them with forces they cannot match, and we shall certainly drive them from the land in disgrace, and they will be utterly humbled'. **38** Solomon said: 'Which of you, nobles, can bring me her throne before they come to me in submission?' **39** Said an afreet of the jinn: 'I shall bring it to you before you rise from your position. I am powerful enough to do it, and worthy of trust'. **40** But the one who was deeply versed in the Book said: 'I shall bring it to you within the twinkling of your eye'. When he saw it standing before him, he said: 'This is by the Grace of my Lord, so as to test me whether I am grateful or ungrateful. He who is grateful [to God] is but grateful for his own good. As for him who is ungrateful... My Lord is self-sufficient, most–generous'. **41** He [then] said: 'Alter the appearance of her throne: let us see whether she will be able to recognise it, or she will remain unguided'. **42** So when she arrived, she was asked: 'Is your throne like this?' She answered: 'It looks as though it were the same'. We were endowed with knowledge before her, and we have surrendered ourselves. **43** Yet that which she used to worship instead of God had kept her away [from the true faith]. She belonged to an unbelieving nation. **44** She was told to enter the court. When she saw it, she thought it was a lake of water, and she bared her legs. Said he: 'It is but a court smoothly paved with glass!' She said: 'My Lord! I have indeed wronged my soul, but now I submit myself, with Solomon, to God, the Lord of all the worlds'. **45** To Thamud We sent their brother, Salih, and he said: 'Worship God alone', but they split into two contending factions. **46** Said [Salih]: 'My people, why do you seek to hasten evil instead of hoping for the good? Why do you not seek God's forgiveness, so that you may be graced with His mercy?' **47** They answered: 'We augur evil from you and those that follow you'. Said he: 'The evil you augur can come only from God. You are indeed people undergoing a test'. **48** There were in the city nine men who did evil deeds in the land, and would not do any good. **49** They said: 'Let us swear a mutual oath by God that we shall suddenly kill him and his household by night; and then we shall boldly say to his next of kin, "We did not witness the destruction of his household; and we are indeed telling the truth".' **50** They devised a scheme; but We also devised a scheme, while they could not perceive it. **51** Behold what all their scheming came to in the end: We destroyed them utterly, together with all their people, and their dwellings are now empty, ruined, because of their wrongdoing. **52** In this there is a clear sign for people of knowledge. **53** And We saved the people who believed and were God-fearing.

54 And Lot said to his people: 'Would you commit this abomination with your eyes open? **55** Would you approach men with lust rather than women? You are a grossly ignorant people'. **56** His people's only answer was: 'Expel Lot's family from your city! They are folk who keep themselves pure'. **57** So We saved him with his household, except for his wife, whom We destined to be among those who stayed behind. **58** And We rained on the others a rain of destruction. Dire indeed was the rain that fell on those who were forewarned.

59 Say: 'All praise be to God, and peace be upon His servants whom He has chosen. Who is more worthy: God or the false [deities] they associate with Him? **60** Or, who is it that has created the heavens and the earth, and sends down for you water from the skies, with which We cause to grow gardens of delightful beauty? You could have never caused such trees to grow. Could there be any deity alongside God? Nay, they are people who swerve from justice. **61** Or, who is it that made the earth a stable abode and caused rivers to run in its midst, and has set upon it firm mountains, and has placed a barrier between the two great bodies of water? Could there be any deity alongside God? Nay, most of them are devoid of knowledge. **62** Or, who is it that responds to the one in distress when he calls out to Him, and who removes the ill, and makes you inherit the earth? Could there be any deity alongside God? Little do they reflect! **63** Or, who is it that guides you in the midst of the deep darkness of land and sea, and sends forth the winds as heralds of His forthcoming grace? Could there be any deity alongside God? Sublimely exalted is God above anything they associate with Him. **64** Or, who is it that creates all life in the first instance, and then brings it forth anew? And who is it that provides you with sustenance out of heaven and earth? Could there be any deity alongside God?' Say: 'Produce your proof, if you are truthful'. **65** Say: 'None in the heavens or earth knows what is hidden except God. Nor can they ever perceive when they shall be raised from the dead'. **66** Indeed the total sum of their knowledge stops short of comprehending the Hereafter. Nay, they are in doubt of it. Nay, they are blind to it. **67** The unbelievers say: 'What! After we have become dust, we and our forefathers, shall we be brought back [to life]? **68** We have been promised this before, we and our forefathers! This is nothing but fables of the ancients'. **69** Say: 'Go all over the earth and see what happened in the end to the guilty'. **70** Do not grieve over them, nor be distressed by what they scheme. **71** They ask: 'When will this promise be fulfilled, if what you say be true?' **72** Say: 'It may well be that something of that which you so hastily demand has already drawn close to you'. **73** Your Lord is indeed most-bountiful to people, but most of them are ungrateful. **74** And indeed your Lord knows all that their hearts conceal and all that they bring into the open. **75** There is nothing that is hidden in the heavens or the earth but is recorded in a clear book. **76** This Qur'an explains to the Children of Israel most of that over which they disagree. **77** And it is indeed guidance and mercy to those who believe. **78** Your Lord will judge between them in His wisdom; for He alone is almighty, all-knowing. **79** So, place your trust in God; for yours is surely the path of the clear truth. **80** Indeed you cannot make the dead hear; and you cannot make the deaf hear your call when they turn their backs and go away. **81** Nor can you lead the blind out of their error. You can only get those who believe in Our signs to listen; and they will then submit themselves [to God]. **82** When the Word comes to pass against them, We will bring forth to them out of the earth a beast which will say to them that mankind had no real faith in Our revelations. **83** On that Day We shall gather from each community a host of those who denied Our revelations; and they shall be lined in ranks. **84** And when they come forth [God] will say: 'Did you deny My revelations even though you did not comprehend them fully; or what was it that you were doing?' **85** And the Word will come to pass against them because of their wrongdoing, and they will be unable to speak. **86** Are they not aware that it is We who have made the night for them to rest in, and the day to give them light? In this there are truly signs for people who will believe. **87** On that Day the Trumpet will be sounded, and all who are in the heavens and the earth will be stricken with terror, except those God wills to exempt. All shall come to Him in utter humility. **88** And you see the mountains, which you deem so firm, pass away as clouds pass away. Such is the work of God who has ordered all things to perfection. He is indeed fully aware of all that you do. **89** Whoever comes [before Him] with a good deed shall have far better than it; and they will be secure from the terror of that Day. **90** And those who come with evil deeds, their faces will be thrust into the Fire: 'Are you now being recompensed for anything other than what you did [in life]?' **91** I am only bidden to worship the Lord of this city who has made it sacred. To Him all things belong. And I am bidden to be one of those who submit themselves [to God]. **92** And to recite the Qur'an. So whoever chooses to follow the right path does so for his own benefit; and if any chooses to go astray, say: 'I am only a warner'. **93** And say: 'All praise is due to God. He will indeed make you see His signs, and you will recognise them. Your Lord is never heedless of what you do'.

Surah 28   The Story

This surah was revealed in Makkah when the Muslims were small in number, suffering persecution at the hands of the powerful unbelievers. To all appearances, they had no chance against such hardliners who were determined to put an end to the message of Islam. The surah begins with a story and ends with another. In both, it tells that God intervenes to show that no power can stand up to His. The surah tells first of the birth of Moses at a time when Pharaoh was at the height of his tyranny, killing the young children of the Israelites to protect his position. The surah shows that his power could avail him of nothing to thwart God's will. In fact, the newborn Moses is taken to Pharaoh's own palace where he is nursed by his own mother and reared by Pharaoh's wife until he grows up. The surah continues the story until Moses receives his message and confronts Pharaoh, calling on him to abandon his claims and to believe in God's Oneness.

At the end, the surah gives us another story showing a different type of tyranny, with Korah [Qarun] the central character. He was given the power of wealth but this made him exceedingly arrogant. Again, God intervenes to crush him.

In between the two stories, the surah shows some of the great signs in the universe that confirm, for all who wish to know, that God is the Creator of the universe and everything in it. He has the power to accomplish what He wills.

The Story

In the Name of God, the Lord of Grace, the Ever-Merciful

1 *Ta. Sin. Mim.* **2** These are verses of the Book that makes things clear. **3** We shall relate to you some of the story of Moses and Pharaoh, setting forth the truth for people who will believe. **4** Pharaoh exalted himself in the land and divided its people into castes. One group of them he persecuted, slaying their sons and keeping their women alive. For certain, he was one who sows corruption. **5** But it was Our will to bestow Our favour upon those who were oppressed in the land and to make them leaders, and to make them the ones to inherit [the land], **6** and to establish them securely on earth, and to let Pharaoh, Haman and their hosts experience at their hands the very things against which they were taking precaution. **7** We revealed to the mother of Moses:

'Breast-feed him, and then when you have cause to fear for him, cast him in the river, and have no fear and do not grieve. We shall restore him to you, and shall make him one of Our messengers'. **8** Pharaoh's household picked him up; and so [in time] he would become an enemy to them and a source of grief. Pharaoh, Haman and their hosts were sinners indeed. **9** Pharaoh's wife said: 'A joy to the eye he will be for me and for you. Do not kill him. He may well be of use to us, or we may adopt him as our son'. They had no inkling [of what was to happen]. **10** By the morning an aching void came over the heart of Moses' mother, and she would indeed have disclosed his identity had We not strengthened her heart so that she could continue to have faith. **11** She said to his sister: 'Follow him'. So she watched him from a distance, while they were unaware. **12** Right from the very beginning We caused him to refuse all nurses' breasts. So, his sister said: 'Shall I direct you to a family who might bring him up for you and take good care of him?' **13** Thus We restored him to his mother, so that she might rejoice in him and grieve no more, and that she might know that God's promise always comes true; even though most people do not know this. **14** When he attained his full manhood and became fully mature, We bestowed on him wisdom and knowledge. Thus do We reward those who do good. **15** One day he entered the city at a time when its people were unaware [of his presence]. He found there two men fighting, one belonging to his own people and the other to his enemies. And the one from his own people cried out to him for help against the one from his enemies, whereupon Moses struck him down with his fist and killed him. He said: 'This is of Satan's doing! Indeed, he is an open foe, seeking to lead man astray'. **16** He then prayed: 'My Lord! I have certainly wronged myself, so forgive me'. So He forgave him. He alone is much-forgiving, ever-merciful. **17** He said: 'My Lord! For all that with which You have blessed me, never shall I give help to wrongdoers'. **18** Next morning, he was in the city, fearful, vigilant, when he saw the man who sought his help the day before again crying out to him for help. Moses said to him: 'Indeed, you are clearly a quarrelsome fellow'. **19** But then, when he was about to strike the one who was their enemy, the latter exclaimed: 'Moses! Do you want to kill me as you killed another man yesterday? You want only to become a tyrant in the land, and you do not want to be one who sets things right'. **20** Then a man came at speed from the farthest end of the city. He said: 'Moses! The nobles are plotting to kill you. So get yourself away. I am giving you sincere advice'. **21** So he left the city in fear, vigilant. He prayed: 'My Lord! Save me from all wrongdoing folk'. **22** And as he turned his face towards Madyan, he said: 'I do hope that my Lord will guide me to the right path'. **23** When he arrived at the wells of Madyan, he found there a large group of people drawing water [for their herds and flocks], and at some distance from them he found two women who were keeping back their flock. He asked them: 'What is the matter with you two?' They said: 'We cannot water [our animals] until the herdsmen drive home. Our father is a very old man'. **24** So he watered their flock for them, and then he withdrew into the shade and prayed: 'My Lord! Truly am I in dire need of any good which You may send me'. **25** One of the two women then came back to him, walking shyly, and said: 'My father invites you, so that he might duly reward you for having watered our flock for us'. And when [Moses] went to him and told him his story, he said: 'Have no fear. You are now safe from those wrongdoing folk'. **26** Said one of the two women: 'My father! Hire him; for the best person that you may hire is one who is strong and worthy of trust'. **27** [The father] said: 'I will give you one of these two daughters of mine in marriage on the understanding that you will remain eight years in my service. If you should complete ten years, it will be of your own choice. I do not wish to impose any hardship on you. You will find me, if God so wills, an upright man'. **28** Answered [Moses]: 'This is agreed between me and you. Whichever of the two terms I fulfil, I trust I shall not be wronged. God is the witness to all we say'. **29** When Moses had fulfilled his term, and was travelling with his family, he perceived a fire on the slope of Mount Sinai. So he said to his family: 'Wait here, for I perceive a fire. Perhaps I may bring you from there some information, or a burning brand from the fire so that you may warm yourselves'. **30** But when he came close to it, he was addressed from the right-side bank of the valley, out of the tree on the blessed site: 'Moses! Truly, I am God, the Lord of all the worlds'. **31** 'Throw down your staff!' But when he saw it moving, as if it were a serpent, he turned and fled, with no thought of turning back. [God said]: 'Moses! Draw near and have no fear! You are certainly secure'. **32** 'Now place your hand inside your garment, and it will come out [shining] white without blemish. Then draw your arm close to your side to allay your fear. These, then, are two proofs from your Lord to Pharaoh and his nobles. They are indeed wicked people'. **33** He said: 'My Lord! I have killed one of them and I fear that they will kill me. **34** And my brother, Aaron, is better in speech than I am. So send him with me as a helper, so that he will confirm what I say, for I fear that they will accuse me of lying'. **35** Said He: 'We shall strengthen your arm with your brother, and will endow both of you with power, so that they will not be able to touch you. By virtue of Our signs shall you two and those who follow you prevail'. **36** When Moses came to them with Our clear signs, they said: 'This is nothing but forged sorcery. Never did we hear of the like of this among our forefathers of old'. **37** Moses replied: 'My Lord knows best who comes with guidance from Him, and to whom the future belongs. Never will the evildoers be successful'. **38** 'Nobles!' said Pharaoh. 'I know of no deity that you could have other than myself. Well, Haman, kindle for me a fire [to bake bricks] of clay, and then build me a lofty tower, so that I may have a look at the god of Moses; even though I am convinced that he is one who tells lies'. **39** Thus arrogantly did he and his hosts behave on earth, against all right, thinking that they would never return to Us. **40** And so We seized him and his hosts and cast them in the sea. Look what happened in the end to those wrongdoers. **41** And We made them leaders who called others to the Fire. No help will they ever receive on the Day of Resurrection. **42** We caused a curse to follow them in this world, and on Resurrection Day they will be among those who are spurned. **43** And so after We had destroyed those earlier generations, We gave Moses the Book providing insight for mankind, as a guidance and grace, so that they may reflect.

44 You certainly were not present on the western side of the Mountain when We issued the Commandments to Moses, nor were you one of those who witnessed [those events]. **45** But We raised up many generations, and long was their span of life. Nor did you dwell among the people of Madyan, reciting Our revelations to them. Rather, it is We who send messengers. **46** Nor indeed were you present on the slopes of Mount Sinai when We called out [to Moses]. Rather, it is an act of your Lord's mercy so that you may warn people to whom no warner has come before you, so that they may perchance reflect. **47** [We have sent you] lest they say when a disaster befalls them as an outcome of what their own hands have wrought, 'Our Lord! If only You had sent us a messenger, we would have followed Your revelations, and would have been among the believers'. **48** Now when the truth has come to them from Us, they say: 'Why has he not been given the like of what Moses was given?' But did they not deny the truth of what Moses was formerly given? Indeed they said: 'These are two kinds of sorcery, each supporting the other'. And they add: 'We reject both of them'. **49** Say: 'Produce, then, a Book from God which would offer better guidance than these two and I shall follow it, if what you say be true!' **50** But if they do not respond to you, then know that they are following only their own whims. Who could be more astray than one who follows his own whims without any guidance from God. Certainly God does not guide those who are wrongdoing. **51** We have indeed caused this word [of Ours] to reach them so that they may reflect. **52** Those to whom We sent the Book before this believe in it. **53** And when it is recited to them, they say: 'We believe in it, for it is the truth from our Lord. Indeed even before this have we submitted ourselves to Him'. **54** These are the ones who shall be given their reward twice for having been patient in adversity, having repelled evil with good, and having spent in charity out of what We have provided for them. **55** And whenever they hear frivolous talk they turn away from it and say: 'To us our deeds and to you yours. Peace be to you! We will have nothing to do with ignorant folk'. **56** Indeed, you cannot guide aright everyone whom you love. It is God who guides whom He wills. He knows best those who are guided aright. **57** They say: 'If we were to follow the guidance along with you, we would be torn away from our land'. Have We not given them a secure sanctuary to which are brought the fruits of all things, as a provision from Us? But most of them have no knowledge. **58** How many a community that exulted in its life [of ease and plenty] have We destroyed. The dwellings they left behind were but scarcely inhabited. It is We who are the only heirs. **59** Your Lord would never destroy a community without first sending them a messenger who would recite to them Our revelations. Never would We destroy a community unless its people are intent on wrongdoing. **60** Whatever you are given is but for the enjoyment of life in this world and for its embellishment, but that which is with God is much better and more enduring. Will you not use your reason? **61** Is the one to whom We have given a goodly promise which he shall certainly see fulfilled comparable to one whom We have given much of the enjoyment of this world but who, on Resurrection Day, will be one of those brought before Us? **62** On that Day, He will call to them and ask: 'Where are those whom you alleged to be My partners?' **63** Those against whom the word [of judgement] has come to pass will say: 'Our Lord! Those whom we have led astray, we only led astray as we ourselves had gone astray. We now disown them before You. It was not us that they worshipped'. **64** They will be told: 'Call on those you alleged to be [God's] partners', and they will call to them, but the latter will not respond to them. They will then see the suffering [that awaits them]. If only they had been open to guidance! **65** On that Day, He will call to them and ask: 'What answer did you give to My messengers?'

66 But to them all information will be blotted out and they will not even ask any questions. **67** However, anyone who repents, believes and does righteous deeds may well be among those who are successful. **68** Your Lord creates and chooses whatever He pleases. Never can they have such choice. Limitless is God in His glory and exalted is He above all those they associate with Him as partners. **69** And your Lord knows all that their hearts conceal and all that they bring out into the open. **70** He is God, other than whom there is no deity. To Him all praise is due at the first and at the last; with Him rests all judgement, and to Him you shall all return. **71** Say: 'Have you considered if God were to make the night perpetual over you, without break, till the Day of Resurrection, is there any deity other than God that could bring you light? Will you not, then, listen?' **72** Say: 'Have you considered if God were to make the day perpetual over you, without break, till the Day of Resurrection, is there any deity other than God that could bring you a night in which to rest? Will you not, then, see?' **73** It is out of His grace that He has made for you the night and the day, so that you might have rest and seek to obtain some of His bounty, and that you may have cause to be grateful. **74** On that Day, He will call to them and ask: 'Where are those whom you alleged to be My partners?' **75** We shall draw from each community a witness, and We shall then say [to the unbelievers]: 'Produce your evidence!' They will then come to realise that all truth belongs to God alone, and all the falsehood they invented will forsake them.

76 Qarun [i.e. Korah] was one of the people of Moses, but he treated them unjustly. We had granted him such treasures that their very keys would have been too heavy a burden for a band of strong men. His people said to him: 'Do not exult [in your riches]; for God does not love those who are exultant. **77** Seek instead, by means of what God has granted you, the good of the life to come, without forgetting your rightful share in this world; and do good just as God has done good to you, and do not seek to spread corruption on earth; for God does not love the ones who spread corruption'. **78** Answered he: 'I have been given this wealth only by virtue of the knowledge that I have'. Did he not know that God had destroyed many a generation that preceded him, and who were far more powerful and greater in wealth than he? The guilty are not questioned about their sins. **79** And so he went forth before his people in all his pomp. Those who cared only for the life of this world said: 'Oh, would that we had the like of what Qarun has been given! He is certainly a man of great fortune!' **80** But those who had been granted true knowledge said: 'Woe to you! God's reward is by far the best for any who believes and does what is right. Yet none can attain this other than those who are patient in adversity'. **81** Then We caused the earth to swallow him, together with his dwelling. He had none to give him support against God, nor was he able to protect himself. **82** By the morning, those who but yesterday had longed to be in his place were now saying: 'Behold! It is indeed God who gives in abundance, or gives in small measure, to whom He wills of His servants. Had not God been gracious to us, He might have caused the earth to swallow us, too. Behold! The unbelievers will not achieve success'. **83** We grant that happy life in the Hereafter to those who do not seek to exalt themselves on earth or to spread corruption. The future belongs to the God-fearing. **84** Whoever comes [before Him] with a good deed shall have far better than it; but anyone who comes with an evil deed will be requited with nothing more than the like of what they have done.

85 He who has made the Qur'an binding on you will surely bring you back to the place of return. Say: 'My Lord knows best who has come with right guidance, and who is lost in obvious error'. **86** You could never hope that this Book would be conferred on you. But it came by your Lord's grace. Hence, lend no support to the unbelievers. **87** Never let them turn you away from revelations after they have been bestowed upon you from on high; but continue to call people to [believe in] your Lord. And never be one of those who associate partners with God. **88** Never call on any deity side by side with God. There is no deity other than Him. Everything is bound to perish except Himself. With Him rests all judgement, and to Him you all shall return.

Surah 29   The Spider

This surah addresses the question of trial to which believers may be subjected by hostile enemies. It suggests this as something that believers may have to endure so as to prove their claims to be believers. It is not enough that one should claim to believe in God. Such a claim must be proven by standing firm in the face of opposition and persecution. The surah refers to the history of several prophets and to others who were hostile to the divine faith. All these references to the Prophets Noah, Abraham, Lot and Shuʿayb, and also to Pharoah, Korah and Haman are very brief. Yet they describe different types of trials endured by believers and different obstacles placed in the way of divine faith.

The surah refers to these forces that try to resist the divine message as flimsy. They may have their day, but they are certain to come to a miserable end. They are compared to a spider and its web, which is the frailest of all homes.

The surah stresses that all those prophets preached what is essentially the same message, taking its final form with the message of Prophet Muhammad (peace be upon him and upon all prophets).

The Spider

In the Name of God, the Lord of Grace, the Ever-Merciful

1 *Alif. Lam. Mim.* 2 Do people think that once they say: 'We are believers', they will be left alone and not put to a test? 3 We certainly tested those who lived before them; and so most certainly God knows those who speak the truth and most certainly He knows those who are liars. 4 Or do those who do evil deeds think that they can escape Us? How ill they judge! 5 Whoever looks forward with hope to meeting God [let him be ready for it]; for the end set by God is bound to come. He alone hears all and knows all. 6 Whoever strives hard [for God's cause] does so for his own good. For certain, God is in no need of anything in all the worlds. 7 As for those who believe and do righteous deeds, We shall most certainly erase their bad deeds, and shall most certainly reward them in accordance with the best that they ever did. 8 We have enjoined upon man goodness towards his parents: yet should they endeavour to make you associate as partner with Me something of which you have no knowledge, do not obey them. It is

to Me that you shall all return, when I shall inform you about all that you were doing [in life]. **9** As for those who believe and do righteous deeds, We shall most certainly admit them among the righteous. **10** Among people, there are those who say: 'We believe in God', yet when any of them is made to suffer in God's cause, he thinks that oppression by man is as grievous as God's punishment. However, should help from your Lord be forthcoming, he is sure to say: 'We have always been with you!' Is not God fully aware of what is in the hearts of all creatures? **11** Most certainly God knows those who truly believe and most certainly He knows those who are hypocrites. **12** The unbelievers say to those who believe: 'Follow our way and we shall indeed take your sins upon ourselves'. But never will they take upon themselves any of their sins. Liars indeed they are. **13** Yet most certainly will they bear their own burdens, and other burdens besides their own; and most certainly will they be called to account on the Day of Resurrection for all their false assertions.

14 We sent Noah to his people and he dwelt among them for a thousand years bar fifty; and then the floods overwhelmed them as they were deep in wrongdoing; **15** but We saved him, together with all those who were in the ark, which We made as a sign for all people. **16** And Abraham said to his people: 'Worship God, and fear Him. This is best for you, if you but knew it! **17** You worship only idols instead of God, and thus you create falsehood. Those that you worship instead of God do not have it in their power to provide sustenance for you. Seek, then, all sustenance from God, and worship Him alone and be grateful to Him. Indeed, to Him you shall return. **18** If you disbelieve, other communities also disbelieved before your time. A messenger of God is not bound to do more than clearly deliver His message'. **19** Are they not aware how God creates [life] in the first instance, and then brings it forth anew? This is indeed easy for God. **20** Say: 'Go all over the earth and see how God has originated His creation in the first instance; and then He will certainly bring about the second life. Most certainly, God has the power over all things. **21** He punishes whom He will, and bestows His mercy on whom He will. To Him you shall be made to return. **22** And never can you elude him, neither on earth nor in the skies. You have none to protect you from God and none to give you support'. **23** Those who deny God's signs and the meeting with Him are indeed the ones who abandon all hope of My mercy. It is for these that painful suffering awaits. **24** [Abraham's] people's only answer was: 'Kill him, or burn him!' But God saved him from the fire. In this there are signs for people who believe. **25** And he said: 'You have taken for worship idols instead of God for no reason other than to have a bond of love between yourselves, in the life of this world. But, then, on Resurrection Day, you shall disown one another and curse one another; and your abode shall be the Fire, and you will have none to support you'. **26** Lot believed in him. He said: 'I shall migrate for the sake of my Lord. He alone is almighty, wise'. **27** We gave him Isaac and Jacob, and caused prophethood and revelation to continue among his offspring. We granted him his reward in this world; and, in the life to come, he will certainly be among the righteous. **28** And Lot said to his people: 'You certainly commit abominations such as none in all the worlds has ever committed before you. **29** Will you approach men [with lust], assault people on the highway, and commit shameful acts in your meeting places?' But his people's only response was to say: 'Bring down upon us God's punishment, if you truly are one who speaks the truth'. **30** He said: 'My Lord! Support You me against these people who spread corruption'. **31** When Our [angel] messengers came to Abraham with happy news, they [also] said: 'We are about to destroy the people of this town, for its people are truly wrongdoers'. **32** He said: 'But Lot lives there!' They answered: 'We know fully well who is there. We shall certainly deliver him and his household, except his wife. She will indeed be among those who stay behind'. **33** Then when Our messengers arrived at Lot's, he was terribly grieved on their account and felt powerless to protect them; but they said: 'Have no fear, and do not grieve. We shall certainly deliver you and your household, except your wife. She will indeed be among those who stay behind. **34** We shall certainly bring down upon the people of this town a horror from heaven in requital of all their wicked deeds'. **35** We made of it a clear sign for people who use their reason. **36** And to the people of Madyan We sent their brother Shu'ayb, who said: 'My people, worship God alone, and look forward to the Last Day, and do not act wickedly to spread corruption on earth'. **37** But they accused him of lying. Thereupon an earthquake overtook them and the morning found them lying lifeless on the ground in their very homes. **38** And 'Ad and Thamud [We also destroyed]. This has been evident to you from their dwellings. Satan had made their evil deeds seem goodly to them, and thus had turned them away from the path [of God] despite their having had the ability to perceive the truth. **39** And Qarun [Korah], Pharaoh and Haman! Moses had come to them with all evidence of the truth, but they behaved with arrogance on earth. Indeed, they could not escape. **40** We took each one of them to task for their sins: upon some of

them We let loose a deadly stormwind; and some were overtaken by
a blast; and some We caused to be swallowed by the earth; and some
We caused to drown. It was not God who wronged them, but it was
they who wronged themselves. **41** Those who take anyone other than
God for their protectors may be compared to the spider which makes
for itself a home. Indeed the spider's home is the frailest of all homes,
if they but knew it. **42** God certainly knows the nature of whatever
people invoke instead of Him. He alone is the Almighty, the Wise.
43 Such are the comparisons We draw for people's benefit, but none
will grasp their meaning except the people of knowledge. **44** God has
created the heavens and the earth in accordance with the truth. Indeed,
in this there is a sign for people who believe. **45** Recite what has been
revealed to you of the Book, and attend regularly to your prayer; for
prayer restrains people from loathsome deeds and from all that is evil.
To remember God is greater still. God knows all that you do.

46 Do not argue with the people of earlier revelations in other
than the most kindly manner, except for those of them who are intent
on wrongdoing; and say: 'We believe in that which has been revealed
to us, as well as that which has been revealed to you, for our God
and your God is one. It is to Him that we submit ourselves'. **47** Thus
it is that We have revealed this Book to you. Those to whom We
have given the Book believe in it, and also among these are some
who believe in it. None knowingly rejects Our revelations other than
the unbelievers. **48** Never have you been able to read a book before
this, nor have you ever been able to transcribe one with your right
hand; or else those who cling to falsehood would have had cause to
doubt. **49** Nay, but this [Qur'an] consists of verses that are clear to the
hearts of those gifted with real knowledge. None knowingly rejects
Our revelations other than the wrongdoers. **50** They say: 'Why have
no miraculous signs ever been bestowed upon him from on high by
his Lord?' Say: 'Signs are in the power of God alone; I am only a
plain warner'. **51** Is it not enough for them that We have revealed to
you this Book which is being read out to them? Indeed there is in it
much grace and a reminder to people who will believe. **52** Say: 'God
is sufficient as a witness between me and you! He knows all that
is in the heavens and the earth; and they who believe in falsehood
and disbelieve in God will certainly be the losers'. **53** They challenge
you to hasten their punishment. Indeed, had not a term been set for
it, that punishment would have already come upon them. Still, it
will most certainly come upon them of a sudden, and they will be
taken unawares. **54** They challenge you to hasten the punishment;

but indeed Hell is encompassing the unbelievers. **55** [That will be] on the Day when suffering will overwhelm them from above and from beneath their feet. He will then say: 'Taste now [the result of] your own doings'. **56** You servants of Mine who have believed! Spacious is My earth: worship Me alone, then. **57** Every soul shall taste death. Then to Us you all must return. **58** Those who believe and do righteous deeds We shall certainly lodge in lofty mansions in Paradise through which running waters flow, therein to abide. **59** Excellent is the reward of those who strive, those who are patient in adversity and in their Lord place their trust. **60** How many a living creature is there that does not bear its sustenance! It is God who provides for them and for you. He alone hears all and knows all. **61** If you were to ask them: 'Who is it that has created the heavens and the earth, and made the sun and the moon subservient [to His laws]?' they will be sure to answer: 'God'. How perverted, then, are their minds! **62** It is indeed God who grants sustenance in abundance, or gives it in small measure, to whom He wills of His servants. God has full knowledge of everything. **63** If you were to ask them: 'Who is it that sends water from the skies, thus giving life to the earth after it had been lifeless?' they will be sure to answer: 'God'. Say: 'All praise is due to God alone!' Yet most of them are without reason. **64** The life of this world is but amusement and play. It is the life to come that is the only true life, if they but knew it. **65** When they embark on a ship, they call to God, sincere in their faith in Him alone; but as soon as He has brought them safe ashore, they begin to associate partners with Him, **66** and thus they show their ingratitude for what We have given them, and go on enjoying their worldly life. Before long they will come to know [the truth]. **67** Are they, then, not aware that We have set up a secure sanctuary while people are being snatched away from all around them? Will they, then, continue to believe in what is false and to deny God's blessings? **68** Who could be more wicked than one who invents lies against God, or denies the truth when it reaches him? Is not Hell the proper abode for the unbelievers? **69** But as for those who strive hard in Our cause, We shall most certainly guide them to paths that lead unto Us. God is indeed with those who do good.

Surah 30   The Byzantines

The surah starts with a reference to a particular event, namely the Byzantines defeat at the hands of the Persian Empire in the early years of the Islamic message. This defeat gave the Arab idolaters in Makkah something to boast about, whereby they said that the Byzantines who believed in one god were defeated by the Persians who, like them, worshipped multiple deities. The surah's opening verses foretell that the Byzantines would be victorious a few years later. It also tells that on that day the believers would rejoice in God's support. This indicates the strong affiliation between the enemies of the divine faith. The idolater Arabs had no love for the Persians and did not follow the Persian religion. Yet they were delighted at their victory against the Byzantines who were Christians, simply because the latter believed in God. Similarly, the bond of faith is clear between those who believe in God's Oneness.

The surah uses all this to drive home the nature of the divine message, referring to a great variety of God's signs in the universe and in man and his nature. It portrays some of the phenomena that appear across the universe. It concludes with a reference to the various stages of man's life and how he develops from a powerless baby to a man full of vigour before weakness creeps again in old age. Believers, however, should remain strong, trusting to God's help.

The Byzantines

In the Name of God, the Lord of Grace, the Ever-Merciful

1 *Alif. Lam. Mim.* 2 Defeated have been the Byzantines 3 in the lands close-by; yet despite this their defeat, they will gain victory within a few years. 4 All power of decision belongs to God before and after. And on that day the believers will rejoice in God's support. 5 He grants support to whomever He wills. He is the Almighty, the Ever-Merciful. 6 This is God's promise. Never does God fail to fulfil His promise; but most people do not know it. 7 They only know the outer surface of this world's life, whereas of the Hereafter they remain unaware. 8 Would they never reflect in their own minds? God has not created the heavens and the earth and all that is between them other than in accordance with the truth and for a specific term set [by Him]. Yet there are many people who deny the truth that they will meet their

Lord. **9** Have they never travelled around the world and seen what was the fate of those who lived before their time? Superior were those in power than they are, and they cultivated the earth and built it up even better than these are doing. To them also came their messengers with all evidence of the truth. Yet, it was not God who wronged them, but it was they who wronged themselves. **10** But then, evil was the end of those who wrought evil, denying God's revelations and deriding them. **11** God originates creation, and then brings it back; then to Him shall you all return. **12** When the Last Hour strikes, the guilty will be speechless with despair, **13** for they will have no intercessors from among those their alleged partners [of God], and they will themselves reject those alleged partners. **14** And when the Last Hour strikes, they will all be divided: **15** as for those who believed and did righteous deeds, they shall be happy in a garden of delight; **16** but as for those who rejected the truth and denied Our revelations and the certainty of the meeting in the Hereafter, they will be brought up for punishment. **17** Extol, then, God's limitless glory both in your evening hours and in your morning hours. **18** To Him is due all praise in the heavens and the earth, at twilight and at noon. **19** He it is who brings forth the living out of that which is dead, and brings forth the dead out of that which is alive, and gives life to the earth after it has been lifeless. Likewise shall you be raised to life. **20** One of His signs is that He created you from dust; and, behold, you become human beings spreading far and wide. **21** And among His signs is that He creates for you spouses out of your own kind, so that you might incline towards them, and He engenders love and tenderness between you. In this there are clear signs indeed for people who think. **22** And among His signs are the creation of the heavens and the earth, and the diversity of your tongues and colours. In this there are clear signs indeed for those who are endowed with knowledge. **23** And among His signs is your sleep, at night and in daytime, as well as your quest for some of His bounty. In this there are clear signs indeed for people who listen. **24** And among His signs is that He displays before you the lightning, giving rise to both fear and hope, and sends down water from the skies, with which He gives life to the earth after it had been lifeless. In this there are clear signs indeed for people who use their reason. **25** And among His signs is that the skies and the earth stand firm at His behest. Then, in the end, when with one call He summons you from the earth, you will all rise. **26** To Him belongs all those in the heavens and the earth: all devoutly obey Him. **27** It is He who creates [life] in the first instance, and then brings it forth anew; and most easy is this for Him. His is the most sublime attribute in the heavens and the earth. He is the Almighty, the Wise. **28** He sets you this comparison, drawn from your own life. Would you have some of those whom your right hands possess as partners in whatever We may have bestowed on you as sustenance, so that you all would have equal shares in it, and you would fear them just as you might fear one another? Thus clearly do We spell out revelations for people who use their reason. **29** Nay, but the wrongdoers follow their own desires, without having any knowledge. Who could guide those whom God has let go astray? They shall have none to support them. **30** Set your face steadily towards the true faith, turning away from all that is false, in accordance with the natural disposition which God has instilled into man. Nothing can change God's creation. Such is the ever-true faith; but most people do not know it. **31** Turn, all of you, to Him, and remain God-fearing. **32** Attend regularly to prayer and do not be among those who associate partners with God, those who have broken the unity of their faith and have become sects, each group delighted with what they hold.

33 When harm touches people they call out to their Lord for help, turning to Him in repentance. But when He gives them a taste of His grace, some of them associate partners with their Lord, [as if] to show their ingratitude for what We have given them. **34** Enjoy, then, your life [as you may]; before long you will come to know [the truth]. **35** Have We ever sent down to them a warrant to confirm what they associate as partners with God? **36** When We give people a taste of grace, they rejoice in it; but if evil befalls them as an outcome of what their own hands have wrought, they lose all hope. **37** Are they not aware that God gives in abundance, or in scant measure, to whom He wills? In this there are clear signs indeed for people who believe. **38** Hence, give his due to the near of kin, as well as to the needy and the traveller in need. This is best for all who seek God's countenance. It is they who shall be successful. **39** Whatever you may give out in usury so that it might increase through other people's property will bring no increase with God, whereas all that you give out in charity, seeking God's countenance, will bring you multiple increase. **40** It is God who has created you, and then has provided you with sustenance, and then will cause you to die, and then will bring you to life again. Can any of those whom you associate as partners with Him do any of these things? Limitless is God in His glory, and sublimely exalted above anything which people may allege to be partner with Him. **41** Corruption has become rife on land and sea in consequence of what people's hands have wrought; and so He will let them taste the consequences of some of their doings, so that they might mend their ways. **42** Say: 'Travel around the world and see what was the fate of those who lived before you. Most of them did associate partners with God'. **43** So set your face steadfastly towards the one true faith before there comes from God a Day which cannot be averted. On that Day all will be divided: **44** he who has denied the truth will have to bear the consequences of his denial, whereas those who did what is right will have smoothed a way [to Paradise] for themselves. **45** And so it is that He might reward, out of His bounty, those who have believed and done righteous deeds. He certainly does not love the unbelievers. **46** And among His signs is that He sends forth the winds bearing good news, so that He might give you a taste of His grace, and that ships might sail at His bidding; so that you might go about in quest of some of His bounty, and that you might have cause to be grateful. **47** We have certainly sent before you messengers to their own peoples, and they brought them clear evidence of the truth. Therefore, We inflicted punishment upon those who deliberately did evil. It is incumbent upon Us to give support to the believers. **48** It is God who sends forth the winds so that they raise clouds, whereupon He spreads them as He wills across the skies, and causes them to break up so that you can see the rain issuing from within it. **49** As soon as He causes it to fall upon whomever He wills of His servants, they rejoice, even though a short while ago, before it was sent down upon them, they had abandoned all hope. **50** Behold, then, the effects of God's grace: how He gives life to the earth after it had been lifeless! It is He who can bring the dead back to life; for it is He indeed who has power over all things. **51** If We send a [scorching] wind and they see it turning yellow, they begin after that to deny the truth. **52** Indeed you cannot make the dead hear; and you cannot make the deaf hear your call when they turn their backs and go away. **53** Nor can you lead the blind out of their error. You can only get those who believe in Our signs to listen; and they will then submit themselves [to God]. **54** It is God who creates you in a state of weakness, and then after weakness He brings about strength in you, and then after strength He brings about your weakness and old age. He creates what He wills; and He alone has all knowledge and power. **55** When the Last Hour strikes, the evildoers will swear that they had not tarried on earth longer than an hour. Thus they used to delude themselves. **56** But those who were endowed with knowledge and faith will say: 'Indeed, you have tarried, in accordance with God's decree, until the Day of Resurrection. This is, then, the Day of Resurrection, but you did not know it'. **57** And so on that Day their excuse will be of no avail to those wrongdoers, nor will they be allowed to make amends. **58** We have set for people in this Qur'an all sorts of illustrations. Yet if you present them with any sign, the unbelievers will say: 'You are but making false claims'. **59** Thus does God seal the hearts of those who do not want to know [the truth]. **60** Therefore, persevere patiently. For certain, God's promise will come true. So, let not the ones deprived of certainty trouble your mind.

Surah 31   Luqman

This surah discusses the central question of faith in four rounds, varying its approach each time. It begins by showing people's different attitudes to belief in God's Oneness and life after death. Those who believe realise that this is a most serious issue and approach it as such, while unbelievers scoff at the signs God has placed in the world around them pointing to the truth. They turn a deaf ear to God's revelations and a blind eye to all that they see of His creation and manifestations of His power. The second discourse (verses 12–19) takes the form of an admonition by Luqman to his son. It is a gentle admonition reminding us of the origin of man and how he is created. It couples this with sound advice to avoid unbecoming practices and to keep to what is likely to be of benefit. The third address (verses 20–28) portrays scenes of the heavens and the earth and the variety of favours God has placed in them for man's benefit. It follows this with reminding people of their accountability and the reward or punishment their actions are certain to earn them. The last presentation employs different scenes from nature and the universe, starting with the succession of day and night. It concludes with the statement that only God knows the timing of the Last Hour, sends down the rain, knows all creatures when they are still in their mothers' wombs, the future actions of every creature and their places of death. None of such information is known to humans.

Luqman

In the Name of God, the Lord of Grace, the Ever-Merciful

1 *Alif. Lam. Mim.* **2** These are verses of the divine Book, full of wisdom, **3** providing guidance and mercy for those who excel in doing good, **4** attend regularly to prayers, give in charity and are indeed certain of the Hereafter. **5** Those are the ones who follow their Lord's guidance, and they are the ones who will be successful. **6** Among people there are some who would pay for idle talk, so as to lead people astray from the path of God, without knowledge, and thus they turn it to ridicule. For such people there is shameful suffering in store. **7** When Our revelations are conveyed to such a person, he turns away in his arrogance as though he had not heard them, as though there were heaviness in his ears. Give him, then, the news of painful suffering.

8 Those who believe and do righteous deeds shall have gardens of bliss in which to abide in accordance with God's true promise. **9** He is the Almighty, the Wise. **10** He has created the skies without any supports that you can see, and has placed firm mountains on earth, lest it sway with you, and has scattered through it all manner of living creatures. We send down water from the skies to cause every kind of goodly plant to grow on earth in pairs. **11** This is all God's creation. Show me, then, what others might have created! Surely, the wrongdoers are in obvious error. **12** We bestowed wisdom on Luqman: 'Be grateful to God; for he who is grateful is only grateful for his own benefit. As for the one who is ungrateful; well, God is self-sufficient, ever to be praised'. **13** Luqman said to his son, admonishing him: 'My dear son! Do not associate any partners with God; for, to associate partners with Him is indeed a great wrong'. **14** We have enjoined upon man goodness to his parents: his mother bore him going from weakness to weakness, and his weaning takes place within two years. Be grateful to Me and to your parents. With Me is the end of all journeys. **15** Yet should they endeavour to make you associate as partner with Me something of which you have no knowledge, do not obey them, but [even then] bear them company in this world's life with kindness, and follow the path of those who turn towards Me. In the end, it is to Me that you shall all return, when I shall inform you about all that you were doing [in life]. **16** 'My dear son! If there be something which is no more than the weight of a grain of mustard seed, and though it be hidden in a rock, or in the skies, or in the earth, God will bring it forth. God is gracious, all-aware. **17** My dear son! Attend regularly to prayer, and enjoin the doing of what is right and forbid the doing of what is wrong, and endure with fortitude whatever befalls you. These are matters that require strong resolve. **18** Do not turn your cheek away from people in false pride, nor walk haughtily on earth. God does not love anyone who is arrogant, boastful. **19** Be of modest bearing in your walk, and lower your voice; for the most hideous of voices is the braying of the ass'.

20 Are you not aware that God has made subservient to you all that is in the heavens and the earth, and has lavished upon you His blessings, outward and inward? Yet some people argue about God without having any knowledge, without guidance, and without any light-giving revelations. **21** When it is said to them, 'Follow what God has revealed', they say, 'No; but we will follow only what we found our forefathers believing in'. Why, even if Satan is beckoning them to the suffering of the blazing Fire. **22** Whoever submits himself to God and excels in good deeds has indeed taken hold of a most firm support. With God rests the final outcome of all events. **23** And whoever disbelieves; let not their unbelief grieve you. To Us they must all return, and then We shall inform them about all that they were doing [in life]. God has full knowledge of what is in people's hearts. **24** We will let them enjoy themselves for a short while, but We shall ultimately drive them into severe suffering. **25** If you were to ask them: 'Who is it that has created the heavens and the earth?', they will be sure to answer: 'God'. Say: 'All praise is due to God alone!' Yet most of them do not understand. **26** To God belongs all that is in the heavens and the earth. Indeed, God is the One who is self-sufficient, worthy of all praise. **27** Were all the trees on earth to be made into pens, and the sea ink, with seven more seas yet added to it, the words of God would not be exhausted. God is indeed almighty, wise. **28** The creation of you all and your resurrection is but like [the creation and resurrection of] a single soul. God hears all and sees all. **29** Do you not see that God causes the night to pass into the day, and the day to pass into the night, and that He has made the sun and the moon subservient [to His laws], each running its course for a set term, and that God is fully aware of all that you do? **30** Thus it is, because God alone is the Ultimate Truth, and all that people invoke beside Him is sheer falsehood, and because God alone is the One Most High, Great. **31** Do you not see that the ships sail the sea by God's blessing, so that He might show you some of His signs? In this there are clear signs indeed for all who are truly patient in adversity and deeply grateful to God. **32** When the waves engulf them like shadows, they call to God, sincere in their faith in Him alone; but as soon as He has brought them safe to land, some of them are restrained in their attitude. Yet none could knowingly reject Our revelations except those who are utterly perfidious or hardened unbelievers. **33** Mankind! Fear your Lord and fear a day when no parent will be of any avail to his child, nor any child will in the least avail his parents! God's promise is most certainly true. Let not, then, the life of this world delude you, and let not deceptive thoughts about God delude you. **34** Indeed with God alone rests the knowledge of when the Last Hour will come; and He it is who sends down rain; and He knows what the wombs contain; whereas no one knows what they will earn tomorrow, and no one knows in what land they will die. God alone is omniscient and takes cognisance of all things.

Surah 32   Prostration

This surah, which was revealed in Makkah, begins by confirming the source of the Qur'an, the Book God has revealed to His last Messenger, Prophet Muhammad (peace be upon him). It asserts that it is the message of the truth, revealed by the Lord of all the worlds. It then speaks of Godhead and shows that He is the Creator of the heavens and the earth and all that they contain. He is the all-powerful who is in full control of everything.

The surah then takes up the question of resurrection after death and the two different ends people face in the life to come. It shows those who were guilty of denying God standing in humility, begging for another chance and promising to do well the next time around. Needless to say, no such chance is given to anyone. Their attitude is contrasted with that of the believers who stand in awe of their Lord and who pray to Him in hope and fear.

The surah concludes with the unbelievers' question of when the warnings given to them will be fulfilled. The answer does not specify a time, but warns them of the inevitability of such fulfilment. They, then, better take heed.

Prostration

In the Name of God, the Lord of Grace, the Ever-Merciful

1 *Alif. Lam. Mim.* 2 The revelation of this Book comes, beyond any doubt, from the Lord of all the worlds. 3 Do they say: 'He has invented it?' It is indeed the truth from your Lord, so that you may warn a community to whom no warner has come before you, and that they may be guided. 4 God it is who created the heavens and the earth and all that is between them in six aeons, and established Himself on the Throne. You have none to protect you from God, and none to intercede with Him for you. Will you not, then, reflect? 5 He regulates and governs all that exists, from the celestial space to the earth; and in the end all shall ascend to Him [for judgement] on a Day the length of which is one thousand years by your reckoning. 6 Such is He who knows all that is beyond the reach of human perception, and all that can be witnessed, the Almighty, the Ever-Merciful, who makes most excellent everything that He creates. 7 He begins the creation of man out of clay; 8 then He causes his progeny to be begotten out of the

essence of a humble fluid; then He fashions him and breathes into him of His spirit. **9** Thus He endows you, mankind, with hearing and sight and hearts. Yet seldom are you grateful! **10** They say: 'What! After we have vanished into the earth, shall we be [restored to life] in a new act of creation?' Nay, they indeed deny that they will be meeting their Lord. **11** Say: 'The angel of death who has been given charge of you will gather you, and then to your Lord you will be brought back'. **12** If you could but see when those wrongdoers will hang down their heads before their Lord and say: 'Our Lord! We have now seen and we have heard. Return us [to our earthly life] and we will do good deeds. We are now firm believers'. **13** Had We so willed, We could indeed have imposed Our guidance on every human being. Instead, My word shall be fulfilled: 'Most certainly will I fill Hell with jinn and humans all together'. **14** 'Taste this, for you [deliberately] forgot you would ever meet this Day. We, too, will forget you; and taste this abiding suffering for all the evil you did'. **15** Only they believe in Our revelations who, whenever they are reminded of them, fall down prostrating themselves in adoration, and extol their Lord's limitless glory and praise; and who are never arrogant; **16** who drag themselves out of their beds at night to pray to their Lord in fear and hope; and who are charitable with what We provide for them. **17** No one can imagine what blissful delights have been kept in store for them as a reward for what they used to do. **18** Is, then, the one who is a believer to be compared to one who is wicked? The two are certainly not equal. **19** Those who believe and do righteous deeds will have the Gardens of repose for an abode in recompense for what they used to do; **20** whereas the wicked have the Fire as their abode: whenever they try to come out of it, they will be thrown back in it, and they will be told, 'Taste this suffering through fire which you always thought to be a lie'. **21** We will certainly let them taste a suffering closer at hand before they experience the greater suffering so that they might return [to the right faith]. **22** Who does a greater wrong than one who is reminded [of the truth] by his Lord's revelations but he, nevertheless, turns away from them? We shall certainly inflict Our retribution on the ones who are guilty. **23** We certainly gave the Book to Moses, so be not in doubt about convergence with it. We made of it guidance for the Children of Israel, **24** and We raised among them leaders who, so long as they remained steadfast and had sure faith in Our revelations, spread guidance in accordance with Our command. **25** Your Lord is certainly the One who will decide between people on the Day of Resurrection with regard to all that on which they differ.

26 Do they not reflect on how many a generation We have destroyed before their time, in whose dwelling places they now walk about? In this there are signs indeed: will they not listen? **27** Are they not aware that it is We who drive water to dry land devoid of herbage, and with it We bring forth crops of which their cattle and they themselves eat? Can they not see? **28** They say: 'When will this judgement be, if you are telling the truth?' **29** Say: 'On the Day when judgement is made no benefit will it be to unbelievers if they then believe; nor will they be granted respite'. **30** Therefore, leave them alone, and wait. They are certainly waiting.

Surah 33   The Confederates

This surah was revealed over a period of four or a little more years during the Madinan period. It is, therefore, largely concerned with the reorganisation of Arab society on Islamic values and principles. It begins with prohibiting the old practice of Arab men who sometimes resorted to what is called *zihar*, whereby a married man would tell his wife that she was to him like the back of his mother, meaning that she was forbidden for him. The surah declares this to be meaningless and forbidden. It also prohibits child adoption as another false claim.

The surah then includes a long passage commenting on the siege of Madinah by the confederate tribes who mobilised a large force to attack Madinah with the declared aim of exterminating Islam and the Muslims. The siege ended with a victory for the Muslims after direct intervention by God to force the unbelievers to abandon their plans.

The surah then speaks about the Prophet's wives and his marriage to his cousin, Zaynab, relating this to the prohibition of adoption. It adds various rules concerning marriage and divorce, as well as the manners to be observed in Muslim society. It includes a condemnation of the practice of some hypocrites who used to try to malign the Muslims. The surah warns them that unless they stop their abominable practices, they will be removed from Madinah.

The surah concludes with the mention of the Last Hour, hinting that it might be close at hand. It adds scenes of the Day of Judgement and finishes with the prospect of suffering for the unbelievers and hypocrites while the believers, men and women, will enjoy God's mercy and forgiveness.

The Confederates

In the Name of God, the Lord of Grace, the Ever-Merciful

1 Prophet! Have fear of God and do not yield to the unbelievers and the hypocrites. God is certainly all-knowing, wise. **2** Follow what is revealed to you by your Lord; for God is well aware of all that you do. **3** Place your trust in God; for God alone is worthy of all trust. **4** Never has God put two hearts in one man's body. Nor does He make your wives whom you declare to be as unlawful to you as your mothers' bodies truly your mothers. Likewise, He does not make your adopted sons truly your sons. These are only words you utter with your mouths, but God says the truth and He alone shows the right path. 5 Call them by their fathers' names; that is more just in God's sight. If you do not know who their fathers are, then treat them as your brethren in faith and your protégés. You shall not be blamed if you make a mistake, but for what your hearts intend. God is indeed much-forgiving, ever-merciful. 6 The Prophet has more claim on the believers than they have on their own selves; and his wives are their mothers. Blood relatives have, according to God's decree, a stronger claim upon one another than other believers [of Madinah] and those who have migrated [for God's sake]. Nonetheless, you are to act with kindness towards your close friends. This is written down in God's decree. 7 We did accept a solemn pledge from all the prophets: from you [Muhammad], and from Noah, Abraham, Moses and Jesus son of Mary. From all did We accept a weighty, solemn pledge. 8 God will question the truthful about the truth [entrusted to them]. He has prepared a painful suffering for the unbelievers.

9 Believers! Remember the blessings God bestowed on you when hosts came down upon you. We let loose against them a windstorm and hosts that you could not see. Yet God sees all that you do. 10 They came upon you from above and from below you. Your eyes rolled [with fear] and your hearts leapt up to your throats, and confused thoughts about God passed through your minds. 11 That was a situation when the believers were sorely tested and severely shaken. 12 The hypocrites and the sick at heart said: 'God and His Messenger promised us nothing but delusions'. 13 Some of them said: 'People of Yathrib! You cannot withstand [the attack] here, so go back'. And a group of them asked the Prophet's permission to leave, saying: 'Our houses are exposed', while they were not exposed. They only wanted to run away. 14 Had their city been stormed from all sides, and had they been asked to renounce their faith they would have done so without much delay. 15 They had previously vowed before God that they would never turn their backs in flight. A vow made to God must surely be answered for. 16 Say: 'Flight will benefit you nothing. If you flee from natural death or from being slain, you will only be left to enjoy life for a little while'. 17 Say: 'Who can keep you away from God if it be His will to harm you, or if it be His will to show you mercy?' Other than God they can find none to protect them or to bring them support. 18 God is indeed aware of those of you who hold others back; and those who say to their brethren: 'Come and join us', while they themselves hardly ever take part in the fighting, begrudging you all help. But then, when danger threatens, you see them looking to

you for help, their eyes rolling as though they were overshadowed by death. Yet when the danger has passed, they will assail you [believers] with sharp tongues, begrudging you all that is good. **19** Such people have not experienced faith. God will bring their deeds to nothing. That is all too easy for God. **20** They think that the Confederates have not withdrawn. Should the Confederates return, they would wish they were in the desert, among the bedouins, asking for news about you. Even if they were with you, they would take but little part in the fighting. **21** In God's Messenger you have a good model for everyone who looks with hope to God and the Last Day, and always remembers God. **22** When the believers saw the Confederate forces they said: 'This is what God and His Messenger have promised us! Truly spoke God and His Messenger'. This only served to strengthen their faith and their submission to God. **23** Among the believers are people who have always been true to what they have vowed before God. Some have already fulfilled their pledges by death, and some are still waiting. They have not changed in the least. **24** God will surely reward the truthful for having been true to their word, and will punish the hypocrites, if that be His will, or accept their repentance. God is indeed much-forgiving, ever-merciful. **25** God turned back the unbelievers in all their rage and fury; they gained no advantage. He spared the believers the need to fight. God is most-powerful, almighty. **26** He brought down from their strongholds those of the people of earlier revelations who aided them, casting terror in their hearts: some you slew, and some you took captive. **27** And He passed on to you their land, their houses and their goods, as well as a land on which you had never yet set foot. God has power over all things.

28 Prophet! Say to your wives: 'If you desire the life of this world and its charms, I shall provide for you and release you in a becoming manner; **29** but if you desire God and His Messenger and the life of the Hereafter, know that God has readied great rewards for those of you who do good'. **30** Wives of the Prophet! If any of you were to be guilty of manifestly immoral conduct, her punishment would be doubled. That is easy for God. **31** But if any of you devoutly obeys God and His Messenger and does good deeds, We shall grant her a double reward, and We have prepared for her most excellent provisions. **32** Wives of the Prophet! You are unlike any other women: if you truly fear God, do not speak too softly, lest any who is sick at heart should be moved with desire; but speak in an appropriate manner. **33** And stay quietly in your homes, and do not display your charms as [women] used to display them in the old days of pagan ignorance. Attend regularly to your prayers, and pay the obligatory charity [zakat], and pay heed to God and His Messenger. God only wants to remove all that is loathsome from you, you members of the [Prophet's] household, and to purify you fully. **34** Bear in mind all that is recited in your homes of God's revelations and wisdom; for God is unfathomable in His wisdom, all aware. **35** For all men and women who have submitted themselves to God – all believing men and believing women, all truly devout men and truly devout women, all men and women who are true to their word, all men and women who are patient in adversity, all men and women who humble themselves before God, all men and women who give in charity, all men and women who fast, all men and women who are mindful of their chastity, and all men and women who always remember God – for them all God has prepared forgiveness of sins and a mighty reward.

36 Whenever God and His Messenger have decided a matter, it is not for a believing man or a believing woman to claim freedom of choice in that matter. Whoever disobeys God and His Messenger strays far into error. **37** You did say to the one to whom God had shown favour and you had shown favour, 'Hold on to your wife and have fear of God'. And thus you would hide in your heart that which God wanted to bring to light. You stood in awe of people, whereas it was God alone of whom you should have stood in awe. Then, when Zayd had come to the end of his union with her, We gave her to you in marriage, so that no blame should attach to the believers for marrying the spouses of their adopted sons when the latter have come to the end of their union with them. God's will must be fulfilled. **38** No blame whatsoever attaches to the Prophet for doing what God has ordained for him. Such was God's way with those who went before him. God's will is always destiny absolute. **39** Those are the ones who convey God's messages and stand in awe of Him, and hold none but God in awe. Sufficient is God to reckon all things. **40** Muhammad is not the father of any one of your men, but is God's Messenger and the seal of all prophets. God has indeed full knowledge of everything. **41** Believers! Remember God always, **42** and glorify him morning and evening. **43** It is He who bestows His blessings upon you, with His angels, so that He might take you out of the depths of darkness into the light. He is truly merciful to the believers. **44** On the Day when they meet Him, they will be greeted with 'Peace', and He will have prepared for them a most generous reward. **45** Prophet! We have sent you as a witness, a bearer of good news and a warner; **46** one who calls people to God by His leave and a light-giving beacon.

47 Give to the believers the good news that a great bounty from God awaits them. **48** Do not yield to the unbelievers and the hypocrites, and disregard their hurting actions. Place your trust in God; for God alone is worthy of all trust.

49 Believers! If you marry believing women and then divorce them before the marriage is consummated, you have no reason to expect them to observe a waiting period. Hence, provide well for them and release them in a becoming manner. **50** Prophet! We have made lawful to you the wives whom you have paid their dowries, as well as those whom God has placed in your right hand through war, as also the daughters of your paternal uncles and aunts, and the daughters of your maternal uncles and aunts, who have migrated with you; and any believing woman who offers herself freely to the Prophet and whom the Prophet might be willing to wed: [this latter] applies to you alone and not to other believers. We well know what We have made obligatory to them in respect of their wives and other women their right hands possess; and thus no blame shall attach to you. God is much-forgiving, ever-merciful. **51** You may defer any of them you please, and take to yourself any of them you please. No blame will attach to you if you invite one whose turn you have previously set aside: this makes it more likely that they will be contented and not distressed, and that all of them will be satisfied with whatever you have to give them. God knows what is in your hearts. God is indeed all-knowing, clement. **52** You [Muhammad] are not permitted to take any further wives, nor to exchange these for other wives, even though you are attracted by their beauty, except for any that your right hand may possess. God keeps watch over all things. **53** Believers! Do not enter the Prophet's homes, unless you are given leave, for a meal without waiting for its proper time. But when you are invited, enter; and when you have eaten, disperse without lingering for the sake of mere talk. Such behaviour might give offence to the Prophet, and yet he might feel too shy to bid you go. God does not shy of stating what is right. When you ask the Prophet's wives for something, do so from behind a screen: this makes for greater purity for your hearts and theirs. Moreover, it does not behove you to give offence to God's Messenger, just as it would not behove you ever to marry his widows after he has passed away. That is certainly an enormity in God's sight. **54** Whether you do anything openly or in secret, [remember that] God has full knowledge of everything. **55** It is no sin for them [to appear freely] before their fathers, their sons, their brothers, their brothers' sons, their sisters' sons, their womenfolk, or such men slaves as their right hands possess. [Wives of the Prophet!] Always remain God-fearing; for God is witness to all things. **56** God and His angels bless the Prophet. Believers! Bless him and give him greetings of peace. **57** Those who affront God and His Messenger will be rejected by God in this world and in the life to come. He has prepared for them a humiliating suffering. **58** And those who malign believing men and women for no wrong they might have done shall have burdened themselves with the guilt of calumny and with a blatant injustice. **59** Prophet! Say to your wives, daughters and all believing women that they should draw over themselves some of their outer garments. This will be more conducive to their being recognised and not affronted. God is much-forgiving, ever-merciful. **60** If the hypocrites, those who are sick at heart and those who spread lies in the city do not desist, We will rouse you against them, and then they will not be your neighbours in this city except for a little while: **61** bereft of God's grace, they shall be seized wherever they may be found, and will be slain. **62** Such has been God's way with those who went before. Never will you find any change in God's way.

63 People ask you about the Last Hour. Say: 'Knowledge of it rests with God alone'. Yet for all you know the Last Hour may well be near. **64** God has certainly rejected the unbelievers and prepared for them a blazing Fire, where they will permanently abide. **65** They will find none to protect or support them. **66** On the Day when their faces shall be tossed about in the Fire, they will say: 'Would that we had obeyed God and obeyed His Messenger'. **67** And they shall say: 'Our Lord! We have paid heed to our masters and our leaders, but they have led us astray from the right path. **68** Our Lord! Give them double suffering, and banish them utterly from Your grace'. **69** Believers! Do not be like those who gave offence to Moses. God showed him to be innocent of whatever they alleged against him. Indeed, he was highly honoured in God's sight. **70** Believers! Have fear of God and say only what is just and true for then He will cause your deeds to be good and sound, and He will forgive you your sins. **71** Whoever obeys God and His Messenger will certainly achieve a great triumph. **72** We offered the trust to the heavens and the earth and the mountains, but they refused to bear it and were afraid to receive it. Yet man took it up. He has always been prone to wickedness, foolish. **73** So it is that God will punish the hypocrites, men and women, as well as the men and women who associate partners with Him; and He will turn in mercy to the believers, both men and women. God is much-forgiving, ever-merciful.

Surah 34   Saba' [Sheba]

The surah begins with praising God who is the Master and Creator of the heavens and earth, and acknowledging that He knows everything that takes place in the universe, even before it happens. It then addresses the question of the Day of Judgement, refuting the arguments of the unbelievers who deny resurrection. The surah quotes their arguments, presenting them as they are stated, before showing how they are without foundation.

The surah presents a glimpse of the story of David and Solomon who showed true gratitude to God for the blessings He bestowed on them. This aspect of the story serves to emphasise the point that no creature, including the jinn and the angels, have any knowledge of what lies beyond the reach of their perception. The jinn did not know of Solomon's death until insects had eaten a part of his stick, causing him to fall down. In contrast to the gratitude shown by David and Solomon, the people of Sheba were ungrateful and they suffered the consequences of the same.

The surah then challenges the unbelievers to call on those whom they claim to be deities to help them with what it is they want. It tells them that such false deities are too weak to even help themselves.

The final part of the surah focuses on the question of revelation and the message God entrusts to His messengers. It states that material riches to which people assign great value are worthless in God's sight. It is good action, based on faith, that gives people what they deserve.

Saba' [Sheba]

In the Name of God, the Lord of Grace, the Ever-Merciful

1 All praise is due to God, to whom belongs all that is in the heavens and the earth; and to Him will be due all praise in the life to come. It is He who is truly the Wise, the All-Aware. **2** He knows all that goes into the earth and all that comes out of it; all that descends from the skies and all that ascends to them. He is the Ever-Merciful, Much-Forgiving. **3** The unbelievers say: 'Never shall the Last Hour come upon us!' Say: 'Yes, by my Lord, it shall most certainly come to you. It is He who knows all that lies beyond the reach of human perception. Not an atom's weight in the heavens or the earth escapes Him; nor is there anything smaller or larger but is recorded in a clear book, so that

He may reward those who believe and do righteous deeds. **4** It is they who shall have forgiveness and generous provisions'. **5** As for those who strive against Our revelations, seeking to defeat their purpose, these shall have a most painful suffering. **6** Those who are endowed with knowledge are well aware that what has been revealed to you by your Lord is indeed the truth, and that it guides to the way that leads to the Almighty, to whom all praise is due. **7** The unbelievers say: 'Shall we point out to you a man who will tell you that, when you have been utterly torn into pieces, you shall be restored to life in a new act of creation? **8** Has he invented a lie about God, or is he a madman?' No! It is those who do not believe in the life to come who are suffering torment as they have gone far in error. **9** Do they not consider how much of the sky and the earth lies open before them and how much lies hidden from them? If We so willed, We could cause the earth to swallow them, or cause fragments of the sky to fall upon them. In all this, there is a sign for every servant of God turning to Him in repentance.

10 We graced David with Our favour. We said: 'You mountains, sing with him God's praises! And likewise you birds!' We caused iron to become soft for him, saying: 'Make coats of mail and measure their links with care. **11** Do good, all of you. I certainly see all that you do'. **12** To Solomon [We made subservient] the wind: its morning course [covered the distance of] a month's journey, and its evening course a month's journey. We caused a fountain of molten brass to flow for him, and some of the jinn worked under his control by permission of his Lord. Whoever of them deviated from Our command We shall make him taste suffering through a blazing flame. **13** They made for him whatever he pleased: shrines and statues, basins as large as watering troughs, and firmly anchored cauldrons. We said: 'Work thankfully, family of David, for few of My servants are truly thankful'. **14** When We decreed his death, nothing showed them that he was dead except an earthworm that gnawed away at his staff. And when he fell to the ground, the jinn saw clearly that, had they understood the reality which was beyond [their] perception, they would not have remained in humiliating servitude. **15** There was a sign for the people of Sheba in their dwelling place: two gardens, one to the right and one to the left: 'Eat of what your Lord has provided for you, and give thanks to Him: a land most goodly and a Lord much-forgiving'. **16** But they paid no heed, and so We let loose upon them a raging torrent and replaced their two gardens with others yielding bitter fruit, tamarisks, and a few lote trees. **17** Thus We requited them for their ingratitude: would We thus requite any but the totally ungrateful? **18** We had placed between them and the cities which We had blessed, towns within sight of one another so that they could travel in measured stages: 'Travel through them by night and day in safety'. **19** But they said: 'Our Lord! Make our journeys longer'. They sinned against their souls; so We caused them to become a tale, and scattered them throughout the land. Surely, there are signs in all this for anyone who is patient in adversity, deeply grateful. **20** Indeed Iblis proved that his opinion of them was right: they all followed him, except for a group of believers. **21** Yet he had no power at all over them; it is only for the end that We might make a clear distinction between those who truly believe in the life to come and those who are in doubt about it. Your Lord watches over all things.

22 Say: 'Call upon those whom you imagine to be partners with God'. They do not have even an atom's weight of authority either in the heavens or the earth, nor have they any share in either, nor does He have any helper from among them. **23** Before Him, intercession is of no avail, except by one to whom He may have granted permission. When the terror is lifted from their hearts, they will ask [one another]: 'What has your Lord ordained?' They will answer: 'The truth. He is the Most High, the Supreme'. **24** Say: 'Who is it that gives you sustenance out of the heavens and the earth?' Say: 'It is God; and either we or you are on the right path or have clearly gone astray!' **25** Say: 'Neither shall you be called to account for whatever we have become guilty of, nor shall we be called to account for whatever you are doing'. **26** Say: 'Our Lord will bring us all together, and then He will lay open the truth between us, in justice. He alone is the One who opens all truth, the All-Knowing'. **27** Say: 'Show me those whom you allege to be partners with Him. Nay! He alone is God, the Almighty, the Wise'.

28 We have sent you to all mankind so that you bring them good news and give them warning; but most people do not understand. **29** They ask: 'When is this promise to be fulfilled, if what you say be true?' **30** Say: 'There has been appointed for you a Day which you can neither delay nor advance by a single moment'. **31** The unbelievers say: 'We will never believe in this Qur'an, nor in any earlier revelations'. If only you could see how the wrongdoers shall be made to stand before their Lord, hurling reproaches at one another. Those of them who were weak on earth will say to those who had deemed themselves mighty: 'Had it not been for you, we would certainly have been believers'. **32** The ones who deemed themselves mighty will say to those who were weak: 'Was it we who prevented you from following right guidance after it had been given you? Certainly not! It was you who were guilty'. **33** Those who were weak will reply to those who deemed themselves mighty: 'Not so! It was your scheming, night and day, ordering us to disbelieve in God and to set up equals to Him'. When they see the punishment awaiting them, they will all harbour utter and unmitigated remorse. We shall put chains round the necks of the unbelievers. Are they to be requited for anything other than what they did? **34** Whenever We sent a warner to any community, those of them who lived in luxury said: 'We do not believe in the message with which you have been sent'. **35** They also say: 'Richer than you are we in wealth, and we have more children. We certainly are not going to be made to suffer'. **36** Say: 'My Lord gives in abundance, or gives in scant measure, to whomever He wills; but most people do not understand'. **37** It is neither your riches nor your children that can bring you nearer to Us: only he who believes and does what is right [comes near to Us]. To these multiple reward will be given for all that they have done. **38** They will dwell in safety in the mansions of Paradise; whereas all who strive against Our revelations, seeking to defeat their purpose, shall be given over to suffering. **39** Say: 'My Lord gives in abundance, or gives in scant measure, to whomever He wills of His servants; whatever you give for His sake He will replace it for you, for He is the best of providers'. **40** On the Day He gathers them all together, He will say to the angels: 'Was it you that these people worshipped?' **41** They will answer: 'Limitless are You in Your glory! You alone are our patron, not they. In fact they worshipped the jinn and most of them believed in them'. **42** Today none of you has any power to benefit or harm another. We will say to the wrongdoers: 'Taste now the suffering through fire which you persistently denied'.

43 When Our revelations are recited to them in all their clarity, they say: 'This is but a man who wants to turn you away from what your forefathers worshipped'. They also say: 'This is nothing but an invented falsehood'. Furthermore, when the truth comes to them, the unbelievers will say: 'This is just plain sorcery'. **44** Yet never have We given them any books to study, nor have We sent them any warner before you. **45** Those who have gone before them likewise denied the truth. These people have not attained even one-tenth of what We gave their predecessors, yet when they denied My messengers, how terrible was My condemnation. **46** Say: 'I counsel you one thing: stand before God, in pairs or singly, and think: there is no madness in your companion [Muhammad]. He is only a warner to you of awesome suffering to come'. **47** Say: 'If I have ever asked you for any reward, you can keep it. My reward rests with none other than God. He is witness to everything'. **48** Say: 'My Lord hurls forth the truth. He has full knowledge of all that is beyond the reach of people's perception'. **49** Say: 'The truth has now come. Falsehood neither creates anything new, nor restores anything'. **50** Say: 'Were I to go astray, I would but go astray to the loss of myself. But if I am on the right path, it is through what my Lord reveals to me. He is all-hearing, ever-near'. **51** If you could but see when they are seized by terror, with nowhere to escape; for they will have been seized from a place nearby. **52** They will say: 'We do believe in it', but how could they attain it from so far away, seeing that they had at first denied it all. **53** They used to cast scorn from far away on what is imperceptible. **54** A barrier will be set between them and all that they desire, just as was done with their kind before. They were lost in perplexing doubt.

Surah 35   The Originator

The very name of this surah explains its subject matter. It speaks about the Creator of the universe who has power over all things. He determines what He creates and how they are created. His will is free, unrestricted by anything mankind may consider to be a law of nature. It is He who has created nature and its laws, and He can override them any time He wills.

Yet He is most-merciful, and when He opens up His grace to man, no power can withhold it. If He chooses not to open it up, no power can do anything to undo what He has determined. Moreover, it is He who gives people what they need for their living.

Throughout the surah, emphasis is given to the fact that God's will is free, unrestricted. It is His will that makes and sustains life, brings into existence, causes death and to Him all shall return.

The surah mentions the Qur'an, God's Book which He entrusts to His chosen servants. All of them benefit by it, including those who wrong themselves by indulging in what Islam does not approve of: the very fact that it is entrusted to them is a great favour granted by God.

The surah concludes with the statement that one of God's favours to mankind is that He gives them respite until an appointed time. Were He to make them instantly accountable for what they do, He would have destroyed them all. This respite gives them a chance to turn to God in repentance and earn His forgiveness.

The Originator

In the Name of God, the Lord of Grace, the Ever-Merciful

1 All praise is due to God, the Originator of the heavens and the earth, who assigns angels to be messengers, endowed with wings, two, or three, or four. He adds to His creation what He pleases. Indeed God has power over all things. 2 Whatever grace God opens up to man, none can withhold it; and whatever He withholds, none other than Him can release. He is the Almighty, the Wise. 3 People! Remember the blessings God has bestowed upon you. Is there any creator other than God who can give you sustenance from heaven and earth? There is no deity other than Him. How can you turn away?

4 If they accuse you of lying, other messengers, who had gone before you, were similarly accused. It is to God that all things return.

5 People! God's promise is true indeed. So do not let the life of the present world delude you, and do not let deceptive thoughts about God delude you. **6** Satan is your enemy, so treat him as an enemy. He only calls on his followers so that they will be among those destined for the blazing Fire. **7** For the unbelievers there is severe suffering in store; while for those who believe and do righteous deeds there is forgiveness of sins and a great reward. **8** How about the one whose evil deeds seem alluring to him so as to regard them as good? God lets go astray him that wills [to go astray], just as He guides him that wills [to be guided]. Therefore, do not waste yourself sorrowing for them. God has full knowledge of all that they do.

9 It is God who sends forth the winds, so that they raise clouds, and We drive them to a dead land and thereby give life to the earth after it had been lifeless. Thus shall resurrection be. **10** Whoever desires might and glory should know that all might and glory belong to God alone. To Him ascend all good words, and He exalts the good deed. For those who plot evil there is severe suffering in store. All their plotting will come to nothing. **11** It is God who creates you all out of dust, then out of a gamete. He then makes you into a couple. No female conceives or gives birth without His knowledge. No one attains to old age or has his life cut short unless it be thus laid down in [God's] decree. All this is easy for God. **12** The two great bodies of water on earth are not alike: one is palatable, sweet and pleasant to drink, and the other is salty and bitter. Yet from each you eat fresh meat and extract ornaments to wear. You also see there ships that plough their course through them so that you may go in quest of some of His bounty and be grateful. **13** He causes the night to pass into the day, and the day to pass into the night; and He has made the sun and the moon subservient [to His laws], each running its course for an appointed term. Thus is God, your Lord: to Him belongs all dominion, while those whom you invoke instead of Him do not own even the skin of a date-stone. **14** If you invoke them they cannot hear your call. Even if they could hear, they would not respond to you. On the Day of Resurrection they will utterly disown your having associated them with God. None can give you information like the One who is all-aware.

15 People! It is you who stand in need of God, whereas He alone is free of all wants, worthy of all praise. **16** If He so wishes, He can do away with you and bring in your place a new creation; **17** this is not difficult for God. **18** No soul will bear the burden of another. If a heavily laden soul should call upon others for help, nothing of its load shall be carried by anyone, not even by a close relative. Hence, you can truly warn only those who stand in awe of their Lord, even though He is beyond the reach of their perception, and attend regularly to prayers. Whoever purifies himself does so for his own benefit. With God is all journeys' end. **19** The blind and the seeing are not equal; **20** nor are darkness and light; **21** nor the [cooling] shade and the scorching heat; and neither are equal the living and the dead. **22** God can make hear whoever He wills, whereas you cannot make those who are in their graves hear you. **23** You are only a warner. **24** We have sent you with the truth, as a bearer of happy news and a warner. There was never a community that has not had a warner. **25** If they accuse you of lying, other communities before them made similar accusations when there came to them messengers with all evidence of the truth, and with books of divine wisdom, and with light-giving revelations; **26** but in the end I took the unbelievers to task: how terrible was My condemnation.

27 Are you not aware that God sends down water from the skies, with which We bring forth fruits of different colours? In the mountains there are streaks of white and red of various shades, as well as others jet-black. **28** Similarly, human beings, beasts and cattle have various colours. It is those who are endowed with knowledge that stand truly in awe of God. Indeed God is almighty, much-forgiving. **29** Those who recite God's Book, attend regularly to prayer, and give in charity, secretly and openly, from what We have provided for them, look forward to a bargain that can never fail, for He will grant them their just rewards, and give them yet more out of His bounty. **30** He is indeed much-forgiving, most-thankful. **31** The Book that We have revealed to you is the truth confirming previous Scriptures. Of His servants God is well-aware, all-seeing. **32** We have given this Book to such of Our servants as We choose: among them are some who wrong their own souls, some follow a middle course; and some who, by God's leave, are foremost in deeds of goodness. That is the greatest favour. **33** Gardens of bliss will they enter, where they will be adorned with bracelets of gold and pearls, and where they will be clad in silk garments. **34** They will say: 'All praise is due to God, who has removed all sorrow from us. Our Lord is certainly much-forgiving, most-appreciative. **35** It is He who, out of His bounty, has settled us in this abode of permanent life, where we shall endure neither toil nor fatigue'. **36** As for the unbelievers, the fire of Hell awaits them. No term shall be determined for them so that they could die, nor shall its suffering be reduced for them. Thus shall We requite all unbelievers.

There they will cry aloud: 'Our Lord! Let us out and we will do good, not like what we did before'. **37** 'Have We not given you lives long enough for anyone who would be warned to take warning? And a warner had come to you. Taste it, then. Wrongdoers shall have none to support them'. **38** God knows all that is hidden in the heavens and earth; He fully knows what is in people's hearts.

39 It is He who made you inherit the earth. Hence, anyone who denies the truth will bear the consequences of his unbelief. In denying Him the unbelievers will have nothing but an increase of their loathsomeness in God's sight; and in denying Him the unbelievers will only add to their loss. **40** Say: 'Have you considered those beings whom you claim to be partners with God and whom you call upon beside Him? Show me what is it that they have created on earth! Or do they have a share in the heavens?' Have We ever revealed to them a book on which they could rely as evidence? No. What the unbelievers promise one another is nothing but delusion. **41** It is God alone who holds the celestial bodies and the earth, lest they deviate [from their courses]. If they should ever deviate, no one else could uphold them after Him. He is indeed ever-clement, much-forgiving. **42** They swear by God with their most solemn oaths that if a warner should ever come to them, they would follow his guidance better than some other community, but when a warner did come to them, they turned away with increased aversion, behaving arrogantly in the land and plotting evil. Yet such evil scheming will engulf none but its authors. Can they expect anything but the way of those unbelievers of old times? **43** No change will you ever find in God's ways; no deviation will you ever find there. **44** Have they not travelled in the land and seen what happened in the end to those before them, even though they were much mightier than them? God can never be foiled by anything whatever in the heavens and the earth. He is all-knowing, infinite in His power. **45** If God were to punish people [at once] for the wrongs they do, He would not leave a single living creature on the surface of the earth. However, He grants them respite for a term set [by Him]. When their term comes to an end, [they realise that] God has all His servants in His sight.

Surah 36   Ya Sin

This surah starts with an explanation of the nature of revelation and the truth of the divine message. This theme runs through the surah from beginning to end. It also gives a clear statement of the fate of those who deny the message and refuse to believe. They condemn themselves by their own actions.

The surah gives an account of a town to which three of God's messengers were sent, but its people continued to reject them and insist on attributing divinity to their idols. Their argument is refuted by a man who comes from the farthest place in the town to put the argument of faith to his people, advising them to believe in order to save themselves.

The question of life after death is repeatedly mentioned in the surah, from start to finish. It draws attention to different aspects of the universe, all of which point to the Creator and endorse the call to believe in His Oneness.

The surah makes clear that the Qur'an has nothing to do with poetry. The unbelievers in Makkah accused Prophet Muhammad of being a poet, but the surah makes clear that he never had such ability. Indeed, it did not behove him, as God's Messenger, to be a poet. What he was given is something far superior. It is this Qur'an, God's word.

Ya Sin

In the Name of God, the Lord of Grace, the Ever-Merciful.

1 *Ya. Sin.* **2** By the Qur'an, full of wisdom, **3** you are indeed one of God's messengers, **4** pursuing a straight way. **5** It is a revelation by the Almighty, the Ever-Merciful, **6** so that you may warn people whose forefathers had not been warned, and who therefore are unaware [of the truth]. **7** The verdict has been passed against most of them, for they will not believe. **8** Around their necks We have put chains, reaching up to their chins, so that their heads are forced up. **9** And We have set a barrier before them and a barrier behind them, and We enshrouded them in veils so that they cannot see. **10** It is all the same to them whether you warn them or you do not warn them: they will not believe. **11** You can truly warn only such a one as follows this reminder and who stands in awe of the Lord of Grace although He is beyond the reach of human perception. To such, then, give the happy news of God's forthcoming forgiveness and a generous reward. **12** It is We who will bring the dead back to life. We record whatever [deeds] they send ahead, as well as the traces they leave behind. We keep an account of all things in a clear record. **13** Cite for them, as a case in point, the people of a township to which messengers came. **14** We sent them two messengers, but they rejected them; so We reinforced them with a third, and they said: 'We are messengers who have been sent to you'. **15** They replied: 'You are nothing but humans like ourselves. Moreover, the Lord of Grace has never revealed anything; you do nothing but lie'. **16** They said: 'Our Lord knows that we have indeed been sent to you. **17** Our only duty is to clearly deliver the message [entrusted to us]'. **18** Said [the others]: 'We augur evil from you. Unless you desist, we will surely stone you and inflict on you a painful suffering'. **19** [The messengers] replied: 'The evil you forebode is within yourselves. [Why do you take this as an evil omen] when you are only being reminded of the truth? Truly, you are going too far'. **20** Then a man came from the farthest end of the city at speed. He said: 'My people! Follow these messengers. **21** Follow those who ask you for no reward, and are themselves rightly guided. **22** Why should I not worship the One who has brought me into being? It is to Him that you will all return. **23** Should I worship other deities beside Him? If the Lord of Grace should will that harm befall me, their intercession will avail me nothing, nor will they save me. **24** Indeed, I should clearly be in error. **25** I do believe in the Lord of you all; so listen to me'. **26** He was told: 'Enter Paradise'. **27** He said: 'Would that my people knew how my Lord has forgiven me my sins, and has placed me among the highly honoured!' **28** After that, We did not send an army from heaven against his people; nor do We send any. **29** Nothing was needed but one single blast, and they fell down lifeless.

30 Alas for mankind! Whenever a messenger comes to them, they level ridicule on him. **31** Are they not aware of how many a generation We have destroyed before them, and that they [who have perished] will never return to them? **32** Yet, they all will be brought before Us. **33** There is a sign for them in the lifeless earth: We give it life and produce out of it grain for them to eat. **34** We place in it gardens of date palms and grapes, and cause springs to gush out of it, so that they may eat of its fruit. **35** It was not their own hands that made all this. Will they, then, not give thanks? **36** Limitless in His glory is He who created all things in pairs: whatever the earth produces, their own human kind and other creatures of which they have no knowledge.

37 Another sign for them is the night: We strip the daylight from it, and they are plunged in darkness. **38** The sun also runs its set course: that is laid down by the will of the Almighty, the All-Knowing. **39** And for the moon We have determined phases until it finally becomes like an old date stalk. **40** Neither the sun can overtake the moon, nor can the night outrun the day. Each floats in its own orbit. **41** And yet another sign for them is that We carry their offspring in laden ships, **42** and that We create things of similar kind for them to ride in. **43** If such be Our will, We may cause them to drown, with none to respond to their cries for help, and then they cannot be saved, **44** unless it be by an act of mercy from Us, leaving them to enjoy life for a while. **45** When they are told: 'Beware of that which lies before you and behind you, so that you may be graced with His mercy', [they pay no heed]. **46** Every single sign that comes to them from their Lord do they ignore. **47** And when they are told: 'Give [in charity] out of what God has provided for you', the unbelievers say to those who believe: 'Are we to feed those whom God could have fed, had He so willed? Clearly, you are lost in error'. **48** They also ask: 'When will this promise be fulfilled, if what you say be true?' **49** All they are waiting for is a single blast that will overtake them while they are still disputing. **50** No time will they have to make bequests, nor will they return to their own people. **51** The Trumpet will be sounded, and out of their graves they will rise and hasten to their Lord. **52** They will say: 'Woe betide us! Who has roused us from our resting place? This is what the Lord of Grace had promised. The messengers told the truth'. **53** It takes nothing but one single blast, and they will all have been brought before Us. **54** Today, no one shall be wronged in the least: you will be requited for nothing other than that which you did in life. **55** Those who are destined for Paradise are today happily occupied. **56** Together with their spouses, they will be in shady groves seated on soft couches. **57** There they have fruit and whatever they ask for: **58** peace and fulfilment through the word of the Lord who is ever-merciful. **59** 'But stand aside today, you guilty ones! **60** Children of Adam! Did I not enjoin on you that you should not worship Satan, as he is your open foe, **61** and that you should worship Me alone? This is the straight path. **62** He had already led astray a great many of you. Could you not, then, use your reason? **63** This, then, is the Hell that you were repeatedly warned against: **64** endure it today for your persistent rejection [of the truth]'. **65** On that Day We shall set a seal on their mouths, but their hands will speak to Us, and their feet will bear witness to whatever they have done. **66** Had it been Our will,

We could have blotted their eyes. They would have striven to find the way, but how could they have seen it? **67** And had it been Our will, We could have paralysed them, right in their places, so that they could not move forward or backward. **68** If We grant long life to a human being, We also cause him to decline in his powers. Will they not use their reason?

69 We have not taught him [the Prophet] poetry; nor is it fitting for him [to be a poet]. **70** This is but a reminder and a Qur'an making all things clear, to warn everyone who is alive, and that the word of God be proved against the unbelievers. **71** Are they not aware that, among all the things Our hands have made, We have created for them cattle which they control. **72** We have subjected these to them, so that some of them they use for riding and of some they may eat, and they have other benefits from them, and [milk] to drink. **73** Will they not give thanks? **74** Yet they have taken to worship deities other than God, hoping for [their] support. **75** They are unable to support them; yet their worshippers stand like warriors to defend them. **76** Let not their words grieve you. We know all that they keep secret as well as all that they bring into the open. **77** Is man, then, not aware that it is We who create him out of a gamete; and then he becomes flagrantly contentious. **78** He comes up with arguments against Us, forgetting how he himself was created. He asks: 'Who could give life to bones that have crumbled to dust?' **79** Say: 'He who brought them into being in the first instance will give them life again. He has full knowledge of every act of creation. **80** It is He who produces for you fire out of the green tree, and from this you kindle your fires'. **81** Is, then, He who has created the heavens and the earth unable to create their like? Of course He can. He alone is the Supreme Creator, the All-Knowing. **82** When He intends something to be, He only says to it, 'Be', and it is. **83** Limitless, then, in His glory is He in whose hand rests the mighty dominion over all things, and to Him you all will be brought back.

Surah 37   Ranged in Ranks

Like all surahs revealed in Makkah, this surah focuses on the main issues of faith: God's Oneness, the Day of Resurrection and individual accountability. However, the surah speaks in particular about a legend that found some popularity among the pagan Arabs in pre-Islamic days. The legend alleges that God married the jinn and they gave birth to the angels who are God's daughters! The surah starts by mentioning certain groups of angels, before it makes a strong denunciation of this legend, making it clear that the jinn were barred from going near heaven, or eavesdropping on angels.

The surah portrays scenes of the universe to make clear that there can only be the One Creator who has no partner. It emphasises the truth of resurrection and individual accountability. It warns the addressees who denied these that past communities also denied them and were severely punished by God. It refers to the people of Noah, Abraham, his sons, Moses, Aaron, Elijah, Lot and Jonah. In all these references, God's grace is shown to be granted in abundance, but those who persistently denied the truth had to face their just punishment.

Towards its end, the surah again refers to the absurd legend, making it clear that there could be absolutely no truth in it. It then concludes by asserting that God's messengers were sure of God's help.

Ranged in Ranks

In the Name of God, the Lord of Grace, the Ever-Merciful

1 By the [angels] ranged in ranks, 2 who rebuke reproachfully 3 and recite God's word 4 most certainly your God is One, 5 Lord of the heavens and the earth and everything between them, Lord of all the points of sunrise. 6 We have adorned the skies nearest to the earth with stars, 7 and have made them secure against every rebellious devil. 8 Thus, they cannot eavesdrop on the ones on high, but shall be repelled from all sides, 9 driven away, with lasting suffering in store for them. 10 If any of them stealthily snatches away a fragment, he will be pursued by a piercing flame. 11 Now ask those [unbelievers]: Are they more difficult to create, or the other beings We have created? Them have We created out of a sticky clay. 12 Whereas you marvel, they scoff; 13 and when they are reminded of the truth, they pay no heed; 14 and when they see a sign, they resort to ridicule; 15 and

say: 'This is nothing but plain sorcery. **16** What! After we have died and become mere dust and bones, shall we be raised back to life? **17** And perhaps our forefathers?' **18** Say: 'Yes, indeed! And you shall be utterly humbled'. **19** There will be just one single cry, and they will all begin to see, **20** and will say: 'Woe betide us! This is the Day of Judgement!' **21** This is indeed the Day of Decision which you used to call a lie! **22** Gather together all those who were bent on wrongdoing, their ilk, and all that they used to worship **23** instead of God, and guide them all to the path of Hell, **24** but halt them a while, for they shall be asked: **25** 'How is it that you do not help one another?' **26** Indeed, on that Day they will be in complete submission. **27** They will turn upon one another accusingly. **28** Some [of them] will say: 'You used to [whisper to us] approaching us from the right!' **29** The others will reply: 'No! It was you who would not believe. **30** We had no power over you; but you were willing to exceed all limits. **31** Now our Lord's word has come true against us, and we are bound to taste [the punishment]; **32** If we led you astray, we ourselves were astray'. **33** On that Day, they all will share in the common suffering. **34** Thus shall We deal with all the guilty ones. **35** Whenever they were told, 'there is no deity other than God', they would turn away in arrogance, **36** and would say: 'Are we to forsake our deities for the sake of a mad poet?' **37** For certain, he has brought the truth, and confirmed the earlier messengers. **38** You will indeed taste grievous suffering, **39** being requited only for what you used to do. **40** Not so God's true servants. **41** Theirs shall be a predetermined sustenance: **42** fruits; and they will be honoured **43** in gardens of bliss, **44** seated on soft couches, facing one another. **45** A cup will be passed round among them with a drink from a flowing spring: **46** clear, delicious to those who drink it, **47** causing no headiness or intoxication. **48** With them will be mates of modest gaze, most beautiful of eye, **49** as if they were hidden eggs. **50** And they will turn to one another with questions. **51** One of them will say: 'I had a close companion on earth **52** who used to ask me: **53** "Do you really believe that after we have died and become mere dust and bones we shall be brought for judgement?"' **54** He adds: 'Would you like to look down?' **55** Then he looks and sees him in the midst of the Fire. **56** He will then say: 'By God! You almost brought me to ruin! **57** But for the grace of God I should have also been brought there'. **58** 'But then is it truly so, that we are not to die **59** except for our first death, and that we are not to suffer? **60** This is indeed the supreme triumph'. **61** Everyone should strive to attain this goal. **62** Is this the better welcome, or the Zaqqum tree? **63** We have made it a test for the wrongdoers. **64** It is a tree that grows in the very heart of the blazing fire of Hell. **65** Its fruit is like devils' heads. **66** They will indeed eat of it, filling their bellies. **67** Then on top of it, they will be given polluted, scalding water to drink. **68** Then again, their ultimate goal is Hell.

69 They found their forefathers astray, **70** and rushed to follow in their footsteps. **71** Most of the people of old went astray before them; **72** although We had sent them warners. **73** Behold what happened in the end to those that had been warned. **74** Not so God's true servants. **75** Noah cried to Us, and We are the best to answer prayer: **76** We saved him and his household from great distress; **77** and caused his offspring to be the survivors. **78** We caused him to be praised by later generations: **79** Peace be upon Noah in all the worlds! **80** Thus do we reward those who do good. **81** He was truly one of Our believing servants. **82** Then We caused the others to drown. **83** Among those who followed his way was Abraham. **84** He turned to his Lord with a sound heart. **85** He said to his father and his people: 'What is this that you worship? **86** Do you choose false deities instead of God? **87** What, then, do you think of the Lord of all the worlds?' **88** Then he cast a glance at the stars, **89** and said: 'Indeed I am sick'. **90** So his people turned away from him and left. **91** He then approached their deities stealthily and said: 'Will you not eat [your offerings]? **92** What is the matter with you that you do not speak?' **93** And then he fell upon them, smiting them with his right hand. **94** His people came to him hurriedly, **95** but he said: 'Do you worship something that you yourselves have carved, **96** while it is God who has created you and all you do?' **97** They said: 'Build him a pyre and throw him into the blazing fire'. **98** They schemed to harm him, but We caused them to be humiliated. **99** And Abraham said: 'I will go to my Lord: He is sure to guide me. **100** Lord! Grant me a righteous son'. **101** We gave him the happy news that he will have a clement son. **102** When the boy was old enough to work with his father, Abraham said: 'My son! I have seen in a dream that I must sacrifice you. Tell me, then, what you think'. [Ishmael] said: 'My father! Do as you are bidden, and, God willing, you will find me to be patient in adversity'. **103** When the two of them had surrendered themselves to the will of God, and Abraham laid him prostrate on his forehead, **104** We called to him: 'Abraham! You have already fulfilled the dream'. **105** Thus do We reward those who do good. **106** All this was indeed a momentous trial. **107** We ransomed [Ishmael] with a noble sacrifice, **108** We caused him to be praised by later generations: **109** Peace be upon

Abraham! **110** Thus do we reward those who do good. **111** He was truly one of our believing servants. **112** We gave Abraham the happy news of Isaac, a prophet and a righteous man; **113** and We blessed him and Isaac; but among their offspring there were those who do good and others who would glaringly sin against their souls. **114** We also bestowed Our favour on Moses and Aaron; **115** We saved them and their people from great distress; **116** We gave them support, so that it was they who achieved victory. **117** We gave them the Scripture which made things clear; **118** We guided them to the right path; **119** We caused them to be praised by later generations: **120** Peace be upon Moses and Aaron! **121** Thus do we reward those who do good. **122** Both were among our believing servants. **123** Elijah too was one of Our messengers. **124** He said to his people: 'Have you no fear of God? **125** How can you invoke Baal and forsake the best of creators, **126** God, your Lord and the Lord of your forefathers?' **127** But they accused him of lying. Therefore, they will certainly be brought [for punishment]. **128** Not so God's true servants. **129** We caused him to be praised by later generations: **130** Peace be upon Elijah! **131** Thus do we reward those who do good. **132** He was truly one of our believing servants. **133** Lot was also one of Our messengers. **134** We saved him and all his household, **135** except for an old woman who stayed behind. **136** Then We utterly destroyed the others. **137** Surely you pass by their ruins at morning-time, **138** as also by night. Will you not, then, use your reason? **139** Jonah too was one of Our messengers. **140** He deserted, going on the laden ship. **141** They cast lots, and he was the one who lost. **142** The whale swallowed him, for he was to blame. **143** Had he not been of those who truly glorified God, **144** he would have remained in the whale's belly till Resurrection Day. **145** We caused him to be cast out, sick, on a barren shore, **146** and caused a gourd tree to grow over him. **147** Then We sent him to [a community of] one hundred thousand or more. **148** They believed, so We let them enjoy life for a while.

149 Now ask the unbelievers if it be true that your Lord has daughters, while they would have sons? **150** Or is it that We have created the angels female in their presence? **151** Out of their falsehood they say: **152** 'God has begotten children'. They are lying indeed. **153** Would He then choose daughters in preference to sons? **154** What is the matter with you? How do you make your judgement? **155** Do you not reflect? **156** Or do you, perhaps, have a clear authority? **157** Bring your scriptures, if you are speaking the truth! **158** They claim that He has kinship with the jinn; yet the jinn themselves know that they will be brought [before God] for judgement. **159** Limitless is God in His glory, above all what people attribute to Him. **160** Not so God's true servants. **161** Neither you nor what you worship **162** can lure away from God any **163** except one who is destined for Hell. **164** Every single one of us has his appointed place: **165** we are ranged in ranks, **166** and we too extol His limitless glory. **167** They have long been saying: **168** 'If only we had before us a tradition from those of old, **169** we would certainly be true servants of God'. **170** Yet they reject it. In time, they will come to know. **171** Our word has already been given to Our servants the messengers: **172** it is they who will be helped, **173** and it is Our forces who will surely be victorious. **174** So, turn away from them for a while, **175** and watch them; in time, they too will come to see. **176** Do they really wish to hasten Our punishment? **177** When it strikes in their midst, terrible will be the morning of those who were already warned. **178** And again, turn away from them for a while, **179** and watch them; in time, they too will come to see. **180** Limitless in His glory is your Lord, the Lord of almightiness, above all what people attribute to Him. **181** And peace be upon all His messengers. **182** All praise is due to God, the Lord of all the worlds.

Surah 38   Sad

In its discussion of the main issues of faith: God's Oneness, life after death and individual accountability, this surah mentions the attitude of the unbelievers in Makkah who expressed amazement at God's choice of one of their number to be His Messenger. The surah tells them at the outset that God's grace is bestowed on whom He wills and no one can interfere with His will. It further tells them that past communities also denied the truth of the divine message and they were severely punished. The unbelievers of the Quraysh could suffer the same sort of punishment which could overwhelm them all of a sudden.

The surah then gives accounts of several prophets, starting with David and Solomon, who were recipients of God's grace. It shows them as ordinary humans who may experience some weakness. However, they soon turn to God in repentance and acknowledge His favours. This is followed by the trial endured by Prophet Job and his patient endurance of his hardship, until God favoured him with His grace.

The surah then contrasts the end of the believers with that of the unbelievers. The latter wonder why they do not see with them in Hell those who were weak in their community but who believed in God and His message. They ridiculed them in this life, but they were the ones to end up in Heaven.

Sad

In the Name of God, the Lord of Grace, the Ever-Merciful

1 *Sad.* By the Qur'an, full of admonition. 2 But the unbelievers are steeped in arrogance and hostility. 3 How many a generation have We destroyed before their time? They all cried out [for mercy], but it was too late to escape. 4 They deem it strange that one from among them has come to warn them. The unbelievers say: 'This is a sorcerer telling lies. 5 Does he make all the gods into one God? This is indeed most strange!' 6 Their leaders go about saying: 'Walk away, and hold steadfastly to your deities: this is an intended design. 7 Never did we hear of a claim like this in any faith of latter days! It is all an invention. 8 Was the message given to him alone out of all of us?' In fact they are in doubt concerning My reminder; they

have not yet tasted My punishment. **9** Or do they own the treasures of your Lord's grace, the Almighty, the Munificent? **10** Or do they have dominion over the heavens and the earth and all that is between them? Let them, then, try to ascend by all conceivable means. **11** Whatever hosts, of any affiliation, may be raised will suffer defeat. **12** Before their time, the truth was rejected by Noah's people, the 'Ad, Pharaoh of the tent-pegs, **13** the Thamud, Lot's people and the dwellers of the wooded dales: these were different groupings; **14** yet each one of them accused God's messengers of lying. Therefore, My retribution fell due. **15** These, too, have but to wait for one single blast; and it shall not be delayed. **16** They say: 'Our Lord! Hasten to us our share of punishment even before the Day of Reckoning'.

17 Bear with patience whatever they say, and remember Our servant David who was endowed with strength. He always turned to Us. **18** We caused the mountains to join him in extolling Our limitless glory in the evening and at sunrise, **19** and likewise the birds in flocks: they all would echo his praise. **20** We strengthened his kingdom; We endowed him with wisdom and decisive judgement. **21** Have you heard the story of the litigants who surmounted the walls of the sanctuary? **22** When they went in to David, he was alarmed. They said: 'Have no fear. We are but two litigants: one of us has wronged the other; so judge between us with justice, and do not be unfair. Show us the way to rectitude. **23** This is my brother: he has ninety-nine ewes and I have only one ewe. Yet he said: "Let me take charge of her", and has been hard on me in his speech'. **24** Said [David]: 'He has certainly wronged you by demanding that your ewe be added to his ewes! Thus do many partners wrong one another, except for those who believe and do righteous deeds, but how few are they!' Then David realised that We were only testing him. He prayed for his Lord's forgiveness, fell down in prostration and turned to God in repentance. **25** We forgave him that, and in the life to come he is to be close to Us and will be well received. **26** David! We have made you a vicegerent on earth: judge, then, between people with justice, and do not follow vain desire, lest it leads you astray from the path of God. Those who go astray from the path of God will have a severe punishment for having ignored the Day of Reckoning. **27** We have not created heaven and earth and all that is between them without a purpose. That is what the unbelievers assume. Woe betide the unbelievers when they are cast in the Fire. **28** Are We to equate those who believe and do righteous deeds with those who spread corruption in the land? Are We to equate the God-fearing with the wicked?

29 This is a blessed Book which We have revealed to you so that people may ponder over its message, and that those endowed with insight may take it to heart. **30** To David We gave Solomon: how excellent a servant of Ours; he would always turn to Us. **31** When, one evening, nobly-bred, swift-footed steeds were brought before him, **32** he kept saying: 'My love of good things is part of my remembering my Lord!' until they disappeared from sight. **33** 'Bring them back to me!' He then stroked their legs and their necks. **34** We had tried Solomon, and placed a body on his throne. He then turned to Us, **35** and prayed: 'My Lord! Forgive me my sins, and bestow upon me such power as shall belong to no one after me. You are indeed the Bountiful Giver'. **36** We made the wind subservient to him, so that it gently sped at his command wherever he wished, **37** and the jinn, including every kind of builder and diver, **38** and others bound together in fetters. **39** This is Our gift; so give or withhold as you please, without account. **40** In the life to come he is to be close to Us and will be well received. **41** Remember Our servant Job who cried out to his Lord: 'Satan has afflicted me with weariness and suffering!' **42** 'Strike [the ground] with your foot! Here is cool water for you to wash with and to drink'. **43** We restored his family to him, and doubled their number as an act of grace from Us, and as a reminder to those who are endowed with insight. **44** 'Take in your hand a bunch of grass and strike with it, and you will not then break your oath.' We found him patient in adversity. How excellent a servant of Ours; he would always turn to Us. **45** Remember Our servants Abraham, Isaac and Jacob: all men of strength and vision. **46** We gave them a specially distinctive quality: the remembrance of the life to come. **47** In Our sight, they were indeed among the elect, the truly good. **48** And remember Ishmael, Elisha and Dhul-Kifl: each belonged to the truly good.

49 Let all this be a reminder. **50** The God-fearing will certainly have a good place to return to: gardens of perpetual bliss, with gates wide open to them. **51** They will be comfortably seated there, and they will call for abundant fruit and drink, **52** having beside them well-matched mates of modest gaze. **53** This is what you are promised for the Day of Reckoning: **54** this, Our provision for you will never end. **55** This is so! Indeed those who transgress the bounds of what is right will have the most evil place to return to: **56** Hell will they have to endure; and how evil a resting place. **57** Let them, then, taste this: a scalding fluid and a dark, disgusting food, **58** and coupled with it, further [suffering] of similar nature. **59** Here is another crowd of people rushing headlong to join you. No welcome to them! They too shall burn in the Fire. **60** These others will say: 'No, but it is you! No welcome to you either! It is you who brought this on us! How vile a place to be in!' **61** They will say: 'Our Lord! Give double punishment in the Fire to whomever has brought this on us'. **62** They will say: 'How is it that we do not see here men whom we considered to be wicked, **63** and whom we made the target of our derision? Or is it that our eyes have missed them?' **64** This is in truth how it will be: the people of the Fire will quarrel among themselves.

65 Say: 'I am but a warner; and there is no deity other than God, the One who conquers all. **66** The Lord of the heaven and the earth and all that is between, the Almighty, the All-Forgiving!' **67** Say: 'This is a great message; **68** yet you turn away from it. **69** No knowledge would I have of what those on high argue. **70** It is only revealed to me that I am here to give clear warning'. **71** Your Lord said to the angels: 'I am about to create a human being out of clay; **72** when I have fashioned him and breathed of My spirit into him, kneel down before him in prostration'. **73** The angels prostrated themselves, all of them together. **74** Not so Iblis. He gloried in his arrogance and was one of those who reject the truth. **75** Said [God]: 'Iblis! What prevents you from bowing down to one whom I have created with My hands? Are you too proud, or do you deem yourself superior?' **76** Answered [Iblis]: 'I am better than he: You have created me out of fire, but created him from clay'. **77** Said He: 'Then get out from it: you are accursed; **78** My rejection shall follow you until the Day of Judgement'. **79** Said [Iblis]: 'My Lord! Grant me a respite till Resurrection Day'. **80** Said He: 'You are one of those granted respite **81** till the Day of the appointed time'. **82** [Iblis] then said: 'I swear by Your very might: I shall certainly tempt them all **83** except Your true servants'. **84** [And God] said: 'This, then, is the truth! And the truth do I state: **85** I will most certainly fill Hell with you and such of them as shall follow you'. **86** Say: 'No reward do I ask of you for this, and I am not one to claim what I am not. **87** This is no less than a reminder to all the worlds, **88** and in time you will certainly come to know its truth'.

Surah 39   The Throngs

This Makkan surah deals with one theme, namely God's Oneness and its essential requirement that people must submit to Him alone, associating no partners with Him. Purity of faith is stressed time and again in various ways.

What is also unique about this surah is that, unlike other Makkan surahs, which portray scenes of the universe, this surah includes but only a few. However, the aura of the life to come pervades the surah from start to finish. Therefore, scenes of the Hereafter are frequent.

The surah refers to human nature and how when man is afflicted by some adversity, he appeals to God declaring his repentance of his past sins and appealing to Him for help. Yet, when his affliction is removed, he forgets his pledges and reverts to his old ways.

The surah concludes with a scene of the Hereafter in which we see the unbelievers and the believers being taken to their different destinations in groups. We see the reception they receive by the angels assigned to both places.

The Throngs

In the Name of God, the Lord of Grace, the Ever-Merciful

1 This Book is bestowed from on high by God, the Almighty, the Wise. **2** It is We who have bestowed on you this revelation from on high, stating the truth. Therefore, worship God alone, sincere in your faith in Him. **3** True devotion is due to God alone. Those who take others besides Him as their protectors say: 'We worship them for no reason other than that they would bring us nearer to God'. God will judge between them concerning all matters on which they differ. God will not grace with guidance anyone who is an ungrateful liar. **4** Had God wished to take to Himself a son, He could have chosen anyone He wanted from whatever He creates. Limitless is He in His glory: the One God who conquers all. **5** He has created the heavens and the earth in accordance with the truth. He causes the night to flow into the day, and the day to flow into the night; and He has made the sun and the moon subservient [to His laws]: each running its course for a set term. He is indeed the Almighty, the All-Forgiving. **6** He has created you all from a single soul, and from it He fashioned its mate; and He has bestowed on you four kinds of cattle in pairs; and He creates you in your mothers' wombs, one act of creation after another, in threefold depths of darkness. Such is God, your Lord: to Him belongs all dominion. There is no deity other than Him. How, then, can you lose sight of the truth? **7** If you disbelieve, God has no need of you; nor is He pleased with disbelief by His servants. If you give thanks, He is pleased with you. No soul will bear the burden of another. In time, to your Lord you all must return, and then He will tell you the truth of all you did. He has full knowledge of what is in people's hearts.

8 When man suffers affliction, he cries out to his Lord, turning to Him for help; but once He bestows upon him a favour by His grace, he forgets what he cried and prayed for earlier, and claims that others are equal to God, thus leading others astray from His path. Say [to him]: 'Enjoy yourself for a while in your disbelief, for you are one of those destined to the Fire'. **9** How about one who devoutly worships God during the hours of the night prostrating himself or standing in prayer, ever mindful of the life to come, and hoping for his Lord's mercy? Say: 'Can those who know and those who do not know be deemed equal?' Only those who are endowed with insight will take heed. **10** Say: '[Thus speaks God:] You servants of Mine who believe! Fear your Lord! Those who do good in this world will have a good reward. Wide is God's earth. Those who are patient in adversity will be given their reward in full, beyond reckoning'.

11 Say: 'I am commanded to worship God, sincere in my faith in Him alone; **12** and I am commanded to be the first to submit myself to Him'. **13** Say: 'Indeed I would dread, were I to disobey my Lord, the suffering of an awesome Day'. **14** Say: 'God alone do I worship, sincere in my faith in Him alone. **15** You can worship whatever you please instead of Him'. Say: 'True losers indeed are those who shall have lost their own selves and their families on Resurrection Day. Such is the ultimate loss'. **16** Above them there shall be layers of fire, and layers of fire shall be beneath them. In this way God puts fear into His servants' hearts: 'My servants! Fear Me!' **17** There is good news for those who shun the worship of false deities and turn to God, so give good news to My servants, who listen carefully to what is said and follow the best of it. **18** These are the ones whom God has graced with His guidance, and these are the ones endowed with insight. **19** How about one on whom God's sentence of punishment has been passed? Can you rescue those who are already in the Fire? **20** As against this, those who are God-fearing will have lofty mansions raised upon mansions high, beneath which running waters flow. This is God's promise. Never does God fail to fulfil His promise.

21 Have you not considered how God sends down water from the skies, and then causes it to travel through the earth to form springs? He then brings with it vegetation of different colours; and then it withers and you can see it turning yellow. In the end He causes it to crumble to dust. In all this there is indeed a reminder for those endowed with insight. **22** How about one whose heart God has opened to Islam, and thus receives light from his Lord? Woe, then, betide those whose hearts harden at the mention of God. These are most obviously in error. **23** God has bestowed from on high the best of all teachings: a Book that is consistent within itself, repeating its statements [of the truth] in manifold forms. It causes the skins of those who stand in awe of their Lord to shiver, but then their skins and hearts soften at the mention of God. Such is God's guidance: He guides with it him that wills, whereas the one whom God lets go astray can never find any guide. **24** How about one who shall have nothing but his bare face to protect him from the awful suffering on Resurrection Day? It will be said to the wrongdoers: 'Taste now what you have earned'. **25** Those who lived before them also disbelieved, and so suffering befell them from where they could not perceive. **26** God gave them a taste of humiliation in this world. Yet much greater will be the suffering of the life to come, if they but knew it! **27** We have set for people in this Qur'an all sorts of illustrations, so that they may reflect. **28** It is an Arabic Qur'an, free from distortion, so that people may become conscious of God. **29** God cites the case of a man who has for his masters several partners at odds with each other, and a man belonging wholly to one person? Can they be deemed equal? All praise is due to God alone, but most of them do not understand.

30 Indeed you are bound to die, and they too are bound to die; **31** and then on the Day of Resurrection you all will dispute with one another in the presence of your Lord. **32** Who could be more wrong than one who invents a lie about God and rejects the truth when it comes to him? Is not there in Hell a proper abode for the unbelievers? **33** It is the one who brings the truth and the one who accepts it as true that are God-fearing. **34** They will have all that they wish for with their Lord: such is the reward of those who do good. **35** God will expunge the worst of their deeds and will give them their reward in accordance with the best that they did.

36 Is not God sufficient for His servant? Yet they would try to frighten you with those who are inferior to Him. He whom God lets go astray can never find any guide; whereas he whom God guides aright can never be led astray. **37** Is God not mighty, capable of inflicting retribution? **38** If you ask them who created the heavens and the earth, they will answer: 'God'. Say: 'Consider these beings you invoke beside Him: if God wills harm to befall me, could they remove the harm He has inflicted? Or, if He wills that mercy should be bestowed on me, could they withhold His mercy?' Say: 'God is enough for me: In Him place their trust those who have a trust to place'. **39** Say: 'My people! Do all that may be in your power, and I will do what I can. **40** You shall come to know who will be visited with humiliating suffering and who shall be smitten by long-lasting suffering'. **41** We have bestowed on you this Book from on high, setting out the truth for mankind. Whoever follows its guidance does so for his own good, and whoever goes astray shall do so at his own peril. You are not responsible for them. **42** God takes away people's souls upon their death, and the souls of the living during their sleep. He keeps with Him the souls of those whose death He has ordained and sends back the others until their appointed time. In all this there are signs for people who reflect. **43** Have they chosen others besides God to intercede for them? Say: 'Why, even though they have no power over anything and no understanding?' **44** Say: 'All intercession belongs to God alone. His alone is the dominion over the heavens and the earth; and to Him you will all in the end return'. **45** Whenever God alone is mentioned, the hearts of those who will not believe in the life to come shrink with aversion; but when others are mentioned side by side with Him, they rejoice. **46** Say: 'God! Originator of the heaves and the earth! You have knowledge of all that is beyond anyone's perception and all that anyone may witness. It is You who will judge between Your servants concerning all that over which they differ'. **47** If the wrongdoers possessed all that is on earth, and twice as much, they would surely offer it all as ransom from the awful suffering on the Day of Resurrection. For God will have made obvious to them something they have never reckoned with. **48** Obvious to them will have become the evil of what they had done; and they will be overwhelmed by that which they used to deride. **49** When man suffers affliction, he cries out to Us; but once We bestow upon him a favour by Our grace, he says: 'I have been given all this by virtue of my knowledge'. By no means! It is but a test, yet most of them do not understand. **50** Those who lived before their time said the same, but of no avail to them was all that they had ever done: for the very evil of their deeds recoiled upon them. Similarly, the wrongdoers among these present people will have the evil of their deeds recoil upon them. **51** They will never be able to frustrate [God's purpose.] **52** Are they not aware that it is God who grants sustenance in abundance, or gives it sparingly, to whomever He wills? In this there are signs to those who believe.

53 Say: '[Thus speaks God]: You servants of Mine who have transgressed against their own souls! Do not despair of God's mercy: God forgives all sins; He alone is much-forgiving, ever-merciful'. **54** Turn towards your Lord and submit to Him before the suffering comes upon you, for then you cannot be helped. **55** Follow the best that has been revealed to you by your Lord before the suffering comes upon you of a sudden, without your being aware of it, **56** lest anyone should say: 'Woe is me for having neglected what is due to God, and for having been one of those who scoffed [at the truth]'; **57** or lest he should say: 'If God had but guided me, I would surely have been among the God-fearing'; **58** or lest he should say, when faced by the suffering [that awaits him]: 'If only I could have a second chance in life, I will be among those who do good'. **59** [God will say]: 'Yes, indeed! My revelations did come to you, but you rejected them. You were filled with false pride and had no faith at all'. **60** On the Day of Resurrection you will see those who invented lies about God with their faces darkened. Is not there in Hell a proper abode for the arrogant? **61** But God will deliver those who are God-fearing to their place of safety: no harm shall afflict them, nor shall they grieve.

62 God is the Creator of everything, and of all things He is the Guardian. **63** His are the keys of the heavens and the earth. Those who deny God's revelations will surely be the losers. **64** Say: 'You ignorant people! Would you bid me worship anyone other than God?' **65** It has been revealed to you, and to those before you, that if you ever associate partners with God, all your works shall certainly come to nothing, and you shall certainly be among the lost. **66** You shall worship God alone, and be one of those who give thanks [to Him]. **67** No true understanding of God have they: on the Day of Resurrection, the whole earth will be a mere handful to Him, and the heavens will be rolled up in His right hand. Limitless is He in His glory, and sublimely exalted above anything which they associate as partner with Him. **68** The Trumpet will be sounded, and all creatures that are in the heavens and the earth will fall down senseless, except those God wills to be spared. It will then be sounded a second time, and they will rise and look around them. **69** The earth will shine bright with the light of its Lord; the Record of Deeds will be laid open; all the prophets and the witnesses will be brought in. Judgement will be passed on them all in justice, and they will not be wronged; for every human being will be repaid in full for whatever they have done. **70** He is fully aware of all that they do. **71** The unbelievers will be led to Hell in throngs. When they reach it, its gates will be opened, and its keepers will ask them: 'Did there not come to you messengers from among yourselves, who recited to you your Lord's revelations and forewarned you of this Day?' They will answer: 'Yes, indeed'. But the sentence of suffering will have already been passed against the unbelievers. **72** They will be told: 'Enter the gates of Hell; there you will abide'. How vile an abode for the arrogant! **73** And the believers will be led to Paradise in throngs. When they reach it, they shall find its gates wide open; and its keepers will say to them: 'Peace be to you! Well have you done. Come in: you are here to stay'. **74** They will say: 'All praise is due to God who has made His promise to us come true and given us this land as our own. Now we may dwell in Paradise as we please'. How excellent is the reward of those who worked hard. **75** You will see the angels surrounding the Throne, extolling their Lord's glory and praise. Judgement will have been passed on all in justice, and it will be said: All praise is due to God, the Lord of all the worlds.

Surah 40   The Forgiving

This surah deals with the issues of truth and falsehood, belief and unbelief, the advocacy of the divine message and its rejection. It also refers to the arrogance shown by those unbelievers who enjoy power and the way God punishes and destroys them.

It starts by presenting some attributes of God that suit its theme. He accepts people's repentance and forgives them their past sins. However, He is also stern in punishment and no one can escape from Him. It then refers to past communities which denied God's messages, reminding people that they face the same fate if they follow their example.

The surah gives a detailed account of a believer who belonged to Pharaoh's household and who tried hard to persuade his people to believe, but they rejected his counsel. The surah shows how he prays for God's help, submitting himself to Him and God protects him against the unbelievers' schemes.

The surah then tells us that those who dispute the divine message are motivated by arrogance; they are too proud to submit to the truth. The surah draws their attention to the great expanse of the universe so that they may feel their insignificance in relation to the universe, which is of God's creation. It then concludes with a directive to the Prophet to remain patient, reminding him that earlier messengers faced the same attitude of rejection.

The Forgiving

In the Name of God, the Lord of Grace, the Ever-Merciful

1 *Ha. Mim.* **2** The revelation of this Book is from God, the Almighty, the All-Knowing, who forgives sins, accepts repentance, is severe in retribution and limitless in bounty. **3** There is no deity other than Him. To Him is the ultimate return. **4** None but the unbelievers dispute God's revelations. Let it not deceive you that they seem to be able to do as they please on earth. **5** Before their time the people of Noah rejected the truth, as did other groups and communities after them. Each of these communities schemed against the messenger sent to them, aiming to lay their hands on him. With false argument they strove to refute the truth, but then I took them to task. How awesome was My punishment! **6** Thus your Lord's word shall come true against the unbelievers: they will be the dwellers in the fire of Hell. **7** Those who bear the Throne and those around it extol their Lord's limitless glory and praise, and have faith in Him, and pray for the forgiveness of all believers: 'Our Lord! You embrace all things with [Your] grace and knowledge. Forgive, then, those who turn to You in repentance and follow Your path, and shield them from the suffering in the blazing Fire. **8** And, our Lord, admit them to the gardens of perpetual bliss You have promised them, together with the righteous from among their ancestors, spouses and offspring. You alone are the Almighty, the Wise. **9** Shield them from all evil. Anyone whom on that Day You shall shield from evil, You shall have graced with mercy. That will be the supreme triumph'. **10** The unbelievers will be addressed: 'Indeed, greater than your present loathing of yourselves is God's loathing of you when you were called to the faith and you rejected it'. **11** They will say: 'Our Lord! Twice have You caused us to die, just as twice You have brought us to life! Now that we have recognised our sins, is there any way out?' **12** [They will be told]: 'This is all because when God alone was invoked, you denied this truth; whereas, when partners were associated with Him, you believed in them! All judgement rests with God, the Exalted, the Supreme One'. **13** He it is who shows you His signs and sends down sustenance from the sky for you. Yet only those who turn to God will take heed. **14** Pray to God, then, sincere in your faith in Him alone, however hateful this may be to the unbelievers. **15** High above all orders [of being] is He, the Lord of the Throne. By His own will does He bestow revelation on whomever He wills of His servants, so as to warn of the Day when all shall meet; the Day when they shall come forth, with nothing about them concealed from God. **16** With whom does sovereignty rest today? With God, the One who holds absolute sway over all that exists. **17** This Day each soul will be requited for what it has earned: no injustice will be done today. God is swift in reckoning. **18** Warn them of the Day that is ever drawing near, when people's hearts will chokingly come up to the throats. The wrongdoers will have neither intimate friend nor intercessor to be heeded. **19** God is well aware of the most stealthy glance, and of everything the heart would conceal. **20** God will judge in accordance with truth and justice, whereas those whom they invoke beside Him cannot judge at all. God alone hears all and sees all.

21 Have they, then, never travelled through the land and beheld what happened in the end to those who lived before them? Greater were they in power than they are, and in the impact which they left on earth. God, however, took them to task for their sins, and they had none to defend them against God. **22** That was because their messengers came to them with all evidence of the truth, yet they rejected it. So God took them to task. He is powerful, stern in retribution. **23** We sent Moses with Our signs and a clear authority **24** to Pharaoh, Haman and Qarun [Korah], but they said: 'A sorcerer, a teller of lies'. **25** When he came to them, setting forth the truth from Us, they said: 'Kill the sons of those who share his faith, and spare only their women'. Yet the schemes of the unbelievers can only go wrong. **26** Pharaoh said: 'Leave it to me to kill Moses, and let him invoke his Lord! I fear that he will change your religion and cause corruption to spread in the land'. **27** Moses said: 'I seek refuge with Him who is my Lord and your Lord from everyone who is too arrogant and will not believe in the Day of Reckoning'. **28** A believing man of Pharaoh's family, who until then had concealed his faith, said: 'Would you kill a man because he says, "God is my Lord", when he has brought you all evidence of the truth from your Lord? If he is a liar, his lie will fall back on him; but if he is speaking the truth, something of what he warns you against is bound to befall you. God will not grace with His guidance anyone who is a lying transgressor. **29** My people! Yours is the dominion today, having the upper hand in the land; but who will rescue us from God's punishment should it befall us?' Pharaoh said: 'I am only putting before you what I see myself; and I am guiding you to none other than the path of rectitude'. **30** Then said the man who believed: 'My people! I fear for you the like of what one day befell earlier communities; the like of what happened to Noah's people, to the 'Ad, and Thamud and those who came after them. **31** God does not will any injustice for His creatures. **32** And, my people! I fear for you the Day [of Judgement] when people will call out to one another [in distress]; the Day when you shall turn back and flee, with no one to defend you against God. **33** He whom God lets go astray can never find a guide. **34** Long before this, Joseph came to you with clear evidence of the truth; but you never ceased to cast doubt on the message he brought you. When he died, you said: "God will never send any messenger after him". In this way God lets go astray those who are transgressors and live in doubt. **35** Those who dispute God's revelations, with no authority granted to them, commit something that is exceedingly loathsome in the sight of God and of those who believe. In this way God sets a seal on the heart of every arrogant tyrant'. **36** Pharaoh said: 'Haman! Build me a lofty tower that I may attain the right means; the means of approach to the heavens, so that I may have a look at this god of Moses. I am convinced that he is lying'. **37** Thus, goodly seemed to Pharaoh the evil of his deed, and he was barred from the right path. Pharaoh's scheming led only to ruin. **38** The man who believed said: 'My people! Follow me: I shall guide you to the path of rectitude. **39** My people! This worldly life is but a brief enjoyment, whereas the life to come is the lasting home. **40** Anyone who does a bad deed will be requited with no more than its like, whereas anyone, be it man or woman, who does righteous deeds and is a believer will enter Paradise where they will receive blessings beyond reckoning. **41** My people! How is it that I call you to salvation, while you call me to the Fire? **42** You call upon me to deny God and to associate with Him others of whom I have no knowledge, the while I call you to the Almighty, the All-Forgiving. **43** There is no doubt that what you call me to is not fit to be invoked either in this world or in the life to come. To God is our return, when the transgressors shall find themselves in the Fire. **44** You shall then remember what I am telling you now. As for me, I commit myself to God: God is well aware of all His servants'. **45** God delivered him from the evils of their scheming, whereas grievous suffering was to encompass Pharaoh's folk: **46** before the Fire they are brought, morning and evening, and then on the Day when the Last Hour comes, it will be said: 'Cast Pharaoh's people into the worst suffering'. **47** They will contend with one another in the Fire: the weak will say to those who were arrogant, 'We have been your followers, so can you relieve us of some share of the Fire?' **48** The arrogant will reply: 'We are all in it together. For God has judged between His creatures'. **49** Those in the Fire will say to the keepers of Hell: 'Pray to your Lord that He lighten this suffering of ours, though it be for one day only'. **50** They will ask: 'Did your messengers not come to you with clear evidence of the truth?' They will say: 'Yes, indeed'. [The keepers of Hell] will say: 'Pray, then!' But the prayers of the unbelievers will be all in vain. **51** We shall indeed support Our messengers and the believers both in this world's life and on the Day when all the witnesses shall stand up. **52** On that Day their excuses will be of no avail to the wrongdoers: their fate will be rejection, and they will have the worst of homes. **53** And indeed, We bestowed Our guidance on Moses, and passed down the Book to the Children of Israel **54** as a guide and a reminder to people of understanding. **55** Therefore, remain patient in adversity, for God's promise always comes true. Ask forgiveness for your sins, and extol your Lord's glory and praise evening and morning.

56 As for those who dispute God's revelations, with no authority granted to them, there is nothing in their hearts but a quest for a greatness they will never attain. Seek, then, refuge with God, for He is the One who hears all and sees all. **57** The creation of the heavens and the earth is indeed greater than the creation of man; yet most people do not understand. **58** The blind and the seeing are not equal; nor can those who believe and do good works and those who do evil be deemed equal. How seldom you reflect. **59** The Last Hour is sure to come: of this there is no doubt. Yet most people will not believe. **60** Your Lord says: 'Call on Me, and I shall answer you. Those who are too proud to worship Me shall enter Hell humiliated'. **61** It is God who has made for you the night in which to rest, and the day to make you see. God is limitless in His bounty to man, but most people do not give thanks. **62** Such is God, your Lord, the Creator of all that exists: there is no deity other than Him. How deluded can you be? **63** Such it is: far deluded are those who knowingly deny God's revelations. **64** It is God who has made the earth a resting place for you and the sky a canopy. He has moulded you into a comely shape and provided you with wholesome things. Such is God, your Lord. So glory be to God, the Lord of all the worlds. **65** He is the Ever-Living. There is no deity other than Him. So call on Him, sincere in your faith in Him. All praise is due to God, the Lord of all the worlds. **66** Say: 'Since all evidence of the truth has come to me from my Lord, I am forbidden to worship those whom you invoke instead of God. I am commanded to submit to the Lord of all the worlds'. **67** It is He who creates you out of dust, then out of a gamete, then out of a clinging cell mass; and then He brings you forth as infants. He then lets you reach maturity, and then grow old – although some of you die earlier. [All this He ordains] so that you may reach your appointed term, and you may use your reason. **68** It is He who ordains life and death. When He wills something to be, He only says to it, 'Be', and it is. **69** Do you not see how those who dispute God's revelations are turned away from the truth? **70** Those who reject the Book and the messages We sent through Our messengers. They will certainly come to know **71** when, with chains and shackles round their necks, they will be dragged **72** into scalding water, and then burnt into the fire of Hell. **73** Then they will be asked: 'Where now are those to whom you ascribed divinity side by side with God?' They will answer: 'They have forsaken us, or rather, what we used to invoke were nothing'. **74** Thus does God let the unbelievers go astray. **75** 'This is because on earth you took delight in things that are untrue and you were insolent. **76** Enter now the gates of Hell, where you shall abide. Evil indeed is the abode of the arrogant.' **77** Hence, remain patient in adversity, for

God's promise always comes true. Whether We show you something of what We hold in store for them or We cause you to die before that, it is to Us that they shall all return.

78 We sent other messengers before your time; some We have given you an account of, while others We have not. No messenger could bring a sign except by God's leave. When God's will becomes manifest, judgement will be passed between them in all justice, and lost will be, then and there, all who have followed falsehood. **79** It is God who provides livestock for you, some for riding and some for your food. **80** You have other benefits in them too. You can reach on them any destination you wish. On them, as on ships, you are carried. **81** And He shows you His signs: which of God's signs can you still deny? **82** Have they not travelled through the land and seen what was the end of those who lived before them? They were more numerous than them, and greater in power and in the impact they left on earth. Yet what they achieved was of no avail to them. **83** When God's messengers came to them with all evidence of the truth, they revelled in what knowledge they had; and so they were overwhelmed by the very thing which they mocked. **84** And then when they saw Our might, they said: 'We believe in God alone, and we renounce those we used to associate as partners with Him'. **85** But accepting the faith after they had seen Our might was not going to benefit them at all. This has always been God's way of dealing with His creatures. There and then the unbelievers will be lost.

Surah 41   Clearly Expounded

This surah speaks about faith, God's Oneness and the life to come, giving strong emphasis to the question of revelation granted to God's Messenger. It adds an element about advocating God's message and highlighting the refined manners of its advocates.

In its discussion of God's Oneness, the surah speaks of creation, giving details of how the heavens and the earth were originally created. The scene fills us with great wonder and amazement. It is followed by reference to some of God's signs in the universe, such as the sun, the moon, the angels and their worship of God, the desolate earth and how it comes into life with repeated rainfall. This is a clear image of resurrection.

The surah speaks about the revelation of the Qur'an, stating that its verses are clearly expounded and its message is stated in perfect clarity. No falsehood may creep into it. Whatever the Qur'an mentions is absolutely true. Nothing that may be added to human knowledge, as a result of any discovery or development, will ever show any flaw in it. How would it be when the Qur'an is the revelation of God whose knowledge is perfect and complete?

The surah mentions the punishment that befell past communities of unbelievers. It also refers to the Day of Judgement and makes clear that its timing is only known to God who knows what every pregnant female will give birth to, just as He knows what every tree and plant will produce. The surah concludes with a promise that God will show people His signs, in the expanse of the universe and within themselves, so that they will know that His message is the truth.

Clearly Expounded

In the Name of God, the Lord of Grace, the Ever-Merciful

1 *Ha. Mim.* **2** A revelation from the Lord of Grace, the Ever-Merciful: **3** a Book, the verses of which have been clearly spelled out as a discourse in Arabic for people of knowledge. **4** It gives good news as well as a warning. Yet, most of them turn away, so that they do not hear. **5** They say: 'Our hearts are veiled from whatever you call us to, and in our ears is deafness, and there is a barrier between us and you. So do you what you will, and so shall we'. **6** Say: 'I am but a human being like yourselves. It has been revealed to me that your God is the

One and only God. Therefore, take the straight path to Him and seek
His forgiveness'. Woe to those who associate partners with Him, and
7 who do not pay zakat [obligatory charity], and who refuse to believe
in the life to come. **8** Those who believe and do good deeds shall have
an unfailing reward. **9** Say: 'Do you indeed disbelieve in Him who
has created the earth in two aeons? And do you claim others to be His
equals? It is He who is the Lord of all the worlds'. **10** He it is who
placed on the earth firm mountains towering above it, and bestowed
His blessings on it, and measured out its varied provisions in four
aeons, ensuring equity for all who seek [such provisions]. **11** Then,
He applied His design to the sky, which was but smoke; and said to it
and to the earth: 'Come, both of you, willingly or unwillingly'. They
both said: 'We do come willingly'. **12** So He decreed that they become
seven heavens in two aeons, and assigned to each heaven its task. We
adorned the sky nearest to the earth with lights, and made them secure.
Such is the design of the Almighty, the All-Knowing. **13** If they turn
away, say: 'I warn you of a thunderbolt like the thunderbolt that struck
the 'Ad and Thamud'. **14** There came to them, from all directions,
messengers saying: 'Worship none but God'. They answered: 'If our
Lord had wished, He would have sent down angels. We will never
believe in your message'. **15** As for the 'Ad, they behaved arrogantly
through the land, against all right, and said: 'Who is mightier than
us?' Did they not realise that God, who created them, was mightier
than them? They continued to reject Our revelations. **16** Therefore,
We let loose upon them a howling gale raging through several days
of misfortune, so as to give them, in the life of this world, a foretaste
of humiliating suffering. Yet the suffering in the life to come will be
even more humiliating, and they will have none to help them. **17** As
for the Thamud, We offered them guidance, but they chose blindness
in preference to guidance. Therefore, the thunderbolt of humiliating
suffering struck them in consequence of what they had wrought.
18 And We saved those who believed and were God-fearing. **19** On
the Day when God's enemies will be gathered together before the
Fire, they will be driven onwards **20** until, when they reach it, their
ears, their eyes and their very skins will bear witness against them,
speaking of what they used to do [on earth]. **21** They will ask their
skins: 'Why did you bear witness against us?' To which they will
reply: 'God, who gave speech to all things, has made us speak. It is
He who created you in the first instance, and to Him you now return.
22 You did not try to hide yourselves so that your ears, eyes and skins
could not be made to testify against you. Yet you thought that God

did not know much of what you were doing. **23** And it is this thought of yours which you entertained about your Lord that brought you to perdition, so that you are now among the lost'. **24** If they resign themselves to patience, the Fire will be their home; and if they pray to be allowed to make amends, they will not be allowed to do so. **25** We have assigned to the unbelievers companions who made their past and present seem goodly to them, but the sentence has fallen due upon them together with bygone generations of jinn and humans. They will indeed be lost. **26** The unbelievers say: 'Do not listen to this Qur'an, but drown it in frivolous talk, so that you may gain the upper hand'. **27** We shall most certainly give the unbelievers a taste of severe suffering; and We shall most certainly requite them according to the worst of their deeds. **28** Such is the requital of the enemies of God: the Fire will be their lasting home: a fit requital for their having knowingly rejected Our revelations. **29** The unbelievers say: 'Our Lord! Show us those jinn and men who have led us astray. We shall trample them under our feet so that they shall be among the lowest of the low'. **30** As for those who say: 'Our Lord is God', and then steadfastly pursue the right way. For these, the angels will descend, saying: 'Have no fear, and do not grieve, but rejoice in the good news of Paradise which you have been promised. **31** We are your guardians in the life of this world and in the life to come. **32** There you shall have all that your souls desire, and all that you ask for, as a ready welcome from Him who is much-forgiving, ever-merciful'. **33** Who speaks better than he who calls people to God, does what is right, and says, 'I am one of those who have surrendered themselves to God?' **34** Good and evil cannot be equal. Repel evil with what is better, and he who is your enemy will become as close to you as a true friend. **35** Yet none will attain this except those who are patient in adversity; none will attain it except those endowed with truly great fortune. **36** If a prompting from Satan should stir you up, seek refuge with God. He is the One who hears all and knows all.

37 Among His signs are the night and the day, and the sun and the moon. Do not prostrate yourselves before the sun or the moon; but prostrate yourselves before God, who has created them, if it is Him you really worship. **38** If the unbelievers are too arrogant, those who are with your Lord glorify Him night and day and never grow weary of that. **39** Another of His signs is this: you see the earth lying desolate, but when We send down rain water upon it, it stirs and swells [with life]. He who brings it to life will surely give life to the dead. He has power over all things. **40** Those who distort the

meaning of Our revelations are not hidden from Us. Who is in a
better state: he who is cast into the Fire, or he who shall come safe
on Resurrection Day? Do what you will; He sees all that you do.
41 Those who reject this reminder [Qur'an] when it comes to them
… It is indeed a sublime Book; no falsehood can ever touch it openly
or in a stealthy manner. **42** It is bestowed from on high by One who
is wise, worthy of praise. **43** Nothing is being said to you other than
what was said to the messengers sent before your time. Your Lord
is the Lord of forgiveness, but He also inflicts painful punishment.
44 Had We willed to make this revelation a discourse in a non-
Arabic tongue, they would have said: 'If only its verses were clearly
spelled out! Why [a message in] a non-Arabic tongue and an Arab
[messenger]?' Say: 'This is guidance and healing for all those who
believe; but as for the unbelievers: there is deafness in their ears, and
they are blind to it'. They are, as it were, being called to from too
far away. **45** We gave the Book to Moses but disputes arose about
it. Had it not been for a decree that had already been issued by your
Lord, judgement would have been passed on them. As it is, they
are in grave, disquieting doubt about it. **46** Whoever does what is
right does so for his own good; and whoever does evil will himself
bear its consequences. Your Lord is never unjust to His creatures.
47 Knowledge of the Last Hour belongs to Him alone. No fruit comes
out of its calyx and no female ever conceives or gives birth without
His knowledge. And so, on the Day when He shall call out to them,
'Where now are those alleged partners of Mine?' They will say, 'We
confess to You that none of us can vouch for them'. **48** Whatever they
used to invoke before will have forsaken them; and they will know
that there is no escape for them. **49** Man never tires of asking for good
[things], but if evil fortune touches him, he abandons all hope, sinking
into despair. **50** Yet whenever We let him taste some of Our grace after
hardship has befallen him, he is sure to say, 'This is but my due!' and,
'I do not think that the Last Hour will ever come; but even if I were to
be taken back to my Lord, the best reward awaits me with Him'. We
shall most certainly give the unbelievers a full account of what they
did, and We shall most certainly give them a taste of severe suffering.
51 When we bestow Our blessings on man, he tends to turn aside
and stay aloof; but as soon as evil touches him, he turns to prolonged
prayer. **52** Say: 'Have you ever thought if this be truly a revelation
from God and yet you deny it? Who could be more astray than one
who places himself so far in the wrong?' **53** We shall show them Our
signs in the wide horizons [of the universe] and within themselves,

so that it will become clear to them that this [revelation] is indeed the truth. Is it not enough that your Lord is witness to everything? **54** They are certainly in doubt as to whether they will meet their Lord. Most certainly, He encompasses everything.

Surah 42   Consultation

The central theme of this surah is revelation and the divine message; every point discussed in the surah is directly relates to this. The surah also speaks of the Day of Resurrection, portrays scenes of the life to come, describes the values and behaviour of believers, and refers to people's provisions whether given in abundance or in small measure. In discussing all these subjects, God's Oneness is emphasised: He is the One Provider, the One Creator, the One who conducts all affairs, and certainly the One who gives revelations. It is He who revealed this Qur'an to Prophet Muhammad, just as He revealed earlier messages to His messengers of old. Thus, God's Oneness is prominent throughout this surah.

The surah makes clear that the divine message in its final form, which was given to Muhammad (peace be upon him), is essentially the same as the messages given to Noah, Abraham, Moses and Jesus, and indeed to all prophets. It concludes with reference to revelation: it comes from God, to whom all creatures shall return.

Consultation

In the Name of God, the Lord of Grace, the Ever-Merciful

1 *Ha. Mim.* 2 *ʿAyn. Sin. Qaf.* 3 Thus has God, the Almighty, the Wise, sent revelation to you, Prophet, and to those who preceded you. 4 His is all that is in the heavens and the earth. He is the Most High, the Supreme One. 5 The heavens are well-nigh rent asunder from above as the angels extol their Lord's limitless glory and praise, and beg forgiveness for all who are on earth. Surely God is much-forgiving, ever-merciful. 6 As for those who take for their protectors beings other than Him, God watches them, and you are not responsible for them. 7 So We have revealed to you a discourse in the Arabic tongue in order that you may warn the Mother City and all who dwell around it; that you may forewarn them of the Day of the Gathering, of which there is no doubt, when some shall be in Paradise and some in the blazing Fire. 8 Had God so willed, He could have made them all one single community, but He admits to His grace whoever He will, whereas the wrongdoers will have no one to protect them and no one to support them. 9 Have they chosen protectors other than Him? God alone is the Protector of all; He is the One who gives life to the dead;

and He has power over all things. **10** Whatever the subject of your disputes, the final word belongs to God. Such is God, my Lord. In Him have I placed my trust, and to Him do I always turn. **11** He is the Originator of the heavens and the earth. He made mates for you from among yourselves, just as He made mates for animals, so that you will multiply. Nothing bears even the slightest comparability to Him. He alone hears all and sees all. **12** His are the keys of the heavens and the earth. He gives abundant sustenance, or gives it in scant measure to whomever He wills. He has full knowledge of everything. **13** In matters of faith, He has ordained for you the same as He had enjoined on Noah – that which We have revealed to you [Muhammad] – and as We enjoined on Abraham, Moses and Jesus: 'Steadfastly uphold the faith and do not divide into factions'. Hard for the idolaters is that which you call on them to accept. God draws to Himself whoever He pleases and guides to Himself everyone who turns to Him. **14** They became divided, out of selfish rivalry, only after the knowledge had reached them. Had it not been for a decree that had already been issued by your Lord, until a term set [by Him], all would have been decided between them. As it is, those after them, who inherited the divine Book, are in grave, disquieting doubt about it. **15** Therefore, call people [to that faith], and follow the straight path as you have been commanded. Do not follow their likes and dislikes, but say: 'I believe in whatever revelation God has bestowed from on high. I am commanded to ensure justice between you. God is our Lord and your Lord. To us shall be accounted our deeds, and to you, your deeds. Let there be no argument between us and you. God will bring us all together, and to Him we shall all return'. **16** As for those who argue about God after He has been acknowledged, their argument is null and void in their Lord's sight: anger will fall upon them and severe suffering awaits them. **17** It is God who has bestowed revelation from on high, setting forth the truth, and established the balance. For all you know, the Last Hour may well be near. **18** Those who do not believe in it seek to hasten it, whereas the believers stand in awe of it and know it to be the truth. Those who argue about the Last Hour have gone far astray. **19** God is most kind towards His creatures. He provides for whoever He will. He is the Powerful, the Almighty. **20** To anyone who desires a harvest in the life to come, We shall grant an increase in his harvest; whereas to the one who desires a harvest in this world, We shall give a share of it, but he will have no share in the life to come. **21** Do they believe in alleged partners [of God] who ordain for them things which God has not sanctioned?

Were it not for God's decree on the final judgement, all would have been decided between them. Painful suffering awaits the wrongdoers. **22** You will see the wrongdoers full of fear on account of what they have done, which is bound to fall back on them. And you will see those who believe and do righteous deeds in the flowering meadows of the Gardens of Paradise. They will have whatever they wish from their Lord. This is indeed the supreme bounty. **23** It is of this [bounty] that God gives good news to His servants who believe and do righteous deeds. Say: 'No reward do I ask of you for this. It is only an act of affection due to kin'. Whoever does good, We shall increase it for him. God is much-forgiving, most-appreciative. **24** Do they say, 'He has invented a lie about God?' If God so willed, He could seal your heart and blot out all falsehood, and establish the truth by His words. He has full knowledge of what is in people's hearts.

25 It is He who accepts the repentance of His servants and who pardons bad deeds. He knows everything you do. **26** He responds to those who believe and do righteous deeds, and gives them much more of His bounty; but as for the unbelievers, severe suffering awaits them. **27** If God were to grant plentiful provisions to His servants, they would behave on earth with much insolence. As it is, He bestows from on high in due measure, as He wills. He is fully aware of His creatures, and He sees them all. **28** It is He who sends down rain when they have lost all hope, and spreads His grace far and wide. He is the Protector, worthy of all praise. **29** Among His signs is the creation of the heavens and the earth, and all the living creatures which He placed in them. He has the power to gather them all whenever He will. **30** Whatever misfortune befalls you is the outcome of what your own hands have done; but God forgives much. **31** Never can you elude Him on earth. You have none to protect you from God and none to give you support. **32** And among His signs are the ships that sail like floating mountains through the seas. **33** If He wills, He stills the wind, and then they lie motionless on the surface of the sea. **34** In this there are signs indeed for all who are patient in adversity and deeply grateful to God; or else He may cause them to perish because of what they have wrought and yet He forgives much. **35** Let those who call Our messages into question know that there is no escape for them. **36** Whatever you are given is but for the enjoyment of life in this world, but that which is with God is much better and more enduring. [It shall be given] to those who believe and place their trust in their Lord; **37** who shun grave sins and gross indecencies; and who, when angered, will forgive; **38** who respond to their Lord, attend regularly to their prayer, conduct their affairs by mutual consultation, and give generously out of what We have provided for them; **39** and who, when oppressed, defend themselves. **40** An evil deed is requited by an evil like it, but the one who forgives and puts things right will have his reward with God. He does not love wrongdoers. **41** However, no blame attaches to those who defend themselves after having been wronged. **42** Blame attaches only to those who oppress other people and transgress in the land against all right. For such, there is painful suffering in store. **43** As for the one who is patient in adversity and forgives; this requires the exercise of a truly strong resolve. **44** He whom God lets go astray will have no one else to protect him. When the wrongdoers come face to face with the suffering [awaiting them], you will see them exclaiming, 'Is there any way of return?' **45** You shall see them brought before the Fire, disgraced and humiliated, looking with a furtive glance. The believers will then say: 'The true losers are the ones who have forfeited themselves and their kindred on this Day of Resurrection'. Indeed the wrongdoers will fall into long-lasting suffering. **46** No protector whatever will they have to help them against God. He whom God lets go astray shall find no way forward. **47** Respond to your Lord before there comes, by God's will, a Day that cannot be put off. There shall be no refuge for you on that Day, nor shall you be able to deny your sins. **48** If they turn away, We have not sent you to be their keeper. Your only duty is to deliver the message [entrusted to you]. When We give man a taste of Our grace, he rejoices in it, but if misfortune befalls him on account of what he has done with his own hands, he is bereft of gratitude. **49** To God belongs sovereignty over the heavens and the earth. He creates what He will. **50** He grants female offspring to whomever He will, and male to whomever He will; Or gives both male and female to whomever He will, and causes whomever He will to be barren. He is all-knowing, infinite in His power. **51** It is not granted to any human being that God should speak to him except through revelation or from behind a veil, or by sending a messenger to reveal by His command what He will. He is exalted, wise. **52** Thus have We revealed a spirit to you [Muhammad] by Our command. You knew neither revelation nor faith, but We made it a light, guiding with it whoever We will of Our servants. You most certainly give guidance to the straight path, the path of God, to whom belongs all that is in the heavens and earth. **53** Most certainly, to God all things shall in the end return.

Surah 43   Gold

This surah deals with some of the problems and difficulties the Islamic message faced in Makkah. It deals with erroneous beliefs and with the arguments the unbelievers made to justify their rejection of the divine message. The pagan Arabs claimed that the angels were God's daughters. The surah asks how they came to this conclusion? What justified attributing females to God when they themselves did not like having daughters? They attributed their practices to God, alleging that they would not have worshipped the angels if God had not wished them to so worship them.

The surah deals with a wide variety of erroneous beliefs and false claims. It states that all God's messengers dissociated themselves from idolatry and the association of partners with God. They all preached the same message of God's Oneness. The surah gives in particular the examples of Abraham, Moses and Jesus. They were all devout servants of God who called on people to submit themselves to God and worship none but Him.

Gold

In the Name of God, the Lord of Grace, the Ever-Merciful

1 *Ha. Mim.* **2** By the Book that makes things clear! **3** We have made the Qur'an a discourse in Arabic so that you may understand. **4** It originates in the source of revelation kept with Us; it is indeed sublime, full of wisdom. **5** Should We ignore you and take away this reminder from you because you are people who transgress beyond bounds? **6** Many a prophet did We send to people of olden times; **7** but they mocked at each prophet who came to them. **8** We destroyed them even though they were mightier than these. Thus their example has gone down in history. **9** Yet if you ask them, 'Who created the heavens and the earth?' they are sure to answer, 'The Almighty, the All-Knowing created them'. **10** It is He who has smoothed out the earth for you and has traced on it paths for you so that you can find your way. **11** And He it is who sends down water from the sky in due measure. With it We raise dead land to life; and thus you will be raised from the dead. **12** And He it is who created all living things in pairs, and provided for you the ships and animals on which you ride, **13** so that when you are seated on their backs you remember your Lord's blessings and say: 'Limitless in His glory is He who has made all this subservient to our use. We could not have done it by ourselves. **14** To our Lord we shall most certainly return'. **15** Yet they assign to Him some of His own servants as offspring. Surely man is clearly hardened in disbelief. **16** Would He, out of all His creation, choose for Himself daughters and favour you with sons? **17** If any of them is given the good news of the birth of what he so readily attributes to the Lord of Grace, his face darkens and he is filled with gloom. **18** [Would they ascribe to God] someone who is brought up among trinkets and cannot put together a clear argument? **19** They claim that the angels, who are themselves but servants of the Lord of Grace, are females! Did they witness their creation? Their testimony will be put on record and they will be questioned about it. **20** They say: 'Had it been the will of the Lord of Grace, we should never have worshipped them'. Of that they have no knowledge: they are blatantly lying. **21** Or have We given them a book before this one to which they are still holding fast? **22** No indeed! They say, 'We found our forefathers following this tradition and we find our guidance by following in their footsteps'. **23** And thus it is: whenever, before your time, We sent a messenger to any community, the wealthy among them said: 'We found our forefathers following this tradition and we are only following in their footsteps'. **24** He said: 'Even though I bring you a guidance better than what you saw your forefathers following?' They replied: 'We reject the message you have been sent with'. **25** Therefore, We inflicted Our retribution on them. Reflect on how those who rejected the truth met their end.

26 Abraham said to his father and his people: 'I renounce what you worship, **27** I worship none other than Him who brought me into being. It is He who will guide me'. **28** He made this an abiding precept among his descendants so that they might always return [to God]. **29** I have allowed these people and their forefathers to enjoy their lives freely until the truth has come to them through a Messenger who makes things clear. **30** Now that the truth has come to them, they say, 'This is all sorcery, and we reject it outright'. **31** They also say, 'Why was not this Qur'an revealed to some great man of the two cities?' **32** Is it they who apportion your Lord's grace? It is We who deal out to them their livelihood in the life of this world, and raise some in rank above others, so that some of them may take others into their service. Your Lord's grace is better than all that they can amass. **33** Were it not that all people would become one community [of unbelievers], We would have provided those who now disbelieve in the Lord of Grace with roofs of silver for houses, stairways on which to ascend, **34** gates, couches on which to recline, and gold ornaments. **35** Yet all this would have been nothing but the fleeting enjoyment of life in this world. It is the life to come that your Lord reserves for the God-fearing. **36** We shall assign to whoever chooses to remain blind to the remembrance of the Lord of Grace an evil one as a comrade. **37** These [evil ones] turn them away from the right path, making them think that they are rightly guided. **38** When such a person comes to Us, he will say [to his comrade]: 'Would that I was as far away from you as the East is from the West'. Evil indeed are you for a comrade! **39** Because of your wrongdoing, it will not be of any benefit to you that you are now to share your suffering. **40** Can you [Prophet] make the deaf hear? Or guide the blind or those who are in manifest error? **41** If We take you away, We shall inflict retribution on them; **42** and if We show you the fulfilment of what We have promised them… We have full power over them. **43** Therefore, hold fast to what has been revealed to you: you certainly are on a straight path; and it is an honour for you and your people. **44** In time, you will all be called to account. **45** Ask any of the messengers We sent before you: 'Did We ever appoint deities to be worshipped other than the Lord of Grace?' **46** We sent Moses with Our message to Pharaoh and his nobles; and he said: 'I am a messenger of the Lord of all the worlds', **47** but when he presented Our signs to them, they laughed at them, yet each sign We showed them was greater than the preceding one. **48** We put them through suffering so that they might return [to the right path]. **49** They said: 'Sorcerer, pray to your Lord for us on the strength of the covenant He has made with you. We shall now follow the right way'. **50** Yet when We removed their suffering they still broke their word. **51** Pharaoh proclaimed to his people, saying: 'My people, is the kingdom of Egypt not mine, with all these rivers flowing at my feet? Do you not see? **52** Am I not better than this contemptible wretch who can hardly make his meaning clear? **53** Why have no bracelets of gold been given to him? Why have no angels come to accompany him?' **54** Thus did he make fools of his people, and they obeyed him. They were people lost in evil. **55** When they incurred Our anger, We inflicted Our retribution on them and drowned them all; **56** and so We made them a thing of the past and an example for later generations.

57 Whenever the son of Mary is cited as an example, your people raise an outcry, saying: 'Who is better: our deities or he?' They cite him only to challenge you. **58** They are contentious people. **59** He was but a servant of Ours whom We had favoured and made an example to the Children of Israel. **60** Had it been Our will, We could have made you angels, succeeding one another on earth. **61** He is a portent of the Last Hour. Have no doubt about it, but follow Me: this is a straight path. **62** Let not Satan debar you; for he is your sworn enemy. **63** When Jesus came with clear signs, he said: 'I have come to you with wisdom, and to make clear to you some of that on which you differ. Therefore, fear God and follow me. **64** God is my Lord and your Lord: so worship Him alone. This is a straight path'. **65** Yet are the sects at variance among themselves. Woe, then, to the wrongdoers for the painful suffering that will befall them on a grievous day. **66** What are they waiting for other than the Last Hour, which will come upon them all of a sudden and take them unawares? **67** On that Day, friends will become enemies to one another, except for the God-fearing. **68** You, servants of Mine, no fear need you have today, nor shall you grieve. **69** You, who have believed in Our revelations and surrendered yourselves to Us, **70** enter Paradise, you and your spouses, in pure happiness. **71** They will be waited upon with trays and goblets of gold; and there will be found all that the souls may desire and the eyes may delight in. There you shall abide; **72** This is the garden that shall be your own on account of what you used to do. **73** You shall have there fruits in abundance, from which to eat. **74** The evildoers shall abide in the suffering of Hell. **75** It will not be lightened for them; they will remain in utter despair. **76** We never wronged them; it was they who have wronged themselves. **77** They will cry, 'Malik, if only your Lord would put an end to us!' He will answer: 'You are here to stay'. **78** We have brought the truth to you, but most of you abhor the truth. **79** If they have resolved on some scheme, We have a scheme of Our own. **80** Or do they think that We do not hear their secret talk and their private counsel? Indeed We do, and Our messengers are with them, recording all. **81** Say: 'If the Lord of Grace had a son, I would be the first to worship him'. **82** Limitless in His glory is the Lord of the heavens and earth, the Lord of the Throne: He is far above their false descriptions. **83** Leave them to indulge in idle talk and play until they face the Day they have been promised. **84** It is He alone who is God in heaven and God on earth; He alone is the Wise, the All-Knowing. **85** Blessed is He to whom sovereignty over the heavens and the earth and all that is between them belongs, and with whom the knowledge of the Last Hour rests, and to whom you shall be brought back. **86** Those whom they invoke beside Him have no power of intercession, unlike those who know the truth and bear witness to it. **87** Yet if you ask them who created them they are sure to answer, 'God'. How is it, then, that they are so misled? **88** And [the Prophet] says: 'My Lord, these are people who will not believe'. **89** Still, bear with them and say, 'Peace', for in time they will come to know.

Surah 44   Smoke

This surah speaks in a direct manner about God's Oneness, the Day of Judgement and the divine message. It begins by stating that the Qur'an was bestowed on a blessed night, the Night of Power, as a manifestation of God's grace. Yet the surah is characterised by a powerful style that aims to shake the human heart and mind into clear reflection on the message. This, so that people will recognise that it is the message of the truth.

The surah warns the unbelievers that God's punishment might overwhelm them all of a sudden, reminding them of the destruction of Pharaoh and his troops.

The surah places strong emphasis on the Day of Resurrection, refuting the unbelievers' argument that there will be nothing after death. It tells them that the universe was not created in vain. Life will come to its appointed end and all mankind will be resurrected in order to receive their just recompense for what they have done in this present life.

Smoke

In the Name of God, the Lord of Grace, the Ever-Merciful

1 *Ha. Mim.* 2 By the Book that makes things clear! 3 We have bestowed it from on high on a blessed night; for, indeed, We have always sent warnings. 4 On that night every matter of wisdom is made clear 5 by Our command; for, indeed, We have always sent messages [of guidance] as a mercy from your Lord. 6 He alone is the One who hears all and knows all; 7 the Lord of the heavens and the earth and all that is between them, if only you were firm believers. 8 There is no deity other than Him; He gives life and deals death. He is your Lord and the Lord of your earliest ancestors. 9 Yet they remain in doubt, playing about. 10 Wait, then, for the Day when the skies shall bring forth a kind of smoke which will make things clear. 11 It will envelop the people. Painful is this suffering! 12 [They will cry]: 'Our Lord! Relieve us from this suffering; for, indeed, we are believers'. 13 How will this remembrance benefit them? A messenger who clearly explained things had previously come to them; 14 but they turned their backs on him and said: 'He is taught by others, a madman!' 15 We shall remove this suffering for a while; but you are

bound to revert [to your old ways]. **16** On that Day We shall deliver
a mighty onslaught; We will indeed exact retribution. **17** We did,
before their time, try Pharaoh's people: there came to them a noble
messenger, **18** who said to them: 'Give in to me, you servants of God!
For, I am indeed a messenger sent to you, worthy of trust! **19** Do not
exalt yourselves against God; for, indeed, I come to you with manifest
authority. **20** I seek refuge with my Lord and your Lord lest you hurl
stones at me. **21** If you do not believe me, stand away from me'.
22 He, then called out to his Lord, saying: 'These people are lost in
sin'. **23** And [God said]: 'Set forth with My servants by night, for
you will surely be pursued; **24** and leave the sea calm behind you; for
their host are destined to be drowned'. **25** How many gardens did they
leave behind, and how many fountains, **26** and fields of grain, and
noble dwellings, **27** and good things in which they used to delight!
28 Thus it was. And We made other people inherit it all. **29** Neither
heaven nor earth shed tears over them, nor were they allowed a respite.
30 We saved the Children of Israel from humiliating suffering,
31 from Pharaoh, who was arrogant and a transgressor. **32** We chose
them knowingly above all other people. **33** And We gave them signs in
which there was a clear test. **34** Now these people assert: **35** 'We shall
die but one death, and we shall not be raised to life again. **36** Bring
back our forefathers, if what you claim be true'. **37** Are they better
than the people of Tubba' and those before them, whom We destroyed
because they were lost in sin? **38** We have not created the heavens and
the earth and all that is between them in mere idle play. **39** We created
them all for nothing other than a true purpose, but most of them do
not understand. **40** The Day of Decision is the time appointed for all
of them. **41** It is a Day when no friend shall be of the least avail to his
friend, and when none shall receive support except those upon whom
God will have bestowed His grace and mercy. **42** He alone is the
Almighty, the Ever-Merciful. **43** The fruit of the Zaqqum tree **44** will
be the food of the sinful; **45** like molten lead will it boil in the belly,
46 like the boiling of scalding water. **47** 'Take him, and drag him into
the midst of the blazing Fire; **48** then pour over his head the suffering
of scalding water! **49** Taste this, you powerful and honourable man!
50 This is the very thing you surely doubted'. **51** The God-fearing
will certainly be in a safe position, **52** amid gardens and fountains,
53 wearing garments of silk and brocade, facing one another. **54** Thus
shall it be. And We shall pair them with pure companions with most
beautiful eyes. **55** There they can call for every kind of fruit, enjoying
peace and security. **56** They shall not taste death there, having had

their one death. He will have preserved them from suffering through the blazing Fire, an act of your Lord's favour. **57** That is the supreme triumph. **58** We have made this Qur'an easy to understand, in your own language, so that they may take heed. **59** Wait, then; they too are waiting.

Surah 45   Kneeling Down

This surah describes the unbelievers' attitude towards the divine message. Some are stubborn in their rejection, unwilling to listen to God's revelations, mock at them and turn a deaf ear to all warnings.

Others, perhaps belonging to earlier divine religions, have obvious misconceptions. They do not have real faith, and they engage in bad deeds. Yet they claim to be loved by God and bound to enjoy His grace. The surah makes it clear that those who have no qualms about committing what is sinful cannot be treated by God on an equal footing with believers who are keen to do only what is righteous.

Others still pay no heed to anything other than the fulfilment of their desires. In fact, their desire becomes the deity they worship. As such, God leaves them to go astray and they soon become deaf to His warnings and their hearts become sealed. They have no way of discerning the truth.

The surah concludes with a powerful statement asserting that God is the Lord of the heavens, the earth and all worlds. He is almighty and wise.

Kneeling Down

In the Name of God, the Lord of Grace, the Ever-Merciful

1 *Ha. Mim.* 2 This Book is bestowed from on high by God, the Almighty, the Wise. 3 Surely, in the heavens and the earth there are signs for those who believe. 4 And in your own creation, and in the animals God scatters on earth there are signs for people of sure faith. 5 And in the alternation of night and day, and in the means of subsistence God sends down from the skies, reviving with it the earth after it had been lifeless, and in the shifting of the winds there are signs for those who use their reason. 6 Such are God's signs that We recount to you, setting forth the truth. In what discourse will they then believe, if they deny God and His revelations? 7 Woe to every lying, sinful person who hears God's revelations being recited to him, and yet persists in his haughty disdain, as though he had not heard them. 8 So, give him the news of painful suffering. 9 When he learns something of Our revelations, he ridicules it. For such people there is humiliating suffering in store. 10 Hell lurks behind them; and all that they may have gained shall be of no avail whatsoever

to them, nor shall any of those which they took for their protectors beside God. Grievous suffering awaits them. **11** This is true guidance; those who reject their Lord's revelations shall suffer a most painful punishment. **12** It is God who has subjected the sea for you, so that ships sail through it by His command, and that you may seek of His bounty, and that you give thanks. **13** And He has subjected to you, as a gift from Himself, all that is in the heavens and on earth. In this there are signs for people who think. **14** Tell the believers that they should forgive those who do not look forward to the Days of God. It is for Him alone to requite people for whatever they may have earned. **15** Whoever does what is right benefits himself; and whoever does evil causes himself harm. In the end to your Lord you will all return. **16** To the Children of Israel We gave revelations, wisdom and prophethood; and We provided them with wholesome things and favoured them above all other nations. **17** We granted them clear indications in matters of faith. It was only after knowledge had been granted them that they began to differ maliciously among themselves. Your Lord will certainly judge between them on Resurrection Day regarding all that on which they differed. **18** And now We have set you on a clear way of religion; so follow it, and do not follow the desires of those who do not know [the truth]. **19** They will be of no help to you against God. The wrongdoers have only one another to protect them, whereas God is the Protector of all who are God-fearing. **20** This [revelation] is a means of insight for mankind, and a source of guidance and grace for people of sure faith. **21** Do those who indulge in sinful deeds think that We shall place them, both in their life and their death, on equal footing with those who believe and do righteous deeds? Flawed is their judgement. **22** God has created the heavens and the earth in accordance with the truth, so that every soul shall be recompensed according to its deeds. None shall be wronged. **23** Consider the one who takes his own desires as his deity, and whom God has [therefore] let go astray despite his knowledge [of the truth], sealing his ears and heart and placing a cover on his eyes: who can guide such a person after God [has abandoned him]? Will you not, then, take heed?

24 They say: 'There is nothing beyond our life in this world. We die, we live, nothing but time destroys us'. Of this they have no knowledge whatsoever. They merely guess. **25** Whenever Our revelations are recited to them in all their clarity, their only argument is to say: 'Bring back our forefathers, if what you claim be true.' **26** Say: 'It is God who gives you life, then causes you to die; and then He will gather you all on Resurrection Day of which there is no doubt, though most people do not understand'. **27** To God belongs the dominion over the heavens and the earth. When the Last Hour strikes, those who follow falsehood will on that Day lose all. **28** You will see every community on its knees. Every community will be summoned to its record: 'Today you shall be requited for all that you did. **29** This Our record speaks of you in all truth; for We have been recording everything you do'. **30** Those who believed and did righteous deeds will be admitted by their Lord into His grace. That will be the manifest triumph. **31** And as for the unbelievers, [they will be asked]: 'When My revelations were recited to you, did you not glory in your arrogance and persist in your wicked ways? For when it was said, "God's promise will certainly come true, and there can be no doubt about the Last Hour", you would answer, "We know nothing of the Last Hour. **32** We think it is all conjecture, and we are by no means convinced".' **33** The evil of their deeds will become clear to them, and they will be overwhelmed by the very thing they used to deride. **34** It will be said to them: 'Today We shall be oblivious of you as you were oblivious of the coming of this your Day! The Fire will be your abode, and you will have no one to help you. **35** Thus it is, because you received God's revelations with ridicule and allowed the life of this world to beguile you'. Therefore, they will not be brought out of the Fire on that Day, nor will they be given a chance to make amends. **36** All praise is due to God, the Lord of heavens, the Lord of the earth and the Lord of all the worlds. **37** His alone is all supremacy in the heavens and the earth. He alone is the Almighty, the Wise.

Surah 46   The Sand Dunes

The surah starts by drawing attention to the creation of the heavens and the earth as well as the great signs in the universe that confirm that God is the Creator of all. Yet the unbelievers continue to pay no heed to the warnings given to them by God's messengers. The surah tells them that their alleged deities are of little use: they can cause them neither benefit nor harm.

The surah then portrays two contrasting types of people brought up by believing parents. The first are dutiful towards their parents and continue on the same line, praying to God to enable them to maintain their way and giving due thanks to God for all His grace. The other are undutiful towards their parents, reject the truth and the divine message describing it as 'legends of the ancients'.

The surah then refers to the punishment that overwhelmed the 'Ad. It describes how they thought that the approaching clouds would bring them rain but instead they brought a devastating storm.

The surah concludes by relating how a number of the jinn listened to the Qur'an, believed in it and went on their way to warn their people, calling on them to believe.

The Sand Dunes

In the Name of God, the Lord of Grace, the Ever-Merciful

1 *Ha. Mim.* 2 This Book is bestowed from on high by God, the Almighty, the Wise. 3 We have not created the heavens and the earth and all that is between them otherwise than in accordance with the truth, and for an appointed term. Yet the unbelievers ignore the warnings they have been given. 4 Say: 'Have you thought of those whom you invoke besides God? Show me what part of the earth they have created, or which share of the heavens they own. Bring me a book revealed before this, or some other vestige of knowledge, if what you claim is true'. 5 Who is in greater error than one who invokes, instead of God, such as will not respond to him till the Day of Resurrection, and are not even conscious of being invoked? 6 When all mankind are gathered [for judgement], these will be enemies to them and will disown their worship. 7 Whenever Our revelations are recited to them in all their clarity, the unbelievers describe the truth when it is delivered to them: 'This is plain sorcery'. 8 Do they say: 'He has

invented it himself'? Say: 'If I have invented it, you cannot be of the least help to me against God. He is fully aware of what you say amongst yourselves about it. Sufficient is He as a witness between me and you. He is indeed much-forgiving, ever-merciful'. **9** Say: 'I am not the first of God's messengers. I do not know what will be done with me or with you. I only follow what is being revealed to me. I am only a plain warner'. **10** Say: 'Have you thought: what if this Qur'an is really from God and you reject it? What if a witness from among the Children of Israel testifies to its similarity [to earlier Scriptures], and has believed in it while you glory in your arrogance? God does not guide wrongdoers'. **11** The unbelievers say of those who believe: 'If this [message] were any good, these people would not have preceded us in accepting it'. Since they refuse to be guided by it, they will always say, 'This is an ancient falsehood'. **12** Yet before this the book of Moses was revealed as a guide and a [sign of God's] grace. This book confirms it in the Arabic tongue, to warn the wrongdoers and to give good news to those who do good. **13** Those who say, 'Our Lord is God', and follow the straight path shall have nothing to fear, nor shall they grieve. **14** They are the ones destined for Paradise where they shall abide as a reward for what they do.

15 We have enjoined upon man to show kindness to his parents: in pain did his mother bear him, and in pain did she give him birth. His bearing and weaning takes thirty months. And so, when he attains to full manhood and reaches the age of forty, he prays: 'My Lord! Grant me that I will be grateful for the blessings which You have bestowed on me and on my parents, and that I may do righteous deeds that will meet with Your goodly acceptance. Grant me good descendants. To You I turn in repentance. I am indeed one of those who submit themselves to You'. **16** It is from such people that We shall accept the best that they ever did, and whose bad deeds We shall overlook. [They shall be] among the people destined for Paradise. True is the promise that has been given them. **17** But there is one who says to his parents: 'Fie on you both! Do you promise me that I shall be resurrected, when generations have passed away before me?' And while they both implore God for help, [and say to him]: 'Alas for you! Believe! God's promise always comes true', he answers: 'All this is nothing but fables of ancient times'. **18** Such are the ones upon whom the verdict is passed, together with other communities of jinn and humans that have passed away before their time. They will be utterly lost. **19** They all shall have their grades in accordance with their deeds; and so, He will repay them in full for their doings, and none shall be wronged.

20 On the Day when the unbelievers will be brought before the Fire, they will be told: 'You have exhausted your share of good things in your worldly life and took your fill of pleasure. So, today you shall be requited with the suffering of humiliation for having been arrogant on earth without any right, and for all your transgression'.

21 Remember that brother of 'Ad who warned his people who lived in the Valley of the Sand Dunes. Other warners have come and gone both before and after him. He said: 'Worship none but God. I fear lest suffering befall you on a terrible Day'. **22** They said to him: 'Have you come to turn us away from our gods? Bring, then, upon us that with which you threaten us, if what you say is true'. **23** He said: 'Only God knows when it will come. I only convey to you the message I am entrusted with; but I see that you are insolent people'. **24** When they saw a cloud approaching their valleys, they said: 'This cloud will bring us rain'. 'No, indeed. It is the very thing you wanted to hasten: a stormwind bearing painful suffering which will destroy everything by the command of its Lord.' **25** When the morning came, there was nothing to see of them except their ruined dwellings. Thus do we requite guilty people. **26** We had securely established them in a manner in which We have never established you; and We had endowed them with hearing, and sight, and hearts. Yet nothing did their hearing, sight and hearts avail them since they persisted in denying God's revelations. They were overwhelmed by the very thing which they had mocked. **27** We have also destroyed other communities that once lived around you, and We gave Our message in various ways so that they might return to the right way. **28** Why did those whom they had set up as deities beside God, hoping that they would bring them nearer to Him, give them no help? Indeed, they utterly failed them. Such were their lies and such their false inventions.

29 We sent to you a group of jinn to listen to the Qur'an. When they heard it, they said to one another, 'Listen in silence!' When the recitation ended, they returned to their people to warn them. **30** 'Our people', they said, 'we have been listening to revelation bestowed from on high after Moses, confirming what came before it. It guides to the truth and to a straight path. **31** Our people! Respond to God's call and have faith in Him. He will forgive you your sins and deliver you from grievous suffering. **32** He who does not respond to God's call cannot elude Him on earth, nor will they have any protector against Him. They are indeed in manifest error'. **33** Are they not aware that God, who has created the heavens and the earth and was not wearied by their creation, has the power to bring the dead back to life? Yes, indeed. He has power over all things. **34** On the Day when the unbelievers will be brought before the Fire, [they will be asked]: 'Is this not the truth?' They will answer: 'Yes, by our Lord'. He will say: 'Taste, then, this suffering, for you were unbelievers'. **35** Remain, then, patient in adversity, just as all messengers endowed with firm resolve bore themselves with patience. Do not seek to hasten their punishment. On the Day when they see what they were promised, it will seem to them as though they had dwelt [on earth] no more than an hour in a single day. This has been made clear. Will, then, any be destroyed except the evildoers?

Surah 47   Muhammad

This surah starts with a statement about the nature of the unbelievers and the believers. The two are shown to be at different ends, particularly as the surah implies that God is an enemy of the former and a friend to the latter. This is followed by clear instructions to the believers to fight the unbelievers who turn people away from God's path. It outlines the ruling concerning captives of war. It then describes the unbelievers' attitude to life and the status of the believers who will be in Heaven.

The surah refers to the hypocrites who pretend to be Muslims when they are not. These are more hostile to Islam and Muslims than unbelievers. They are indeed their worst enemies as they conspire with the open enemies of Islam while pretending to be Muslims. However, God is fully aware of their secret dealings and He will expose them.

The surah ends with a reminder to the believers to remain steadfast and show patience in adversity. They should never lose heart when they meet their enemies in battle. They should remain steadfast for God will bring them victory in due course. They are also encouraged to spend their money in what furthers the cause of Islam. God will reward them richly for such donations.

The verse endings of this surah are unlike any other in the Qur'an. Overall, they impact a particularly strong rhythm, one that is especially apparent in the original Arabic.

Muhammad

In the Name of God, the Lord of Grace, the Ever-Merciful

1 Those who disbelieve and debar others from God's path will have their deeds brought to nothing by Him, **2** whereas those who have faith and do righteous deeds, and believe in what has been revealed to Muhammad, for it is indeed the truth from their Lord – He will forgive them their bad deeds and bring them to a happy state. **3** This is because the unbelievers follow falsehood, whereas those who believe follow the truth from their Lord. Thus does God lay down for mankind their rules of conduct. **4** Now when you meet the unbelievers in battle, smite their necks. Then when you have thoroughly subdued them, bind them firmly. Thereafter, set them free either by an act of grace or against ransom, until war shall lay down its burden. Thus [shall it be]. Had God so willed, He could have punished them Himself, but it is His will that He tests you all by means of one another. And as for those who are slain in God's cause, never will He let their deeds go to waste. **5** He will grant them guidance, and bring them to a happy state, **6** and will admit them to the Garden He has already made known to them. **7** Believers! If you support [the cause of] God, He will support you and will make your steps firm; **8** but as for the unbelievers, ill fortune awaits them as He will bring their deeds to nothing. **9** This is because they hate what God has bestowed from on high, and thus He causes their deeds to go to waste. **10** Have they never travelled through the land and seen what was the end of those who lived before their time? God destroyed them utterly. A similar fate awaits the unbelievers. **11** This is because God protects the believers, while the unbelievers have no one to protect them. **12** God will indeed admit those who believe and do righteous deeds into gardens through which running waters flow, while those who disbelieve will enjoy their life [in this world] and eat as cattle eat; but the Fire shall be their abode. **13** How many cities of greater power than this your city which has driven you out have We destroyed, and they had none to help them. **14** Is he who takes his stand on a clear evidence from his Lord like one to whom the evil of his own deeds seems goodly, or like those who follow their own desires? **15** Such is the Paradise which the God-fearing are promised: in it are rivers of water for ever pure, rivers of milk the taste of which never alters, rivers of wine, a delight for those who drink, and rivers of honey pure and clarified. In it they shall have all kinds of fruit. And they receive there forgiveness by their Lord. Are they to be compared to those who are to abide in the Fire and be given a drink of scalding water that tears their bowels?

16 Some of them listen to you, but no sooner do they leave your presence than they [scornfully] say to those endowed with knowledge: 'What is it that he said just now?' Such are the ones whose hearts God has sealed, and who follow their desires. **17** As for those who accept divine guidance, God increases them in guidance and causes them to grow in the quality of being God-fearing. **18** Are they waiting for the Last Hour to come upon them of a sudden? Its portents have already come; but once it has arrived, what benefit will it then be to them if they take heed? **19** Know, then, that there is no deity other than God, and pray to Him to forgive you your sins, and to forgive all believing men and women. God knows all your comings and goings, as well as your abiding at rest. **20** The believers say: 'Would that a surah had been revealed'. Yet when a surah of clear import is revealed, and fighting is mentioned in it, you see those who are sick at heart staring at you like one who is about to faint for fear of death. Far better for them would be obedience and an appropriate word. **21** Moreover, when fighting is decided upon, it is better for them to be true to God. **22** If you turn away now, is it to be expected of you that you will spread corruption in the land and break your ties of kinship? **23** It is such as these whom God rejects, leaving them deaf and blind. **24** Will they not, then, try to understand the Qur'an? Or are there locks on their hearts? **25** Those who turn their backs after guidance has been given to them are seduced by Satan who fills them with false hopes. **26** That is because they say to those who abhor all that God has revealed, 'We will obey you in some matters', but God knows all their secret schemes. **27** How will they feel when the angels gather them in death, striking their faces and their backs. **28** That is because they follow what incurs God's anger, and hate what pleases Him. Therefore, He will surely make all their deeds come to nothing. **29** Do those who are sick at heart assume that God will never bring their malice to light? **30** Had We so willed, We could have pointed them out to you, and you would have recognised them by their marks; but you will most certainly recognise them by the tone of their speech. God knows all that you people do. **31** Most certainly We shall put you to the proof to see who of you strive hard and remain firm; and We shall test the truth of your assertions.

32 Those who disbelieve and debar others from the path of God, and take a hostile stand against the Prophet after they have seen the light of guidance, can in no way harm God; but He will surely make all their deeds come to nothing. **33** Believers, obey God and obey the Messenger, and do not let your deeds come to nothing. **34** Those who disbelieve and debar others from the path of God, and in the end die unbelievers shall not be granted forgiveness by God. **35** Therefore, do not lose heart or sue for peace. It is you who have the upper hand, and God is with you. He will never let your deeds go to waste. **36** The life of this world is but play and amusement, but if you believe and are God-fearing, He will grant you your reward. He does not ask you to give up all your possessions. **37** If He were to ask you all and press you hard, you would grow tight-fisted, and He would bring your malice to light. **38** You are called upon to give in God's cause, but some among you will turn out to be miserly. Whoever is miserly [in God's cause] is miserly towards himself. God is the source of all wealth, whereas you are the ones in need. If you turn away, He will substitute other people for you, and they will not be like you.

Surah 48   Victory

This surah was revealed towards the end of Year 6 AH, shortly after the conclusion of the al-Hudaybiyah Peace Treaty between the Muslims and the unbelievers in Makkah. The Prophet and his Companions went to Makkah aiming to perform 'umrah and offer worship at the Ka'bah, but the Quraysh tried to stop them entering Makkah, despite their age-old commitment not to bar anyone wishing to visit the Ka'bah for worship. After a long standoff and futile attempts by various emissaries to achieve an agreed accommodation, the Quraysh sent a delegation to negotiate a treaty. Acting on God's instructions, the Prophet accepted all the terms the Quraysh required and the treaty was signed, declaring the cessation of hostilities for ten years. The Muslims were restless when the treaty was signed because they felt that some of the terms the Prophet accepted were unfair to the Muslims.

The surah declares the agreed arrangements to be 'a glorious victory'. It speaks of the hypocrites in Madinah who did not join the Prophet and the Muslims on their mission, thinking that they would be crushed by the Quraysh. It denounces their attitude, which always looked for immediate gain.

The surah also praises the Prophet's Companions who pledged to him that they would fight to the end, should there be any need. This was at a certain point before the negotiations had started. At this juncture, the Muslims were under the impression that their envoy, 'Uthman, had been killed by the Quraysh.

The surah states the reason why God stopped the Muslims from fighting the Quraysh despite their assured victory in any battle that might have ensued. It transpires there were Muslims in Makkah who had had to conceal their belief. They were unknown to the Madinah Muslims and they might have got caught and been killed in any battle that ensued.

The surah concludes with an assertion that the dream the Prophet had about the Muslims visiting the Ka'bah for worship will come true. Its final verse describes the model Muslim society established by the Prophet and his Companions.

Victory

In the Name of God, the Lord of Grace, the Ever-Merciful

1 We have granted you a glorious victory, **2** so that God may forgive you all your faults, past and future, bestow upon you the full measure of His blessings and guide you on a straight way. **3** God will certainly grant you His mighty support. **4** It is He who sent down tranquillity into the hearts of the believers, so that they may grow more firm in their faith. To God belongs all the forces of the heavens and the earth; He is indeed all-knowing, wise. **5** He will admit the believers, both men and women, into gardens through which running waters flow, there to abide, and He will forgive them their bad deeds. That is, in God's sight, a great triumph. **6** God will also inflict suffering on the hypocrites and the idolaters, men and women, who harbour evil thoughts about God. Evil encompasses them from all sides, and they incur God's anger. He has rejected them and has prepared for them Hell, an evil destination. **7** To God belongs all the forces of the heavens and the earth; He is indeed almighty, wise. **8** We have sent you [Muhammad] as a witness, a bearer of good news and a warner **9** so that you [people] may believe in God and His Messenger, support Him, honour Him and extol His limitless glory morning and evening. **10** Those who pledge their allegiance to you are actually pledging their allegiance to God: God's hand is over their hands. He who breaks his pledge does so to his own detriment; but to the one who fulfils his pledge to Him, God will grant a rich reward. **11** The desert Arabs who stayed behind will say to you, 'Our property and our families kept us busy; do then ask God to forgive us'. Thus they say with their tongues what is not in their hearts. Say: 'Who, then, can avert from you anything that God might have willed, whether it be His will to harm you or to confer a benefit on you? No! God is fully aware of what you do'. **12** No! You thought that the Messenger and the believers would never return to their families and this thought seemed pleasing to your hearts. You entertained such evil thoughts because you have always been devoid of goodness. **13** As for those who will not believe in God and His Messenger, We have prepared a blazing fire for the unbelievers. **14** To God belongs the dominion over the heavens and the earth. He forgives whoever He will and punishes whoever He will. God is much-forgiving, ever-merciful. **15** When you set forth on a course that promises war gains, those who previously stayed behind will say: 'Let us come with you'. They thus seek to alter God's words. Say: 'You shall not come with us. God has already said so'. They will then say: 'You begrudge us [our share]'. How little they understand. **16** Say to the desert Arabs who stayed behind: 'You will be called upon to fight against a people of great prowess in war: you will have to fight them unless they surrender. If you obey, God will reward you well; but if you turn away as you have done before, He will inflict on you painful suffering'. **17** No blame attaches to the blind, nor does blame attach to the lame, nor does blame attach to the sick. Whoever obeys God and His Messenger shall be admitted by Him into gardens through which running waters flow; but the one who turns away will He severely punish.

18 God was indeed well pleased with the believers when they pledged their allegiance to you under the tree. He knew what was in their hearts and so He sent down tranquillity upon them, and rewarded them with a speedy victory, and with many war gains for them to take. **19** God is almighty, wise. **20** God has promised you [people] many war gains that you shall achieve. He has hastened this gain for you and He has held back the hands of hostile people from you, so that this may become a sign for the believers. He will guide you on a straight way. **21** There are still other gains to come, which are still beyond your power. God has full control over them. God has power over all things. **22** Were the unbelievers to fight you, they would have turned their back in flight. They shall find none to protect or support them. **23** Such was God's way which operated in the past; and never will you find any change in God's way. **24** It is He who, in the valley of Makkah, stayed their hands from you, and your hands from them, after He gave you the advantage over them. God sees all that you do. **25** They were the ones who disbelieved, and who debarred you from the Sacred Mosque and prevented your offering from reaching its place of sacrifice. Had it not been for the fact that there were among them believing men and women unknown to you and whom you might have unwittingly trampled underfoot, and on whose account you would have unwittingly incurred guilt... God will admit to His grace whomever He wills. Had they stood apart, We would have inflicted on the unbelievers among them truly painful suffering. **26** The unbelievers fanned fury in their hearts, the fury of ignorance. Meanwhile, God sent down tranquillity on His Messenger and on the believers, and made the word of piety binding on them. They were most worthy of it and deserved it well. God has full knowledge of all things. **27** God has shown the truth in His Messenger's true vision: most certainly you shall enter the Sacred Mosque, if God so wills, in full security, with your heads shaved or your hair cut short, without fear. God knew what you did not, and He granted you, besides this, a speedy victory. **28** It is He who sent His Messenger with guidance and the religion of truth so as to make it prevail over all religions. Sufficient is God as a witness. **29** Muhammad is God's Messenger; and those who are with him are firm and unyielding towards the unbelievers, full of mercy towards one another. You can see them bowing down, prostrating in prayer, seeking favour with God and His good pleasure. They bear on their faces the marks of their prostrations. This is how they are pictured in the Torah. And in the Gospels, they are like a seed that brings forth its shoot, strengthens it, grows thick and stands firm on its stem, delighting the sowers. Through them God will enrage the unbelievers. To those of them who believe and do righteous deeds God has promised forgiveness and a rich reward.

Surah 49   Private Apartments

This surah was revealed in Madinah and it describes the community Islam brings into existence: its values, practices, customs and traditions. It is a community where the finest values are observed. In this community people know their position in relation to God and His Messenger. They abide by the rules of conduct when they refer or speak to them.

In a Muslim community, no one is taken on suspicion. Any statement or accusation concerning any individual must be ascertained before action is taken. On the other hand, if friction, leading to hostilities, erupts between two groups of Muslims, reconciliation should be brought about between them so that the proper qualities of the Muslim community, making all Muslims parties to a bond of brotherhood, is restored.

It is a community where the rights of the individual are respected and doubts are removed. Fine manners are valued and observed.

The surah makes clear that God created mankind in different peoples and nations so that they may get to know one another, not fight over worldly gains.

The surah concludes with a statement of what genuine belief in the true faith means, and its requirements. As we recite the surah we realise that to be a believer is a great blessing we achieve through God's guidance.

Private Apartments

In the Name of God, the Lord of Grace, the Ever-Merciful

1 Believers! Do not behave presumptuously in the presence of God and His Messenger. Have fear of God: God hears all and knows all. 2 Believers! Do not raise your voices above the voice of the Prophet, nor speak loudly to him as you would speak loudly to one another, lest all your deeds should come to nothing without your perceiving it. 3 Those who lower their voices in the presence of God's Messenger are the ones whose hearts God has tested for piety. Forgiveness and a rich reward await them. 4 Those who call out to you from outside your private apartments are for the most part people who do not use their reason. 5 If they had the patience to wait until you went out to them, it would be for their own good. Still, God is much-forgiving,

ever-merciful. **6** Believers! If any transgressor comes to you with a piece of news, make sure of it first, lest you should wrong others unwittingly and then regret your action. **7** And know that God's Messenger is among you. Were he to comply with your inclinations in many a case, you would surely come to harm. But God has caused [your] faith to be dear to you, and has given it beauty in your hearts, and has made hateful to you unbelief, wrongdoing and disobedience of God. Such indeed are they who follow the right course. **8** [All this is indeed part of] God's bounty and favour. God is all-knowing, wise. **9** If two groups of believers fall to fighting, make peace between them. But then, if one of the two goes on acting wrongfully towards the other, fight against the one that acts wrongfully until it reverts to God's commandment; and if they revert, make peace between them with justice, and deal equitably with them. Indeed, God loves those who act equitably. **10** All believers are but brothers. Hence, make peace between your two brothers, and remain God-fearing, so that you may receive [God's] mercy. **11** Believers! No men shall deride other men: it may well be that those [whom they deride] are better than themselves. And no women [shall deride other] women: it may well be that those [whom they deride] are better than themselves. And neither shall you defame yourselves, nor insult one another by [opprobrious] epithets. Ill-seeming is a name connoting wickedness [to be used of one] after he has believed. Those who do not repent are indeed wrongdoers. **12** Believers! Avoid suspicion as much as possible, for, some such suspicion is a sin. And do not spy on one another, nor backbite one another. Would any of you like to eat the flesh of his dead brother? Surely you would loathe it. And remain God-fearing. God is certainly the One who accepts repentance, and He is ever-merciful. **13** Mankind! We have created you all out of a male and a female, and have made you into nations and tribes, so that you might come to know one another. Truly, the noblest of you in the sight of God is the one who is most genuinely God-fearing. God is all-knowing, all-aware. **14** The Bedouins say: 'We have attained to faith'. Say [to them]: 'Believers you are not. Rather say, "We have submitted ourselves", for true faith has not entered your hearts. But if you truly pay heed to God and His Messenger, He will let nothing of your deeds go to waste. God is indeed much-forgiving, ever–merciful'. **15** True believers are only those who have believed in God and His Messenger, and never then entertained any doubt, and who strive hard in God's cause with their possessions and their lives. Those are the ones who are true to their word. **16** Say: 'Do you, perchance, want to inform God of your faith, when God knows all that is in the heavens and earth? Indeed, God has full knowledge of everything'. **17** They think that they have bestowed a favour upon you by having embraced Islam. Say: 'Do not count your embrace of Islam a favour to me. It is indeed God who bestows a favour upon you by showing you the way to faith, if you are men of truth'. **18** God certainly knows the hidden reality of the heavens and the earth; and God sees all that you do.

Surah 50   Qaf

The Prophet used to recite this surah as his speech before Friday or Eid Prayer, and on some other occasions when there were large numbers of people in attendance. It has a very powerful rhythm and speaks about man. Man is always under God's watchful eye, from birth to his last breath in this life. It is full of images of life, death, resurrection, the gathering of all mankind, and accountability. It portrays all these against a background of flourishing life in the universe, how the blessed water falls from the sky to give life to the earth and, as a result, gardens flourish, trees grow and yield their fruits, and grains are produced in plenty. All this should serve as eye openers and reminders for everyone who turns to God for guidance.

Qaf

In the Name of God, the Lord of Grace, the Ever-Merciful

1 *Qaf.* By the glorious Qur'an. **2** But the unbelievers deem it strange that a warner from among themselves should have come to them and they say: 'This is indeed most strange! **3** When we have died and become dust…? Such a return [to life] is too far-fetched'. **4** We know very well what the earth takes away from them. We have an unfailing, comprehensive record. **5** Yet they deny the truth when it comes to them; and so they are in a state of confusion. **6** Do they not look at the sky above them: how We have built it and adorned it, leaving no flaws in it. **7** We spread out the earth and set upon it firm mountains, and caused every kind of delectable plants to grow on it, **8** so that it serves as a lesson and a reminder to everyone who wishes to turn to God. **9** We send down from the skies water rich in blessings, and We produce with it gardens and fields of grain, **10** and tall palm trees laden with clusters of dates, providing sustenance suitable for people. **11** Thus We bring dead land to life. So will [people] come forth from the dead. **12** Long before these unbelievers Noah's people also disbelieved, as did the people of al-Rass, Thamud, **13** 'Ad, Pharaoh, Lot's brethren, **14** the dwellers of the wooded dales and the people of Tubba': They all disbelieved God's messengers, and therefore My warnings came true. **15** Were We worn out by the first creation? Yet they are still in doubt about a renewed creation. **16** It is We who have created man, and We know what his soul whispers to him. **17** We are closer to him than his jugular vein; with two receptors set to record, one on his right and one on his left, **18** every word he utters [is noted down by] an ever-present watcher. **19** The stupor of death brings with it the full truth: 'This is what you tried to escape'. **20** The Trumpet will be blown: 'This is the Day [you were] warned of'. **21** Every soul will come attended by one who will drive it on and another to bear witness. **22** 'Of this you have been unmindful, but We have lifted your veil and sharp is your sight today.' **23** And his companion will say: 'Here is what I have recorded'. **24** 'Cast into Hell every hardened unbeliever, **25** everyone who hindered good, was a sinful aggressor, fomenter of doubt, who set up another deity alongside God. **26** Cast him into severe suffering.' **27** His companion will say: 'Our Lord! I did not make him transgress. He had already gone far astray'. **28** God will say: 'Do not argue in My presence, for I had forewarned you. **29** My word will not be altered; but never do I do the least wrong to My creatures'. **30** On that Day We will ask Hell, 'Are you full?' and it will reply, 'Are there no more?' **31** And Paradise will be brought close to the righteous and will no longer be distant: **32** 'This is what you have been promised; this is for everyone who used to turn to God and to keep Him in mind, **33** who used to stand in awe of the Lord of Grace although He is beyond the reach of human perception, and who comes before Him with a heart full of devotion. **34** Enter Paradise in peace; this is the Day when everlasting life begins'. **35** There they shall have all that they desire, and We have even more for them. **36** How many a generation, far greater in power, have We destroyed before these [unbelievers]? They wandered through the lands seeking a place of refuge. **37** In this there is a reminder for everyone who has an alert heart, or one who attentively listens and sees. **38** We have indeed created the heavens and the earth and all that is in between in six aeons. No weariness could ever touch Us. **39** Bear, then, with patience whatever they may say, and extol your Lord's limitless glory before the rising of the sun and before its setting; **40** and in the night, too, extol His glory, and at the end of every prayer. **41** And listen out for the Day when the caller will call from a nearby place, **42** the Day when they will in truth hear the Mighty Blast; that is the Day when they will come out [of their graves]. **43** It is We who grant life and deal death; and to Us all shall return. **44** On the Day when the earth will be rent asunder all around them, letting them rush out. That gathering will be easy for Us. **45** We are fully aware of what they say. You are not one to use coercion with them. Therefore, remind, with the Qur'an, those who fear My warning.

Surah 51   The Scattering Winds

This surah sets for itself the objective of strengthening man's bond with God so that man looks up to Him for everything he needs. When man is freed from worrying about his needs, he is able to turn to God with sincerity and determined purpose. The surah reassures man that God has assigned to people their provisions and they will receive them, because it is God who is the powerful provider.

The surah draws an image of God's righteous servants and the end they are expected to have in the life to come. This will be their recompense for the way they behave in this life.

The surah also draws attention to what befell past communities when they rejected the message of the truth after it was delivered to them through God's messengers. It further mentions the creation of the heavens and the earth as manifestations of God's power.

The Scattering Winds

In the Name of God, the Lord of Grace, the Ever-Merciful

1 By the winds that scatter far and wide; 2 by those [clouds] that are heavily laden; 3 by those that speed along with gentle ease; 4 by those that distribute by command; 5 that which you are promised is true indeed, 6 and, for certain, judgement is bound to come. 7 By the sky and its starry pathways 8 you people are at variance in what you say, 9 abandoned by whoever wishes to turn away. 10 Perish the ones given to blind guessing 11 who are steeped in error, heedless of the truth. 12 They ask: 'When will this Day of Judgement come?' 13 That will be a Day when they will be sorely tried by the Fire. 14 Taste this your trial! This is what you were keen to hasten. 15 The God-fearing will be amid gardens and springs. 16 They will happily receive what their Lord will grant them; for they were keen to do good. 17 They would sleep but little at night, 18 and would pray for forgiveness at the time of dawn, 19 and would give a rightful share of their possessions to the one who asks [for help] and the one who is deprived. 20 On earth there are signs for those with sure faith, 21 and in yourselves too: can you not see? 22 And in the sky is your sustenance and all that you are promised. 23 By the Lord of the heavens and the earth, all this is the very truth, just as true as you are endowed with speech. 24 Have you heard the story of Abraham's honoured guests? 25 They went in

to see him and bade him peace. He answered, 'Peace', [and added to himself] 'These are strangers'. **26** He turned quickly to his household and brought out a fat calf. **27** He placed it before them, saying: 'Will you not eat?' **28** He then became apprehensive of them, but they said: 'Do not be afraid'. They gave him the good news of [the birth of] a son who would be endowed with knowledge. **29** His wife then came in with a loud cry, struck her face, and said: 'A barren old woman!' **30** Replied they: 'Thus will it be. This is what your Lord said. He is the Wise, the All-Knowing'. **31** Said Abraham: 'What is your errand, messengers?' **32** They replied: 'We have been sent to a people lost in sin, **33** to bring down on them stones of clay, **34** marked as from your Lord for those who transgressed all bounds'. **35** We brought out such believers as were there; **36** but We did not find there any who had surrendered themselves to Us apart from a single house. **37** We left there a sign for those who fear the grievous suffering. **38** In Moses, too, there is a sign: We sent him to Pharaoh with clear authority; **39** but Pharaoh turned away in the pride of his power and said [of Moses]: 'He is but a sorcerer, or maybe a madman'. **40** We seized him and his hosts, and cast them all into the sea: he was the one to blame. **41** In the 'Ad there is another sign: We let loose against them a life-destroying wind **42** which reduced to dust everything it came upon. **43** And in Thamud, too, when they were told: 'You can enjoy your life for a while', **44** but they insolently defied their Lord's commandment. So, the thunderbolt struck them while they were helplessly looking on. **45** They were unable even to rise; nor could they defend themselves. **46** And the people of Noah before them: they too were people lost in evil. **47** We built the sky with power; and We gave it a vast expanse; **48** and We spread out the earth: how well have We prepared it! **49** All things We have created in pairs, so that you may take thought. **50** Flee, then, to God! I am sent by Him to give you clear warning; **51** and do not associate partners with Him: I am sent by Him to give you clear warning! **52** Thus whenever a messenger came to those that lived before them, they also said: 'He is but a sorcerer, or maybe a madman'. **53** Have they, perchance, handed down this legacy to one another? No! They are people who transgress all bounds. **54** Turn, then, away from them: you shall incur no blame; **55** and go on reminding all. Such a reminder will benefit those who believe. **56** I have not created the jinn and mankind to any end other than that they may worship Me. **57** No sustenance do I require of them, nor do I require that they should feed Me. **58** God is indeed the Provider of all sustenance, the Lord of Power, the Ever-Mighty. **59** The wrongdoers shall have their share [of evil] like their predecessors. Let them not ask Me to hasten it. **60** Woe betide the unbelievers on the Day they have been promised.

Surah 52   Mount Sinai

The surah begins with an oath by some sacred things in this world and others in the world beyond our perception. The oath gives an air of great seriousness. The surah then tells us what the oath is about: it is the inevitability of God's punishment for those who deserve it. Nothing can avert it from them. This is followed by an image of gloom as those to be punished are thrust into Hell.

The surah follows this with a scene describing the status of the believers who coupled their belief with good action throughout the present life. They will enjoy a life of eternal bliss. The surah then refutes all arguments that make people hesitate to believe. This is a very powerful scene that leaves no argument justifying any hesitation about acceptance of the divine faith.

At the end, the surah reassures the Prophet of God's care and directs him to extol God's praises at all times.

Mount Sinai

In the Name of God, the Lord of Grace, the Ever-Merciful

1 By Mount Sinai; 2 by a Scripture inscribed 3 on unrolled parchment; 4 by the much-visited House; 5 by the vault raised high; 6 by the swelling sea; 7 your Lord's punishment will indeed come to pass. 8 Nothing can stop it. 9 On the Day when the sky will shake and reel, 10 and the mountains will move away. 11 Woe on that Day to those who deny the truth, 12 who idly play with vain trifles. 13 On that Day they will be irresistibly thrust into the fire of Hell, 14 [and told:] 'This is the Fire you used to deny! 15 So is this sorcery, or do you not see? 16 Burn in it! It will be the same whether you bear it with or without patience. You are being requited for what you have done'. 17 The believers will be in gardens and in bliss, 18 rejoicing in all that their Lord will have granted them; for their Lord will have warded off from them the suffering of the blazing Fire. 19 'Eat and drink with healthy enjoyment as a reward for what you have done.' 20 They will recline on couches arranged in rows, and We shall pair them with companions having most beautiful eyes. 21 As for the believers whose offspring follow them in faith, We shall unite them with their offspring; and We shall not deny them anything of the reward for their deeds. Yet every individual will be held in pledge for his own deeds.

22 We provide them with fruit and meat as they desire. **23** They pass around a cup which will not lead to idle talk or to sin. **24** They will be waited upon by youths of their own, [as pure] as pearls hidden in their shells. **25** They will turn to one another, asking each other. **26** They will say: 'When we were still living with our kinsfolk, we were full of fear, **27** and so God has been gracious to us, and warded off from us suffering through the scorching wind. **28** We used to pray to Him: He is the Beneficent, the Ever-Merciful'. **29** So, [Prophet,] remind people. By the grace of your Lord, you are neither a soothsayer nor a madman. **30** Or do they say, 'He is but a poet; let us await whatever misfortune time will bring him'. **31** Say: 'Wait if you will. I too am waiting'. **32** Is it their reason that prompts them to take this attitude; or are they simply arrogant people? **33** Or do they say, 'He has fabricated it himself?' They certainly do not believe. **34** Let them, then, produce a discourse like it, if what they say is true. **35** Were they created out of nothing? Were they the creators? **36** Did they create the heavens and the earth? No. They have no faith. **37** Do they possess your Lord's treasures? Or are they in ultimate control? **38** Or have they a ladder to climb, in order to eavesdrop [on heaven's secrets]? Let their eavesdropper produce a clear proof. **39** Is He to have only daughters and you sons? **40** Do you [Prophet] demand a payment from them that would leave them burdened with debt? **41** Do they have knowledge of the hidden reality so that they can write it down? **42** Or do they want to entrap you? It is the unbelievers who are truly entrapped. **43** Have they, then, any deity other than God? Exalted is God far above anything they associate with Him. **44** Even if they see a part of the sky falling down, they would say, 'It is but a mass of clouds!' **45** Leave them, then, until they face the Day when they will be thunderstruck; **46** the Day when none of their scheming will be of any avail to them, when they will receive no support. **47** Closer at hand more suffering awaits the wrongdoers, but most of them are not aware of it. **48** So, await in patience your Lord's judgement; for you are under Our watchful eyes. Extol your Lord's limitless glory and praise when you rise, **49** and extol His glory at night, and at the time when the stars retreat.

Surah 53   The Star

The surah starts by explaining the nature of revelation, stressing the fact that the Prophet saw the Angel Gabriel who brought him God's revelations. It mentions two situations when the Prophet met Gabriel to drive the point home that there was real contact between them, and that the Prophet witnessed some of God's greatest signs.

The surah then speaks about the alleged deities the unbelievers claim to be God's partners. It refers to their legends about the angels stating that their claims are without foundation. The Prophet is then instructed to pay no heed to those who turn away from God and remain preoccupied with the present material world. They deserve to be nothing but totally ignored.

The surah's last passage mentions the essence of divine faith which has always remained the same: from the earliest to the last. It is a message based on God's Oneness, resurrection for a second life when justice will be administered to all.

The Star

In the Name of God, the Lord of Grace, the Ever-Merciful

1 By the star when it sets. 2 This fellow-man of yours has not gone astray, nor is he deluded. 3 He does not speak out of his own fancy. 4 That [which he delivers to you] is nothing less than a revelation sent down to him, 5 something that a very mighty one has taught him, 6 [an angel] of surpassing power, who stood 7 on the highest horizon, 8 and then drew near, and came close, 9 until he was two bow-lengths away, or even closer, 10 and revealed to God's servant what he revealed. 11 [Muhammad's] heart did not belie what he saw. 12 Will you, then, contend with him over what he sees? 13 Indeed, he saw him a second time 14 by the lote tree of the farthest limit, 15 near to the Garden of Abode, 16 when the lote tree was shrouded with whatever shrouded it. 17 The eye did not waver, nor was it too bold; 18 he certainly saw some of the greatest signs of his Lord. 19 Have you considered al-Lat and al-ʿUzza, 20 and Manat, the third other? 21 Are you to have the male and He the female? 22 That would then be an unfair division. 23 These are nothing but names which you have invented – you and your forefathers – for which God has given no authority. They [who disbelieve] follow nothing but surmise and

the whims of their own souls, even though right guidance from their Lord has now come to them. **24** Is man to have all that he may wish for, **25** when both the life to come and this present life belong to God alone? **26** Numerous are the angels in the heavens, yet their intercession will avail nothing until God has given leave to whomever He wills and with whom He is pleased. **27** Those who do not believe in the life to come give the angels female names. **28** Yet of this they have no knowledge. They follow nothing but surmise, but surmise can never take the place of truth. **29** So, ignore those who turn away from Our message and care only for the life of this world. Such is the sum of their knowledge. **30** Your Lord knows best who strays from His path, and He knows best who follows right guidance. **31** Indeed, to God belongs all that is in the heavens and the earth. He will requite those who do evil in accordance with what they did, and will reward those who do good with what is best. **32** As for those who avoid grave sins and shameful deeds, apart from casual indulgence, your Lord is abounding in forgiveness. He is fully aware of you when He brings you into being out of the earth, and when you are still hidden in your mothers' wombs. Do not, then, assert your own goodness. He knows best those who are truly God-fearing. **33** Consider the one who turns away: **34** he gives little at first then hardens and stops. **35** Does he have knowledge of what lies beyond the reach of human perception so that he can clearly see? **36** Has he never been told of what is written in the revelations given to Moses, **37** and to Abraham who was true to his trust: **38** that no soul shall bear the burden of another; **39** that man will only have what he strives for; **40** that his labour will be seen **41** and he will be given the fullest reward for it; **42** that with your Lord is the ultimate end; **43** that it is He who causes [people] to laugh and weep; **44** and it is He who deals death and gives life; **45** that it is He who creates the two sexes, male and female, **46** from a seed as it is lodged in place; **47** that it is He who brings about a second life; **48** that it is He who gives riches and possessions; **49** that He is the Lord of Sirius; **50** that it is He who destroyed the ancient 'Ad; **51** and Thamud, leaving no trace of them; **52** as well as Noah's people before them, for these were truly most unjust and most overweening; **53** that it is He who brought down the ruined cities **54** enveloping them with whatever came over them. **55** Which, then, of your Lord's blessings do you still doubt? **56** This is a warning like those warnings given in former times. **57** The imminent Hour draws ever nearer. **58** None but God can remove it. **59** Do you find this discourse strange? **60** Do you laugh instead of weeping, **61** and pay no heed? **62** Prostrate yourselves before God and worship Him alone.

Surah 54   The Moon

Whilst this surah sounds like an onslaught on those who deny the divine message, it nonetheless gives perfect reassurance to the believers. At the beginning, the surah portrays a scene of the Day of Judgement and ends with another. In between, it mentions the punishment meted out to some past communities when they persisted in denying the truth, despite being given what should have convinced them of God's Oneness. Yet after each one of these episodes, the surah reminds people that the Qur'an is given to them with its clear message. They only need to reflect on it and the truth will appear in front of their eyes.

The Moon

In the Name of God, the Lord of Grace, the Ever-Merciful

1 The Last Hour draws near, and the moon is split asunder. **2** Yet when the unbelievers see a sign, they turn away and say, 'Yet another act of continuous sorcery'. **3** They deny the truth and follow their own desires. Yet everything is ultimately settled. **4** There has come to them tidings that should have restrained [their arrogance], **5** far-reaching wisdom, but warnings have been of no avail. **6** So turn you away from them. On the Day the Summoner will summon them to something unknown, **7** with eyes downcast, they will come out of their graves like swarming locusts rushing towards the Summoner. **8** The unbelievers will say: 'Hard indeed is this day'. **9** Before them, Noah's people rejected the truth. They rejected Our servant, saying: 'He is mad!' and he was harshly rebuffed. **10** Therefore, he called out to his Lord: 'I am overcome. Grant me help!' **11** So We opened the gates of heaven with water pouring down in torrents, and caused the earth to burst forth with springs. **12** Thus the waters met for a preordained purpose. **13** We carried him in a vessel made of planks and nails **14** which floated under Our eyes: a reward for him who had been rejected. **15** We have left this as a sign: will anyone take heed? **16** How grievous was My punishment and how true were My warnings. **17** We have made the Qur'an easy to bear in mind: will anyone take heed? **18** The people of 'Ad also rejected the truth. How grievous was My punishment and how true were My warnings. **19** We sent against them a howling, cold wind on a day of unceasing misfortune: **20** it swept people away as though they were uprooted palm trunks. **21** How grievous was My punishment and how true were My warnings. **22** We have made the Qur'an easy to bear in mind: will anyone take heed? **23** The people of Thamud also rejected [My] warnings. **24** They said: 'Are we to follow one single mortal from among ourselves? In that case, we would surely be in error, lost in utter folly. **25** Could a message have been sent to him alone out of all of us? No, he is indeed an insolent liar'. **26** 'Tomorrow they will know who is the insolent liar. **27** We shall send them a she-camel as a test. So watch them and be patient. **28** Tell them that the water is to be equitably shared between them: each should drink in turn.' **29** They called their friend, who took something and slew her. **30** How grievous was My punishment and how true were My warnings. **31** We sent against them a single blast, and they became like the dry twigs of the sheepfold builder. **32** We have made the Qur'an easy to bear in mind: will anyone take heed? **33** Lot's people also rejected [My] warnings. **34** We sent a stone-bearing wind against them, and only Lot's family did We save at the break of dawn, **35** as an act of grace from Us: thus do We reward the thankful. **36** He warned them of Our punishment, but they were in doubt about his warnings. **37** They even asked him to hand his guests over to them, so We sealed their eyes. 'Taste, then, My punishment and [the fulfilment of] My warnings.' **38** At daybreak abiding suffering befell them. **39** 'Taste, then, My punishment and [the fulfilment of] My warnings.' **40** We have made the Qur'an easy to bear in mind: will anyone take heed? **41** Pharaoh's people also received warnings. **42** They rejected all Our signs; so We took them to task as only the Almighty, who is able to carry out His will, can take to task. **43** Are your unbelievers better than those others? Or have you been given an immunity in the Sacred Books? **44** Or do they say, 'We are a great host and we will be victorious?' **45** Their hosts will be routed, and they will turn tail and flee. **46** But the Last Hour is their appointed time, and the Last Hour is most calamitous and most bitter. **47** The evildoers are indeed in error and in raging flames of Fire. **48** On the Day when they are dragged into the Fire, their faces down, [they will be told], 'Taste now the touch of Hellfire'. **49** We have created everything in due measure. **50** Our command is but once, like the twinkling of an eye. **51** We destroyed people like you in the past. Will anyone take heed? **52** Everything they do is noted in their records. **53** Every single thing, small or great, is recorded. **54** The God-fearing will be in gardens and running waters, **55** in a seat of truth, in the presence of an all-powerful Sovereign.

Surah 55   The Lord of Grace

This surah reminds people of the grace God bestows, in abundance, on mankind and indeed on all that exists. It tells us about the blessings He grants to all people at all times and in all circumstances. His grace and blessings are to be found everywhere, all around us, and in every natural phenomenon. Everything in the universe and everything in the world around us testify to God's grace: the sun, the moon, the succession of day and night, the balance that allows life to continue, the trees that grow from small seeds, the plentiful grains, and all that lives. His grace is granted even to those who deny Him and disbelieve in Him. The surah concludes with blessing the name of God, who is full of majesty and who always bestows His grace.

Note in this surah the repetition of the verse that wonders at those who deny God when they see His blessings and favours all around them. Such repetition gives the surah its unique character and adds to the feeling that God's mercy always surrounds us.

The Lord of Grace

In the Name of God, the Lord of Grace, the Ever-Merciful

1 [It is] the Lord of Grace **2** who has taught the Qur'an. **3** He created man **4** and taught him to articulate [thought and speech]. **5** The sun and the moon function in due measure. **6** The stars and the trees prostrate themselves [before Him]. **7** He has raised the skies high, and has set the balance, **8** so that you may not exceed the balance. **9** Weigh, therefore, with justice and do not fall short in the balance. **10** He has laid the earth for His creatures, **11** with all its fruits, its palm trees with sheathed clusters, **12** its husked grain and its sweet-smelling plants. **13** Which, then, of your Lord's blessings do you both deny? **14** He created man from dried clay, like pottery, **15** and created the jinn from raging flames of fire. **16** Which, then, of your Lord's blessings do you both deny? **17** He is the Lord of the two risings and the Lord of the two settings. **18** Which, then, of your Lord's blessings do you both deny? **19** He has given freedom to the two great bodies of water, so that they may meet; **20** yet between them is a barrier which they do not cross. **21** Which, then, of your Lord's blessings do you both deny? **22** Pearls and corals come from both. **23** Which, then, of your Lord's blessings do you both deny? **24** His are the lofty ships that sail like floating mountains through the seas. **25** Which, then, of your Lord's blessings do you both deny? **26** All that lives on it perishes; **27** but forever will remain the Face of your Lord, full of majesty, granting grace. **28** Which, then, of your Lord's blessings do you both deny? **29** Everyone in heaven and earth entreats Him. Everyday He manifests Himself in some wonderful way. **30** Which, then, of your Lord's blessings do you both deny? **31** We shall attend to you two huge communities [of jinn and mankind]. **32** Which, then, of your Lord's blessings do you both deny? **33** Jinn and mankind, if you can pass beyond the regions of heaven and earth, then do so. You cannot pass beyond them without authority. **34** Which, then, of your Lord's blessings do you both deny? **35** A flash of fire will be sent against you, and molten brass, and you will be left without support. **36** Which, then, of your Lord's blessings do you both deny? **37** When the sky is rent asunder and becomes rose-red like [burning] oil. **38** Which, then, of your Lord's blessings do you both deny? **39** On that Day neither mankind nor jinn will be asked about their sins. **40** Which, then, of your Lord's blessings do you both deny? **41** The guilty ones will be known by their mark and shall be seized by their forelocks and their feet. **42** Which, then, of your Lord's blessings do you both deny? **43** This is the Hell which the guilty deny. **44** They will go round between its flames and scalding water. **45** Which, then, of your Lord's blessings do you both deny? **46** For those who stand in fear of their Lord's presence there shall be two gardens. **47** Which, then, of your Lord's blessings do you both deny? **48** With shading branches. **49** Which, then, of your Lord's blessings do you both deny? **50** With a pair of flowing springs. **51** Which, then, of your Lord's blessings do you both deny? **52** With every kind of fruit in pairs. **53** Which, then, of your Lord's blessings do you both deny? **54** They will recline on carpets lined with rich brocade; and the fruit of both these gardens will be within easy reach. **55** Which, then, of your Lord's blessings do you both deny? **56** In both [gardens] will be mates of modest gaze, whom neither man nor jinn will have touched before. **57** Which, then, of your Lord's blessings do you both deny? **58** [These mates look] like rubies and corals. **59** Which, then, of your Lord's blessings do you both deny? **60** Shall the reward of good be anything but good? **61** Which, then, of your Lord's blessings do you both deny? **62** Besides these two there are two other gardens. **63** Which, then, of your Lord's blessings do you both deny? **64** Both of the deepest green. **65** Which, then, of your Lord's blessings do you both deny? **66** With two gushing springs. **67** Which, then, of your Lord's blessings do you both deny? **68** With fruits, date-palms and pomegranate trees. **69** Which, then, of your Lord's blessings do you both deny? **70** There will be in [these gardens] all things most excellent and beautiful. **71** Which, then, of your Lord's blessings do you both deny? **72** [They will have] dark-eyed and modest companions, sheltered in pavilions. **73** Which, then, of your Lord's blessings do you both deny? **74** Neither man nor jinn will have touched them before. **75** Which, then, of your Lord's blessings do you both deny? **76** They will recline on green cushions and fine carpets. **77** Which, then, of your Lord's blessings do you both deny? **78** Blessed is the name of your Lord, full of majesty, granting grace.

Surah 56   The Inevitable Event

This surah begins by describing the resurrection as something that will inevitably take place and will determine the position of every individual, raising some people high and sending others down. It then tells of three groups of people and where they end. These are the ones 'to the fore', the 'people of the right' and the 'people of the left'.

The surah then speaks about faith itself and re-confirms the inevitability of resurrection, seeking to make it clear and acceptable to people by drawing their attention to what they see in the world all the time. It reminds them first of how they are born, then draws their attention to what they plant and harvest, and to the rain and water without which no life can take place. It also mentions the fire in which they burn their old trees. At this point, the surah reminds them of the life to come and the Fire that is in waiting for unbelievers.

The surah states a great oath that the Qur'an is God's Book which He revealed to Prophet Muhammad (peace be upon him). Finally, the surah paints an image of a person who is about to die and his relatives stand around him, helpless, unable to prevent the inevitable end.

The Inevitable Event

In the Name of God, the Lord of Grace, the Ever-Merciful

1 When that which is certain to happen will have come to pass **2** no one will then deny its having come to pass, **3** abasing [some], exalting [others]. **4** When the earth is violently shaken **5** and the mountains crumble away **6** and scatter abroad into fine dust, **7** you shall be divided into three classes: **8** There are the people of the right side; what people are they? **9** And the people of the left side; what people are they? **10** And there are those to the fore, who shall be foremost. **11** These will be brought nearest to God, **12** in gardens of bliss. **13** A good many of them are from earlier times **14** and a few from later generations. **15** On gold-encrusted couches **16** they will recline facing each other. **17** Immortal youths shall wait upon them **18** with goblets, ewers, and cups filled with water from unsullied springs. **19** From it they will not be dispersed, nor will they be in short supply. **20** And with fruit of any kind they may choose, **21** and with the meat of any fowl they may desire. **22** There will be for them companions with large beautiful eyes **23** like hidden pearls: **24** a reward for what they used to do. **25** There they will hear no idle talk, no sinful speech, **26** only the saying, 'Peace! Peace'. **27** As for those on the right, what people are they? **28** They will dwell amid thornless lote trees **29** and flower-clad acacias **30** with extended shade, **31** constantly flowing water, **32** abundant fruits, **33** unfailing, never out of reach, **34** [reclining on] couches raised high. **35** We will have brought forth [their mates] in perfect creation, **36** making them virgins, **37** full of love, of matching age, **38** for those on the right. **39** A good many of them are from earlier times **40** and a good many from later generations. **41** And those on the left, what people are they? **42** They will dwell amid scorching wind and scalding water **43** in the shadows of black smoke, **44** neither cool nor refreshing. **45** In times gone by, they overindulged in luxury **46** and persisted in heinous sin, **47** saying, 'What! When we have died and become mere dust and bones, are we to be raised up again? **48** And our forefathers, too?' **49** Say: 'All people of the earliest and latest generations **50** will indeed be gathered together at an appointed time on a specific Day. **51** Then, you who have gone astray and denied the truth **52** will eat from the fruit of the Zaqqum tree, **53** filling your bellies with it, **54** and will drink scalding water; **55** yet you will drink it like insatiably thirsty camels drink'. **56** Such will be their dwelling place on the Day of Judgement. **57** It is We who have created you: will you not believe? **58** Consider the semen you discharge: **59** do you create it, or are We the Creator? **60** We have decreed that death shall be among you. Nothing can prevent Us **61** from replacing you by others like yourselves or bringing you into being anew in a way unknown to you. **62** You have learned how you have come into being in the first instance. Why, then, do you not reflect? **63** Consider the seeds you sow in the ground: **64** is it you who makes them grow, or We? **65** Were it Our will, We could turn it into chaff and leave you to wail, **66** 'We are burdened with debt; **67** we have been deprived'. **68** Consider the water you drink: **69** is it you who brings it down from the clouds, or We? **70** Were it Our will, We could make it salty and bitter. Why, then, do you not give thanks? **71** Consider the fire you kindle: **72** is it you who grows its tree, or We? **73** We made it a reminder [for man], and a comfort for desert travellers. **74** Extol, then, the glory of the name of your Lord, the Supreme. **75** I do swear by the positions of the stars **76** – a mighty oath, if you but knew it! – **77** that this is indeed a most honourable Qur'an, **78** in a well-guarded record **79** that only the purified can touch: **80** a revelation from the Lord of all the worlds. **81** Would you look on this discourse with disdain? **82** Do you make it your livelihood that you persistently deny it? **83** When the soul [of a dying person] comes up to the throat **84** while you are helplessly looking on **85** We are closer to him than you, although you do not see Us. **86** Why, if you think you are not to be judged, **87** can you not restore that [ebbing life], if what you claim is true? **88** If that dying person is one of those who are drawn close to God, **89** he will have repose, fulfilment and a garden of bliss. **90** If he is one of those on the right, **91** a greeting of peace will welcome you by the ones on the right. **92** But if he happens to be one of those who denied the truth and went astray, **93** he will be welcomed with scalding water, **94** and the heat of a blazing fire. **95** This is surely the indubitable truth. **96** Extol, then, the glory of the name of your Lord, the Supreme.

Surah 57   Iron

This surah, which was revealed in Madinah, calls on the Muslim community to live up to their faith. They need to make sure of what their acceptance of the Islamic faith means to them and what changes it brings into their lives. They have to fulfil the duties Islam assigns to them, particularly in their way of life and what they allocate of their money to spend for God's cause.

The surah makes a distinction between those who accepted Islam at the beginning, when it was facing powerful enemies seeking to crush and put an end to it, and those who accepted it after it had become the leading power in Arabia. Yet both groups are assured that they will be in Heaven.

The surah seeks to give Muslims a clear concept of life, telling them that the life of this world is no more than some play, a passing delight, a beautiful show, some boasting and a quest for more riches and children. It is incomparable to life in Heaven, which is a great expanse, full of pure bliss.

The surah concludes with a reference to earlier messengers who advocated the true faith based on God's Oneness.

Iron

In the Name of God, the Lord of Grace, the Ever-Merciful

1 Everything in the heavens and earth extols God's limitless glory. He is the Almighty, the Wise. 2 His is the dominion over the heavens and the earth. He grants life and causes death; and He has power over all things. 3 He is the First and the Last, the Outer and the Inner. He has full knowledge of all things. 4 It is He who created the heavens and the earth in six aeons and established Himself on the throne. He knows all that goes into the earth and all that comes out of it; all that descends from the skies and all that ascends to them. He is with you wherever you may be; and God sees all that you do. 5 His is the dominion over the heavens and the earth. Everything goes back to God. 6 He causes the night to pass into the day, and the day to pass into the night; and He has full knowledge of what is in people's hearts. 7 Believe in God and His Messenger, and give [in charity] of that of which He has made you trustees. Those of you who believe and give [in charity] will have a great reward. 8 Why should you not believe in God when

the Messenger calls upon you to believe in your Lord, and He has already taken a pledge from you, if you are true believers? **9** It is He who bestows from on high clear revelations to His servant, to lead you out of the deep darkness into light. God is indeed most compassionate to you, ever-merciful. **10** Why should you not spend freely in the cause of God, seeing that God's alone is the heritage of the heavens and the earth? Those of you who gave and fought [for God's cause] before the victory are not like others: they are higher in rank than those who gave and fought afterwards, although God has promised the ultimate good to all of them. God is well aware of all that you do. **11** Who will offer God a generous loan, which He will repay in multiples and will generously reward him? **12** On the Day when you see all believers, men and women, with their light spreading rapidly before them and to their right, [they will be told], 'The good news for you today is that you shall for ever abide in gardens through which running waters flow. This is indeed the supreme triumph'. **13** On that Day the hypocrites, men and women, will say to the believers, 'Wait for us! Let us have a ray of your light!' They will be told: 'Turn back and seek some other light'. A wall with a gate will be raised between them: within it will be mercy, and outside will be suffering. **14** [Those without] will call out to those [within], 'Were we not with you?' They will reply, 'Yes, but you allowed yourselves to be led into temptation, you wavered, you doubted, and you were deceived by false hopes until God's command came to pass, and indeed you let your deceptive thoughts about God delude you'. **15** Today no ransom will be accepted from you or from the unbelievers. The Fire shall be your home: it is where you belong; and how evil a destination! **16** Is it not time for believers that their hearts should feel humble at the remembrance of God and the truth that has been bestowed from on high, and not to be like those who were granted revelations before them and whose hearts have hardened with the passing of time? Many of these are now transgressors! **17** Know that God restores the earth to life after it has been lifeless. We have made Our revelations clear to you so that you may use your reason. **18** Those who give generously in charity, men and women, and thus offer a goodly loan to God, [their loan] will be repaid in multiples, and they will have a generous reward. **19** Those who believe in God and His messengers are the ones who uphold the truth, and who will bear witness to it before their Lord. They will have their reward and their light. Those who disbelieve and deny Our revelations are the dwellers of the blazing Fire. **20** Know that the life of this world is but a play, a passing delight, a beautiful show, a cause of boasting among you and a quest for more riches and children. It is like the rain that causes the plants to grow, and thus gives delight to the sowers. Then it withers, and you can see it turn yellow, and in the end it crumbles into dust. In the life to come there is terrible suffering, as well as God's forgiveness and His goodly acceptance. The life of this world is no more than an illusory pleasure. **21** Vie with one another in seeking to attain your Lord's forgiveness, and a Paradise as vast as the heavens and the earth, prepared for those who believe in God and His messengers. Such is God's bounty which He grants to whomever He pleases. God's bounty is great indeed. **22** No incident can take place, either on earth or in yourselves, unless it be recorded in a decree before We bring it into being – that is easy for God – **23** so you need not grieve for what you miss or be overjoyed at what you gain. God does not love those who are arrogant and boastful; **24** [nor] those who are miserly and bid others to be miserly. Those who turn away should remember that God alone is self-sufficient, worthy of praise. **25** We sent Our messengers with clear evidence of the truth, and through them We bestowed the Book from on high, setting the balance, so that people could uphold justice. We have also sent down iron, with its mighty strength and diverse uses for mankind. Thus God may mark out those who would stand up for Him and His messengers, even though He is beyond the reach of human perception. God is indeed powerful, almighty. **26** And We sent Noah and Abraham, and gave prophethood and revelation to their descendants. Among them there are some who were rightly guided, but many who were transgressors. **27** We sent other messengers to follow in their footsteps. After these We sent Jesus, son of Mary. We gave him the Gospel and put compassion and mercy in the hearts of those who truly follow him. As for monastic asceticism, We did not enjoin it upon them. They invented it themselves out of a desire for God's goodly acceptance. Even so, they did not observe it as it should properly be observed. So We gave those of them who truly believed their due reward, but many of them were transgressors. **28** Believers, remain God-fearing and believe in His Messenger. He will then give you a double measure of His mercy, and will provide you with a light to walk in, and will forgive you. God is much-forgiving, ever-merciful. **29** The people of earlier revelations should know that they have no power whatever over any of God's bounty. All bounty is in God's hand: He grants it to whomever He wills. God's bounty is limitless.

Surah 58   The Pleading

This surah begins with attending to a special situation that occurred during the time when the Muslim community in Madinah was still developing. It was the case of a particular woman whose husband had resorted to the abominable practice of olden days when a pagan Arab might tell his wife that she was no longer a wife to him, but rather that she was to him like the back of his mother. Thus all marital relations between the two were put to an end. The woman in this case complained to the Prophet, who could offer her no solution, until this surah was revealed to tell him, the Muslims and mankind whereby God, in His majesty, had listened to the woman's plea. The surah makes clear that this practice was forbidden in Islam and outlines the measures to be taken in such cases.

The surah then speaks about those who were secretly conspiring against the Muslim community and warns them against God's severe punishment. It concludes with a clear distinction between the believers and those who take a hostile attitude towards God, His Messenger and the Islamic message. No friendly relationship can exist between the two.

The Pleading

In the Name of God, the Lord of Grace, the Ever-Merciful

1 God has heard the words of the woman who pleads with you concerning her husband, and complained to God. God has heard what you both had to say. God hears all and sees all. 2 Even if any of you say to your wives, 'You are to me like my mother's back', they are not your mothers; their only mothers are those who gave them birth. What they say is iniquitous and false. Yet God pardons and forgives. 3 Those who separate themselves from their wives by saying, 'You are as unlawful to me as my mother,' and then go back on what they have said, must atone by freeing a slave before the couple may resume their full marital relations. This is an admonition to you, and God is fully aware of all that you do. 4 However, he who does not have the means shall fast instead for two consecutive months before the couple may resume their full marital relations; and he who is unable to do so shall feed sixty needy people; this, so that you may prove your faith in God and His Messenger. Such are

the bounds set by God. Painful suffering awaits those who will not believe. **5** Those who contend against God and His Messenger shall be brought low as those who lived before them were brought low. We have bestowed from on high clear revelations. Shameful suffering awaits the unbelievers on the Day when God will raise them all from the dead and tell them exactly all that they did in life. **6** God will have taken it all into account, even though they may have forgotten it. God is witness to all things. **7** Are you not aware that God knows all that is in the heavens and all that is on earth? Never can a secret conversation take place between three people where He is not the fourth; nor between five where He is not the sixth, nor between less or more than that without Him being with them, wherever they may be. On the Day of Resurrection He will tell them the truth of what they used to do. God has full knowledge of everything. **8** Have you not seen how those that have been forbidden to hold secret conversations still revert to what they have been forbidden? They conspire with one another with a view to sinful doings, aggressive conduct and disobedience of God's Messenger? When these people come to you they greet you with words God does not use to greet you. They say to themselves, 'Why does God not punish us for what we say?' Hell will be punishment enough for them. They will burn there. How vile a journey's end! **9** Believers, when you converse in secret, do not do so with a view to sinful doings, aggressive conduct and disobedience of God's Messenger, but rather hold counsel to promote righteousness and God-consciousness. Always remain God-fearing; to Him you will be gathered. **10** [All other kinds of] secret conversation is the work of Satan, designed to cause grief to the believers. Yet he cannot harm them in the least, unless it be by God's leave. In God, then, let the believers place their trust. **11** Believers, when you are told to make room for one another in your gatherings, then do so, and God will make room for you. If you are told to rise up, then do so. God will elevate, by many degrees, those of you who believe and those who have been given knowledge. God is fully aware of all that you do. **12** Believers, when you wish to speak to God's Messenger in private, offer something in charity before you speak to him. That is better for you and more conducive to purity. If you do not have the means, God is much-forgiving, ever-merciful. **13** Do you hesitate to offer charity before you speak with the Prophet? Since you did not offer charity, and God has turned to you in His mercy, attend regularly to prayer and pay your zakat [obligatory charity] and obey God and His Messenger. God is well aware of your actions. **14** Have you not seen those who would be friends with people who have incurred God's anger? They belong neither to you nor to them. They knowingly swear to falsehood. **15** God has prepared for them grievous suffering. Evil indeed is what they do. **16** They use their oaths as a cover [for their falseness], and they turn people away from the path of God. Hence, shameful suffering awaits them. **17** Neither their wealth nor their children will be of the least avail to them against God. They are destined for the Fire, where they will abide. **18** On the Day when God will raise them all from the dead, they will swear before Him as they swear now before you, thinking that they have something to stand upon. It is they who are indeed liars. **19** Satan has gained mastery over them and thus caused them to remain oblivious of the remembrance of God. They are the party of Satan. It is the partisans of Satan who will truly be the losers. **20** Those who contend against God and His Messenger will be among the most abject. **21** God has thus ordained: 'I shall most certainly prevail, I and My messengers'. God is indeed powerful, almighty. **22** You shall not find people who truly believe in God and the Last Day on friendly terms with those who contend against God and His Messenger, even though they may be their fathers, sons, brothers, or kindred. These are the people in whose hearts God has inscribed faith, and whom He has strengthened with a spirit of His own. He will admit them into gardens through which running waters flow, where they will abide. Well pleased is God with them, and they with Him. They are the party of God. It is the partisans of God that will be truly successful.

Surah 59   The Gathering

The surah begins and ends with glorifying God, the Almighty, the Wise. Its subject matter is the evacuation of the Jewish al-Nadir tribe from Madinah. When the Prophet settled in Madinah, he established a pluralist society bound by a document, which was the first written constitution in human history. This treaty, or constitution, committed the Jews to defend Madinah alongside the Muslims against any external attack.

The al-Nadir, however, violated this treaty, plotting instead to assassinate the Prophet when he visited their quarters. The hypocrites in Madinah, who pretended to be Muslims but were trying hard to undermine Islam and the Muslim community, encouraged the Jews of al-Nadir to challenge the Prophet's order requiring them to evacuate Madinah, promising them full support. However, no such support was forthcoming. The Muslims besieged the Jews in their forts for twenty-six days, at the end of which the Jews agreed to evacuate Madinah. They were then allowed to leave in safety.

The surah comments on these events and relates them to the principles of faith. At the end, the surah highlights a number of God's attributes and mentions the Qur'an and its powerful effect.

The Gathering

In the Name of God, the Lord of Grace, the Ever-Merciful

1 Everything in the heavens and everything on earth extols God's limitless glory. He is the Almighty, the Wise. 2 It is He who drove the unbelievers among the people of earlier revelations out of their homes at the first gathering. You never thought they would go; while they thought that their fortifications would protect them against God. God came upon them from where they had not expected, casting terror into their hearts. Thus, they destroyed their homes by their own hands, as well as the hands of the believers. Learn from their example, you who are endowed with insight. 3 Had it not been for God having decreed exile for them, He would surely have inflicted [greater] suffering on them in this world. In the life to come they will still endure suffering through the Fire 4 because they have defied God and His Messenger. Whoever defies God – well, God is severe in retribution. 5 Whatever of their palm trees you [believers] may have cut down or left standing

on their roots, it was done by God's leave, so that He might disgrace the transgressors. **6** Whatever gains were taken from them God has turned over to His Messenger; you did not have to spur horse or riding-camel for its sake. God gives His messengers mastery over whomever He wills. God has power over all things. **7** Whatever gains God turns over to His Messenger from the people of the townships belong to God, the Messenger, kinsfolk, orphans, the needy and the traveller in need. Thus, they would not just circulate among those of you who are rich. Whatever the Messenger gives you, take it; and whatever he forbids you, abstain from it. Remain God-fearing; for God is severe in retribution. **8** [Such gains are for] the poor migrants who have been driven out of their homes and possessions, seeking God's favour and His goodly acceptance, and who help God and His Messenger. These are the ones who are true. **9** And to those who were already firmly established in the Home and in faith, those who love the ones that seek refuge with them and harbour no desire in their hearts for whatever the others may have been given. They give them preference over themselves, even though they are in want. Those who are saved from their own greed are truly successful. **10** Those who come after them pray: 'Our Lord! Forgive us and forgive our brethren who preceded us in faith. Leave no malice in our hearts towards those who believe. Lord, You are compassionate, ever-merciful'. **11** Are you not aware of those hypocrites who say to their brethren who disbelieve among the people of earlier revelations, 'If you are driven out, we shall most certainly go with you, and shall never pay heed to anyone against you; and if you are attacked, we shall most certainly come to your aid?' God bears witness that they are indeed liars. **12** If they are driven out, they will not go with them; and if they are attacked, they will not help them. Even if they come to their aid, they will most certainly turn their backs in flight; and in the end they will have no help. **13** You, [believers] arouse in their hearts a fear more intense than their fear of God, because they are devoid of understanding. **14** They will never fight you even united except from within fortified strongholds or from behind walls. Strong is their internal hostility. You may think that they are united when in fact their hearts are at odds with one another, because they are people who will not use their reason. **15** Like those who, a short while before them, had to taste the evil that came from their own doings. Painful suffering is in store for them. **16** Like Satan, who says to man, 'Reject the faith!' Yet when man disbelieves, Satan says, 'I here and now disown you. I fear God, the Lord of all the worlds'. **17** Both will end up in the Fire, where they will abide. Such is the reward of the wrongdoers. **18** Believers, have fear of God. Let every soul consider carefully what it sends ahead for tomorrow. Remain God-fearing, for God is fully aware of all that you do. **19** Be not like those who forget God, so God causes them to forget their own souls. They are the transgressors. **20** Not equal are the ones destined for the Fire and the ones destined for Paradise. Those who are destined for Paradise are indeed the ones who will triumph. **21** Had We brought down this Qur'an upon a mountain, you would have seen it humble itself and break asunder for fear of God. We put such images before people so that they may reflect. **22** He is God: there is no deity other than Him. It is He who knows all that is beyond the reach of anyone's perception, as well as all that which can be witnessed. He is the Lord of Grace, the Ever-Merciful. **23** He is God: there is no deity other than Him, the Sovereign, the Holy, the Source of Peace, the Giver of Faith, the Guardian over all, the Almighty, the Compeller, to whom all greatness belongs. Exalted is God in His limitless glory above anything they associate as partner with Him. **24** He is God: the Creator, the Maker who gives shape and form to all. His are the most gracious names. Everything in the heavens and earth extols His limitless glory. He alone is the Almighty, the Wise.

Surah 60   Women Tested

This surah seeks to define relations between believers and unbelievers. It tells the believers that they must not take God's enemies, who are also their enemies, for their friends. There is a great gulf between the two and it cannot be bridged by simple gestures of friendship. The surah exposes the real intentions of the unbelievers who drove the Prophet and the Muslims out of their homes for no reason other than their beliefs.

The surah cites the example of Prophet Abraham and his followers who dissociated themselves from their people who persisted in worshipping deities other than God and who refused to believe in God's Oneness. Yet the surah does not preclude the possibility that a change of heart may occur or that hostility between the two groups may be replaced by friendship. For this to happen, the unbelievers must cease their hostility.

The surah makes clear that friendship can be maintained with unbelievers who are at peace with the Muslim community. It is only when unbelievers are hostile and go to war against Muslims that such friendship cannot be permitted.

The last four verses of the surah provide legislation concerning believing women who migrated to join the Muslim community and others who pledged allegiance to the Prophet.

Women Tested

In the Name of God, the Lord of Grace, the Ever-Merciful

1 Believers! Do not take My enemies, who are your enemies as well, for your friends, showing them affection when they have rejected the truth you have received, and have driven the Messenger and yourselves out only because you believe in God, your Lord. If you have left your homes to strive in My cause and to seek My pleasure, then do not secretly lean towards them with affection. I well know all that you conceal and all that you reveal. Whoever of you does this has already strayed from the right path. **2** If they get the better of you, they will remain your enemies and stretch out their hands and tongues to you with evil. They dearly wish to see you unbelievers. **3** Neither your kinsfolk nor your own children will be of any benefit to you. On the Day of Resurrection He will decide between you. God sees all that you do. You have a good example in Abraham and those who followed him, when they said to their people: 'We disown you and what you worship instead of God. We reject you. The enmity and hate that have arisen between us and you will last until you believe in God alone'. The only exception was Abraham, when he said to his father, 'I shall pray for forgiveness for you, although it is not in my power to be of any avail to you against God'. **4** 'Our Lord! In You we have placed our trust, and to You do we turn, and with You is the final destination. **5** Our Lord! Do not make of us a test for the unbelievers. Forgive us, Lord. You are the Almighty, the Wise.' **6** In them, indeed, you have a good example for everyone who looks forward with hope to God and the Last Day. Anyone who turns away should remember that God is truly self-sufficient, worthy of all praise. **7** It may well be that God will bring about affection between you and those who are now your enemies. God is all powerful; God is much-forgiving, ever-merciful. **8** God does not forbid you to deal kindly and with full equity with those who do not fight you on account of your faith, nor drive you out of your homes. God loves those who behave equitably. **9** God only forbids you to turn in friendship towards those who fight against you because of your faith, and drive you from your homes, and help others to drive you out. Those of you who turn towards them in friendship are indeed wrongdoers. **10** Believers! When believing women come to you as migrants, test them. God knows best their faith. If you ascertain that they are believers, do not send them back to the unbelievers. They are no longer lawful [as wives] for the unbelievers, and these are no longer lawful to them. None the less, hand back to the unbelievers the dowries they have paid them. It is no offence for you to marry them after giving them their dowries. Do not hold on to marriage ties with unbelieving women. Ask for repayment of the dowries you have paid, just as they have the right to ask for repayment of their dowries. Such is God's judgement. He judges between you in equity. God is all-knowing, wise. **11** Should any of your wives go over to the unbelievers and you subsequently acquire gains from them, then pay those whose wives have gone away the equivalent of whatever dowry they had paid. Fear God, in whom you believe. **12** Prophet! When believing women come and pledge to you that they will not associate any partner with God, nor steal, nor commit adultery, nor kill their children, nor lie about who fathered their children, nor disobey you in anything reasonable, then accept their pledge of allegiance and pray to God to forgive them. God is much-forgiving, ever-merciful. **13** Believers! Do not take as friends any people with whom God is angry. They despair of the life to come just as the unbelievers despair of those buried in their graves.

Surah 61   The Ranks

This surah seeks to establish in every Muslim's consciousness the conviction that their faith is the true faith. It is a faith that provides a way of life for mankind ensuring their happiness in this life and in the life to come. Earlier versions of this system were given but the communities to whom it was entrusted, particularly the Children of Israel, deviated from it, introducing into it matters that did not belong to it. The surah mentions the Prophets Moses and Jesus and their missions. Islam is the final divine message which God wants to prevail over all religions.

The other purpose of the surah is to make clear to Muslims that they must be true to their faith and be ready to sacrifice for its cause their lives and their possessions. Only when they are so ready, are they true to their declared intention of being true believers.

The surah invites them to take part in the most profitable business any person can undertake. They can ensure such great profits when they firmly believe in God and His Messenger and strive for God's cause. This will give them the greatest prize of all: Heaven with all its bliss and a victory soon in the coming. They only need to be supporters of God's cause and to give of their maximum.

The Ranks

In the Name of God, the Lord of Grace, the Ever-Merciful

1 All that is in the heavens and in the earth extols God's limitless glory: for He alone is the Almighty, the Wise. **2** Believers! Why do you say what you do not do? **3** Most loathsome is it in the sight of God that you say what you do not do! **4** God loves indeed those who fight in His cause in solid ranks, as though they were a firm and compact building. **5** Now when Moses spoke to his people, he said: 'My people! Why do you cause me grief, when you know that I am a messenger God has sent to you?' So, when they swerved from the right way, God let their hearts swerve from the truth. God does not bestow His guidance upon evildoers. **6** And also Jesus, the son of Mary, said: 'Children of Israel! I am God's messenger to you, [sent] to confirm the Torah revealed before me, and to give news of a messenger that will come after me, whose name shall be Ahmad'. But when he came to them with all evidence of the truth, they said: 'This is plain sorcery'. **7** Who could be more wicked than one who invents a falsehood about God, when he is only being called upon to submit to Him? God does not bestow His guidance upon the wrongdoers. **8** They aim to extinguish God's light with their mouths, but God will spread His light in all its fullness, however hateful this may be to the unbelievers. **9** It is He who has sent His Messenger with guidance and the religion of truth, so that He may cause it to prevail over all other religions, however hateful this may be to the idolaters. **10** Believers! Shall I point out to you a bargain that will save you from painful suffering? **11** You are to believe in God and His Messenger, and to strive hard in God's cause with your possessions and your lives. This is for your own good, if you but knew it. **12** He will forgive you your sins, and [in the life to come] will admit you into gardens through which running waters flow, and into goodly mansions in the Gardens of Eden. That is the supreme triumph! **13** And [He will grant you] yet another thing that you dearly love: help from God and a victory soon to come. Give you the good news to the believers. **14** Believers! Be helpers [in the cause] of God; just as Jesus, the son of Mary, said to the disciples: 'Who will be my helpers in God's cause?' The disciples said: 'We shall be [your] helpers in God's cause'. And so some of the Children of Israel came to believe whereas others denied the truth. But We have given those who believed strength over their enemy and they were the ones to prevail.

Surah 62   The Congregation

This surah makes clear that the Muslims are the community entrusted with the divine message. It must be grateful to God for bestowing this honour on it. It makes clear that a community that is given the trust of the divine message but is unfaithful to its task does not deserve to be in a position of favour with God.

The Jews in Madinah used to claim that they were the ones who were God's true friends. The Prophet is instructed in this surah to challenge them to a mutual supplication for death. Needless to say, friends of God will be in a better situation when they die, as God will admit them to Heaven. The surah makes clear that they could never wish for death because they know that their deeds put them in a position of disfavour with God.

The final part of the surah deals with a special situation that took place in Madinah, when a trade caravan arrived as the Prophet was addressing the Muslim community. The believers left him to attend to the caravan. Here, the surah tells them that such actions must be stamped out.

The Congregation

In the Name of God, the Lord of Grace, the Ever-Merciful

1 All that is in the heavens and all that is on earth extol the limitless glory of God, the Sovereign, the Holy, the Almighty, the Wise. **2** It is He who has sent to the unlettered people a Messenger from among themselves to declare to them His revelations, to purify them and to instruct them in the Book and in wisdom, yet before that they were indeed in manifest error, to them and to others yet to join them. **3** He is indeed the Almighty, the Wise. **4** Such is God's favour: He grants it to whom He will. God is One who bestows great favours. **5** Those who were entrusted with the burden of implementing the Torah but then failed to do so are like an ass that carries a load of books. Wretched is the example of those who deny God's revelations. God does not guide the wrongdoers. **6** Say: 'You who follow the Jewish faith! If you truly claim that out of all people you are God's friends, then wish for death, if your claim is true'. **7** But they will never wish for it because of what their hands have wrought in this life. God is well aware of the wrongdoers. **8** Say: 'The death from which you are trying to run away will certainly overtake you. You will then be returned to the One who knows what is beyond human perception and that which can be witnessed. He will then tell you all that you have done'. **9** Believers! When the call to prayer is made on Friday, go straightaway to the prayer and leave off your trading. This is best for you, if you but knew it. **10** When the prayer is finished, disperse in the land and seek God's bounty. Remember God often so that you may be successful. **11** Yet when people see some trade or entertainment, they head off towards it, leaving you standing there. Say: 'That which is with God is far better than any entertainment or trade. God is the best of providers'.

Surah 63   The Hypocrites

Although this surah is given this title and is devoted to the discussion of what the hypocrites in Madinah used to do to undermine the Muslim community and Islam, practically every surah revealed in Madinah has something to say about the hypocrites. They certainly did much to create division and discord. They allied themselves with the Jews who were also scheming against the Muslim community. The surah refers to some of their statements and their efforts to set one group of Muslims against another.

The surah concludes with a directive to Muslims to allow nothing to interfere with their certainty of faith.

The Hypocrites

In the Name of God, the Lord of Grace, the Ever-Merciful

1 When the hypocrites come to you, they say, 'We bear witness that you are indeed God's Messenger'. God knows that you are truly His Messenger and He bears witness that the hypocrites are indeed liars. **2** They use their oaths as a cover [for their falseness], and they turn people away from the path of God. Evil indeed is what they do. **3** That is because they professed to believe, then they renounced faith. So, a seal has been set on their hearts and therefore they are devoid of understanding. **4** When you see them, their outward appearance may please you; and when they speak, you listen to what they say. They are like propped-up timbers. They think that every shout is directed against them. They are the real enemy; so beware of them. May God destroy them! How perverse they are! **5** When they are told, 'Come, so that God's Messenger may ask forgiveness for you', they turn their heads away. You see them drawing back in arrogance. **6** As for them, it is all the same whether you pray for their forgiveness or you do not pray. God will not forgive them; for God does not bestow His guidance on such transgressing folk. **7** They are the ones who say [to one another]: 'Do not give anything to those who are with God's Messenger, so that they may abandon him'. To God belong the treasures of the heavens and the earth, but the hypocrites cannot understand. **8** They say, 'When we return to Madinah, the more honourable will surely drive out those who are contemptible'. All honour belongs to God, His Messenger and the believers, but the hypocrites do not know. **9** Believers! Do not let your riches or your children make you oblivious of the remembrance of God. Those who do so will surely be the losers. **10** Give, then, out of what We have provided for you, before death comes to any of you, and then he says, 'My Lord, if You would grant me a delay for a short while, I would give in charity and be one of the righteous'. **11** God does not grant a delay to any soul when its term has come. God is fully aware of all that you do.

Surah 64   Mutual Loss and Gain

Although this surah was revealed in Madinah, it addresses the issues that the Makkan surahs focus on, such as clarity of faith and the essential concepts of the divine message. Its style is very similar to Makkan surahs. Only the last five verses adopt the Madinan style, urging the Muslims to spend for God's cause.

This similarity is not accidental, because the issues of God's Oneness, resurrection and accountability are basic issues and Muslims and non-Muslims need to be frequently reminded of them. They are, indeed, present throughout the part of the Qur'an revealed in Madinah, alongside legislative issues.

Mutual Loss and Gain

In the Name of God, the Lord of Grace, the Ever-Merciful

1 All that is in the heavens and all that is on earth extol the limitless glory of God; all sovereignty belongs to Him and all praise is due to Him. He has power over all things. **2** It is He who has created you, yet some of you are unbelievers and some do believe. God sees all that you do. **3** He has created the heavens and the earth in accordance with the truth, and fashioned you, giving you a comely appearance. To Him all shall return. **4** He knows what is in the heavens and the earth; and He knows what you conceal and what you reveal. God has full knowledge of the secrets of all hearts. **5** Have you not heard of those who disbelieved in earlier times? They tasted the evil consequences of their own doings. Painful suffering still awaits them. **6** That is because their messengers came to them with clear signs, but they said, 'Shall mere humans be our guides?' So, they denied the truth and turned away. God is free of all need. God is self-sufficient, worthy of all praise. **7** The unbelievers allege that they will not be raised from the dead. Say, 'Yes indeed! By my Lord, you will certainly be raised from the dead, and then you will certainly be told of all that you have done. This is easy for God'. **8** Believe then in God and His Messenger, and in the light which We have bestowed from on high. God is fully aware of what you do. **9** [Think of] the time when He will gather you all together for the Day of the Gathering, the Day of mutual loss and gain. For anyone who shall have believed in God and done what is right, He will efface his bad deeds and will admit him into gardens through which running waters flow, where they will abide for ever. That is the supreme triumph. **10** But those who disbelieve and deny Our revelations are destined for the Fire where they will abide. How miserable an end! **11** No calamity can ever befall anyone except by God's leave. He will guide the heart of anyone who believes in Him. God has full knowledge of all things. **12** So obey God, and obey the Messenger. If you turn away, know that Our Messenger's only duty is to deliver his message in full clarity. **13** God: there is no deity other than Him. In God, then, let the believers place their trust. **14** Believers, some of your spouses and children are enemies to you; so beware of them. Yet if you overlook their faults, pardon and forgive, God is much-forgiving, ever-merciful. **15** Your wealth and children are only a trial and a temptation, whereas with God there is a great reward. **16** Therefore, remain God-fearing as best as you can, listen, obey and be charitable. That will be best for you. Those that are preserved from their own meanness are the ones who will achieve success. **17** If you make a goodly loan to God, He will repay you in multiples, and will forgive you your sins. God is ever-thankful, forbearing. **18** He knows all that is beyond the reach of human perception and all that is witnessed; the Almighty, the Wise.

Surah 65   Divorce

Surah 2 gives many rulings about divorce and what it entails. This surah complements these rules, giving details about different situations. It starts by making it clear that divorce must be done in accordance with Islamic legislation, with regard to its timing and the arrangements that follow. It states that the proper time for divorce is when the woman to be divorced can begin her waiting period, which means that she must not be in her monthly period, nor in a period of cleanliness from menses during which she has had sexual intercourse with her husband. The surah outlines certain rulings about the waiting period before it legislates for what may affect any children, particularly suckling children after the divorce.

It includes a warning against following in the footsteps of communities that abandoned God's laws and stood in opposition to His messengers. They rued the consequences of their attitude. The surah concludes with affirming that the universe is of God's creation and that His power is supreme and His knowledge is total and perfect.

Divorce

In the Name of God, the Lord of Grace, the Ever-Merciful

1 Prophet! When you[18] divorce women, divorce them with a view to their prescribed waiting period, and reckon the period accurately. Be conscious of God, your Lord. Do not drive them out of their homes, nor shall they themselves leave, unless they commit a flagrant indecency. These are the bounds set by God. Whoever transgresses God's bounds wrongs his own soul. You never know; after that, God may bring about some new situation. **2** When they have completed their appointed term, either retain them in fair manner or part with them in fair manner. Call to witness two people of known probity from among yourselves; and do yourselves bear witness before God. Thus is admonished everyone who believes in God and the Last Day. For everyone who fears God, He will grant a way out, and will provide for him whence he does not expect. **3** God will be sufficient for everyone who puts his trust in Him. God always attains His purpose. God has

---

18   The plural form is used here indicating that the address is to the Muslim community as a whole.

set a measure for everything. **4** As for those of your women who are beyond the age of monthly courses, as well as for those who do not have any courses, their waiting period, if you have any doubt, is three months. As for those who are with child, their waiting term shall end when they deliver their burden. For everyone who is God-fearing, God makes things easy. **5** Such is God's commandment which He has revealed to you. God will pardon the bad deeds of everyone who is God-fearing and will grant him a richly reward. **6** Let them dwell wherever you dwell, according to your means, and do not harass them so as to make their lives a misery. If they are with child, maintain them until they have delivered their burden. If, after that, they suckle your infants, pay them for it. Take counsel with one another in a fair manner. If some of you make things difficult, let another woman suckle the child. **7** Let the one who has ample means spend in accordance with his means; and let the one whose provisions are restricted spend according to what God has given him. God does not burden anyone with more than He has given them. After hardship, God will grant ease. **8** Many a community that insolently defied the commandment of their Lord and His messengers We have brought to account in a severe manner and inflicted on them terrible suffering. **9** Thus they tasted the outcome of their own conduct. Yet the end of their conduct was ruin. **10** God has prepared a severe punishment for them. So, you who are endowed with insight, you who have faith, fear God. God has bestowed on you a reminder from on high. **11** [He has sent you] a Messenger who recites to you God's revelations that make things clear, so that He may lead those who believe and do righteous deeds out of the depths of darkness into the light. God will admit everyone who believes in Him and does righteous deeds into gardens through which running waters flow, where they will abide for ever. God will have granted them a most excellent provision. **12** It is God who has created seven heavens and a similar number of the earth. His command descends through them all, so that you may learn that God has power over all things, and that God encompasses all things with His knowledge.

Surah 66   Prohibition

This surah refers to an incident in the private life of the Prophet and his wives. God chose that His last Messenger should be, like all previous messengers, a human being with all the desires, motives, incentives and dislikes a man may have. However, his life was made an open book, and we know of it more than any of us would like to be publicly known of our private affairs. The incident relates to jealousy between the Prophet's wives, which is a normal feeling between wives of the same husband.

The surah then includes important directives to the Muslim community, encouraging people to turn to God in repentance. In its final part, it gives examples of wives who were married to prophets but they themselves were unbelievers. By contrast, Pharaoh who claimed to be a god had a wife who was a true believer. Virgin Mary is also cited as a good model for believers.

Prohibition

In the Name of God, the Lord of Grace, the Ever-Merciful

1 Prophet, why do you prohibit yourself something that God has made lawful to you in your desire to please your wives? God is much-forgiving, ever-merciful. 2 God has already ordained for you [believers] a way to release you from such oaths. God is your Lord Supreme. He alone is the All-Knowing, the Wise. 3 The Prophet told something in confidence to one of his wives. When she divulged it, and God made this known to him, he spoke of a part of it and passed over a part. When he thus let her know of that, she asked, 'Who has told you this?' He said: 'The All-Knowing, the All-Aware told me'. 4 Would that you two turn to God in repentance, for your hearts have swerved! But if you support each other against him, know that God is his protector, and that, therefore, Gabriel, all righteous believers and the angels will stand behind him. 5 Were he to divorce you, his Lord may well give him in your stead spouses better than you: women who surrender themselves to God, true believers, devout, penitent, who worship in humility and reflect thoughtfully, be they women previously married or virgins. 6 Believers! Guard yourselves and your families against a fire fuelled by people and stones, over which are appointed angels, stern and mighty, who never disobey

God in whatever He commands them and always do what they are bidden to do. **7** Unbelievers! Make no excuses today. You will only be requited for what you used to do. **8** Believers! Turn to God in sincere repentance. It may well be that your Lord will efface your bad deeds and admit you into gardens through which running waters flow, on a Day when God will not disgrace the Prophet or those who believed with him. Their light will spread out before them, and on their right. They will say: 'Our Lord! Perfect our light for us and forgive us. You certainly have power over all things'. **9** Prophet, strive hard against the unbelievers and the hypocrites, and press hard on them. Their ultimate abode is Hell, and how vile a journey's end. **10** God has given examples of unbelievers: Noah's wife and Lot's wife. They were married to two of Our righteous servants but betrayed them. Their husbands could be of no avail to them against God. They were told: 'Enter both of you the Fire with all those who will enter it'. **11** God has also given examples of believers: Pharaoh's wife, who said: 'My Lord! Build me a mansion in heaven near You, and save me from Pharaoh and his doings, and save me from the wrongdoing folk'. **12** And Mary, the daughter of 'Imran, who guarded her chastity; and We breathed of Our spirit into her. She accepted the truth of her Lord's words and His revealed Books. She was truly devout.

Surah 67   Dominion

The first verse gives us the key to this surah: God has dominion of the universe and all that it contains, and He has power over all things. Thus, everything is in His hand and subject to His will. Moreover, there is much that is beyond what we can see, hear or perceive, and all this exists, functions and operates by God's will. Whatever takes place in our world and the world beyond reflects God's dominion and power. Life and death occur all the time, but how do they come about? We see countless stars and planets, and there are far more of them beyond the ken of all our means of reaching out. How do they function and what is the purpose of their existence? How come the earth can support human life while no other planet in the solar system can? We see the birds flying and we think little of their ability, yet a little reflection will tell us that there is much more to it than the apparent movement of wings and a tail.

The surah invites people to reflect on God's power and dominion and to realise that the message given to them is the truth and they will do well to make it the constitution for their lives on earth.

Dominion

In the Name of God, the Lord of Grace, the Ever-Merciful

1 Blessed be He in whose hand all dominion rests; **2** who has power over all things; who has created death as well as life, so that He may put you to a test to show who of you is best in conduct. He alone is the Almighty, Much-Forgiving. **3** He created seven heavens in layers. No fault will you see in what the Lord of Grace creates. Turn up your eyes: can you see any flaw? **4** Then look again, and again: your vision will come back to you dull and weary. **5** We have adorned the lowest heaven with lamps and made them missiles to pelt the devils with. We have prepared for them suffering through the blazing Fire. **6** Suffering in Hell awaits those who deny their Lord: an evil destination. **7** When they are thrown in it, they will hear it drawing in its breath as it boils up, almost bursting with fury. **8** Every time a group is thrown in it, its keepers will ask them, 'Did no one come to warn you?' **9** 'Yes', they will reply, 'a warner did indeed come to us, but we did not believe him. We said, "God has revealed nothing. You are in total error"'. **10** They will further say, 'Had we but listened, or reasoned, we would not now be among the inhabitants of the blazing Fire'. **11** Thus they shall confess their sins. Far [from God's mercy] are the inhabitants of the blazing Fire. **12** Those who stand in awe of their Lord although He is beyond the reach of human perception will have forgiveness and a rich reward. **13** Whether you keep your words secret or state them openly, He has full knowledge of what is in all hearts. **14** How could it be that He who has created should not know all? He is above all comprehension, yet is all-aware. **15** He it is who has made the earth easy to live upon. Go about, then, in all its highlands and eat of His provisions. To Him you will be resurrected. **16** Do you feel secure that He who is in heaven will not cause the earth to swallow you up when it quakes? **17** Or do you feel secure that He who is in heaven will not let loose against you a sandy whirlwind. You will come to know the truth of My warning. **18** Those who lived before them also disbelieved. How terrible was My rejection of them? **19** Do they not see the birds above them, spreading their wings and drawing them in? None but the Lord of Grace holds them up. He sees everything. **20** What army is there to come to your aid, except for the Lord of Grace? The unbelievers are truly lost in self-delusion. **21** Who will provide for you, if He were to withhold His provision? Yet they persist in their arrogance and in rebellion. **22** Is he who goes grovelling on his face better guided than the one who walks upright on a straight path? **23** Say: 'It is He who has brought you into being, and given you hearing, sight and hearts. Yet seldom are you thankful. **24** And He it is who caused you to multiply on earth; and to Him you shall be gathered'. **25** They say: 'When is this promise to be fulfilled, if what you say be true?' **26** Say: 'God alone has knowledge of this. I am only a plain warner'. **27** When they see it close at hand, the unbelievers' faces will be stricken with grief, and it will be said: 'This is what you were calling for'. **28** Say: 'Just think: whether God destroys me and those who follow me, or bestows mercy upon us, who will protect the unbelievers from painful suffering?' **29** Say: 'He is the Lord of Grace: in Him we believe, and in Him we place our trust. You will come to know who is in manifest error'. **30** Say: 'Just think: if all your water were to sink underground, who would give you clear flowing water?'

Surah 68   The Pen

This surah appears to have been revealed in the early Makkan period, perhaps in the fourth or fifth year after the start of the Islamic message. It comforts and reassures the Prophet and the fledgling Muslim community. They were facing stiff opposition from the Quraysh and other unbelievers, and such opposition included slander, false accusations and defamation. The surah asserts the Prophet's noble character, denouncing his detractors.

The surah tells a story about some rich people who wished to give nothing of the produce of their garden to the poor, but God destroyed their harvest. They then realised their mistake and turned to God in repentance. The unbelievers could do well to follow their example and heed the numerous signs that encourage them to believe in God and mend their ways. The surah concludes with an emphatic statement that the Qur'an is given as a reminder to all mankind.

The Pen

In the Name of God, the Lord of Grace, the Ever-Merciful

1 *Nun*. By the pen, by all they write, 2 you are not, by your Lord's grace, a madman. 3 And indeed you shall have a never-ending reward. 4 Most certainly, yours is a sublime character. 5 You shall before long see, as they will see, 6 which of you is afflicted with madness. 7 Your Lord knows best who has strayed from His path, as He knows the ones who are rightly guided. 8 So pay no heed to those who deny the truth. 9 They would love that you compromise with them, so that they will also compromise. 10 Furthermore, pay no heed to any contemptible swearer, 11 slanderer, going about with defaming tales, 12 hinderer of good, aggressor, sinful, 13 cruel and, on top of all that, given to evil. 14 Just because he has wealth and children, 15 when Our revelations are recited to him, he says, 'Fables of the ancients!' 16 We shall brand him on the snout. 17 We try them as We tried the owners of a certain garden, who vowed that they would harvest its fruits on the morrow, 18 and made no allowance. 19 A visitation from your Lord came upon that garden while they were asleep, 20 so that by morning it was stripped bare and looked desolate. 21 At daybreak they called out to one another: 22 'Go early to your tilth if you wish to gather all its fruits'. 23 So they went off, whispering to one another, 24 'Make sure

that no needy person enters the garden today'. **25** Early they went, strongly bent on their purpose. **26** When they saw it, they exclaimed: 'Surely we have lost our way! **27** No! We are utterly ruined'. **28** The wisest among them said, 'Did I not tell you, "Will you not extol God's limitless glory?"' **29** They said, 'Limitless in His glory is our Lord! Truly, we were doing wrong'. **30** Then they turned upon each other with mutual reproach. **31** They said: 'Woe betide us! We have done great wrong. **32** It may be that our Lord will grant us something better instead. To our Lord we truly turn in hope'. **33** Such is the suffering [in this life], but greater indeed is the suffering in the life to come, if they but knew it. **34** For the God-fearing there shall be gardens of bliss with their Lord. **35** Should We treat those who submit themselves to Us as We treat the guilty? **36** What is the matter with you? On what basis do you judge? **37** Or have you a divine book which you study, **38** and in which you find that you shall have all that you choose? **39** Or have you received solemn oaths, binding on Us till the Day of Resurrection, that you will get whatever you yourselves decide? **40** Ask them which of them will vouch for this. **41** Or have they partners? Let them produce their partners, if what they say is true. **42** On the Day when matters become so dire, they will be asked to prostrate themselves, but they will not be able to do so. **43** Their eyes will be downcast, with ignominy overwhelming them. They were invited to prostrate themselves when they were safe. **44** Therefore, leave to Me those who deny this revelation. We shall bring them low, step by step, in ways beyond their knowledge. **45** I will allow them more time: My scheme is truly firm. **46** Do you [Prophet] demand a payment from them [and so they fear] that they would be burdened with debt? **47** Do they have knowledge of the hidden reality so that they can write it down? **48** So, await in patience your Lord's judgement; and do not be like the man in the whale who called out in distress. **49** Had not grace from his Lord reached him, he would have been left upon that barren shore in a state of disgrace. **50** His Lord, however, chose him and made him one of the righteous. **51** The unbelievers well-nigh trip you up with their eyes when they hear this reminder. They say, 'He is surely mad'. **52** Yet it is but a reminder to all mankind.

Surah 69   The Inevitable Truth

This surah imparts a feeling of grave seriousness as it talks about the punishment that befell earlier communities who denied the truth of the life to come. It further speaks about resurrection, individual accountability and judgement, the way the guilty ones are driven to Hell and the ultimate assertion, in great emphasis, of the origin of the Qur'an and that it is God's Book imparted by a noble angel to a noble prophet. Such grave seriousness is felt most in the final verses as they speak of what would happen to anyone who invents lies and attributes them to God. However, the Qur'an remains as a reminder to those who are God-fearing and a cause of bitter regret to the unbelievers. The concluding verse gives an order to the Prophet, and indeed to every believer, to extol the name of God, the Supreme Lord of all worlds.

The Inevitable Truth

In the Name of God, the Lord of Grace, the Ever-Merciful

1 The Inevitable Truth! **2** What is the Inevitable Truth? **3** Would that you knew what the Inevitable Truth is! **4** The people of Thamud and 'Ad denied the Striker. **5** Thamud were destroyed by an overwhelming event, **6** while 'Ad were destroyed by a furiously howling wind, which He caused to rage upon them for seven nights and eight decisive days. **7** You could see their people lying dead, like uprooted trunks of hollow palm trees. **8** Can you see any trace of them now? **9** Pharaoh, too, and those before him, and the ruined cities – all indulged in sin, **10** and disobeyed their Lord's messenger; and so He took them to task with an ever-tightening grip. **11** When the waters rose high, We carried you in the floating Ark, **12** making it all a lasting reminder for you, so that attentive ears may take heed. **13** When the Trumpet is sounded a single time, **14** and the earth and mountains are lifted up and with one mighty crash are flattened, **15** that which is certain to happen will on that Day have come to pass. **16** The sky will be rent asunder, for, it will have become frail on that Day. **17** The angels will stand on all its sides and, on that Day, eight of them will bear aloft the Throne of your Lord. **18** On that Day you shall be brought to judgement and none of your secrets will remain hidden. **19** He who is given his record in his right hand will say, 'Come you all! Read this my record. **20** I certainly knew that one day I would have to face my account'. **21** He will be in a happy state of life, **22** in a lofty garden, **23** with its fruits within easy reach. **24** 'Eat and drink to your hearts' content as a reward for what you have done in days gone by.' **25** But he who is given his record in his left hand will say, 'Would that I had never been shown my record **26** and knew nothing of my account! **27** Would that death had been the end of me! **28** Nothing has my wealth availed me. **29** I am now bereft of all my power'. **30** 'Lay hold of him and shackle him, **31** and burn him in the fire of Hell, **32** and then fasten him in a chain seventy cubits long.' **33** He did not believe in God Almighty, **34** and he never encouraged feeding the needy. **35** So, no friend has he here today, **36** nor any food except the filth **37** that none other than the sinners eat. **38** I need not swear by what you can see **39** and what you cannot see: **40** this [Qur'an] is the word of a noble Messenger, **41** not the word of a poet – how little you believe! **42** nor the word of a soothsayer – how little you reflect! **43** This [Qur'an] is a revelation from the Lord of all the worlds. **44** Had he attributed some fabrications to Us, **45** We would indeed have seized him by the right hand **46** and cut off his life-vein, **47** and none of you could have saved him. **48** This [Qur'an] is indeed a reminder to the God-fearing. **49** We well know that among you are some who deny its truth. **50** Yet it will be a cause of bitter regret for the unbelievers. **51** It is indeed truth absolute. **52** Extol, then, the glory of the name of your Lord, the Supreme.

Surah 70   Ways of Ascent

Like the surah before it, this surah also deals with the question of the Day of Judgement in a very serious manner, but it derives its images from within the human soul. Thus, man's preoccupations and inner feelings are highlighted. Indeed, Hell itself is shown to be a living being that beckons unbelievers to come to it. Even the torment that befalls the unbelievers is largely psychological.

The surah also paints an image of the believers and here again it describes inner feelings as well as obvious characteristics. It shows the great difference in the psychology of the believers and unbelievers, and how they react to situations of happiness and adversity. It also mentions that the unbelievers entertain thoughts of being admitted to Heaven. Thus, the Qur'an gives its message in a variety of ways so as to leave no excuse for anyone who denies the truth it clearly states.

Ways of Ascent

In the Name of God, the Lord of Grace, the Ever-Merciful

1 An inquirer has asked about a suffering which is bound to befall **2** the unbelievers. Nothing can ward it off, **3** as it comes from God, the Lord of the Ways of Ascent. **4** All the angels and the Spirit will ascend to Him, on a day the length of which is fifty thousand years. **5** Therefore, endure all adversity with goodly patience. **6** People think it to be far away, **7** but We see it near at hand. **8** On the Day when the sky will be like molten lead, **9** and the mountains like tufts of wool, **10** when no friend will ask about his friend, **11** though they may be within sight of one another. The guilty one will wish he could ransom himself from the suffering on that Day by sacrificing his own children, **12** his wife, his brother, **13** the kinsfolk who gave him shelter, **14** and all those on earth, if it could save him. **15** But no! It is the raging Fire **16** that tears the skin away. **17** It will claim all who turn their backs, and turn away from the truth, **18** amass riches and hoard them. **19** Man is born with a restless disposition: **20** when misfortune befalls him, he is fretful; **21** and when good fortune comes his way, he grows tight-fisted. **22** Not so those who pray, **23** and always attend to their prayers; **24** who give a due share of their possessions **25** to the one who asks [for help] and the one who is deprived; **26** who believe in the Day of Judgement; **27** who stand in fear of their Lord's punishment, **28** for none may feel totally secure from their Lord's punishment; **29** who guard their chastity **30** except with those joined to them in marriage, or those whom they rightfully possess – for then, they are free of all blame, **31** whereas those who seek to go beyond that [limit] are indeed transgressors; **32** who are faithful to their trusts and to their pledges; **33** who stand up for the truth when they bear witness; **34** and who attend to their prayers without fail. **35** They are the ones to be honoured in the Gardens of Paradise. **36** What is wrong with the unbelievers, that they run confusedly before you, **37** from the right and the left, in crowds? **38** Does every one of them hope to enter a garden of bliss? **39** No! We have created them from the substance they know. **40** By the Lord of all star risings and settings, We certainly have the power to replace them with better people. **41** There is nothing to prevent Us from doing so. **42** Leave them to indulge in idle talk and play until they face the Day they have been promised, **43** the Day when they shall come in haste from their graves, as if rallying to a flag, with eyes downcast, with ignominy overwhelming them. **44** Such is the Day they have been promised.

Surah 71   Noah

This surah relates the story of Prophet Noah and his advocacy of the divine message among his people. He was met with stubborn rejection and unwavering denial of the truth. We learnt in other surahs that he advocated his message for not less than 950 years (29: 14) and that only a small number of his people actually believed (11: 40). Here he speaks of how varied his methods of advising his people and inviting them to believe in God were, and he describes how he set before them all the blessings God had given them. He mentions how he drew their attention to God's creation and how it all points to the truth of God's Oneness and the inevitability of resurrection and accountability. He describes their arrogance and their stubborn rejection. Ultimately, he prays to God to punish them for their attitude.

This is a great episode in the history of the divine message. When we read it we realise the great blessing God has bestowed on mankind by sending Prophet Muhammad with His final message. He was a Messenger full of compassion. When he was hard pressed by his opponents, He prayed to God to guide them.

Noah

In the Name of God, the Lord of Grace, the Ever-Merciful

1 We sent Noah to his people: 'Warn your people, before painful suffering befalls them'. **2** He said: 'My people, I am here to warn you plainly. **3** Worship God alone and fear Him, and obey me. **4** He will forgive you your sins and grant you respite for an appointed term. When God's appointed term comes, it can never be put back, if you but knew it'. **5** He said: 'My Lord! I have been pleading with my people night and day, **6** but the more I call them, the further they run away. **7** Whenever I call on them, so that You may forgive them, they thrust their fingers into their ears, draw their garments over their heads, grow obstinate and become even more arrogant and insolent. **8** I have called them openly; **9** I have preached to them in public, and I spoke to them secretly, in private. **10** I said: "Ask your Lord for forgiveness: He is ever-forgiving. **11** He will let loose the sky over you with abundance, **12** and will give you wealth and children; and will provide you with gardens and rivers. **13** What is the matter with you? Why do you behave with such insolence towards your Lord,

14 when it is He who has created you in successive stages? **15** Do you not see how God has created seven heavens in layers, **16** placing in them the moon for a light and the sun for a lantern? **17** God has made you spring from the earth like a plant, **18** and He will return you into it and then bring you out again. **19** God has made the earth a vast expanse for you, **20** so that you may walk along its spacious paths"'. **21** Noah said: 'My Lord! They have disobeyed me and followed those whose wealth and children lead them increasingly into ruin. **22** They have devised a mighty plot, **23** and said to each other: "Do not ever renounce your gods! Do not abandon Wadd, Suaʿ, Yaghuth, Yaʿuq or Nasr". **24** They have led many astray. Lord, grant the wrongdoers increase in nothing but error'. **25** Because of their sins, they were drowned, and were made to enter the Fire. They found none besides God to support them. **26** And Noah said: 'Lord! Do not leave a single unbeliever on earth. **27** If you spare them, they will lead Your servants astray and beget none but sinners and hardened unbelievers. **28** My Lord! Forgive me, my parents and everyone who enters my house as a believer. Forgive all believing men and women. To the wrongdoers grant You no increase except in perdition'.

Surah 72   The Jinn

This surah speaks of a very significant incident which the Qur'an relates to the Prophet, telling him that a group of the jinn listened to the Qur'an as he was reciting it. Immediately thereafter, they returned to their own people to inform them of what they had heard, advising them to believe in it. The surah reports what the jinn said to their people. From this surah we learn much that is true about the jinn as it quotes their description of themselves.

The unbelievers in Makkah used to allege that some of the jinn taught the Prophet the Qur'an, claiming this was so as the jinn had taught their poets. They also believed that the jinn knew about future events and assigned to them powers that are far superior to those of human beings. Indeed, such beliefs were prevalent in many societies, and some of them still exist in our modern world, even in some sections of advanced countries.

From the jinn's discourse in this surah and in Surah 46, which also mentions their listening to the Qur'an and giving the news of the Prophet's message to their people, we learn that the jinn did not know anything of or about the Qur'an until they listened to the Prophet reciting it in prayer. They do not know the future. Some of them believe and others do not. Indeed, some foolish ones among them do what some foolish humans do whereby they say outrageous things about God. They acknowledge, however, that they have no means of escaping God's will.

Some people deny the existence of the jinn, claiming that this is nothing but superstition. Such denial, however, is not founded on any certain knowledge. The fact that so many superstitions have been weaved around the jinn make people deny their existence. Yet the same people do not claim to have known all creatures on earth, let alone elsewhere in the world around us, in order to be able to support their denial. We, therefore, believe in the jinn's existence, as it is confirmed by the Qur'an's true statements.

The Jinn

In the Name of God, the Lord of Grace, the Ever-Merciful

1 Say: 'It has been revealed to me that a group of the jinn listened in and then said: "We have heard a wondrous discourse, giving guidance to what is sagacious, and we have come to believe in it. **2** We shall never associate partners with our Lord. **3** Sublimely exalted is the glory of our Lord! He has taken to Himself neither consort nor son. **4** Some foolish ones among us have been saying some outrageous things about God. **5** Yet we had thought that no man or jinn would ever utter a lie about God. **6** True, in the past some among mankind sought refuge with some of the jinn, but they caused them further trouble. **7** They thus came to think, just like you thought, that God will not raise anyone. **8** We tried to reach heaven, but found it full of mighty guards and shooting stars. **9** We used to take up positions there to listen, but whoever tries to listen now will find a shooting star in wait for him. **10** We do not know if this bodes evil for those who live on earth, or if their Lord intends to guide them to what is right. **11** Some among us are righteous and others less so: we follow widely divergent paths. **12** We know that we can never elude God on earth, and we can never elude Him by flight. **13** When we heard the guidance, we came to believe in it. Whoever believes in his Lord need never fear loss or injustice. **14** Some of us submit to Him and others are unfair. Those who submit to God are the ones who have endeavoured to attain what is right. **15** But those who are unfair will be the fuel of Hell-fire"'. **16** 'Had they established themselves on the right way, We would have given them abundant water to drink, so as to test them by this means. **17** Anyone who turns away from his Lord's revelation will be made to endure uphill suffering. **18** Places of worship are for God alone; therefore, do not invoke anyone other than God'. **19** Yet when God's servant stood up to pray to Him, they pressed in on him in multitude. **20** Say: 'I invoke my Lord alone, and I associate no partners with Him'. **21** Say: 'It is not in my power to cause you harm or to set you on the right course'. **22** Say: 'No one can ever protect me from God, nor can I ever find a place to hide from Him'. **23** My task is only to deliver what I receive from God and His messages'. Whoever disobeys God and His Messenger will have the fire of Hell, where they will abide for ever. **24** When they see what they have been promised, they will realise who has the lesser help and is smaller in number. **25** Say: 'I do not know whether that which you have been promised is imminent, or whether my Lord has set for it a distant term'. **26** He alone knows that which is beyond the reach of human perception, and He does not disclose His secrets to anyone except to a messenger whom He has been pleased to choose. **27** He then sends watchers to walk before and behind him, to know that they have delivered their Lord's messages. **28** He has full knowledge of all they have. He takes count of everything.

Surah 73   The Enfolded One

This surah is delivered in two parts, with the second part, consisting of just the last verse, revealed one year later than the first. It tells the Prophet to stand in night worship, spending half of it, or even more or a little less, in prayer. The Prophet complied and so did his Companions who believed in his message. They were small in number, but they were the vanguard of a great community of believers. This duty was imposed on them as preparation for the hard task ahead, namely the delivery of the message and its defence. Such preparation through prayer at a time when the world around them was fast asleep gave them clear vision and spiritual strength. This served them well when they faced the unbelievers' stiff opposition to their message; they who persecuted them in Makkah and who raised armies to crush them when they had established their state in Madinah.

The order to stand up in night worship was relaxed after one year, but it remains a strongly recommended practice for advocates of Islam, particularly when they are faced with powerful enemies or placed under much pressure.

The Prophet continued to spend a considerable part, normally one-third, in night worship for the rest of his life. When his wife asked him why he did so when God had already forgiven him his sins, if any, he answered: 'Should I not be God's grateful servant?'

The Enfolded One

In the Name of God, the Lord of Grace, the Ever-Merciful

1 You enfolded one! 2 Stand in prayer at night, all but a small part of it, 3 half of it, or a little less, or add to it. 4 Recite the Qur'an calmly and distinctly. 5 We shall bestow on you a weighty message. 6 The night hours are strongest of tread and most upright of speech. 7 During the day you have a long chain of things to attend to. 8 Therefore, remember your Lord's name and devote yourself wholeheartedly to Him. 9 He is the Lord of the east and the west. There is no deity other than Him. Take Him for your guardian. 10 Endure with patience what people may say, and leave their company with noble dignity. 11 Leave to Me those who deny the truth and enjoy the comforts of this life. Bear with them for a little while. 12 We have heavy fetters and a blazing fire, 13 food that chokes and painful suffering

14 on the Day when the earth and the mountains will shake, and the mountains will crumble into heaps of shifting sand. **15** We have sent you a messenger to be your witness, just as We sent a messenger to Pharaoh. **16** Pharaoh disobeyed the messenger, and so We inflicted on him a severe punishment. **17** How will you, if you continue to disbelieve, guard yourselves against a Day that will turn children's hair grey? **18** That is the Day when the skies shall be rent asunder. God's promise will certainly be fulfilled. **19** This is but a reminder. Let him who will, take the way to his Lord. **20** Your Lord knows that you stand in prayer nearly two-thirds of the night, or one-half or a third of it, as do some of your followers. It is God who determines the measure of night and day. He is aware that you will not be able to keep a measure of it, and therefore He turns towards you in His grace. Recite of the Qur'an as much as may be easy for you. He knows that some of you will be sick, others will go about in the land seeking God's bounty, and others will be fighting for God's cause. Therefore, recite whatever you may do with ease. Attend regularly to prayer, pay your zakat [obligatory charity], and give God a goodly loan. Whatever good you may offer on your own behalf, you shall find it with God to be better and richer in reward. Seek God's forgiveness, for God is much-forgiving, ever-merciful.

Surah 74   Wrapped in a Cloak

This surah also addresses the Prophet and it commands him to arise and give warning. This was the task assigned to all prophets and God's messengers. It warns all people that they will have to face a hard day. It then specifies a single unbeliever making clear that he will suffer God's punishment in Hell. The surah gives the reason for making his fate clear. He deliberated over the Qur'an, acknowledging its power and sound argument, but then led the efforts to turn people away from it.

    The surah makes clear the difference between the believers and the unbelievers and the outcome each group will merit on the Day of Judgement. It adds a confession by the unbelievers of what they used to do in this present life, one which spelled out their doom.

Wrapped in a Cloak

In the Name of God, the Lord of Grace, the Ever-Merciful

1 You, wrapped in your cloak, **2** arise and give warning. **3** Glorify your Lord's greatness; **4** clean your garments; **5** stay away from all filth; **6** do not hold up what you give away, showing it to be much; **7** but to your Lord turn in patience. **8** When the Trumpet is sounded **9** that will be a Day of anguish, **10** far from easy for the unbelievers. **11** Leave to Me the one I created alone, **12** to whom I have granted vast wealth, **13** and sons by his side, **14** making life smooth and easy for him; **15** yet he greedily desires that I give him more. **16** No! He has set himself stubbornly against Our revelations. **17** I will constrain him to endure a painful uphill climb! **18** He thought and he schemed. **19** Damn him, how he schemed! **20** Again, damn him, how he schemed! **21** He looked around, **22** then he frowned and glared, **23** then he turned his back and gloried in his arrogance, **24** and said, 'This is just sorcery handed down from olden times! **25** This is nothing but the word of a mere mortal!' **26** I will cast him into the scorching Fire. **27** Would that you knew what the scorching Fire is like! **28** It leaves nothing, and spares nothing; **29** it appears before mankind, **30** guarded by nineteen. **31** We have appointed none other than angels to guard the Fire, and We have made their number a test for the unbelievers. Thus those who have been granted revelations in the past may be convinced and the believers may grow yet more firm in their faith; and so those who have been granted revelations and the believers will entertain no doubt; but the sick at heart and the unbelievers will ask, 'What could God mean by this image?' Thus God lets go astray whomever He wills, and guides whomever He wills. No one knows your Lord's forces except Him. This is all but a reminder for mankind. **32** No! by the moon! **33** By the night when it departs, **34** and the shining dawn! **35** It is indeed one of the mighty things, **36** a warning to all mankind, **37** to those of you who choose to go ahead or to lag behind. **38** Every soul is held in pledge for what it has wrought, **39** except for those on the right hand. **40** They will be in gardens, and will ask **41** about the guilty ones: **42** 'What brought you into the scorching Fire?' **43** They will answer: 'We were not among those who prayed, **44** neither did we feed the needy; **45** but we indulged with others in vain talk, **46** and we denied the Day of Judgement **47** until there came upon us that which is certain'. **48** So, of no benefit to them could be the pleas of any intercessors. **49** What is the matter with them that they turn away from all admonition **50** like terrified asses **51** fleeing from a lion? **52** Every one of them demands to be given revelations unfolded before him. **53** No! They do not fear the life to come. **54** No! This is indeed an admonition. **55** Let him who will, take heed. **56** They, however, will not take heed unless God so wills. He is the Lord to be feared, the Lord of forgiveness.

Surah 75   The Day of Resurrection

This surah begins with a note referring to the Day of Resurrection followed by another referring to the human soul. These two continue to be at the core of the surah's discourse. Shortly after this opening, the surah mentions that man asks about the timing of the Day of Resurrection, and then it paints a powerful scene of man's predicament when he realises its inevitability and that there is no escape.

The surah also paints another powerful scene of man as death approaches and he realises that nothing he may have of power, wealth, or other resources can prevent or delay it.

As it approaches its end, the surah reminds man of his creation: how conception takes place leading to the development of the embryo, then males and females are born. This ends with a rhetorical question making it clear that the One who has initiated this process of bringing man out of this very humble origin can certainly bring the dead back to life.

The Day of Resurrection

In the Name of God, the Lord of Grace, the Ever-Merciful

1 I need not swear by the Day of Resurrection **2** and I need not swear by the self-reproaching soul! **3** Does man think that We will not put his bones together again? **4** Yes, indeed! We are able to put in perfect order his very fingertips! **5** Yet man wants to deny what lies ahead of him. **6** He asks: 'When will this Day of Resurrection be?' **7** When the sight is dazzled **8** and the moon eclipsed, **9** when the sun and the moon are brought together, **10** on that Day man will say: 'Where to flee?' **11** But no! There is no refuge. **12** On that Day, to your Lord all shall return. **13** Man will be told on that Day all that he put forward and all that he put back. **14** Man will be a witness against himself, **15** even though he may put up his excuses. **16** Do not move your tongue repeating its words in haste. **17** We shall see to its collection and recitation. **18** When We recite it, follow its recitation. **19** Then it will be for Us to make its meaning clear. **20** Yet you love this fleeting life, **21** and give no thought to the life to come. **22** Some faces will on that Day be radiant with happiness, **23** looking towards their Lord; **24** and some faces will on that Day be overcast with despair, **25** realising that a great calamity is about to befall them. **26** Yet when the departing soul comes up to the throat, **27** when it is said, 'Can any charmer [do something now]?' **28** When he knows it is the final parting, **29** and one leg will be joined with another, **30** to your Lord he will on that Day be driven. **31** He neither believed nor prayed, **32** but denied the truth and turned away, **33** then he went back to his people full of arrogance. **34** Your doom, man, comes nearer and nearer, **35** and ever nearer and nearer. **36** Does man think that he will be left without purpose? **37** Was he not a mere drop of emitted sperm? **38** It then became a clinging cell mass, and then God created and shaped it, **39** fashioning out of it the two sexes, male and female. **40** Is He not, then, able to bring the dead back to life?

Surah 76   Man

This surah begins with a reminder to man of three things: 1) There was a time when he was not in existence; 2) He has a very humble origin, but God gave him his different abilities and faculties; and 3) God showed him the way and left him to choose to either be a grateful believer or an unbelieving ingrate.

The surah then delivers a very short statement of what awaits the unbelievers, but follows it with a very detailed description of what the believers will enjoy in Heaven. This is perhaps the most detailed scene of the comforts and bliss that awaits God's good servants.

The surah follows this with an emphatic statement that the Qur'an was revealed by God, and gives instructions to the Prophet to remain patient as he continues with his task of delivering God's message. He is to glorify God at all times and to offer worship during the long night. It concludes by stating that God will bestow His grace on whomever He wills, while the wrongdoers will face severe punishment.

Man

In the Name of God, the Lord of Grace, the Ever-Merciful

1 Was there not a period of time when man was not yet something to be thought of? **2** We have created man from a drop of mingled fluid, so that We might try him. Therefore, we have endowed him with hearing and sight. **3** We have shown him the way, [giving him the choice] to be thankful or ungrateful. **4** For the unbelievers, We have prepared chains and shackles, and a blazing Fire. **5** The righteous shall drink from a cup mixed with *kafur*,[19] **6** a fountain where God's servants shall drink, making it flow in abundance. **7** They are the ones who fulfil their vows and stand in awe of a day of woes that fly far and wide, **8** who give food – though they need it themselves – to the needy, the orphan and the captive, [saying within themselves,] 'We feed you for the sake of God alone. **9** We desire neither recompense from you, nor thanks. **10** We fear the Day of our Lord: a bleak, distressful day'. **11** God will save them from the woes of that Day, and will grant them radiance and joy, **12** and will reward them for their

---

19   A sweet-smelling substance extracted from beautiful flowers.

patience in adversity with a garden and [garments of] silk. **13** They will recline there on soft couches, feeling neither burning sun nor severe cold. **14** Its shades will come low over them, and its clusters of fruit will hang low, within easy reach. **15** They will be served with silver plates and goblets that seem to be crystal, **16** crystal-clear, but made of silver, the measure of which they are the ones to determine. **17** They will be given to drink of a cup flavoured with ginger, **18** from a spring there called Salsabil. **19** They will be waited upon by immortal youths. If you see them, you would think they were scattered pearls. **20** If you were to look around, you would see only bliss and a vast kingdom. **21** They shall be arrayed in garments of fine green silk and brocade; and adorned with bracelets of silver. And their Lord will give them a most pure drink. **22** This is a reward for you. Your endeavours are well appreciated. **23** It is We who have bestowed the Qur'an upon you by gradual revelation. **24** Await, then, your Lord's judgement in all patience, and pay no heed to any of these sinners and unbelievers. **25** Remember your Lord's name morning and evening. **26** At night prostrate yourself before Him, and extol His limitless glory throughout the long night. **27** These people love the fleeting life, and leave behind them a Day that will be heavy. **28** It is We who have created them and strengthened their constitution. If it be Our will, We can replace them entirely with others of their kind. **29** This is but a reminder. Let him who will, take the way to his Lord. **30** Yet you cannot will except by the will of God. God is indeed all-knowing, wise. **31** He admits to His grace whoever He will, but for the wrongdoers He has prepared painful suffering.

Surah 77   Sent Forth

Just as Surah 54 repeats a question about God's punishment meted out to past communities of unbelievers, and Surah 55 repeats a reference to God's blessings, this surah repeats the warning that those who deny the truth will face grave punishment in the life to come.

This surah consists of several sections of short verses and varying rhymes, but it is characterised by a powerful rhythm and strong beat. It describes great celestial events that herald the Day of Judgement, refers to the punishment of past nations, mentions the origins of man, the inevitable death and what awaits those who deny the message and disbelieve in God's Oneness. There is a short section about believers and their reward, but it concludes by rebuking the unbelievers.

Sent Forth

In the Name of God, the Lord of Grace, the Ever-Merciful

1 By those sent forth in swift succession; **2** and those tempestuously storming on; **3** and those scattering far and wide; **4** and those separating [right and wrong] with all clarity; **5** and those giving a reminder, **6** with an excuse and a warning, **7** what you have been promised shall be fulfilled. **8** When the stars are dimmed, **9** and the sky is rent asunder, **10** and the mountains are scattered like dust, **11** and the messengers are given their appointed time… **12** For what day has all this been set? **13** For the Day of Distinction. **14** Would that you knew what the Day of Distinction is! **15** Woe on that Day betide those who deny the truth. **16** Did We not destroy those people of old? **17** We shall certainly cause later ones to follow them. **18** Thus do We deal with the guilty. **19** Woe on that Day betide those who deny the truth. **20** Have We not created you from a humble fluid, **21** placing it in a safe lodging **22** for a pre-determined term? **23** Thus have We determined; excellent indeed is how We determine. **24** Woe on that Day betide those who deny the truth. **25** Have We not made the earth an abode **26** for the living and the dead? **27** We have placed on it firm, lofty mountains and provided you with fresh water to drink. **28** Woe on that Day betide those who deny the truth. **29** Go to that which you used to deny! **30** Go to a shadow rising in three columns; **31** giving no shade, nor relief from the flame. **32** It throws up sparks as huge as forts, **33** as bright as yellow camels. **34** Woe on that Day betide those who deny the truth. **35** On that Day they will not utter a word, **36** and they will not be allowed to offer any excuse. **37** Woe on that Day betide those who deny the truth. **38** This is the Day of Distinction: We have gathered you with all those people of old. **39** If you have a scheme left, then use it against Me now. **40** Woe on that Day betide those who deny the truth. **41** The God-fearing shall dwell amid cool shades and springs, **42** and fruits as they may desire. **43** Eat and drink to your hearts' content in return for what you did. **44** Thus do We reward those who do good. **45** Woe on that Day betide those who deny the truth. **46** Eat and enjoy your life for a little while, for you are certainly guilty. **47** Woe on that Day betide those who deny the truth. **48** When they are told to bow down before God, they do not bow down. **49** Woe on that Day betide those who deny the truth. **50** In what message, after this, will they believe?

Surah 78   The Tidings

This surah begins with a question about something over which people differ. It gives it an air of greatness and mystery, without explaining it. It then moves away from the question to remind people of how the world around them came into existence, and how its various components fall into place and serve the common cause of preserved existence. It provides a long list of images of creation before it returns to explain that the great event which raised their questions and caused their differences is inevitable and will take place at its appointed time. This is the Day of Judgement when everyone will receive their different judgements according to what they have done in their present lives.

After portraying a scene of the suffering of the people doomed to Hell, the surah gives another image of the God-fearing who will enjoy His mercy and who will be in Heaven. It then concludes with a majestic scene showing the angels standing in rank none uttering a word except with God's permission.

The Tidings

In the Name of God, the Lord of Grace, the Ever-Merciful

1 About what are they asking? **2** About the fateful tiding **3** on which they dispute. **4** No indeed; they shall certainly know! **5** Again, no indeed; they shall certainly know! **6** Have We not spread and levelled the earth, **7** and made the mountains as pegs? **8** We created you in pairs, **9** and made your sleep a cessation of activity. **10** We made the night a mantle, **11** and appointed the day for gaining a livelihood. **12** We built above you seven mighty ones, **13** and placed therein a blazing lamp. **14** We send down out of the rain-clouds water in abundance, **15** by which We bring forth grain and varied plants, **16** and gardens thick with trees. **17** Fixed is the Day of Distinction. **18** On that Day the Trumpet is blown and you shall come in crowds, **19** and heaven is opened, and becomes gates, **20** and the mountains are made to move away, and seem to have been a mirage. **21** Hell stands as a vigilant watch guard, **22** a final resort for those who transgress all bounds. **23** Therein they shall abide for ages, **24** tasting neither coolness nor any drink, **25** except boiling fluid and decaying filth: **26** a fitting recompense. **27** They did not expect to be faced with a reckoning, **28** and roundly denied Our revelations. **29** But We have placed on record every single thing, **30** [and We shall say]: 'Taste this, then, the only increase you shall have is increase of torment'. **31** The God-fearing shall have a place of security, **32** gardens and vineyards **33** and high-bosomed maidens, of equal age, for companions, **34** and a cup overflowing. **35** There they shall hear no idle talk, nor any falsehood. **36** Such is the recompense of your Lord: a truly sufficient gift. **37** Lord of the heavens and earth and all that lies between them, the Lord of Grace, with whom they have no power to speak. **38** On the Day when the Spirit and the angels stand in ranks, they shall not speak, except those to whom the Lord of Grace has given leave, and who shall say what is right. **39** That Day is a certainty. Let him who will, seek a way back to his Lord. **40** We have forewarned you of an imminent scourge, on the Day when man will behold what his hands have forwarded and the unbeliever will cry: 'Would that I were dust!'

Surah 79   The Pluckers

This surah's opening is engulfed with mystery. It speaks about certain things that commentators have variably explained, with some saying that they refer to the angels and others suggesting that they are stars. This is followed by a still more mysterious report of events that herald the Day of Judgement. The first scene of that Day is one of people dreading the outcome.

After this start, with all its mystery, the surah mentions Moses and his encounter with Pharaoh and the destruction of the latter and his troops. This should serve as a clear lesson to whoever reflects on it. The surah then draws people's attention to the creation of the universe and its perfect structure.

The destiny of people is explained and attached to their chosen ways. The ones who transgress and seek the pleasures of this present life will have nothing to boast of in the life to come. On the other side are the ones who fear God and work for the life to come. These will be in Heaven.

The surah concludes with a reference to the question people always ask: When is the Last Hour to come. It makes clear that no one knows its timing except God.

The Pluckers

In the Name of God, the Lord of Grace, the Ever-Merciful

1 By those that pluck out vehemently, 2 and those that move forward rapidly; 3 by those that float along at ease, 4 and those that outstrip swiftly, 5 and those that conduct matters. 6 On the Day when a violent convulsion will [be overwhelming], 7 to be soon followed by a further [convulsion], 8 all hearts shall be filled with terror, 9 and all eyes shall be downcast. 10 They say, 'What! Are we being restored to our former state, 11 even though we have become [no more than] hollow bones?' 12 They say, 'That will be a return with loss'. 13 But with just one blast 14 they shall be alive on earth. 15 Have you heard the story of Moses? 16 His Lord called out to him in the sacred valley of Tuwa, 17 saying: 'Go to Pharoah: he has transgressed all bounds, 18 and say to him: "Would you like to reform yourself? 19 I will guide you to your Lord, so that you may be in awe of Him"'. 20 He showed Pharaoh the mightiest miracle, 21 but Pharaoh cried lies and

rebelled. **22** He then turned away hastily. **23** He summoned all his men and made a proclamation to them: **24** 'I am your supreme Lord,' he said. **25** God smote him with the scourge of both the life to come and this life. **26** Surely in this there is a lesson for the God-fearing. **27** Which is stronger in constitution: you or the heaven He has built? **28** He raised it high and gave it its perfect shape, **29** and gave darkness to its night, and brought out its daylight. **30** After that He spread out the earth. **31** He brought out water from it, and brought forth its pastures; **32** and the mountains He set firm, **33** for you and your cattle to delight in. **34** Then, when the great, overwhelming event comes to pass – **35** on that Day man will clearly remember what he has done, **36** when Hell is brought in sight of all who are looking on; **37** then, he who transgressed the bounds of what is right, **38** and chose this present life **39** will have Hell for his dwelling place. **40** But he who feared that he will stand before his Lord and forbade his soul its base desire **41** will dwell in Paradise. **42** They question you about the Last Hour, when will it come to pass? **43** But why should you be concerned with its exact timing? **44** The final word concerning it belongs to your Lord. **45** Your mission is merely to warn those who fear it. **46** On the Day when they see that hour, it will seem to them that their life on earth had spanned only one evening, or one morning.

Surah 80   The Frowning

The opening of this surah speaks about an incident that took place in the early years of the Islamic message, when the Prophet was engaged with a few of the dignitaries in Makkah, explaining to them the message of Islam. He stored high hopes for his message if those people would accept it. During this meeting, a blind Muslim man came over and interrupted the Prophet, asking him to teach him something of the Qur'an. The Prophet was displeased at the interruption and his displeasure showed on his face. He did not express his feeling in words. Needless to say, the blind man did not feel anything for he saw nothing. However, the surah was revealed to censure the Prophet's behaviour and to tell him that it was not right that he should attend to those men in preference to a believer who was God-fearing and who sought to learn more.

The surah goes on to speak about man and his usual attitude to faith and life. It invites man to reflect on what he takes for granted in this life, starting with the food he eats and how it comes about. It concludes with confirming the serious nature of the Day of Judgement when everyone will be preoccupied with his or her own destiny, forgetting even their closest relatives.

The Frowning

In the Name of God, the Lord of Grace, the Ever-Merciful

1 He frowned and turned away **2** when the blind man came to him. **3** How could you tell? He might have sought to purify himself. **4** He might have been reminded and the reminder might have profited him. **5** But to the one who considered himself self-sufficient **6** you were all attention. **7** Yet the fault would not be yours if he remained uncleansed. **8** As to him who comes to you with zeal, **9** and with a feeling of fear in his heart, **10** him you ignore. **11** No indeed! This is an admonition. **12** Let him who will, bear it in mind. **13** It is written on honoured pages, **14** exalted, purified, (**15-16**) by the hands of noble and devout scribes. **17** Perish man! How ungrateful he is! **18** Of what did God create him? **19** Of a drop of sperm. He created him and proportioned him. **20** He makes his path smooth for him. **21** He then causes him to die and to be put in his grave. **22** He will surely bring him back to life when He pleases. **23** But by no means has man fulfilled His bidding.

24 Let man reflect on the food he eats: **25** how We pour down the rain in torrents, **26** then cleave the earth in fissures; **27** how We bring forth the grains, **28** the grapes, and the fresh vegetation, **29** the olive and the palm, **30** the dense-treed gardens, **31** the fruit-trees and the green pastures, **32** for you and your cattle to delight in. **33** But when the stunning blast is sounded, **34** on that Day everyone will forsake his brother, **35** his mother and his father, **36** his wife and his children: **37** for each one of them will on that Day have enough preoccupations of his own. **38** Some faces on that Day shall be beaming, **39** smiling and joyful. **40** Some other faces on that Day shall be covered with dust, **41** veiled with darkness. **42** These shall be the faces of the unbelievers, the hardened in sin.

Surah 81   The Darkening

This surah consists of two parts, each of which focuses on a fundamental concept of the Islamic faith. The first part speaks about the Day of Judgement and the great universal upheaval that ushers it in. The upheaval affects the sun, stars, mountains, oceans, the earth, the skies, beasts and, naturally, man.

The second part focuses on the truth of revelation, describing the angel who brought it and the Prophet who received it. It also refers to the people who are addressed by this divine revelation and their attitude to it. It concludes with mentioning the divine will which gave people their nature and gave them the Qur'an, God's revelation.

The Darkening

In the Name of God, the Lord of Grace, the Ever-Merciful.

1 When the sun is darkened, **2** when the stars fall and disperse, **3** when the mountains are made to move away, **4** when the camels, ten months pregnant, are left untended, **5** when the wild beasts are brought together, **6** when the seas are set alight, **7** when people's souls are paired [like with like], **8** when the infant girl, buried alive, is asked **9** for what crime she was slain, **10** when the records are laid open, **11** when the sky is stripped bare, **12** when Hell is made to burn fiercely, **13** when Paradise is brought near, **14** every soul shall know what it has put forward. **15** I swear by the turning stars, **16** which move swiftly and hide themselves away, **17** and by the night as it comes darkening on, **18** and by the dawn as it starts to breathe, **19** this is truly the word of a noble and mighty messenger, **20** who enjoys a secure position with the Lord of the Throne. **21** He is obeyed in heaven, faithful to his trust. **22** Your old friend is not mad. **23** He saw him on the clear horizon. **24** He does not grudge the secrets of the unseen. **25** It is not the word of an accursed devil. **26** Whither then are you going? **27** This is only a reminder to all mankind, **28** to those of you whose will is to be upright. **29** Yet, you cannot will except by the will of God, Lord of all the worlds.

Surah 82   Cleaving Asunder

This surah too mentions the great universal upheaval that ushers in the Day of Judgement but paints it in a shorter version, because this surah takes a calmer approach than the last, remonstrating with man. This remonstrance, however, is coupled with a veiled warning, because man takes God's favours for granted, not showing gratitude for them. The surah then states the reason for this attitude, which is denial of the Day of Judgement. If man believes in the Day of Judgement and individual accountability, his attitude will be totally different. The surah confirms that it is certain to come and people will have two different ends. Furthermore, no one can avail another of anything.

Cleaving Asunder

In the Name of God, the Lord of Grace, the Ever-Merciful

1 When the sky is cleft asunder, **2** when the planets are scattered, **3** when the oceans are made to explode, **4** when the graves are hurled about, **5** every soul shall know its earlier actions and its later ones. **6** O man, what has lured you away from your gracious Lord, **7** who created and moulded you and gave you upright form? **8** He can give you whatever shape He wills. **9** Shun it! But you deny the Last Judgement. **10** Yet there are guardians watching over you, **11** noble recorders, **12** who know all that you do. **13** Surely the righteous shall be in bliss, **14** while the wicked shall be in a blazing fire, **15** which they shall enter on the Day of Judgement; **16** nor shall they ever be absent from it. **17** Would that you knew what the Day of Judgement is! **18** Oh, would that you knew what the Day of Judgement is! **19** It is the Day when no soul can be of any help to any other soul; for on that Day all sovereignty is God's alone.

Surah 83   The Stinters

The surah speaks about an abominable practice that may be found in any community if belief in the Day of Judgement and individual accountability is lacking. It is namely defrauding others. The surah warns such practitioners of severe punishment.

The surah then describes the ultimate fates of the transgressors and the righteous, showing the first group enduring their punishment in Hell, while the righteous enjoy what God grants them of His favours in Heaven.

The surah concludes by showing the unbelievers how, in this present life, they scoff at believers. This situation is reversed in the life to come, when the believers are given their reward of pure happiness.

The Stinters

In the Name of God, the Lord of Grace, the Ever-Merciful

1 Woe to the stinters 2 who, when others measure for them, exact in full, 3 but who, when they measure or weigh for others, defraud them. 4 Do such people not think that they will be raised to life 5 on a great Day, 6 the Day when all mankind shall stand before the Lord of all worlds? 7 No indeed; the record of the transgressors is in Sijjin 8 would that you knew what Sijjin is! 9 It is a record inscribed. 10 Woe on that Day to those who deny the truth, 11 who deny the Day of Judgement. 12 None denies it but the guilty aggressors, the evildoers, 13 who, when Our revelations are recited to them, cry: 'Fables of the ancients!' 14 No indeed! Their own deeds have cast a layer of rust over their hearts. 15 No indeed! On that Day they shall be shut out from their Lord. 16 They shall enter the blazing Fire, 17 and will be told: 'This is [the reality] which you denied!' 18 But the record of the righteous is in 'Illiyun. 19 Would that you knew what 'Illiyun is! 20 It is a record inscribed, 21 witnessed by those who are closest to God. 22 The righteous will surely be in bliss. 23 [Reclining] on couches, they will look around them. 24 In their faces you shall mark the glow of bliss. 25 They will be given to drink of a pure-drink, securely sealed, 26 with a seal of musk, for this let the strivers emulously strive. 27 It is a drink mixed with the waters of Tasnim, 28 a fountain at which those who are closest to God will drink. 29 Those who are given to sinful practices scoff at the faithful

30 and wink at one another as they pass by them. **31** When they go back to their folk they speak of them with jests, **32** and when they see them they say: 'These have indeed gone astray!' **33** Yet they have not been assigned the mission of being their guardians. **34** So on this Day [of Judgement] the faithful will laugh at the unbelievers, **35** as they recline upon their couches and look around them. **36** Shall the unbelievers be requited for what they were wont to do?

Surah 84   The Rending

This surah starts with scenes of the universal upheaval portrayed in Surahs 81 and 82, but they are shown here in an atmosphere of submission by the heavens and earth. The surah then addresses man in a calm way so that he may turn towards God in obedience and submission, just like the sky and the earth. It tells him about the two different ends man faces in the life to come, drawing his attention to scenes of this world that should make him realise that God is the Creator of the universe and that He controls everything in it. The last part of the surah wonders at those who continue to disbelieve in the truth of God's Oneness and the life to come. It tells us that God is aware of everyone's inner thoughts.

The Rending

In the Name of God, the Lord of Grace, the Ever-Merciful

1 When the sky is rent asunder, 2 obeying her Lord in true submission; 3 when the earth is stretched out 4 and casts forth all that is within her and becomes empty, 5 obeying her Lord in true submission! 6 O man! You have been toiling towards your Lord, and you shall meet Him. 7 He who is given his record in his right hand 8 will in time have a lenient reckoning 9 and return rejoicing to his people. 10 But he who is given his record behind his back 11 will in time call down destruction upon himself 12 and will enter the fire of Hell. 13 He lived joyfully among his people. 14 He surely thought he would never return. 15 Yes, indeed; his Lord was watching over him. 16 I swear by the twilight, 17 and by the night and what it envelops, 18 and by the moon in her full perfection, 19 that you shall certainly move onward, stage after stage. 20 Why then do they not accept the faith? 21 Or, when the Qur'an is read to them, they do not fall down in prostration? 22 But the unbelievers persist in rejecting [the truth], 23 yet God knows very well what they are hiding. 24 So give them the tidings of a grievous suffering, 25 except for those who believe and do good deeds; for theirs is an unfailing reward.

Surah 85   The Constellations

The surah refers to an incident involving a community of believers who were burnt to death by unbelievers, only because they believed in God. Those unbelievers sat and watched the believers being thrown into the great fire they had lit for them. They were pleased with their actions, thinking it was right for them to do what they did.

The surah makes clear that those who persecute the believers and punish them for their beliefs will suffer God's punishment. The believers on the other hand will enjoy great success as they earn God's pleasure and are rewarded for their beliefs and actions.

The surah asserts that God's punishment is severe. Nonetheless, He is loving and forgiving to those who turn to Him in repentance.

The Constellations

In the Name of God, the Lord of Grace, the Ever-Merciful

1 By the heaven with its constellations, **2** by the promised Day, **3** by the witness and that which is witnessed, **4** slain be the people of the pit **5** of the fire abounding in fuel, **6** when they sat around it, **7** watching what they did to the believers. **8** They took vengeance on them for no reason other than that they believed in God, the Almighty, to whom all praise is due, **9** to whom the dominion of the heavens and the earth belongs. But God is witness of all things. **10** Those who persecute the believers, men and women, and do not repent shall suffer the punishment of Hell, and suffer the punishment of burning. **11** But those who believe and do righteous deeds shall have gardens through which running waters flow; that is the supreme triumph. **12** Stern indeed is your Lord's vengeance. **13** It is He who brings into being, and then restores to life. **14** He is the Much Forgiving, the All-Loving, **15** Lord of the Throne, the Glorious, **16** He does whatever He wills. **17** Have you heard the story of the hosts, **18** of Pharaoh and Thamud? **19** Yet the unbelievers persist in their denial [of the truth]. **20** But God surrounds them all. **21** This is indeed a glorious Qur'an, **22** inscribed on an imperishable tablet.

Surah 86   The Night Visitor

This surah has a strong rhythm characterised by a hard beat. Even the Arabic word for the 'night visitor', *al-tariq*, is derived from a root that means 'to knock'. The surah emphasises that every soul is watched over. It invites man to look at the way he is created from gushing fluid and then how he is born. Man, then, should reflect that the One who created him from such a humble origin is able to bring him back to life after he has died and perished.

The surah then gives an oath that the resurrection is real and inevitable. It concludes with giving the unbelievers respite, but makes it clear that they will not escape their end.

The Night Visitor

In the Name of God, the Lord of Grace, the Ever-Merciful

1 By the heaven and by the night visitor. **2** Would that you knew what the night visitor is! **3** It is the star that pierces through darkness. **4** For every soul there is a guardian who watches over it. **5** Let man then reflect: of what he is created. **6** He is created of gushing water; **7** he issues from between the loins and the chest bones. **8** God is well able to bring him back [to life]. **9** On the Day when consciences are tried, **10** man shall be helpless, with no supporter. **11** By the heaven with its returning rain, **12** by the earth ever splitting with verdure, **13** this is surely a decisive word; **14** it is no idle talk. **15** They devise many an artful scheme, **16** but I too have My schemes. **17** So give respite to the unbelievers; leave them alone for a while.

Surah 87   The Most High

This surah speaks about God, the Most High and states some manifestations of His creation. It gives the Prophet certain assurances which greatly pleased him and for which he was most grateful to God. The first gift mentioned is that he would not forget the Qur'an that was being revealed to him.

He was assured that God would smooth his way to whatever is easy in all his own affairs and the affairs of the message which was entrusted to him. These were truly valuable gifts that could only be given by God.

The surah includes the essential elements of the Islamic concepts of God, man, revelation, resurrection and life after death.

The Most High

In the Name of God, the Lord of Grace, the Ever-Merciful

1 Extol the limitless glory of the name of your Lord, the Most High, **2** who creates and proportions well, **3** who determines and guides, **4** who brings forth the pasturage, **5** then turns it to withered grass. **6** We shall teach you and you shall not forget **7** except what God wills. He knows what is manifest and what is kept hidden. **8** And We shall smooth your way to perfect ease. **9** Give warning, therefore, [regardless of] whether such warning is of use. **10** He who fears God will heed it, **11** but the most hapless wretch will turn aside from it, **12** who shall be cast into the great Fire, **13** in which he shall neither die nor remain alive. **14** Successful will be he who purifies himself, **15** and glorifies the name of his Lord and prays. **16** Yet you prefer this present life, **17** while the life to come is better and longer lasting. **18** All this has indeed been stated in earlier revelations; **19** the Scriptures of Abraham and Moses.

Surah 88   The Enveloper

'The Enveloper' is yet another name used in the Qur'an to refer to the Day of Judgement. The surah begins with a question addressed to the Prophet, one whereby he is asked whether he had heard the story of the Enveloper. It then proceeds to give some scenes and images of what will happen on that day, when people face the outcome of their deeds in this life. It describes the results facing unbelievers and the happy end of believers.

The surah refers to some of the great scenes of the world around us which need only to be reflected upon to guide man to the inescapable conclusion that God is the Creator of all.

The Enveloper

In the Name of God, the Lord of Grace, the Ever-Merciful

1 Have you heard the story of the Enveloper? 2 Some faces on that Day are downcast, 3 labour weary, worn out, 4 about to enter a scorching fire, 5 made to drink from a boiling fountain. 6 Their only food shall be nothing but dry thorns, 7 which will neither nourish nor satisfy their hunger. 8 Other faces on that Day are jocund, 9 well-pleased with their striving, 10 in a sublime garden, 11 where they hear no babble. 12 A running fountain shall be there, 13 and raised couches, 14 and goblets placed ready, 15 and cushions laid in order, 16 and carpets spread out. 17 Let them reflect on the camels, how were they created; 18 and heaven, how it is raised aloft; 19 and the mountains, how they are hoisted; 20 and the earth, how it is spread out. 21 Therefore exhort them; your task is only to exhort. 22 You are not their overseer. 23 But he who turns his back and disbelieves, 24 God shall inflict on him the greatest suffering. 25 To Us they shall surely return, 26 when We shall bring them to account.

Surah 89   The Dawn

This surah begins with an oath that gives an air of calm and serenity, describing the dawn and the night before it. Yet some of its scenes are violent and hard hitting. It gives brief references to a few past communities that suffered God's punishment for their rejection of the truth advocated by His messengers.

The surah describes man's attitude to his own situation when he does not base himself on belief in God and His Oneness. It exposes the unbelievers' situation which leads them to adopt such an attitude.

The surah concludes with a gentle address to the believing soul, inviting it to return to its Lord, pleased and well pleasing. It is to enter Heaven with God's servants who are true believers.

The Dawn

In the Name of God, the Lord of Grace, the Ever-Merciful

1 By the dawn, 2 by the ten nights, 3 by that which is even and that which is odd, 4 by the night as it journeys on! 5 Is there not in that an oath for a man of sense? 6 Have you not heard how your Lord dealt with the 'Ad. 7 The people of Iram, the many-pillared [city], 8 the like of whom has never been created in the whole land? 9 And with the Thamud, who hollowed out rocks in the valley? 10 And with Pharaoh, of the tent-pegs? 11 They were all transgressors throughout their lands, 12 bringing about much corruption there. 13 Therefore, your Lord let loose on them the scourge of suffering. 14 Your Lord surely observes all. 15 As for man, whenever his Lord tries him by His generosity and with a life of ease, he says, 'My Lord is bountiful to me'. 16 But whenever He tries him by stinting his means, he says, 'My Lord has disgraced me'. 17 No indeed; but you are not generous towards the orphan, 18 nor do you urge one another to feed the needy. 19 You devour the inheritance [of others] greedily, 20 and you love wealth passionately. 21 No indeed! When the earth is systematically levelled down, 22 and your Lord comes, with the angels rank on rank, 23 and on that Day, Hell is brought near, then man will remember, but how will that remembrance avail him. 24 He shall say, 'Oh, would that I had prepared for my life!' 25 On that Day, none will punish as He punishes, 26 and none will bind with chains as He binds. 27 'Oh soul at peace! 28 Return to your Lord, well pleased and well pleasing. 29 Enter, then, together with My servants! 30 Enter My Paradise!'

Surah 90   The City

This surah starts with an oath by 'this city', which is Makkah, where His Messenger is a dweller. It speaks of man and his creation. It reminds man of God's favours as He has given him his faculties of perception and shown him the two ways of right guidance and error.

The surah then urges man to look as high as his faculties equip him to reach. This can only be done by extending help to those in need, and by building a community based on compassion and perseverance.

The City

In the Name of God, the Lord of Grace, the Ever-Merciful

1 I swear by this city, 2 this city in which you are a dweller, 3 by parent and offspring: 4 indeed, We have created man in affliction. 5 Does he think that no one has power over him? 6 He says: 'I have spent abundant wealth'. 7 Does he think that none observes him? 8 Have We not given him two eyes, 9 a tongue, and two lips, 10 and shown him the two paths. 11 Yet he would not scale the Ascent. 12 Would that you knew what the Ascent is. 13 It is the freeing of a slave, 14 or the feeding, on a day of famine, 15 of an orphaned near of kin, 16 or a needy man in distress, 17 and to be of those who believe and enjoin on one another to be patient in adversity, and enjoin mercy on one another. 18 Those who do this shall be on the right hand. 19 And those who deny Our revelations shall be on the left hand, 20 with fire closing in upon them.

Surah 91   The Sun

This surah focuses on the human soul and the fact that both the way to goodness and success and the way to evil are open to it. It makes clear that man chooses either way in all freedom and as a result he bears the consequences of his choice.

The surah sets this fact against a background of natural phenomena pointing to God's Oneness and His creation of the universe. It then refers to the story of the Thamud and how they denied the divine message, disobeying God and His messenger. Therefore, they deserved the punishment that befell them.

The Sun

In the Name of God, the Lord of Grace, the Ever-Merciful

1 By the sun and his morning brightness, **2** by the moon as she follows him, **3** by the day, which reveals his splendour, **4** by the night, which veils him. **5** By the heaven and its construction, **6** by the earth and its spreading, **7** by the soul and its moulding **8** and inspiration with knowledge of wickedness and righteousness. **9** Successful is the one who keeps it pure, **10** and ruined is the one who corrupts it. **11** In their overweening arrogance the people of Thamud denied the truth, **12** when their most hapless wretch broke forth. **13** God's messenger said to them: 'It is a she-camel belonging to God, so let her have her drink'. **14** But they rejected him, and cruelly slaughtered her. For this their sin their Lord let loose His scourge upon them, and razed their city to the ground. **15** He does not fear what may follow.

Surah 92   The Night

The surah highlights the fact that man writes his own destiny, as he chooses his way in this life. When he makes his choice, God facilitates his way to the natural end of his choice. It is man who condemns himself, by his actions, to severe punishment in Hell, and it is man who saves himself and enjoys a life of bliss in Heaven. This is all determined by the sort of life man leads in this world.

As there are two ways leading to two different ends, the surah starts with an oath by two opposite natural phenomena: the night as it covers the world with its darkness and the day in its full splendour. Thus, the surah provides an example of the harmony the Qur'an establishes between the subject matter it discusses and the background against which it is set.

The Night

In the Name of God, the Lord of Grace, the Ever-Merciful

1 By the night when she lets fall her darkness, 2 by the day in full splendour, 3 by Him who created the male and the female: 4 surely your endeavours have divergent ends. 5 As for him who gives and is God-fearing 6 and believes in the truth of the ultimate good, 7 We shall smooth the way to perfect ease. 8 But as for him who is a miser and deems himself self-sufficient, 9 and rejects the truth of the ultimate good, 10 We shall smooth the way to affliction. 11 What will his wealth avail him when he goes down [to his grave]. 12 It is for Us to give guidance, 13 and Ours is the life to come, and this first life. 14 I warn you, therefore, of the raging Fire, 15 which none shall have to endure but the most hapless wretch, 16 who denies the truth and turns away. 17 Kept away from it will be him who is God-fearing, 18 who gives away his money to purify himself, 19 not in recompense of any favours done him by anyone 20 but only out of a longing for the countenance of his Lord, the Most High. 21 He shall indeed be well pleased.

Surah 93   The Morning Hours

The surah starts with an oath that aims to spread an air of ease and comfort, because it aims to comfort the Prophet and assure him of God's unfailing care. It reminds him of how God took care of him when he was a young orphan, providing him with guidance. Orphan is the equivalent of the Arabic term *yatim*. However, *yatim* only applies to a child who has lost its father, while, strictly speaking, in English 'orphan' means a child who has lost both parents. Prophet Muhammad lost his father before he was born, and his mother died when he was only six years old. So, both the Arabic and English terms applied to him. He is instructed to show proper care for those who need it and to tell of God's favours, thereby showing his gratitude.

The Morning Hours

In the Name of God, the Lord of Grace, the Ever-Merciful

1 By the bright morning hours, 2 and the night when it grows still and dark, 3 your Lord has neither forsaken you, nor does He hate you. 4 Surely the life to come will be better for you than this present life. 5 And, certainly, in time your Lord will be bounteous to you and you will be well pleased. 6 Has He not found you an orphan and given you a shelter? 7 And found you in error, and guided you? 8 And found you poor and enriched you? 9 Therefore do not wrong the orphan, 10 nor chide away the beggar, 11 but speak of your Lord's favours.

Surah 94   Solace

Like the surah before it, this surah comforts the Prophet who was facing stiff opposition as he called on his people to believe in God and discard the false deities they considered to be His partners. The surah reminds the Prophet that God's help is always forthcoming, and hardship will be overcome by ease. Therefore, he should turn to God with love and resume his efforts to deliver his message and call on all people to accept it. Needless to say, the Prophet did this for the rest of his life.

Solace

In the Name of God, the Lord of Grace, the Ever-Merciful

1 Have We not opened up your heart, **2** and relieved you of your burden, **3** which weighed heavily on your back? **4** And have We not given you high renown? **5** With every hardship comes ease. **6** Indeed, with every hardship comes ease. **7** When you have completed your task resume your toil, **8** and to your Lord turn with love.

Surah 95   The Fig

This surah states that God has created man in the finest form and given him guidance in order to fulfil his role. Man, however, brings himself to the lowest of the low by rejecting God's guidance and refusing to follow the way that earns the highest prize: admittance into Heaven.

The Fig

In the Name of God, the Lord of Grace, the Ever-Merciful

1 By the fig and the olive, 2 and by Mount Sinai, 3 and by this secure city, 4 We indeed have created man in the finest form, 5 then We brought him down to the lowest of the low, 6 except for those who believe and do good deeds; for theirs shall be an unfailing recompense. 7 Who, then, can henceforth cause you to deny the Last Judgement? 8 Is not God the Most Just of judges?

Surah 96   The Clinging Cell Mass

The first five verses of this surah are the first Qur'anic revelation ever. When they were given to Muhammad (peace be upon him), he became a prophet. This was a great event, and indeed the greatest event in human history, as it heralded the provision of divine guidance for man, guidance available to him for the rest of human life.

The opening verses state the relationship between God and man. Man is God's creation and He gives him the faculty of learning and obtaining new knowledge.

The rest of the surah was revealed later, as is clear from its references to events that took place after the Prophet began to advocate his message and call on people to believe.

The Clinging Cell Mass

In the Name of God, the Lord of Grace, the Ever-Merciful

1 Read in the name of your Lord who has created 2 – created man out of a clinging cell mass. 3 Read – for your Lord is the most Bountiful One, 4 Who has taught the use of the pen, 5 taught man what he did not know. 6 Indeed, man becomes grossly overweening, 7 once he thinks himself self sufficient. 8 Surely to your Lord all must return. 9 Look at the one who tries to prevent 10 a servant of God from praying! 11 Think: does he follow the right guidance 12 and enjoin [others to be] God-fearing? 13 Think: if he denies the truth and turns his back, 14 does he not realise that God sees all? 15 Nay, if he does not desist, We will most certainly drag him by his forelock, 16 his lying, sinful forelock. 17 Then let him call his henchmen. 18 We will call the guards of Hell. 19 No, pay no heed to him, but prostrate yourself and draw closer to God.

Surah 97   Power

This surah speaks of the Night of Power which commemorates the revelation of the Qur'an. It was a night of great blessing given to mankind, as it signalled the provision of everlasting guidance, ensuring that man can build a fine community that seeks to achieve the highest standard of a noble way of life whenever he wants. Such a community needs only to set the Qur'an as its guide and abide by its teachings and implement its rulings.

Muslims are encouraged to spend this night, which occurs during the month of Ramadan, in worship. Their reward for such worship is better than that of one thousand months. This is an aspect of God's limitless generosity.

Power

In the Name of God, the Lord of Grace, the Ever-Merciful

1 From on high have We bestowed it [the Qur'an] on the Night of Power. **2** Would that you knew what the Night of Power is! **3** The Night of Power is better than a thousand months. **4** On that night the angels and the Spirit by their Lord's leave descend with all His decrees. **5** That night is peace, till the break of dawn.

Surah 98   The Clear Proof

This surah was revealed in Madinah and it refers to the unbelievers' attitude towards the divine faith. It tells us that unbelievers, whether belonging to earlier divine religions or polytheists, persist in their erring ways until they have clear proof in the form of a messenger from God reciting His revelations.

The surah makes clear that the divine religion is essentially one, based on simple facts and clear rules. There was never a cause for division or conflict. People, however, go too far in error and thus create division and conflict. The result is that the unbelievers are the worst of mankind, while those who believe and do righteous deeds are the best of mankind.

The Clear Proof

In the Name of God, the Lord of Grace, the Ever-Merciful

1 It is inconceivable that the unbelievers among the people of earlier revelations and the idolaters could have ever changed their ways until there had come to them the clear evidence of the truth: **2** a messenger from God reciting revelations blessed with purity, **3** wherein are sound decrees of high value. **4** The people given revelations in the past broke up their unity only after such clear evidence of the truth had been given to them. **5** Yet they were ordered to do nothing more than to serve God, to worship Him alone with sincere dedication and purity of faith, to attend to their prayers and to pay their zakat. That is surely the right religion, pure and straight. **6** The unbelievers among the people of earlier revelations and the idolaters will be in the fire of Hell, where they will abide. They are the worst of all creatures. **7** But those who believe and do righteous deeds are the best of all creatures. **8** Their reward [awaits them] with their Lord: the Gardens of Eden through which running waters flow, in which they will abide forever. God is well pleased with them and they with Him. This is for him who is God-fearing.

Surah 99   The Earthquake

As it mentions the final earthquake that rocks the earth, the surah produces a similar quake within people's hearts. It shakes them so that they realise where they are going. They will come to a Day when everyone will have to account for their deeds throughout their lives on earth. They will, indeed, be shown all their deeds. Even an atom weight of good or evil they do in this life will be shown to them on that day. None will be able to complain about the fate to which they bring themselves.

The Earthquake

In the Name of God, the Lord of Grace, the Ever-Merciful

1 When the earth is rocked by her [final] earthquake, 2 when the earth shakes off her burdens, 3 and man asks: 'What is the matter with her?' 4 On that Day she will tell her news, 5 for your Lord will have inspired her. 6 On that Day people will come forward, separated from one another, to be shown their deeds. 7 Whoever does an atom's weight of good shall see it then, 8 and whoever does an atom's weight of evil shall see it then also.

Surah 100   The Coursers

This surah starts with a quick scene describing running horses that raid an enemy at the break of dawn. This serves as an introduction to a statement about the condition of man who is ungrateful to his Lord and who passionately loves wealth. It ends with a scene of the start of the Day of Judgement when the contents of graves are scattered and people's secrets are laid bare.

The Coursers

In the Name of God, the Lord of Grace, the Ever-Merciful

1 By the snorting coursers, **2** striking sparks of fire, **3** rushing to assault at dawn, **4** raising a trail of dust, **5** storming into any army: **6** man is surely ungrateful to his Lord, **7** and to this he himself bears witness; **8** and truly, he is passionate in his love of wealth. **9** Does he not know that when the contents of the graves are scattered about, **10** and what is in the breasts is brought out – **11** that on that Day their Lord [will show that He] is fully aware of them?

Surah 101   The Striker

The surah speaks of the Day of Judgement, giving it yet another name. It mentions the fact that people will face their destiny according to what they do during their lives on earth. Those who do well and believe will have a comfortable life, but those who go through life disobeying God and doing what He has forbidden will face a terrible end; suffering punishment in the scorching Fire.

The Striker

In the Name of God, the Lord of Grace, the Ever-Merciful

1 The Striker! 2 What is the Striker? 3 Would that you knew what the Striker is! 4 The Day when people will be scattered moths, 5 and the mountains like tufts of carded wool. 6 Then he whose weight [of good deeds] is heavy in the balance 7 shall enjoy a happy life. 8 But he whose weight is light in the balance, 9 shall have the abyss for his home. 10 Would that you knew what this is like! 11 It is a scorching fire.

Surah 102   Rivalry for Worldly Gain

This surah has a majestic rhythm, as it seeks to awaken people who are so preoccupied with their worldly gains, seeking more and more, to the fact that they will be resurrected on a Day of Judgement. Then, they will have to account for what they have done in this life.

Rivalry for Worldly Gain

In the Name of God, the Lord of Grace, the Ever-Merciful

1 You are preoccupied by greed for more and more, **2** until you go down to your graves. **3** Nay, in time you will come to know! **4** Again, in time you will come to know! **5** Indeed, were you to know [the truth] with certainty... **6** You would, most certainly, see the fire of Hell. **7** Again, you will, most certainly, see it with your very eyes. **8** Then on that Day you will certainly be questioned about your joys and comforts.

Surah 103   The Declining Day

Short as this surah is, it provides the essential elements of the Islamic constitution for human life. Its third verse describes the nature of the Muslim community, its role and essential characteristics. This constitution applies to man at all times, all communities and all civilisations. Faith, good action, mutual counselling to follow the truth and endure adversity are the essential components of this constitution.

The Declining Day

In the Name of God, the Lord of Grace, the Ever-Merciful

1 I swear by the declining day, that man is a certain loser, 3 except for those who have faith and do righteous deeds and counsel one another to follow the truth and counsel one another to be patient in adversity.

Surah 104   The Slanderer

This surah describes a certain type of man. He gets rich but he is mean, selfish and lacks dignity. He counts his money time and again, thinking that it gives him status and nobility. He, therefore, makes fun of people, taunts them and backbites. He has no respect for social values. His end is certain to be grim.

The Slanderer

In the Name of God, the Lord of Grace, the Ever-Merciful

1 Woe to every taunting, slandering backbiter, 2 who amasses wealth and keeps counting it again and again, 3 thinking that his wealth will make him immortal. 4 By no means! He will indeed be flung into the crushing one. 5 Would that you knew what the crushing one is! 6 It is God's own kindled fire, 7 which will rise over people's hearts. 8 It will close in upon them, 9 in towering columns.

Surah 105   The Elephant

This surah refers to an event that took place in the same year the Prophet was born. Abrahah, the Governor of Yemen, wanted the Arabs to switch their pilgrimage from the Ka'bah in Makkah to a church he built for them in Yemen. The Arabs refused. He marched at the head of an army, declaring his intention to destroy the Ka'bah. When he arrived close to Makkah, flocks of birds attacked his army, bombarding them with small stones. Anyone who was hit by a stone was killed, including Abrahah. The surah reminds the Arabs of this event, which they knew very well, telling them that God's power is limitless.

The Elephant

In the Name of God, the Lord of Grace, the Ever-Merciful

1 Are you not aware how your Lord dealt with the people of the Elephant? 2 Did He not utterly confound their treacherous plan, 3 and send against them flocks of birds, 4 which pelted them with stones of sand and clay? 5 Thus He made them like stalks of devoured leaves.

Surah 106   The Quraysh

This surah reminds the Arabs, particularly the Quraysh, the most distinguished Arab tribe, of God's favour. He gave them a secure city where they lived in peace, and He facilitated for them their trade trips to Syria in summer and to Yemen in winter, earning them much and ensuring plentiful provisions and secure homes.

The Quraysh

In the Name of God, the Lord of Grace, the Ever-Merciful

1 For the tradition of the Quraysh, **2** their tradition of travelling in winter and summer. **3** Let them worship the Lord of this House, **4** who provided them with food against hunger, and with security against fear.

Surah 107   Small Kindness

This surah shows that Islam is an integrated faith that links beliefs to proper attention to worship and to mutual social security within the Muslim community. Belief that does not encourage a Muslim to look after the needy in his community has no substance. Hence, the one who ill-treats an orphan and does not feed the poor is one who denies religion altogether. The surah also delivers a warning to those who do not attend properly to their prayer. They are hypocrites and they need to mend their ways.

Small Kindness

In the Name of God, the Lord of Grace, the Ever-Merciful

1 Have you seen him who denies religion? **2** It is he who thrusts the orphan away **3** and does not urge others to feed the needy. **4** Woe, then, to those who pray **5** but are heedless of their prayers; **6** who put on a show of piety **7** but refuse to give even the smallest help to others.

Surah 108   Abundance

Like Surahs 93 and 94, this surah is given to the Prophet to comfort and assure him of God's care. It tells him that God has given him abundance of goodness. He, therefore, should give thanks to God. It tells him how such thanks are to be given. The surah sets values on a proper footing, stating that divine guidance gives an increase of every good thing while error and going astray leads to being cut off.

Abundance

In the Name of God, the Lord of Grace, the Ever-Merciful

1 We have certainly given you abundance. **2** So pray to your Lord and sacrifice to Him. **3** Surely, he who hates you is the one cut off.

Surah 109   The Unbelievers

At one stage when the Prophet was facing stiff opposition to his message by the Arabs in Makkah, some of the elders of the Quraysh suggested to him a compromise: you worship our deities for some time and we worship your God. They told him that in this way, the two parties would each reap the benefit of both ways and both religions. The surah replies to this offer most emphatically, stating that no such arrangements are acceptable under the divine faith. Religion is a very serious matter. It must remain pure.

The Unbelievers

In the Name of God, the Lord of Grace, the Ever-Merciful

1 Say: 'Unbelievers! **2** I do not worship what you worship, **3** nor do you worship what I worship. **4** I shall never worship what you worship, **5** nor will you ever worship what I worship. **6** You have your own religion and I have mine'.

Surah 110   Divine Help

This surah, which was revealed in Madinah, gave the Prophet the happy news that victory for the divine message was assured. People will embrace the faith in large numbers. This actually took place during the Prophet's own lifetime. The whole of Arabia was Muslim before the end of his blessed life, and Islam was making inroads elsewhere as well.

The surah also makes clear that Islam elevates its community to a high level of goodness, sincerity and dedication. Never can any human community attain such a high summit except under Islam.

Divine Help

In the Name of God, the Lord of Grace, the Ever-Merciful

1 When God's help and victory come, **2** and you see people embracing God's religion in large numbers then extol your Lord's limitless glory, and praise Him, and seek His forgiveness. **3** He is the One who accepts repentance.

Surah 111   Fire Flames

Abu Lahab was one of the Prophet's uncles, but he was adamantly opposed to him and his message. Essentially, he spared no effort in dissuading people from following his nephew's message. When the Prophet addressed other tribes during the pilgrimage season, explaining to them the message of Islam, Abu Lahab also went to them but only to accuse the Prophet of lying and being mad. He said to them that he, his uncle, and his people knew Muhammad very well and were determined to oppose him. The surah sealed his fate, however, and neither Abu Lahab, nor his wife who placed harmful objects in the Prophet's way, embraced Islam before their deaths.

Fire Flames

In the Name of God, the Lord of Grace, the Ever-Merciful

1 Doomed are the hands of Abu Lahab; doomed is he. 2 His wealth and his gains shall avail him nothing. 3 He shall have to endure a flaming fire, 4 and his wife, the carrier of firewood, 5 shall have a rope of palm fibre round her neck.

Surah 112   Purity of Faith

Composed of four very short verses, this surah sums up one-third of the Qur'an, which is devoted to asserting God's Oneness. It sets in perfect clarity the concept of His Oneness, yet it uses truly extraordinary concise and precise form of expression. One that sets out His qualities of oneness, eternality, absoluteness and incomparability. One that established He has neither ancestor nor offspring.

Purity of Faith

In the Name of God, the Lord of Grace, the Ever-Merciful

1 Say: He is God, the One and only God **2** the Eternal, the Absolute. **3** He begets none, nor is He begotten, **4** and there is nothing that could be compared to Him.

Surah 113   The Daybreak

This surah, as also the next, direct the Prophet, and all believers, to seek refuge with God from everything that makes them fear or worry, whether apparent or hidden, known or unknown. It is like saying to mankind: come to God to enjoy His protection. With Him no harm can touch you from any quarter. With Him, you will be safe and secure.

The Daybreak

In the Name of God, the Lord of Grace, the Ever-Merciful

1 Say: 'I seek refuge in the Lord of the Daybreak, **2** from the evil of anything that He has created; **3** from the evil of darkness when it gathers; **4** from the evil of the conjuring witches; **5** from the evil of the envious when he envies'.

Surah 114   Mankind

Here, refuge is sought with God, the Lord, King and only deity of mankind from the evil of Satan, the slinking prompter who tries hard to lead people astray. He whispers to people, urging them to do what displeases God, painting it as giving them pleasure and happiness. The attributes of God mentioned in this surah are those that are certain to repel evil. Hence, they are especially appropriate.

Mankind

In the Name of God, the Lord of Grace, the Ever-Merciful

1 Say: 'I seek refuge in the Lord of mankind, **2** the King of mankind, **3** the God of mankind, **4** from the mischief of the slinking prompter, **5** who whispers in the hearts of mankind, **6** from among jinn and mankind'.

Index